y Johnston doesn't just preach authentic Christianity—he lives it. *Jesus Called* thought-provoking and encouraging look at what the body of Christ should *can* be in this dark and desperate culture."

—JIM DALY, President, Focus on the Family

Called is an answer to prayer that I'm already putting into practice. Ray ston does a masterful job of showing the true picture of the church as a nt, relevant, uncompromising agent of change in our world. I love this book, know you will too. Get ready to be transformed in your thinking."

DALE C. BRONNER, Pastor, Word of Faith Cathedral, Atlanta, and Author, *Change Your Trajectory*

ohnston is a living and loving example of a compassionate leader who wants meet the Jesus that most people miss. You will discover the true meaning of atness of the Christian journey, and you will not want to live any other way. ges are filled with prescriptions to remedy what Christians are missing."

—DAVID E. BIXBY, President, Azusa Pacific University

ohnston's *Jesus Called* is moving and motivating, a consummate nent."

—LEONARD SWEET, Author; E. Stanley Jones Professor of vangelism, Drew University; Professor, George Fox University and Tabor College; Chief Contributor, PreachTheStory.com

hout scripture, God's prophets used their gift to inspire and encourage nply to do what God created them to do. Ray Johnston's book is a pro- l to American churches today, and really to Christians throughout the nply to do what Jesus told us to do. I'm pleased to endorse *Jesus Called* you'll read it, then *do* it!"

—DOUG BEACHAM, General Superintendent, International Pentecostal Holiness Church

esus Called, I found myself convicted, inspired, and helped. It's filled information, helpful analyses, and inspiring stories. But, on a deeper ead the book, I heard Jesus calling to my heart—the inner chamber ns and visions are too easily covered over by fear and complacency— rds, 'I want my church back. Even more, Doug, I want *you* back.'"

—DOUG MEYE, Developing Pastors Lead, Transformation Ministries

JOHN GRAHAM

Praise for *Jesus Called—He Wants His C*

"We love Ray Johnston, and his new book reminds us of w
meant to be from the very beginning."

—MARK BURNETT AND

Executive Producers, *Ben-Hur*, United Ar

"At a time when everyone is trying to be nonoffensive to
refreshing to hear from a man like Ray who is bold enou

—FRANCIS CHAN, Author of *Crazy Love*

"I know you; you believe in Jesus and make it to church
Johnston's latest sharing will reset you and your church
engaging like never before. *Jesus Called* will also fill in t
show how you can enjoy Him even more."

—MIKE NOVAK, President/CEO,

"Ray Johnston totally gets it! In *Jesus Called—He W*
provides a truth mirror to see why people don't enc
to many churches. But he doesn't leave it there. As
speaks compellingly into what it will take for chur
and radiate Jesus fully."

—SANTIA

President, C

"Ray Johnston is a thriving leader, a thriving vision
of a revolutionary and thriving church. In this b
to rethink the church and Christ for greater kin
world in need of real life transformation. Take th

—EFREM SMITH, Pre

and Author, *The Post-*

"Ray Johnston shines a bright light on the
produces the kind of church where Jesus isn
actually shows up. With wisdom and pract
ades of powerful local church ministry, he cr
church leaders and members to invite Jesus

—LARRY

"As a skilled architect, Ray Johnston examines and exposes the cracks in the foundation of the church Jesus promised to build. With practical and prophetic accuracy, he almost painfully uncovers the flaws in the efforts of the church to remain faithful to the evangelistic enterprise of the kingdom of our Lord. Johnston challenges the church to stand firm and in power on the original design of the Master and to receive new applications to the Master's original revelation."

—KENNETH C. ULMER, Former President, The King's University, and Senior Pastor/Teacher, Faithful Central Bible Church, Los Angeles, CA

"My friend Ray Johnston has written what will be his bestselling book ever. *This* is the book he was destined to write. Ray is a lover of Jesus and a lover of the church that was meant to be. Many of us still love Jesus but are pretty ticked off at His bride. Ray had me at the first paragraph and never let me go. Read this book and fall in love with Jesus and His church all over again. I'm hoping every student in my school and every Christian in the nation will read this book."

—JOHN JACKSON, President, William Jessup University, and Author, *Leveraging Your Leadership Style*

"Ministering with compassion and working with governments shows us that to make a national impact, either spiritually or politically, the church must return to our first love—Jesus and His Word. I applaud Ray Johnston for encouraging and urging us further ahead in order to get us back to the simple words of Jesus."

—DOUG STRINGER, Founder, Somebody Cares International, Houston, TX

"*Jesus Called* is a book that comes from the heart of a pastor who loves Jesus' church. Its intent is not to bash and tear down what some are doing but to encourage all of us to try to be what God desires—communities that love Jesus and live like Him. I have personally benefitted from my friend Ray's heart of encouragement, and now we *all* can! I loved the book. Ray's call is for *all* of us to take a step toward Jesus and see what He unleashes in us. May we have the courage to be faithful to this beautiful challenge to answer Jesus' call."

—STEVE CLIFFORD, Pastor, Westgate Church, Saratoga, CA

"Ray Johnston is a high-energy Christ follower. In *Jesus Called*, he energizes readers to live more significant lives by being obedient to the words and works of Jesus. What could be more simple—or more challenging? I recommend this book to churchgoers and to pastors everywhere."

—GARRETT BOOTH, Pastor, Grace Church, Houston, TX

"This fascinating missive hugs the highway of foundational Christian truth while brilliantly navigating the twists and turns of religion and tradition, ultimately reaching its destination: the love of Christ and His plan for the church from the beginning. Bold, thought provoking, compelling; a must-read for believer and unbeliever alike!"

—K. FRANCIS SMITH, Lead Pastor,
Kingdom Builders Covenant Church, Conyers, GA

"Everything Ray Johnston leads his church to do is about touching lives with the love of the gospel. In *Jesus Called*, he shows how anytime we take our eyes off of Jesus, things deteriorate. Through indifference, ignorance, and neglect of Jesus, the church has been marginalized. When a church reveals Jesus' love so the world can see Him, the mission of the original church becomes clear."

—G. HENRY WELLS, DMin, DD, Pastor Emeritus,
Fair Oaks Presbyterian Church, Sacramento, CA

"Pastor Ray is one of the most gifted pastor/leaders I have known in more than forty years of ministry. He loves people and God's church. And he has done it again! What his book *The Hope Quotient* does for the disheartened and down, his new book, *Jesus Called*, can do for Christians and churches. Read it, digest it, and take its challenge to heart. The future direction of the church is at stake."

—JACK HAMILTON, Executive Pastor, High Desert Church

"Once again God has used Ray to freshly inspire pastors like me, as well as followers of Jesus, to embrace the heart of Jesus for His church. Get ready to be aroused, encouraged, and equipped to join Jesus in building His church. There was a cauldron burning inside of me as I read this book. I was gently reproved, greatly enthused, and wonderfully aligned with the turning of each page."

—GARY L. GADDINI, Lead Pastor,
Peninsula Covenant Church

"I was introduced to Ray Johnston through his book *Hope Quotient*, which stopped me in my tracks. With *Jesus Called*, Ray Johnston has messed me up again. I'm wanting to stop my own studies and totally devote myself to these truths. Yes, *Jesus Called* is a good book, but more importantly, it's a vital Jesus-blood transfusion that can purify the body of Christ afresh. Let it flow through your veins!"

—ROD ANDERSON, Senior Pastor,
Commonwealth Church, London, England

"Ray Johnston is an unbelievably gifted teacher, and he's at his absolute best in his new book. Do yourself a favor and read this one . . . every word."

—JOHNNIE MOORE, President, The KAIROS Company

"The state of Jesus' church is a *huge* deal to Him. It ought to be a *huge* deal to us! After fifteen years doing church the way Ray does, I'm more passionate than ever about Jesus and His church. Now you have the same opportunity. My hope is that this moves you enough to share the book with others, and that the state of Jesus' church would become a big deal to everyone who wears His beautiful name."

—LINCOLN BREWSTER, Recording Artist and Worship Leader

"I like it when a man believes the Great Commission, says '*Go!*' and make disciples. If we do this, we can see cities and even nations transformed, as the early church did. If ever there was a time for the power of the gospel to bring change in society, it is now, starting in the church. Ray gives us a great reminder to take Jesus literally at His Word and do what He sent us to do. Thank you, Ray Johnston, for this refreshing view of the work of the today's church, to get in step with Jesus."

—ROBERT BARRIGER, Founding Pastor, Camino de Vida, Lima, Peru

"When I first read the title I wondered whether this might be a church-bash, but I was wrong. Ray Johnston, as a lover of the local church, has put together a timely, prophetic plea that, if heeded, will change the church both in America and globally. His high energy and wit pave the way for the words of a deep-thinking leader of leaders. This is a 'must-read' for everyone interested in the future of the church."

—MICHAEL MURPHY, Founder, Leaderscape Sydney Australia,
and Leader, ARC Australia

"Instead of overwhelming us with what's wrong, this book is inspirational, with the real life stories of those who have acted and how God has worked through them. It's obvious a book like this comes from practicing what you preach. Ray and his church have done just that. I'm buying this book for our ministry team, Christian friends, and seekers. I've no doubt once you've read it you'll do the same."

—DON BREWSTER, Agape International Missions, Roseville, CA

"We need Ray Johnston's book because sermons don't set you free—truth does. Playing it safe has gotten us where we are in the Western church. We're the proof that soft and safe *doesn't work*! Truth sets us free, gives us courage, gives us energy, opens our eyes, enlarges our hearts, expands our worldviews, stretches our spirits. Truth is fearless. And, thank God, so is Ray. This book is like joining the gym in January. It's the hurt you need."

—PAUL LOUIS COLE, President,
Christian Men's Network International, Dallas, TX

"We've made church so complicated. It's embarrassing how far we've drifted from what Jesus intended. In *Jesus Called*, Ray Johnston leaves very little wiggle room in his conviction to get us back on track to what Christ intended His church to be."

—LANCE HAHN, Pastor, Bridgeway Church, Rocklin, CA,
and Author, *How to Live in Fear*

"I have known Ray Johnston for more than thirty years. His life is built around his deep love for God's church. This book is a wake-up call for the American church to be reintroduced to Jesus and the 'passion, power, grace, truth, vision, freedom, and power' He makes available to His people—His church. Ray tackles issues in the Christian life and church that many would sidestep. He is direct in how we can give Jesus His church back and be a vibrant testimony in doing so."

—JON WALLACE, President, Azusa Pacific University

JESUS CALLED—
HE WANTS HIS
CHURCH BACK

JESUS CALLED—HE WANTS HIS CHURCH BACK

What Christians and the American Church Are Missing

RAY JOHNSTON

W Publishing Group

An Imprint of Thomas Nelson

Published in Nashville, Tennessee, by W Publishing, an imprint of Thomas Nelson.

Author is represented by the literary agency of Alive Communications, Inc., 7680 Goddard Street, Suite 200, Colorado Springs, CO 80920, www.alivecommunications.com.

Thomas Nelson titles may be purchased in bulk for educational, business, fund-raising, or sales promotional use. For information, please e-mail SpecialMarkets@ThomasNelson.com.

All italics in direct Scripture quotations are the author's emphasis.

Library of Congress Cataloging-in-Publication Data

Names: Johnston, Ray, 1952-
Title: Jesus called - He wants his church back : what Christians and the American church are missing / Ray Johnston.
Description: Nashville : W Publishing Group, an imprint of Thomas Nelson, 2016.
Identifiers: LCCN 2015024756 | ISBN 9780718079567 (hardcover)
Subjects: LCSH: United States--Church history--21st century.
Classification: LCC BR526 .J655 2016 | DDC 277.3/083--dc23
LC record available at http://lccn.loc.gov/2015024756

Printed in the United States of America

16 17 18 19 20 RRD 9 8 7 6 5 4 3 2

To the staff, board, and church family at Bayside:
I am grateful for your courageous and contagious love for Christ. I always wanted to be part of a church that loved Jesus enough to impact its world—and now I pastor the exact church I always wanted to attend.
I am grateful for your vision and generosity. We have shut down for weekends to serve the community . . . moved our services to ARCO Arena to rebuild inner-city schools . . . added forty-five day camps every summer to reach kids . . . added 125 teenagers to our staff every summer . . . conducted five Compassion First campaigns so we could give away millions to help hurting people around the world—and you have refused to settle for less.
I am grateful for your love for my family and me. All four of my kids have made commitments to Christ and been challenged to follow Him because of your example and encouragement. As a dad of four—thank you!
And it still feels like we are just getting started . . .

Contents

Foreword

IF YOU WERE TO LOOK IN A DICTIONARY AT A SECTION IN between the words *encouragement* and *energy*, what you would find is a picture of Ray Johnston. Because they define the beginning and the end of the force that is Ray in the world, and they define what you will receive as you read this book.

Ray is passionate about the church. He loves it with his whole heart. He loves it just the way it is, but he loves it too much to let it stay that way (kind of like Jesus in that regard).

The energy that vibrates in these pages is the energy of the prophet. Prophets were always animated by their passion for what the people of God could be, their sorrow for how far the people of God fall short, and their urgency about closing the gap. That is Ray.

Another mark of good prophets: not only do they challenge God's people to live up to God's calling, but they also share in themselves the humility and repentance of falling short. (Interestingly, the only prophet who fails to identify with the people in their sinfulness is the runaway prophet Jonah.) Here, too, Ray hits the good-prophet standard. His candor and humility are part of what makes this book so readable.

In fact, Jesus has been calling to ask for his church back ever since he went into ascension mode. Churches are always losing their first love or quarreling over what kind of meat to eat or which spiritual gift counts the most or which party to vote for or which show not to watch. And Jesus is forever calling his people back to the main thing.

One of the reasons Ray is such an urgent yet winsome voice for this cause is that Ray is not simply an ivory-tower thinker about the church. He has rolled up his sleeves and has gotten a job and is actually doing it. There's something about being in the trenches, about finding out what actually makes a sermon or a small group or a program or a resource *helpful* to real people, that deepens a leader's learning in a way quite different than words forged in the abstract lab of theory rather than in the furnace of actual ministry.

I know. I get to work in the same little part of the world. I get to sneak over to his church sometimes and watch the lives being changed. I've talked to folks from his church when I was down in Mexico and experienced their passion to serve. I get to receive encouraging words from him at the most unexpected moments, just because that's who he is. He and the church he serves are the real deal.

Dietrich Bonhoeffer wrote that all people who enter a church tend to carry what he called a "wish-dream," an illusion about the ideal kind of church I feel entitled to be a part of. Ideal churches don't exist, mostly because all real churches are made up of real people. Bonhoeffer writes that until someone dies to that wish-dream—until we become "dis-illusioned" in the best sense of that word—we will be dangerous to ourselves and to other people inside the church and out.

So allow Ray to dis-illusion you, and then to captivate and inspire and re-enchant you with the beauty of the church, with the energy and encouragement brought in a way only he can bring.

I hope this book gets read by millions. Let's start with you. Turn the page. What are you still reading this for?

—John Ortberg

Read This First

JESUS IS POPULAR IN AMERICA. AFTER TWO THOUSAND YEARS, He is still a global favorite and sits at the top of the US polls. He's more popular than rugby, soccer, or football. He's more popular than Beyoncé, Frank Sinatra, or Mozart. His reputation is more sterling than that of St. Augustine, Abraham Lincoln, or Mother Teresa. He's been more closely watched than *I Love Lucy, Seinfeld,* or *Breaking Bad*. He is quoted more often than Winston Churchill, Woody Allen, or Forrest Gump's mom.

More people know the philosophies of Jesus than those of Mahatma Gandhi, Karl Marx, or Friedrich Nietzsche. More people are familiar with Jesus' words than those of Aristotle, Albert Einstein, or Dr. Seuss.

Most everyone thinks Jesus is one of the greatest moral teachers of all time. Christians consider Him their leader. Muslims consider Him a great prophet. World leaders consider Him a model. Orators consider Him a mentor. Radicals consider Him a member.

In our world, it's okay to tear down presidents, police officers, and pop stars. It's acceptable to fault your colleagues, teachers, and even your own kids. It's perfectly appropriate to criticize Taylor Swift's latest song, Barack Obama's latest executive order, and the NFL's latest bad boy.

But with all His popularity, hardly anyone ever finds fault with Jesus . . .

Or obeys Him.[1]

Read This Second

A RECENT PEW RESEARCH POLL SHOWS THAT CHRISTIANITY IN America is in a sharp decline, while atheism has doubled.[1] Though these results are troubling, there is a deeper truth. The people who have left Christianity are those who called themselves Christians but did not live the life. They've finally given up the pretense.

Yet these should be the best of times! The Christian faith in America should be breaking records. Why?

- **We have better resources.** We have Christian schools, Christian universities, Christian camps, Christian cruises, Christian publishing, Christian conferences, Christian dating websites, Christian musicians, and Christian amusement parks.
- **We have world-class buildings.** We have better church campuses, featuring better seating and lighting, better parking, and better coffee. Some even have sports fields and bowling alleys.
- **We have corporate-level leadership.** Huge denominations function as multinational corporations. Megachurches pastored by megapastors with megasized staffs are now in every city in America.
- **We have better communications.** Technology has exploded. Almost every church has a website, a Twitter account, and sermons available via podcast. We own Christian radio

networks, television networks, and individual stations. We have professionally produced television ministries, some with superstar pastors. And now, thanks to some preachers in LA, we even have our own reality show.

The list is endless.

The American church has never had more resources. These should be the best of times. These should be days in which Christians and churches experience explosive growth and unparalleled influence.

So why do we see headlines like this one from the *Huffington Post*?

WHY NOBODY WANTS TO GO TO CHURCH ANYMORE[2]

What has gone wrong? I had to go to South Africa to find out.

PART 1

A World Without Jesus

CHAPTER 1

Finding Jesus in South Africa

Behold, I am making all things new!
—JESUS, REVELATION 21:5 ESV

SOUTH AFRICA WAS HEAVY WITH ANTICIPATION. NELSON Mandela was free. The constitution was being rewritten. Decades of suffocating apartheid were over, and nobody knew what the future would hold. Carol and I got off a plane in Cape Town, prepared to spend two tension-filled weeks training pastors and leaders in South Africa's Dutch Reformed churches.

The teaching of the Dutch Reformed Church had formed the ideological basis that inspired apartheid. They were the oppressors. All the prime ministers during the apartheid era had come from the Dutch Reformed Church. Then times changed, apartheid died, and the church desegregated in principle—but it stayed segregated in practice. Church leaders officially apologized for their role in apartheid, but old habits die hard.

As a result, Carol and I became more and more depressed going from one dead, segregated church to another. Tradition reigned. Pastors were frustrated. Change seemed impossible. Youth pastors kept telling us, "It's a nightmare" and "It's hopeless!" And it was. The situation was a total disaster.

Then everything changed.

On our last weekend there, I was invited to preach at the largest Dutch Reformed church in the country. We pulled into the parking lot expecting another segregated, lifeless, uptight, condemning, all-white, old-fashioned, tradition-driven church.

Instead, we were stunned.

We walked in and saw thousands of people joyfully worshiping together. The atmosphere was *electric*. We were shocked to see the crowd was *diverse*. Whites, blacks, teenagers, adults, rich, and poor were all standing side by side, singing in English and other languages. I couldn't believe it. This place didn't look like anything we had seen in the entire country.

I leaned over, elbowed the pastor, and asked, "How long have you been pastor of this church?"

"Ten years," he said.

"Was it this way when you got here?"

"Oh no," he said. "It was like every other church in the country."

I had to know. "What happened?"

As the worship team started a new song, the pastor told me the whole story. He said the change took place with just one conversation. He walked into his first church board meeting, went to the head of the table where a chair was reserved for him, and turned to his leaders.

"I'm not sitting in that chair," he said. "No one will ever sit in that chair again. That's Jesus' chair. It's supposed to be His church. From what I can tell, this church has been running without Him, and that's going to stop right now. Since it's His church, why don't we give it back to Him? And since it's His church, from now on we will only ask one question: *What does Jesus want us to do?*

"Our decisions will no longer be determined by South African culture or our own tradition or our own preferences. Beginning this moment, we are recommitting our lives and our church to Jesus, and from now on we will do only what Jesus wants to do!"

Two hundred years of cultural conditioning and church history had been thrown right out the window—*gone!*

The pastor put his arm around my shoulder and said, "None of our traditions or preferences mattered anymore. We just gave the church back to Jesus." Then he swept his arm across the still-worshiping congregation and added, *"And this is just what Jesus wanted to do!"*

I have never recovered from that service.

Walking away from that amazing group of South African Christ-followers, I was more convinced than ever that the greatest need of any Christian is to rediscover the power unleashed by reconnecting with and actually following Jesus.

> *The greatest need of any Christian is to rediscover the power unleashed by reconnecting with and actually following Jesus.*

I wondered if the same thing could happen in America.

CHAPTER 2

Seven Lost Decades

You are the earth's salt. But if the salt should become tasteless, what can make it salt again?
—Jesus, Matthew 5:13 PHILLIPS

RECENTLY I WALKED INTO MY HOUSE AND INSTANTLY THOUGHT something was on fire. The whole house smelled like smoke. I walked into the kitchen and saw that something *was* burning. A thin layer of smoke hovered under the ceiling. Everyone in my family was at home, but no one had noticed the smoke because it happened so gradually.

People fail to notice toxic stuff all the time because it can be even more gradual and less obvious than smoke from a fire. It's nearly invisible. Sometimes it's even underground.

The famed Niagara Falls were threatened in 1898 when developer William T. Love started digging a canal nine miles away to divert water and create hydroelectric power. An economic downturn ended his project and saved the falls. But then the city repurposed the abandoned mile-long ditch as a dump, allowing layer after layer of chemicals, twenty-one thousand tons in all, to be deposited over decades. In 1953, they closed and sealed the dump, then covered the area with dirt. The school board built two schools on it, and developers built neighborhoods there. In 1962, an expressway was built on the site. Happy residents filled the area. But as the water table rose, the chemical seals, broken by construction, started seeping chemicals. Pools of oil and poisonous puddles began to dot the neighborhoods. In 1978, the federal government declared the area a disaster, relocated residents, demolished many of the homes, and then resealed and fenced the land of what is now the infamous Love Canal.[1]

The frightening thing about this situation, considered to be one of the worst environmental disasters in America, is this: the cause of the danger was not visible. Decades passed while chemical toxins gradually built up and made a deadly foundation on which people built their lives. But nobody knew it—until the damage was done. Thousands of people had their lives disrupted or destroyed by something under the surface that they were completely unaware existed.

In the last seventy years, America has accumulated layer upon layer of toxins upon which our spiritual, emotional, and relational lives are built. For the most part, people have felt the impact but are unaware of where the causes originated.

SEVEN DECADES THAT HAVE CHANGED EVERYTHING

American culture is changing—and changing fast. And during each of the last seven decades, Americans have lost something that they desperately can't afford to lose.

The 1950s—Americans Lost Innocence

In the 1950s, Americans lost innocence. World War II was over. The population grew rapidly. Rock music was born. Teenagers were liberated from their parents by cars. And in the fifties an entertainment explosion resulted in Hollywood becoming the number one shaper of values in America.

Seven decades later the results look like this:

- 96.7 percent of American homes have at least one television set.[2]
- The average American consumes almost 60 hours of digital content each week across TV, radio, computer, and mobile devices.[3]
- By age five, the average American child will watch 8,190 hours of TV—almost one full year of life.[4]
- By age eighteen, that same kid will view 200,000 violent acts and 16,000 murders on TV.[5]

This exposure to media continues to shape values and lifestyles in ways no one anticipated. Six professors at Calvin College studied the impact of this media explosion and discovered it has resulted in these things:

- Immaturity—Television culture rewards youthfulness and criticizes maturity.
- Materialism—Media creates the idea we can buy happiness.
- Passivity—We do television by watching. (That carries over to church. How do we do Christianity? Go to church, sit, watch.)
- Teaching and entertainment have become inseparable.
- Personalities are more important than ideas—This is impacting political elections in ways we are just beginning to understand.
- Instant gratification is now accepted as the norm—Everything on television is condensed and resolved *now.* Today's American child has no concept of the future.
- Television provides people with their value structure.[6]

American kids and teenagers today are growing up in a brave new world with unlimited access to everything. As one parent told me, "My kid recently watched one hour of music videos and in that hour saw more sex and violence than his grandparents could have ever imagined."

We have lost innocence. Maybe that's why we are now dealing with the first generation in history that is sophisticated but not mature.

The 1960s—Americans Lost Authority

In the 1960s, America seemed to be on the eve of destruction. It was a decade of significant events:

- The Vietnam War
- Massive protests
- Haight-Ashbury and the "Summer of Love"
- LSD and psychedelic drugs
- Woodstock
- The riots in Los Angeles, Detroit, Chicago, and Memphis
- The assassinations of President John F. Kennedy, Martin Luther King Jr., and Robert Kennedy

The result? People lost respect for authority. People stopped trusting authority. In short, people lost faith in authority in almost any form.

The battle cry of the sixties was, "Don't trust anyone over thirty!" In the song of the era, Pete Townshend's "My Generation," The Who lead singer Roger Daltrey sang that he hoped he would die before he got old. Pete and Roger, incidentally, are both grandfathers now, many times over. But the total lack of respect for authority they put into song in the 1960s became the national mood.

Unfortunately, that attitude has never changed. This is why Jesus' prescription for spiritual health, which requires submitting to the authority of God and the authority of Scripture, is a foreign language to today's generation.

The 1970s—Americans Lost Love

Some historians refer to the decade of the 1970s as "the decade that never happened."[7] As comedians have quipped, "If you remember the seventies, you weren't there."

The seventies was a decade of excess and self-centeredness. As the Vietnam War fizzled out, Americans stopped thinking they could change the world, and, freed from all restraints, people started following

Timothy Leary's mantra: "Turn on, tune in, drop out." Dress, disco, and drugs exploded into the culture.

During the "me decade," television, movies, and magazines (like *Self* magazine) promoted a new era of sensitivity and feelings, but self-actualization turned into self-absorption, and families in the 1970s came apart (despite reading *Jonathan Livingston Seagull*). Americans learned from *Love Story* that "love means never having to say you're sorry," but ironically it was during this "free love" decade that they lost the one thing talked about most: love.

Americans were bombarded with the message that sexual purity is for prudes and losers. To paraphrase what social scientists said in following decades, Americans starving for love settled for sex. This poisonous idea has robbed future generations of the kind of commitment and integrity essential for developing lasting relational intimacy.

The free love "gift" from the 1970s is a gift that has never stopped *taking*!

The 1980s—Americans Lost Values

As people became preoccupied with glamour, fashion, wealth, and media, the 1980s introduced them to the fast lane of rapid change.

- Hollywood helped everybody get in touch with his or her inner "Valley girl."
- The launch of the first space shuttle led to global communications.
- The rapid development of technology sparked cultural and social revolutions that went on to impact the world.

The rise of technology and communications led to an expansion of wealth and the use of easy credit, which created the most intense consumer culture in history. As Americans worked harder, we consumed more. Houses filled with consumer goods, and people began parking in their driveways because the garage was now full. Storage facilities popped up everywhere to keep up with our demand for places to put more stuff.

If the 1970s taught us to care about ourselves first, then the 1980s taught us to start caring about how much we owned. A movie that symbolizes the eighties is *Wall Street*, with Michael Douglas starring as Gordon Gekko. Gekko summarized the entire 1980s with one phrase: "Greed is good." The mantra of the eighties was "Life, liberty, and the purchase of happiness."

The 1990s—Americans Lost Faith

The 1990s was a jarring decade of highs and lows. The Persian Gulf War, O. J. Simpson's Ford Bronco chase, and the LA riots kept Americans glued to their televisions. And unthinkably, in the heartland of America, bombers attacked the Alfred P. Murrah Federal Building in Oklahoma; then students massacred their classmates at a high school in Littleton, Colorado.

One parent told me, "What is happening in our country? I am afraid to send my kid to school." In the 1990s, Americans lost faith.

The 2000s—Americans Lost Security

Time magazine listed the 2000s as "The Decade from Hell."[8] They had a point. As January 1, 2000, dawned, Americans feared Y2K, the computer bug expected to wreak havoc when electronic calendars clicked over to the new millennium. But after the big lead-up, when the year finally changed over from 1999 to 2000, nothing happened.

I have a friend who sold everything he owned and moved to the country. Many people stockpiled food. (My wife and I didn't. I figured with four kids and a minivan, there was enough food stashed in the crevices of that car to feed our family for a month.)

The decade started with only a scare, but our worst fears were realized when, on September 11, 2001, terrorists took down United Flight 93, hit the Pentagon, and destroyed the Twin Towers.

The towers weren't the only things that came down that day. For many

Americans, 9/11 is the day they lost all sense of personal security. And since that day, Americans in homes with security systems in neighborhoods with security gates have thought, *I feel insecure even in my own country.*

The 2010s—Americans Lost Hope

By the time the year 2010 rolled around, the United States was grappling with the Great Recession, which nearly toppled the world financial system. With the economy teetering, millions of people lost their jobs, their homes, and their retirement funds. Out of work and out of luck, many Americans have lost the one thing they need most—hope.

- 63 percent of Americans today believe the economy is getting worse.
- 62 percent indicate they are very concerned for their own job security.
- 91 percent report being "deeply concerned" about the economic outlook for their kids.[9]

For the first time in American history, young people are predicting their lives won't be as good as their parents'.

When people lose faith in the future, they lose hope in the present.

WHY THIS MATTERS FOR OUR COUNTRY

The past seven decades have shaken America. Largely unseen, sometimes buried deep underground, these seven cultural shifts that have changed everything have created a moral "Love Canal" in our country.

And the real problem is this: In each decade, Americans have lost one thing that is *essential for emotional, relational, and spiritual health!*

> In each decade, Americans have lost one thing that is essential for emotional, relational, and spiritual health!

It is impossible to be emotionally healthy . . .

It is impossible to be relationally healthy . . .
It is impossible to be spiritually healthy . . .

without . . .

innocence
authority
love
values
faith
security
hope

- Try raising good kids without *innocence* . . . or *values* . . . or *authority*.
- Try leading a team, business, or country without respect for *authority*.
- Try building a healthy marriage without *love* . . . or *values* . . . or *faith*.
- Try building a better future without *faith* and *hope*.
- Try being emotionally healthy without *security* or *hope*.
- Try being happy without *hope*.

Americans are starving for these seven things and have no clue where to find them.

WHY THIS MATTERS FOR CHRISTIANS

I believe that Americans are feeling the effects of the loss of these seven things in ways they never have before. I also think it has created an openness for something—*anything*—that actually works.

> We could be on the front edge of the greatest decade for people to turn to Jesus.

This next decade could see the greatest impact for the Christian faith in centuries. Why? Because most people, especially parents, are reeling from the loss of these seven things. And most people have a sneaking suspicion they won't be restored by the government, culture, or a new technological advancement.

What a great decade to point people to Jesus! Why?

- Where do you find *innocence*? In the forgiveness of God.
- Where do you find *authority*? In the character of God.
- Where do you find *love*? In the unlimited love of God.
- Where do you find lasting *values* you can build your life on? In the Word of God.
- Where do you find *faith*? In the promises of God.
- Where do you find *security*? In the faithfulness of God.
- Where do you find *hope*? All of the above!

We could be on the front edge of the greatest decade for people to turn to Jesus. But, as we will see in the next chapter, there is going to be some stiff competition.

CHAPTER 3

Building on a Cracked Foundation

Everyone who hears these words of mine
and puts them into practice is like a wise
man who built his house on the rock.
—Jesus, Matthew 7:24

THE YEAR 1937 SAW COMPLETION OF ONE OF THE MOST recognizable architectural works in the world, the Golden Gate Bridge. Last week, I drove to San Francisco on business and came over the rise where that world-renowned bridge first comes into view. Clouds crowned the very top of the two famous upswept towers. Their gigantic cables draped from the clouds to the roadway beneath, gleaming in the morning sun, stopping high above a sparkling ocean. I have experienced that breathtaking scene, one of the most photographed in the world, hundreds of times. But I still had to stop the conversation I was in and say, "Just look at *that*!"

Against all odds, the Golden Gate Bridge was built above a treacherous strait with raging currents beneath and powerful winds above. To construct its two towers, dynamite and divers had to blast through the bedrock beneath the ocean, level it, and sink a deep foundation. The bridge sits adjacent to the San Andreas Fault—a fault zone that causes thousands of earthquakes each year—so it had to be built not only with durability but also with flexibility. From the middle of its suspension, the roadway sways from side to side as much as twenty feet.

Visitors get spooked when they feel the bridge vibrating and swaying. But its movement is proof of the bridge's sturdy construction. When I lived near the bridge, an engineer friend told me that if a major earthquake ever hit Northern California, the Golden Gate Bridge would be the safest place to be. Either there or Nebraska.

Why? He explained the Golden Gate Bridge has two things going for it that create stability. First, it is anchored in the bedrock. Second, above the foundation it has flexibility. I thought, *What an unbeatable combination! Flexible but anchored firmly to a rock-solid foundation.*

Everyone reading this book has three things in common:

1. **You are building something.** You may be building a career, building a marriage, building a family, building a ministry, or building your character—but you're building.
2. **It isn't getting easier.** Difficulties include changing values, economic downturns, the influence of the media, and taxes—and by the time you're reading this, the price of gas may be ten dollars per gallon.
3. **You want a solid foundation.** Everyone wants a solid foundation for their homes, for their marriages, for their kids' values, and for their futures.

Jesus capped off His most famous message, the Sermon on the Mount, with a story about building a solid foundation. He said:

> Therefore everyone who hears these words of mine and puts them into practice is like a wise man who built his house on the rock. The rain came down, the streams rose, and the winds blew and beat against that house; yet it did not fall, because it had its foundation on the rock. But everyone who hears these words of mine and does not put them into

> practice is like a foolish man who built his house on sand. The rain came down, the streams rose, and the winds blew and beat against that house, and it fell with a great crash. (Matthew 7:24–27)

Jesus was teaching us far more than an architectural lesson. He was asking the most important question anyone will ever ask. Jesus was saying, in essence, *If you reject Me and My words for the foundation of your life, then what do you propose to replace them with that is going to be able to hold you up for a lifetime?*

What Jesus is conveying to us is this: *your ultimate worldview matters.*

THE POWER OF A FOUNDATIONAL WORLDVIEW

Sayyid Qutb is not a household name.

Even though he died fifty years ago, he has had a profound effect on your life. Sayyid was an Egyptian educator and politician with a worldview of hatred and violence, especially against Jews, Christians, and the West. He communicated his worldview through twenty-four books, numerous articles, his relationships, and his politics. Arrested for plotting to assassinate the Egyptian president, he continued spewing his radical theories for another decade from prison before he was finally hanged in 1966.

This would have been the end of Sayyid—except his brother, Muhammad Qutb, was a university professor who started teaching, publishing, and promoting his brother's teachings in Saudi Arabia. You probably have never heard of either of those brothers, but the entire world has heard of their star pupil, Osama bin Laden. Bin Laden took their worldview and acted on it, and because of that we now live in a different world.[1]

> What Jesus is conveying to us is this: your ultimate worldview matters.

Today we live in an age of terrorism because of the worldview of one man who was executed by his own countrymen. *One* man. All these decades later, we are reaping the effects of it.

Every time you take off your shoes in an airport, it's because of one man's worldview. Every time you have to take ten forms of identification to get a driver's license or passport—and even then they might not give it to you—it is because of one man's worldview.

Worldviews have consequences. A worldview is the set of beliefs you build your life upon. Your worldview determines your thoughts regarding life and death, and the past, present, and future. Your worldview determines what you think about relationships, time, and money. Your worldview determines your thoughts about happiness. Your success level, your stress level, your sense of confidence, and your peace of mind all come from your worldview.

Everything depends on a person's worldview—and everyone has one. That's why Jesus spent so much time challenging them. In the fifth chapter of Matthew alone, Jesus repeated this one phrase five different times:

"You have heard that it was said . . . *But I tell you* . . ." (vv. 21–22).

"You have heard that it was said . . . *But I tell you* . . ." (vv. 27–28).

"It has been said . . . *But I tell you* . . ." (vv. 31–32).

"You have heard that it was said . . . *But I tell you* . . ." (vv. 33–34).

"You have heard that it was said . . . *But I tell you* . . ." (vv. 38–39).

CHRISTIANITY'S GREATEST COMPETITION

What alternative worldviews compete with the one Christ sets for us? Here are six of the most common, and sometimes the most destructive, American worldviews that bombard us in classrooms, books, entertainment, and advertising. (A note of gratitude to my friend Rick Warren, who preached a sermon on this ten years ago. It's been bothering me ever since—so I thought I would let it bother you for the next decade.)

Hedonism

Let's start with the number one American worldview—hedonism. The catchphrase for hedonism is, "If it feels good, do it!" In the last couple of decades, *party* has become a verb instead of a noun. We live in an instant-gratification age where the *Playboy* philosophy of loving pleasure more than loving God is now a given.

Hedonism states that the most important thing in life is how you feel. If you feel good, then what you're doing is good. If you feel bad, then what you're doing is bad. In hedonism, everything is ruled by feelings.

Even people who believe themselves to be committed to Christ can live a hedonistic worldview without realizing it:

- If I am a Christian but I am living a self-centered life, I'm a hedonist.
- If my aim is to work to make enough money so I can have fun and pursue pleasure, I'm a hedonist.
- If my life goal is retirement, I'm a hedonist.
- If my future plan is to sit back and do nothing, I'm a hedonist.

There are only three options in life: Live to please yourself. Live to please others. Live to please God. Each is a worldview with distinct consequences.

Living to please yourself promises joy but delivers misery. Self-absorbed, happy people don't exist.

Living to please other people fills you with anxiety. Does anyone really want to spend their entire life worried about what other people are thinking about them? It would be like being sentenced to spending your entire life in junior high school.

Maybe that is why Jesus taught the opposite of hedonism. Jesus said, "What good is it for someone to gain the whole world, yet forfeit their soul?" (Mark 8:36).

People weren't created by God to merely live pleasure-seeking, self-centered lives.

Materialism

The materialism worldview can be summed up in one word—"More!" It's the worldview that says, "The one who dies with the most toys wins."

Thousands of television and Internet commercials every year convince Americans that happiness and fulfillment are just one purchase away. People start thinking, *I will be worth more when I own more.* People with a materialistic worldview confuse their value with valuables.

Materialists have bought into the illusion that having more will make you happier and more secure. But all having more does is give you more to fix, or more to worry about losing, or more to find new places for.

If materialism were an effective worldview choice, the richest people would be the happiest people. We know that is not true. So did J. Paul Getty, who was the wealthiest man in the world in 1966 but said, "I would gladly give all my millions for just one lasting marital success."[2]

Jesus challenged the conventional wisdom of the materialist when He said, "Life does not consist in an abundance of possessions" (Luke 12:15). In other words, the greatest things in life aren't things at all.

Individualism

The worldview of individualism can be summed up in two words—"Me first!" This worldview is the darling of advertisers who make big bucks in the serve-yourself world by dishing up slogans that appeal to individualism, such as, "Have it your way." "We do it all for you." "Obey your thirst."

What was once called the "me generation" gave birth to what historian Christopher Lasch called the "culture of narcissism."[3] Individualism is what leads people to say, "I don't care what it does to you or to the children—I'm walking out on this marriage." Individualism is a me-first, my-way, I-have-to-think-of-my-own-happiness thought pattern. This self-centered way of life ignores what is best for the community, for other people, for the family, or for the church, because of an attitude that says, "I only do what's best for me."

Jesus taught a totally different worldview. He said, "Whoever wants to save their life [and their self-centered living] will lose it, but whoever loses their life for me will find it" (Matthew 16:25).

Significance does not come from status, salary, success, or serving yourself. It comes from serving God and others. Jesus taught that you will begin to live only when you begin to give yourself away. He said, "Whoever wants to become great among you must be your servant, and whoever wants to be first must be slave of all. For even the Son of Man did not come to be served, but to serve, and to give his life as a ransom for many" (Mark 10:43–45).

After all, if the me-first worldview worked well, the happiest people in the world would be the most selfish.

Pragmatism

The most common phrase embracing pragmatism is, "Whatever works!" Pragmatism says, "It might not be my thing, but if it works for you, great!"

In our Hollywood-shaped, media-saturated, pluralistic, postmodern society, this philosophy is in vogue. Nobody wants to be the one to say, "That's not right." Yet there are two reasons this view is not only problematic but also destructive.

First, there are things in the world that are evil. The prevalent view is that if you have the nerve to suggest that something is actually wrong, then you're being an intolerant "hater." But when there is evil, a stand has to be taken and a warning has to be issued.

Second, all ideas have consequences, and pragmatism makes truth relative and correction impossible. Under pragmatism, Christianity and truth lose their power and are just another option in the marketplace of ideas.

We all live at the mercy of our ideas about how things are. What you *believe* . . . determines how you *behave* . . . which determines what you *become*. Everything you become in life is ultimately driven by what you believe.

> What you believe . . . determines how you behave . . . which determines what you become.

Jesus challenged this worldview, saying, "You have let go of the commands of God and are holding on to human traditions" (Mark 7:8).

Centuries ago, the wisest man who ever lived wrote, "There is a way that appears to be right, but in the end it leads to death" (Proverbs 14:12).

Humanism

The anthem to humanism is Frank Sinatra's hit song "My Way." In humanism, people are their own ultimate authority, and they write their own truths. It's the worldview that states, "I'm the master of my own fate" and "My will [not Thy will] be done."

New Age spiritualists love to say, "You're divine." "You are your own truth." And people love to hear it.

A while back I was speaking on this subject in a message titled "The New Age Rage." As I got up to speak at our eleven thirty Sunday service, a woman in the back jumped out of her seat and walked the length of the stands yelling, "Don't listen to this man!" She threw the message notes in the air and stormed out. What a sermon introduction. There wasn't a person asleep in the room!

The point of the message that morning was this: if you're going to call yourself a Christian, you can only have one God—and you're not Him. This is exactly what the original temptation was when Satan told Eve, in essence, "Eat this and you'll be like God."

Jesus left room for only *one* way, and it's not "my way." He said, "This, then, is how you should pray . . . 'your will be done, on earth as it is in heaven'" (Matthew 6:9–10).

Fatalism

The worldview of fatalism can be summarized in four words that crush dreams. They replace hope with discouragement. They replace confidence with cynicism. What are those words?

"Things will never change."

A fatalistic worldview is cancer of the spirit. With that worldview, dreams for the future are squelched. Fatalistic people do not have hope or faith. Rather than live with a vibrant faith in an unlimited God, they live totally dominated by their prior experiences with discouragement. Fatalism, stoicism, and cynicism—these are all related.

Jesus' teachings flew in the face of the fatalistic worldview. He said, "With man this is impossible, but not with God; all things are possible with God" (Mark 10:27).

One of the main problems undermining American Christianity is this: people become Christians, join the church, put Christian bumper stickers on their cars—but stop short of letting Jesus make a fundamental change in their foundational beliefs, their worldviews. Their lives don't reflect the values taught and lived by the Jesus they claim to follow.

Another way to put it is this: until Jesus changes your worldview, He will never change your life. Real change happens only when there is a fundamental change in your foundational worldview.

A lot of Christians pick and choose what worldview they'll adopt. When they're out on a date—"I'm a hedonist!" Then at work, when they're closing the deal—"I'm a pragmatist!" When they get their paycheck—"I'm a materialist!" We pull out the appropriate worldview we think will make us happy at the moment.

One national survey by Barna Research Institute suggested that a large share of our nation's problems is directly attributable to the absence of a biblical worldview among Americans. Out of 2,033 adults surveyed, only 4 percent had a biblical worldview.[4] Only 4 percent had a foundation of biblical truth on which to base a decision. We may wonder why people don't act right in our nation. It's because they don't think right!

Even more shocking was that only 9 percent of born-again Christians actually hold to a biblical worldview that influences how they make decisions.[5]

Flitting through worldviews and choosing a different one for each situation creates a shifting foundation, leading to confusion and stress and all kinds of negative emotions in your life.

THREE WAYS TO STRENGTHEN YOUR FOUNDATION

At five thirty on the morning of June 27, 2009, in Shanghai, China, an apartment building nearing completion toppled intact onto the wet turf, resulting in one death. Because no one had moved into the apartments yet and the neighboring buildings were just far enough away to keep from creating a domino effect, no one else was killed. Six people were sentenced to prison for their negligence in the avoidable accident.

Following a thorough investigation, the real estate manager was imprisoned along with the safety officer and other members of the construction crew. The finding was that construction had been rushed in order to make more money for the developers. The ground had not been properly prepared before the building went up. Piles of earth were left on one side of the building while a pit was dug on the other. The lack of solid ground beneath the building caused it to collapse. It should have been obvious that you can't construct a building on uneven, shifting ground.[6]

Here are three things you can do to shore up your foundation.

1. Saturate Your Life with God's Truth

In California, we have incredible beaches and awesome mountains, and we occasionally have life-altering, freeway-destroying, building-collapsing, World Series–delaying earthquakes. The 1989 Loma Prieta Earthquake struck the Bay Area just as the World Series was set to begin. When the shaking stopped, the game was canceled. Candlestick Park was damaged. Electricity was out. Fires erupted, and tens of thousands found themselves suddenly homeless. Six people lost their lives, and 671 people were injured. Damage was estimated at $433 billion. The magnitude 6.9 earthquake was felt over an area of about four hundred thousand square miles.[7]

People who live in California get used to the idea that the ground underneath them may shift—and when it does, everything changes. But every person everywhere is going to experience different kinds of quakes. Financial quakes, spiritual quakes, health quakes, relationship quakes, moral quakes, maybe career quakes, and—if you're married—definitely marital quakes will shake you to the core. If your foundation is not built solidly on truth that doesn't change, then you're going to listen to one thing one day, another on another day, and you're going to cave in. Nothing is more important than a foundation of truth. The Bible says, "Buy the truth and do not sell it—wisdom, instruction, and insight as well" (Proverbs 23:23).

You can build your life on truth, or you can build your life on trends.

When you receive Christ, you are completely forgiven, you're given a brand-new start, and you get a new identity. "Therefore, if anyone is in Christ, he is a new creation" (2 Corinthians 5:17 ESV). That is a new identity.

After that part, though, the rest of the verse reads, "The old has passed away; behold, the new has come" (ESV). After you become a Christ-follower, a new worldview has to match your new identity. If you base your life on a faulty worldview, you're still going to have disaster.

America is plagued with truth decay right now. Jesus said, "You will know the truth, and the truth will set you free" (John 8:32). The more you know the truth, the firmer a foundation you will have. Just like you stop tooth decay in your mouth, it's time you stop truth decay in your brain.

Not long ago, I read about a court case in which the jury deadlocked and the judge had to dismiss charges against a mother who cut off the arms of her ten-month-old baby, who died from her injuries. The reason the mother wasn't prosecuted further and the jury deadlocked was because the jurors became convinced that the mother did not know the difference between right and wrong.[8]

The idea that there is no such thing as truth is called postmodernism, or relativism. The pragmatic worldview says, "What's true for you may not be true for me." This is a philosophy of convenience, because it means we can do whatever we want to do—even chop off a baby's arms—and we're off the hook.

When Jesus said, "You will know the truth and the truth will set you free," He was talking about *The Truth.* Not *a* truth, not *any* truth, not the truth you make up for your own agenda. That's not the truth that sets you free. It is *The Truth* that sets you free.

A pilot can fly into the side of a mountain if he becomes disoriented and believes the plane's altitude is greater than it actually is. No matter how much the pilot believes he is higher, the truth doesn't change—and a mountain isn't going to move either.

We're constantly discovering truth. We're just now discovering new facts about DNA and genomes and all kinds of science. But it's been there all along. We just didn't know it.

It's time to get a foundation of truth under you by studying the Bible, reading good Christian books, going to church, and taking classes at church or online. Get truth.

2. Learn to Spot Counterfeit Truth

People who need to know how to spot a counterfeit dollar bill, such as retailers, spend a great deal of time handling genuine dollar bills. One of the most obvious ways a counterfeit is spotted is due to the feel of the bill. The printing press used for dollar bills creates a unique texture to the paper that a counterfeit doesn't have. When people who handle a lot of dollar bills pick up a fake, they may not know exactly why they recognize it as counterfeit, but they just know it's not real.

The best way to discern what is false is to spend a lot of time handling truth. "Dear friends, do not believe every spirit, but test the spirits to see whether they are from God, because many false prophets have gone out into the world" (1 John 4:1).

The Bible wants us to test what we listen to. One of the ways you can test for worldview is to look at the results. When you study the great philosophers, you learn that some of them committed suicide or went insane. For example, Friedrich Nietzsche was the guy who said, "God is dead," but Nietzsche went insane. Sigmund Freud committed suicide.

Professor Paul Vitz from New York University penned a book titled *Faith of the Fatherless*. He studied one hundred famous atheists to see if they had anything in common. What he discovered was that they all hated their fathers. They were either abandoned, ridiculed, or rejected by their fathers, or their fathers died at an early age.[9] When we pray, "Our Father in heaven . . ." (Matthew 6:9), people with a father wound will say, "If God is like my father, no thanks!"

Never accept a belief without looking at the lifestyle behind it.

3. Commit Yourself to Living Truth

Make God the priority in your life, and you'll see amazing things. Jesus said, "Seek his [God's] kingdom, and these things will be given to you as well" (Luke 12:31). He says, in essence, "Make the Father your main priority, and I'll take care of all the rest."

There are benefits to having a Jesus-based worldview. The great theologian Dallas Willard said:

> People who believe in the virgin birth do not get points for believing in the virgin birth. They live in a different world—a world where virgin births occur is a different world from one in which they don't. A world where Jesus Christ rises from the dead, a world where we have a reliable word from God in the scriptures . . . this is different from a world where these things aren't true. And when we believe in the true world, we gain the riches and realities that God has provided. When we don't believe we live in that world, we are simply restricted to what we can work on our own.[10]

When we have a worldview that God exists and is real, that Christ is who He claimed to be, and that we can build our lives based on His Word, then we get to live in a world where. . . .

- God keeps His promises.
- You matter to God.
- Your past can be forgiven.
- Your future can be secure.
- Transformation is possible.
- Your life can matter.
- You know that you are loved and cherished by God!

Carol and I took our daughters to Germany to visit our son at Bible school. While he was in class, we took a day trip down to Dachau, where the first Nazi concentration camp was built. By the end of the war, more than thirty-two thousand Jews and other political prisoners were killed there.

The day we went, the sky was oppressively dark and gray. The weather was freezing. We walked under the haunting "welcome" sign that said Work Will Set You Free, then spent half the day in those stark, thoroughly depressing grounds. Nobody said much as they were touring. The dreariness of the day underscored the blanket of somberness that descended on us. There was no laughter, no joy in that whole compound.

We listened to the recorded tour as we walked into rooms where experiments were done on people. We walked into gas chambers, into places where people were hanged, into barracks where people were practically stacked on top of one another, and into shower rooms where people were killed.

I stood in the middle of Dachau and thought, *What can we learn from this?*

What I learned was this—ideas have consequences. The saying "What you believe doesn't matter as long as you're sincere" could not be further from the truth. The Nazis believed they were a superior race. They believed they were justified in what they did to people. Their actions were the result of ideas they believed.

A lot is at stake in what you believe.

Ideas have consequences. You cannot build a solid Christian life on a shaky foundation. You cannot base your life on a faulty worldview without experiencing disastrous results. With a shaky foundation, the pillars of your life—your faith, your family, your work—will lack the emotional and spiritual support they need.

PART 2

Christianity Without Jesus

CHAPTER 4

"I'm a Non-Christian, Just Like Most Christians"

It is not everyone who keeps saying to me "Lord, Lord" who will enter the kingdom of Heaven.
—JESUS, MATTHEW 7:21 PHILLIPS

ONE OF THE WONDERS OF THE WORLD IS THE TAJ MAHAL. THE shah who built the Taj Mahal in 1629 was heartbroken over the death of his favorite wife. To commemorate her, he ordered this magnificent memorial to be built. This building is so grand that we now use the name "Taj Mahal" to describe buildings of spectacular proportions or indescribable beauty.

Before he started building, the shah placed his wife's casket in the middle of the construction site so the memorial would be built on top of her remains. As he built, he became enamored of his project. He worked on it with great passion, making it better, bigger, grander, and more expensive than anything ever imagined.

During construction, workers excavated portions of the land to sink the foundation. As the story goes, the shah stumbled over the corner of a box in the dirt. Irritated, he had it removed to make way for the memorial. The result is that the building was erected, but when it was finished, the woman's remains were nowhere to be found. He'd built the building, but he forgot to hang on to the woman it was meant to commemorate.[1]

How often has Jesus Christ been thrown out while Christians built things that were supposed to honor Him?

The very one the Taj Mahal was built to honor was discarded during construction. That's not the only time this has happened. How often has Jesus Christ been thrown out while Christians built things that were supposed to honor Him?

I wonder if maybe we have developed a watered-down version of the Christian faith where we have lost . . .

> the grace of Jesus,
> the love of Jesus,
> the truth of Jesus,
> the passion of Jesus,
> the sacrifice of Jesus, and
> the joy of Jesus.

SEVEN SIGNS OF CHRISTIANITY WITHOUT JESUS

We've arrived at something I call "Christianity without Jesus." Where did we go wrong? The signs are everywhere. Here are seven.

1. American Christians Don't Look Much Like Jesus

American Christians, in general, don't look much like Jesus . . . or love like Him . . . or lead like Him . . . or live like Him.

We may be *believers*, but we're not *becomers*. We may show up to church, but for the rest of the week we don't practice Jesus' words.

For many Christians, the Bible has become their *message* book but not their *method* book. I've met many Christians who base their *opinions* on the Bible but don't base their *actions* on the Bible. To them, the Bible affects their *beliefs* but not their *behavior.*

It isn't often that I agree with *Politically Incorrect* television host Bill Maher, but when I heard one of his scathing rants against evangelical Christians, I had to admit it—Maher hit the nail with his head. He took off about Christians applauding the killing of Osama bin Laden and went on to observe that many people claim to follow Jesus while ignoring almost everything He said.

Here is an edited portion of what Maher said. See if this doesn't ring true:

> For almost two thousand years, Christians have been lawyering the Bible to try and figure out how "love thy neighbor" can mean "hate thy neighbor" and how "turn the other cheek" can mean "screw you, I'm buying space lasers." . . .
>
> If you rejoice in revenge, torture, and war . . . you cannot say you're a follower of the guy who explicitly said, "Love your enemies" and, "Do good to those who hate you". . . .
>
> Nonviolence was kind of Jesus' trademark. Kind of His big thing. To not follow that part of it is kind of like joining Greenpeace and hating whales.
>
> There's interpreting, and then there's just ignoring.

Then the rant took an unexpected turn. In response to Obama's support for bin Laden's assassination, Maher said,

> I say "hallelujah" because my favorite new government program is surprising violent religious zealots in the middle of the night and shooting them in the face . . .
>
> But you see, I can say that, because *I'm a non-Christian—just like most Christians.*
>
> And Christians . . . I know you hate this, and you want to square

this circle, but you can't. I'm not even judging you, *I'm just saying logically that if you ignore every single thing Jesus commanded you to do, you're not a Christian, you're just auditing. You're not Christ's followers, you're just fans.*[2]

Although Maher was picking his favorite peeves, he obviously dislikes the inconsistencies of Christians. He is not alone.

2. Many Americans Are Fed Up with Christians

Many Americans are fed up with Christians, with good reason. Regular, irreligious people flocked to Jesus, but they stay away from Christians today in droves. People desperately need Jesus, yet some of the ones who represent Him actually repel people. I recently experienced this myself.

Last year, some friends helped me fulfill a lifelong dream to attend the Masters Golf Tournament. It was just as memorable as I expected. But what I'll never forget was the preacher standing at the gate!

We joined masses of sweaty fans hiking through the enormous parking lot across the street from the gates. As we got nearer, we could hear someone yelling, "The wages of sin is death!" He kept screaming it over and over where hundreds gathered to enter. There were a few people with him holding a cheery sign that said, "Hell is full of both pagan and religious who thought Jesus would not judge them." It was hot out there, and I thought, *Man, they'd be better off just handing out bottles of water to people and blessing them in Jesus' name!*

He was there every day, so I finally went over to talk to him. I thought I could help. I wanted him to add the rest of the verse, the part with the good news: "The wages of sin is death, *but the free gift of God is eternal life through Jesus Christ our Lord.*" But he wouldn't stop screaming to talk to me. I went to the man standing behind him, who seemed as though he was in charge, but he wouldn't talk to me either. I finally said, "You don't like to have conversations, do you?"

For many Americans, that's how they view Christians—people who are self-righteously headed for heaven but won't deal with issues here on earth. Two recent polls illustrate this. The percentage of Americans who have a favorable impression of Jesus is a soaring 90 percent.[3] That's great! But a second poll showed that only 42 percent like evangelical Christians.[4] More people like Jesus than they like Christians.

Why is that?

3. American Christians Are Known More for What They Are Against Than What They Are For

Today, Christians have turned off a lot of people by being more concerned with what they are against than what they are for. Author Sheldon Vanauken, who found Jesus with the help of C. S. Lewis, penned:

> The best argument for Christianity is Christians: their joy, their certainty, their completeness. But the strongest argument *against* Christianity is also Christians—when they are sombre and joyless, when they are self-righteous and smug in complacent consecration, when they are narrow and repressive, then Christianity dies a thousand deaths. But, though it is just to condemn some Christians for these things, perhaps, after all, it is not just, though very easy, to condemn Christianity itself for them. Indeed, there are impressive indications that the positive quality of joy is in Christianity—and possibly nowhere else. If that were certain, it would be proof of a very high order.[5]

Bona fide reasons exist for such colorful cultural depictions of Christians. Over the history of the American church, we've been known to be against the following:

- Dishwashers
- SpongeBob SquarePants
- Music, drums, guitars, shorts, sandals
- Spitting

- Wearing clothes with stripes
- Wedding rings
- Dancing
- Playing cards, billiards, dominoes
- Gambling
- Sports (or any activity) on Sunday
- Going to movies
- Watching television, listening to the radio
- Tattoos
- Long hair on men, short hair on women
- Abolition of slavery
- Right of women to vote
- Caffeine
- Rock music
- Harry Potter
- Wearing makeup or earrings

The list of things Christians have protested or boycotted is endless. To name a few: Disney, the Beatles, all rock music, Teletubbies, Santa, the Easter Bunny, Procter and Gamble products, and Marriott hotels. Some denominations have come against the circus, interracial dating, mixed bathing, and even shaving (the cast of *Duck Dynasty* must love that).

4. Some American Christians Are Eeyores

H. L. Mencken once described a Puritan as "a person with a haunting fear that someone, somewhere, is happy."[6]

When you walk into the average church, it is so somber, so lifeless, it makes you want to ask, "Who died?" not "Who lived?"

When did we . . .

- . . . decide that things like joy, grace, and celebration should be banned?

- . . . replace enjoying God with enduring life?
- . . . trade grace for legalistic rules?
- . . . decide that worship should be somber or boring?

At the church where I pastor, the leadership team works hard to stop religious attitudes. People notice! The women's ministry director from our church walked into a supermarket recently and struck up a conversation about Jesus with another woman in line. Eventually the woman said, "Where do you go to church?"

Rachel told her, and the lady's face brightened. "Oh, you go *there*? That's fantastic! Now I can go there!"

Rachel said, "What do you mean?"

The woman said, "I went to church there a month ago, and it was so much fun. The people were so alive. There was so much laughter in the building. I just assumed it couldn't be a Bible-believing church, so I haven't been back. But I can tell that you're a Bible-believing Christian, and now that I know you go there, I'll go too!"

Doesn't it sometimes feel like we have ignored the verse of Scripture that says, "The joy of the Lord is your strength" (Nehemiah 8:10)? Or that we're no longer worshiping the same God who made King David dance with all his might (2 Samuel 6:14)? It makes you wonder if the same committee that instituted the NFL's "no celebration" rule has taken over American churches as well. "Let's win! But let's be really quiet about it . . ."

5. American Christians Have Started Caring About All the Wrong Things

A sermon became famous some years ago because the preacher started by saying that thirty thousand children died of starvation yesterday. Then he added, "and most of you don't give a [expletive]." Then he said, "What's worse is that you're more upset with the fact that I said [expletive] than the fact that thirty thousand kids died last night."

Those words hit a nerve and went viral. He's not alone in those thoughts. I recently had a conversation with a very bright twenty-five-year-old Christian leader. She was brilliant but disillusioned by the church. When I asked why, she said, "Make a list of the top things most Christians are passionate about, and justice issues never make the top ten!"

I said, "What do you mean?"

She said, "Most American Christians are far more passionate and concerned about prayer in schools than they are that millions of American schoolchildren have no access to food, books, computers, or a good future."

She's right. Four years ago, our congregation decided to become the number one resource that ensured every kid in our region could read.

Two weeks after we launched the program, I received a letter from a church member criticizing our efforts and saying we shouldn't interfere in what is the government's responsibility. The only problem was, their point didn't solve the problem. If the kids' parents, government, or teachers don't teach them to read, then who will? Christians!

6. Some American Christians Have Replaced Relationship with Ritual

Maybe it's because we've replaced relationship with ritual that we get so caught up in tradition and legalism, all the while sounding so spiritual. Adding extra rules to the Bible will kill any Christian's freedom and joy, and it will eventually replace a soft heart with a rock-hard, bitter spirit.

Two things are in danger of taking over the average church. The first is *ceremonial Christianity.* Now, there is nothing wrong with ceremony, ritual, or tradition. They can help people in their worship or spiritual disciplines, and some people may simply prefer them. But the truth is, *God doesn't care about ceremony.* He cares about your heart.

I know a guy who grew up believing he had to dress up for church. He would never consider going to church barefoot. Then he went to India and tried to walk into a church with shoes on, and the Indian Christians stopped him. In India, you take off your shoes before entering. Which tradition does God care about? Did He change His mind? No, He cares about your heart.

God doesn't care if you dress up or down, if you have a cross on your church or not, or if you worship in a monument built to Him or in a warehouse. Jesus is searching for worshipers who worship Him "in spirit and in truth" (John 4:23).

Real relationship is always more important than any religious ritual.

The second thing taking over the average church is *religious legalism*. Television producers Mark Burnett and Roma Downey have become friends whom I greatly admire. Recently, we were on the mission field together in Nicaragua and had some great conversations. I'm proud of the way they're handling their media empire. When they came out with the *Son of God* movie and *The Bible* television series, they were ready for a media backlash. But they said the angriest letters they received were from Christians!

Real relationship is always more important than any religious ritual.

I understand it. The angriest letters I have ever received, from the bitterest people, were from Christians telling me what, in their opinion, I was doing wrong. Yet I've never had one letter saying, "You aren't patient," or "You're not kind," or any other fruit of the Spirit. Why are we so worked up about our own agendas and so blasé about Jesus' agenda?

In the popular television program *The Simpsons*, the Simpsons' neighbors, the Flanders family, are Christians. One day Maude Flanders returned home from a trip. Homer Simpson asked her, "Where have you been?" Maude Flanders answered, "I've been away at Bible camp, learning how to be more judgmental."[7]

Legalists will always judge you for not keeping their rules.

Christians have been doing this to one another for centuries. Centuries ago in Geneva, Switzerland, the great John Calvin tried to build a totally Christian society. That doesn't sound too bad, right? Church attendance was required of everybody. Sensible. Laws regulated how many dishes could be served at a meal, because having too many courses was considered a sign of gluttony. That's a bit harsh, but it went on from there.

They had rules about the appropriate colors for clothes. They didn't allow singing, pictures, statues, church bells, organs, theater, hunting, or wearing rouge or lace, among other infractions. One new father named his son Claude, but because there was no St. Claude in the Bible, the father was jailed. A woman was jailed for wearing a hairdo that was of such a height it was judged to be immoral.[8] I'd have loved to have seen *that*!

One legalistic group says, "We don't believe in wearing makeup." Another group says, "It's okay to wear makeup, but you can't play cards." Another group says, "Of course it's okay to play cards, but you can't go to movies." Another group says, "Movies are fine, but you can't go to dances."

The problem with all forms of legalism is that the focus is on human performance rather than on God's love and grace. The important thing about any teaching is its origin—did it come from God or from man?

The great Baptist pastor from Atlanta, Charles Stanley, who is no stranger to Christian rules and regulations, wrote in the most transparent and gentle terms about a life-changing experience he had:

> I was in my late forties and working hard as a pastor, but I knew something was lacking in my walk with the Lord. I began searching my heart to see if anything was hindering my relationship with God, but I was left with only the keen awareness of the void in my heart. . . .
>
> I revealed every piece of personal information to my friends. After the group reflected upon what I had said, one member asked me to elaborate on the death of my father, who had died when I was nine months old. After I finished, he told me to close my eyes. Then he said, "Picture this: your father has just picked you up in his arms and is holding you. What do you feel?" . . .
>
> That meeting with my friends took place decades ago, but I remember it vividly. I cried. *I felt warm, loved, and secure. I had never felt the amazing depth of my heavenly Father's love until then. I was saved at twelve years of age, but that meeting with my friends was the first time I*

felt with all my heart that God truly loved me. Not as a distant, impersonal God, but as a loving Heavenly Father.[9]

That's the heart of Christianity. It is about relationship, not rituals.

7. Many American Christians Give Simplistic Answers to Complex Situations

God tells us there are secrets He is keeping, such as the date and time of Christ's return, and there are secrets He has revealed to us, which we understand by prayerful study of His Word. But some Christians claim to know every certain answer to every deep question that Christians have struggled with for centuries. This attitude is not only arrogant and misguided but it also doesn't meet people's needs, especially when answers hurt rather than help.

When a tragedy occurs, these people try to explain exactly what happened from a spiritual point of view. What we really need in tragedy is not clarity for unknown and unknowable truths, but the certainty of known truth.

A young woman from our church got pregnant. Early in the pregnancy, the doctor told her and her husband that the baby was missing some genetic material. "Your baby likely will not survive the pregnancy," the doctor said. "If it does, it will die right after you deliver it. This baby can't live, so we recommend ending the pregnancy."

The couple prayed about it and didn't feel right about intervening, so they decided to let God do whatever He was going to do. A lot of friends prayed for them. They decided to name their son Isaac, because they were offering him up to the Lord as Abraham had done with his son Isaac.

With a lot of bed rest, the woman made it through the pregnancy. Then, to the amazement of the medical professionals, she delivered a live baby. The doctor said, "Go ahead and hold the baby now, but he might live only a few minutes."

They held their son, but he didn't die. The parents spent the night in the hospital, and Isaac lived through the night. After a second night, they asked the doctor, "Can we take Isaac home? At least he'll die with us."

The doctor said, "Yes, but be prepared, because the baby will die. You're not going to have a long-term life with this child."

Isaac lived another day at home, so his parents made a decision. Their son would not be with them long, so they wanted to cram an entire lifetime into the short time they would have with him. They threw a one-week birthday party for Isaac instead of a one-year party. They started throwing parties at the end of each week, celebrating him.

They thought about what other kids got to do in their lives, and they started doing it all. They took trips and wheeled their infant son around the zoo, the beach, and the redwoods. Isaac lived for nine weeks. I'll never forget racing over to their home when I got the phone call that Isaac was gone. His mother was still holding him. His mom and dad had done so well in the face of tragedy, yet it was no less tragic.

Before I left, they asked if I would speak at Isaac's memorial service. That brought me up short. I couldn't imagine what I could say. I prayed for the next few days, then I felt God drop this message on my heart for the service:

> First, I'm really sorry.
>
> Second, you are a strong bunch of people. You're amazing.
>
> The problem is this: there is a difference between certainty and clarity. When something like this happens, everyone wants clarity. Why would God let this happen? Why us? And a lot of well-meaning Christians have all kinds of stupid, trite answers. They are all happy to tell you what they are. I don't have all the answers, and they don't have the answers either. What they say usually makes things worse.
>
> I don't have clarity, but what I do have is certainty. So I've made a list of what I'm certain of, and I'd like to read this to you:
>
> - I am certain that your son was loved every second of every day of his life, as much or more than any kid I've ever met.

- I am certain that God was honored and blessed by the kinds of decisions you made.
- I am certain that you have been surrounded by support from relatives, neighbors, and friends who love you.
- I am certain that the right road is never the easy road, and that if every parent in America cared as much about their kids as you cared about your son, we would be a much better nation.
- I am certain that no life ever is devoid of meaning, no matter how short, and that somehow God used and will continue to use Isaac in ways we can't comprehend.
- I am certain that Isaac's last breath here was followed by his first breath there in the arms of Jesus.
- I am also certain that the next time he is in your arms, he, and you, will be more alive than you have ever been.
- I am certain that God is close to you, because I am certain that the God Christians worship understands what it means to lose a son.
- I am certain of this great verse: "Let the little children come to me."
- And I am certain that is where Isaac is right now.

Let's face it: sometimes there are no simple answers. It does no good to try to live our faith without following the very source of it, because . . .

- . . . without Jesus' love, we become critical.
- . . . without Jesus' sacrifice, we become selfish.
- . . . without Jesus' grace, we become legalists.
- . . . without Jesus' direction, we become driven by opinion.
- . . . without Jesus' values, we care about all the wrong things.
- . . . without Jesus' wisdom, we become unbalanced.
- . . . without Jesus' passion, we become boring.
- . . . without Jesus' joy, we become lifeless.

And, by the way, so does His church.

CHAPTER 5

Fed Up with Church

For you set aside the commandment of God,
and hold tightly to the tradition of men.
—Jesus, Mark 7:8 WEB

A YEAR AGO, I PULLED UP TO A STOPLIGHT, AND A WHITE VAN pulled up right next to me. I can still see the huge red letters on the side that spelled out two words: *Church Sucks.*

In this chapter, I want to make sure you understand that I am not bashing the church. I am a fan. (More about that later.) Growing up far outside the Christian faith, I had no knowledge of Christ or His church. Atheism, alcoholism, and alienation through divorce were the central lifestyle options for my family, passed on from generation to generation. Without the Christian church I have no clue where I would be, or where my marriage or family would be, today. I have grown as a Christ-follower, as a husband, as a father, and as a leader primarily as a result of being deeply connected to the Christian church.

That said, the words printed on the side of that truck make a statement we had better not ignore. Why? It's a point of view more and more people agree with.

THE UNDERWHELMING AMERICAN CHURCH

One Halloween, a local outdoor mall set up tables between its stores and handed out free candy. Kids dressed up and got chocolate, the stores got business, parents got free entertainment, and dentists got the profits a month later. But our church got a huge opportunity. Some volunteers set up a table and laid out candy; then I started talking to people while other volunteers started writing.

I'd start with, "Hey, do you have time for a quick three-question survey?" If they said yes, I asked, "Are you an active member of a local church?" If they said yes, the survey was over.

In the American church, we sometimes get it all wrong.

If they said no, they didn't attend church, then I'd say, "That's fascinating. You're obviously a sharp person, so why don't you go to church?" We wrote down everything they said.

The third question was, "What would it take for a church to attract somebody like you?"

Their answers gave us a huge education in one afternoon. We summarized the top reasons they didn't attend church as the following:

1. "I don't want to be badgered for money."
2. "They're all hypocrites."
3. "I don't want to be talked down to by some preacher who acts like he's better than I am."
4. "The music is awful."
5. "The sermons are boring."
6. "I'm busy, so why would I waste an hour?"

What would attract people to church had basically one big answer: "If you could help my kids and help my family, I might show up."

FIVE REASONS THAT PEOPLE ARE FED UP WITH CHURCH

I think what the people who painted the side of that van were saying is that in the American church, we sometimes get it all wrong. Here are five things people are sick and tired of.

1. People Are Fed Up with Churches That Treat People Like Outsiders

One Sunday, about three hundred people were standing around the courtyard of our church when I walked through. A guy smoking a cigarette spotted me and yelled across the courtyard, "Hey, Ray! That was a hell of a sermon!"

I recognized him from the local golf course. It was probably his first time in a church. I walked right up to him, shook his hand, and thanked him for coming. Think of the churches he'd be kicked out of! Jesus loves transforming these kinds of people. I am convinced he's going to connect with Jesus, get in the men's Bible study, and start using his gifts to serve—and in another year, he will phrase that sentiment differently. Right now, I'm glad he's there.

For too long, American churches have majored in making people feel like outsiders. We have created an alien environment that seems designed to communicate to the vast majority of Americans that they are outsiders who don't belong. We have insider customs. We sing insider songs. We use insider language, which often gets really pretentious.

- Bible study becomes *hermeneutics.*
- Preaching becomes *homiletics.*
- Teaching the Christian faith becomes *apologetics.*
- A church service becomes a *liturgy.*
- The Ten Commandments become the *Decalogue.*
- Loving Jesus becomes *Christology.*

- Church life becomes *ecclesiology.*
- Talk about the universe, and it's *cosmology.*
- Have a faith-based worldview, and it's *epistemology.*
- Christ's return becomes *eschatology.*
- The closing song is the *doxology.*
- Talk about the Holy Spirit, and you're *pneumatological.*
- Teach about salvation, and you're *soteriological.*
- Get together with another church, and you're *ecumenical.*
- Tell others about Jesus, and you're *missional.*
- The Bible becomes *the canon.*

The more unchurched people who pile into our church today, the more we realize our phrases are unintelligible. "Turn to Joshua," I'll say. Then they look around to find a guy named Joshua. We mention "general revelation," and they think we're talking about a Civil War hero.

And it all adds up to creating an elitist, foreign environment guaranteed to make most Americans feel like they don't belong.

2. People Are Fed Up with Churches That Are Disconnected from the Real World

Every community has churches that emphasize and put money into buildings, choir robes, stained glass, and other things to make their religious experience more pleasant, instead of helping the very people God put in their own community.

You could shut the doors of the average church and the community wouldn't even know they were gone. Why? Because most Christians and churches are disconnected from the people and needs in their own community.

The Bible teaches us to be separated from the world, but as author Ed Cole wrote, "We preach separation, but practice isolation."[1] Somehow the separation of church and state has separated the church from almost everyone in the state.

In my area, 87 percent of people do not attend any church, and it seems like it doesn't really bother anyone. This is amazing to me.

- If 87 percent of people were keeping their kids out of school . . .
- If 87 percent of Apple computers weren't functioning . . .
- If 87 percent of Toyotas broke down their first year . . .
- If 87 percent of people who went to a hospital for help died . . .

. . . everyone's alarm bells would go off! Any one of those would be considered a crisis. Yet somehow it never dawns on American churches that the same kind of ordinary people who flocked to Jesus two thousand years ago are now staying away in droves. Forget the church bells—our alarm bells should be ringing off the walls.

I was standing on a golf course with three businessmen who had never met before. Of course the conversation started with what everyone did for a living. I spoke last and gave my usual answer to spark a conversation: "I pastor a church for people who don't like church."

Everyone laughed. One guy said, "Must be a big church! Let's admit it, nobody wants to go to church!"

To which I said, "It is, and you're right." He wasn't being *rude*—he was just being *real.* We're the ones who have disconnected from real people like him.

3. People Are Fed Up with Churches That Are All About Money

People are tired of churches that keep score with money. I know of a church that prints all the members' names in the bulletin at the end of the year with everything they have given over the last twelve months. The pressure on those people is off the charts.

Christians are called to be generous, but the church is never called to *manipulate* people into generosity. I heard about someone with a radio "ministry" who usually spent ten minutes talking about Jesus and twenty minutes talking about money. Then one week the manipulative host took it up a notch. He said, "We need seventy thousand dollars. We also believe that God will give you ten times what you send in. So, figure out what you need, send a tenth, and God will give you ten times that amount."

A listener wrote to him:

> Dear Sir,
>
> I understand you need seventy thousand dollars. I also understand you believe God will give you ten times what you give. The good news is this: I have a solution to your problem. Send me a check for seven thousand dollars, and God will give you the seventy thousand. I will be waiting for your reply.

He's still waiting.

A God-honoring pastor, Rick Cole, is helping build support for Sacramento's "sanctuary movement." During the winter, one night each month a church hosts the homeless in their building, thirty churches in all. To pull it off, the administration and logistics cost about three hundred thousand dollars each year, and it's worth every penny.

Recently Rick lived on the streets downtown for two weeks to raise money for the project. One night, he slept in an area with trash bins. At 2:00 a.m., someone woke him up, saying, "Ya got any weed?" (To my knowledge, he didn't.)

The next day, Rick called me out on Facebook. He said, "Ray Johnston, I know you have 13,000 people in your church. They should each give $1." It was a great challenge for a great cause. We were happy to collect what was needed and deliver a check!

Rick is leading by example. The entire city is focusing on his campaign, and it made national news. Our mayor, former NBA All-Star Kevin Johnson, joined Rick downtown with his support. Why? Because genuine servanthood, self-sacrifice, and generosity attracts the attention of the world.

This is the secret Paul uncovered when he wrote, "They exceeded our expectations: They gave themselves first of all to the Lord, and then by the will of God also to us" (2 Corinthians 8:5). They gave of themselves first to the Lord, then to others. Their spiritual commitment led to compassion.

4. People Are Fed Up with Churches That Have Convictions but No Compassion

Someone told me the story about an African American man who moved into an all-white community, not realizing how unwelcome he would be. On Sunday he went to a local church, but no one talked to him. He went the next week, and they still didn't talk to him. He went for four straight weeks and then made an appointment with the pastor.

"I've been coming to church here, but I'm having a really hard time connecting," the man said.

The pastor looked at him and said, "Well, maybe God doesn't want you at this church."

Four weeks later the guy ran into the pastor in a store. The pastor said, "Hey. I haven't seen you. Did you pray about it? What did God tell you?"

The guy said, "I prayed about it, and God told me, 'Don't worry about it. I've been trying to get in that church for years, and they won't let Me in either.'"

The Bible is crystal clear that there is no male, no female, no ethnic differences, no "Jew nor Gentile," no rich, no poor, but we are all one in Christ (Galatians 3:28). Churches are sometimes not as clear about that.

People respond to the church when our compassion breaks down barriers. In Sacramento a few years ago, white "Christian" supremacists firebombed three Jewish synagogues. Shortly after the attack, I was driving home after church and felt as though God whispered, *So-called Christians destroyed those synagogues. Real Christians ought to rebuild them.*

> *People respond to the church when our compassion breaks down barriers.*

The next week, I announced that we were going to receive an offering on the following Sunday to rebuild those synagogues. Word of the offering spread across our part of the state. People drove from all over Northern California to be part of our services in order to give to that offering.

A Jewish couple drove for hours to sit through the service and hear for themselves what was happening. After the service, they came up to me and said, "We drove three hours to see this. We have never heard of any Christian doing anything nice for a Jewish person—*ever.* We couldn't believe this was actually happening. We had to come and see it for ourselves. We want to say thank you. We didn't think Christians like this existed."

The offering was huge—not enough to rebuild three buildings in the State of California, but it was a significant help to those Jewish leaders. Yet as soon as it was over, I received one of the angriest letters from a Christian I've ever received. It said, in effect, "How dare you raise money for *those* people!"

That person would have said nothing if we compromised on helping others and spent the money on new church carpet for ourselves.

5. People Are Fed Up with Churches That Replace Truth with Tradition

One time I served as an interim pastor while a church was looking for a new pastor. A couple of great, godly college students helped me. During a weekend service, I had these interns serve Communion to the church.

A longtime church member came to me after the service and let me have it. "How dare you have these guys serve Communion!" he said. "They're not ordained in our denomination or our church."

"I'll make you a deal," I said. "Please go through any Bible and see if you can find where it says you have to be ordained in our denomination and church to serve Communion. If you find that, I'll stand up next week, apologize, and step down."

Week after week he sat there, most likely stewing and waiting to outlast me so he could set the new pastor straight.

If a practice or issue isn't outlined in the Bible, then it is a preference, or merely a habit based on tradition.

Jesus said, "You set aside the commandment of God, and hold tightly to the tradition of men" (Mark 7:8 WEB). The minute that happens, the church becomes petrified, the preferences of people replace the principles in God's Word, and the people who need the church the most grace it with their absence.

THE AMERICAN CHURCH IN DECLINE

What do the following things have in common?

- VCRs
- Flip phones
- Answering machines
- Folding maps
- Floppy discs
- Drafting tables
- Movie rental stores
- Analog TV
- Phone books
- Landlines
- Kim Kardashian and Damon Thomas
- Kim Kardashian and Kris Humphries

What do all of these have in common? *Great start—lousy finish.* Unfortunately, we have to add one more item to that list:

- The American church

The sad truth today is that the church is at the lowest point in its American life. The percentage of people unaffiliated with faith doubled from 1990 to 2009. The percentage of people willing to describe themselves as atheist or agnostic grew fourfold during those same years.[2] American Christians today have the least amount of influence they have ever had, are plummeting in likability, are burning out pastors, are seeing their teenagers walk away from faith, and have all but lost their impact on culture.

- Between 4,000 and 7,000 churches close their doors every year, and it's getting worse. Thom Rainer, president and CEO of LifeWay Christian Resources, predicts the annual rate of church closings will continue to soar to 10,000 churches.[3]
- The percentage of self-professed Christians is down 13 percent over two decades.[4]
- Less than 20 percent of Americans regularly attend church.[5]
- American church attendance is steadily declining.[6]
- Established churches, 40 to 190 years old, are in rapid decline.[7]
- In 2050, the percentage of the US population attending church will be almost half of what it was in 1990.[8]

Newsweek magazine concluded that the Christian God "is less of a force in American politics and culture than at any other time in recent memory."[9]

A few years ago, my wife and I took a trip to Nairobi, Rome, Paris, London, Zurich, Munich, Florence, and Fresno. The trip was exhilarating—with one major exception. We visited church after church and cathedral after cathedral. They had magnificent art, majestic architecture, stunning stained glass, icons, pageantry, and historic religious rituals. There was only one thing missing—people!

Like a lot of American churches, the buildings were beautiful but barren. They had everything but were empty.

It's enough to make Jesus roll over in His empty grave.

The Bible tells about a rich church in the wealthy city of Laodicea, a community with many of the conveniences we have today, including the equivalent of indoor plumbing, shopping malls, and huge sports stadiums. Perhaps the church also had beautiful grounds, gifted preachers, and the applause of the people.

The only thing this church was missing was the one thing it needed—the blessing of God. Ultimately, the reason that was missing, in the words of Jesus, was that they were "lukewarm" (Revelation 3:16).

CHAPTER 6

Lukewarm and Loving It!

Love the Lord your God with all your heart and
with all your soul and with all your mind.
—Jesus, Matthew 22:37

THE HISTORIC NOTRE-DAME CATHEDRAL, HERALDED IN 1323 AS "the sun among stars," presides in architectural glory over a bend of the Seine River in the heart of Paris. Notre-Dame's builders and artisans took almost two hundred years to craft its iconic towers, sweeping arches, stained glass tableaus, ornate statuary, and engravings. In seven hundred years, church leaders embellished it with magnificent bells, revolutionaries ravaged it, and patriots restored it. The once-vibrant outside colors are now peeled and faded, leaving the familiar, warm gray stone that will be seen by almost fourteen million visitors this year.

A while back I spent two fantastic hours sitting in a coffee shop across the street. I watched hundreds of people stream through the massive front doors—old, young, loud, or meditative; a mix of ethnicities, styles of dress, attitudes, and languages. Most will exit in about an hour under the gaze of dozens of centuries-old church leaders watching in silence from stone eyes. The visitors leave awestruck, amazed, appreciative, and for the most part, *unchanged.*

What is the difference between Notre-Dame Cathedral and a typical American church on any given Sunday? Not much. Each week, millions of American Christians walk through the doors of beautiful church buildings constructed with the earnest intent to glorify God. They observe and follow the motions, then walk out about an hour later, most without having their spiritual lives ignited in any meaningful way.

Sixty years ago, writer and professor Chad Walsh wrote about this kind of Christianity. The end is so powerful that I added italics for you:

> Millions of Christians live in a sentimental haze of vague piety, with soft organ music trembling in the lovely light from stained-glass windows. Their religion is a thing of pleasant emotional quivers, divorced from the will, divorced from the intellect, and demanding little except lip service to a few harmless platitudes. I suspect that Satan has called off the attempt to convert people to agnosticism. If a man travels far enough away from Christianity he is always in danger of seeing it in perspective and deciding that it is true. *It is much safer, from Satan's point of view, to vaccinate a man with a mild case of Christianity, so as to protect him from the real thing.*[1]

Christians seem to want to attend church but not necessarily follow Jesus. We want our kids to be good, but we don't expect them to be *that* good. Will Willimon, dean of the Chapel at Duke University, learned this when he received a call one day from an upset parent.

"I hold you personally responsible," the father said.

"Me?" Will asked.

The father was hot because his graduate school–bound daughter had just informed him that she was going to put her school plans on hold ("throw it all away" was the way the father described it) and do mission work in Haiti instead.

"Isn't that absurd?" shouted the father. "A degree in mechanical engineering from Duke and she's going to dig ditches in Haiti."

"Well, I doubt that she's received much training in the engineering department here for that kind of work, but she's probably a fast learner and will get the hang of ditch-digging in a few months," Will said.

"Look," said the father, "this is no laughing matter. You are completely irresponsible to have encouraged her to do this. I hold you personally responsible."

Dr. Willimon finally said, "You were the one who started the ball rolling. You're the one who introduced her to Jesus, not me."

To which the father replied meekly, "But all we ever wanted her to be was a good Presbyterian."[2]

When given a choice, the vast majority of people will take lukewarm over hot or cold every time. On cold winter days in Sacramento, we turn on the heat in our worship center to warm it up so it gets lukewarm. On scorching summer days, we turn on the air conditioning to cool it down until it's lukewarm. Why do we do all of this? Because people don't like extremes. And why do we like things lukewarm? Because it's *comfortable*. But settling for comfortable will paralyze your spiritual life every time.

That may be why millions of American Christians are so anemic spiritually. They don't take the Bible seriously, not because of any great theological conviction but simply because it makes them uncomfortable. Working with the poor or connecting with people who are "different" takes us outside our comfort zones. Sharing our faith, tithing, giving, serving, caring, stretching, connecting, and praying are all *essential* for a living faith but often don't happen, usually because they are risky, inconvenient, or difficult. We'd rather put our faith in neutral, give in to compromise, and settle for a lifeless, boring faith than experience the kind of discomfort that creates growth.

We'd rather put our faith in neutral, give in to compromise, and settle for a lifeless, boring faith than experience the kind of discomfort that creates growth.

C. S. Lewis said it this way:

> If we consider the unblushing promises of reward and the staggering nature of the rewards promised in the Gospels, it would seem that Our Lord finds our desires not too strong, but too weak. We are half-hearted creatures, fooling about with drink and sex and ambition when infinite joy is offered us, like an ignorant child who wants to go on making mud pies in a slum because he cannot imagine what is meant by the offer of a holiday at the sea. We are far too easily pleased.[3]

The amazing thing is this: almost no one starts out this way. Few brand-new Christians are lukewarm. Most new believers have a vibrant faith. Worship is fresh and new. The Bible is becoming an open book. Stunned by God's amazing grace, they can't wait to help their friends experience the same. Then something happens. Their romance with God turns to routine. Delight turns to disillusionment. Enjoying God is replaced by enduring life. And another church-attending, cross-wearing, lukewarm Christian is produced. What happened? They have fallen prey to one or more of the seven things that destroy spiritual growth and health.

SEVEN HABITS OF HIGHLY DEFECTIVE CHRISTIANS

Here are seven problems the American church is mass-producing today.

1. Undeveloped Faith

✓ MATTHEW 10:38 NLT	✗ 1 HALLUCINATIONS 1:17
"If you refuse to take up your cross and follow me, you are not worthy of being mine."	"Do not let your hearts be troubled. Believe in God. Believe also in whatever you want."

The fastest-growing religion in America is not Christianity or Islam or Buddhism or Hinduism or Amway. It's not even atheism or agnosticism. According to researchers with the National Study of Youth and Religion at the University of North Carolina at Chapel Hill, the fastest-growing faith, especially with the youth of America, is something they identified as "Moralistic Therapeutic Deism."[4] It is so pervasive, it's shaping the faith of Christians whether they know it or not. MTD, as it is called, has three components.

Moralistic means that God wants people to be morally good and kind to people. The problem is pinning this down. What does that "goodness" look like? That's a bit uncertain. Nobody knows.

Therapeutic means the central goal is to be healthy, happy, and feel good about yourself. What exactly does appropriate health and happiness look like? Well, that's also unclear.

Deism means there is a god who exists, but he isn't necessarily involved in your daily life. The MTD god doesn't really place demands on us but is always available when we have a problem.

Author Christian Smith says that what's so dangerous about this religion is that many people in Christian churches think of themselves as Christians but are really embracing MTD.[5] And this "religion" clashes head-on with Jesus, who said things like, "The Son of Man did not come to be served, but to serve, and to give his life as a ransom for many" (Matthew 20:28).

Unwitting victims of this new, politically correct orthodoxy are missing out on the real adventure of true Christianity. MTD is not following Jesus. It's not biblical faith. It's not God-honoring living. It's a watered-down version of the Christian faith that isn't Christ-centered.

Recently, our church held a Compassion First campaign, when we call everyone to give sacrificially. Every child in the church took part in a parade where they brought the money they had saved or raised to give toward thirty-one different community projects. Carol Holt, our children's minister, said one boy walked down the aisle clutching his bank all the way and repeating, "I don't want to give Jesus my money. I don't want to give my money to Jesus." Cute kid, but let's admit it: we've all felt like that before.

MTD declares, "You don't have to sacrifice. You don't have to listen to the tough stuff Jesus said." This is a direct clash with Jesus, who said,

"Whoever wants to be my disciple must deny themselves and take up their cross daily and follow me" (Luke 9:23).

2. Uncommitted Hearts

✓ MATTHEW 15:8

"These people honor me with their lips, but their hearts are far from me."

✗ 1 HALLUCINATIONS 6:5

"Love the Lord your God with most of your heart and with some of your soul and with a bit of your mind."

Imagine a football coach gathering his team and challenging them by saying, "Guys, we are going for the championship. This is our year! And let me tell you what it's going to take—I'm gonna need you to give . . . a *50 percent effort*."

Or imagine a guy standing in front of his bride at the altar and saying, "I promise to honor you and cherish you. And I promise before God and these witnesses to be faithful to you pretty much some of the time."

None of us would settle for this attitude in any other area of life, so it's amazing how we tolerate this spiritually.

Some friends had a young woman live with them for a couple of years. She started dating a young man, and it got serious. One day the girl came home from seeing the boy. She said, "He's acting weird. I need to check where we are."

The next time she was out with him, she said, "Hey, you seem distant. What's happened?"

He said, "I'm really struggling right now in our relationship. All my life I've had an image of the girl I'd end up with. Growing up in Southern California, I always thought I'd have this blonde, hot, beach-babe kind of girl. And I'm really struggling now. Because I'm trying to figure out if I should hold out for my dream girl . . . *or if I should settle for you*."

She came home, told my friend, and he said, "Don't you dare tell me you told him that was okay!"

She said, "Don't worry. I told him, 'Let me make this decision real easy for you. Good-bye!'"

God gets treated like this all the time. Many of us treat Jesus the same way, and many churches cater to people just like that. They say, "Come to our service and it won't cost you anything. We will keep it so short it's almost like you weren't even here. We won't take an offering, because somebody might be ticked off that we believe in generosity. And we won't ever teach anything calling for change or commitment. Please come, and we will water down our message so that no one could possibly ever be offended, challenged, or changed!"

God doesn't want you to settle for Him. God doesn't want 10 percent of your life. He doesn't want 50 percent. Not even 99 percent will do. He wants *all* of your life!

3. Undeveloped Character

✓ MATTHEW 5:29

"If your right eye causes you to stumble, gouge it out and throw it away. It is better for you to lose one part of your body than for your whole body to be thrown into hell."

✗ 1 HALLUCINATIONS 5:29

"If your right eye causes you to stumble, try to downplay it. It is far better to have two eyes than to be uncomfortable."

I love cars—especially old ones. For the last three decades, I have driven a 1965 Mustang convertible (and after sending four kids through college, it may have to last another couple of decades). I love going to car shows, where automakers display the new models they hope you will buy.

They also have two other kinds of cars. And that's where it gets interesting.

Concept cars are the wild cars some engineer dreamed up. Maybe they're made out of fiberglass with wild tail pipes or painted flames, or maybe they have a hot tub in them. They're designed for just one purpose—to get people to ooh and ahh and drool over them. But you can't buy one, because the company has no intention of making any more. It's one of a kind. Unique. They are a blast to look at, but there is no way anyone is actually making that car-boat-plane-espresso maker for your garage anytime soon.

Then there are *prototype cars*. You've never seen a car like the prototype car either, but there is a difference: the prototype is intended to be the first of many thousands that are modeled on that one car.

Often we look at Jesus as a concept car. One of a kind. We see Jesus and know that no one else will ever be like Him. But the apostle Paul says nope, Jesus was not a concept car. Jesus was a prototype, the firstborn, the model for thousands and perhaps millions that will come after Him.

Jesus was meant to be the firstborn among many brothers and sisters. In other words, God's goal is for you and me to become like Jesus!

The apostle Paul confirms this: "For those God foreknew he also predestined to be conformed to the image of his Son, that he might be the firstborn among many brothers and sisters" (Romans 8:29). Now, what he means is this: as remarkable, unselfish, kingdom-centered, and incredible as Jesus Christ Himself was, that is what God intends for *all* of us to become.

> No one is more committed to helping you grow as a Christian than God.

Paul also wrote, "Being confident of this, that he who began a good work in you will carry it on to completion until the day of Christ Jesus" (Philippians 1:6). This verse indicates that God is working behind the scenes, twenty-four hours a day, to bring about this kind of change in your life.

This should be a great encouragement to those of us who think that spiritual growth and maturity is unattainable. No one is more committed to helping you grow as a Christian than God, and He's working night and day behind the scenes to transform you.

4. Unrepentant Lifestyles

✓ JOHN 14:23

"Anyone who loves me will obey my teaching. My Father will love them, and we will come to them and make our home with them."

✗ 1 HALLUCINATIONS 3:4

"Never change, for God accepts you just the way you are. Therefore, just stay like you are."

I doubt you like the word *repent*. Neither did I. We'll come back to that in a minute.

Millions of American Christians have settled for a faith that comforts them but doesn't challenge or change them. Settling for a watered-down version of Christianity leaves them the same year after year. This isn't new. Two thousand years ago, Paul wrote two long letters to the most gifted and least mature church, the church at Corinth, to identify the root reason so many people attend church but remain unchanged.

It still happens in our day, when people say, "We want a version of Christianity that doesn't command us to repent. It tolerates our lifestyle and also affirms it." People who think this way don't exist to glorify God. To them, God exists to grant permission to do whatever they want.

Paul said people basically fall under three types, outlined in 1 Corinthians:

1. **People who know God** (1 Corinthians 2:12–13). These people are forgiven, filled with the Spirit of God, and beginning to live a God-honoring life.
2. **People who don't know God** (1 Corinthians 2:14). These people are disconnected or distant from God.
3. **People who know God, but live like they don't** (1 Corinthians 3:1–4). These are "infants in Christ" who

require the "milk" of the Word and not "solid food." They are people of faith; however, they lack faithfulness.

Somehow, American Christianity has been corrupted by the widespread teaching that the only thing that matters to God is *what you believe.* Almost all Christian churches, fellowships, colleges, and organizations require adherence to a statement of faith. That is a good thing, because the Bible is clear: *what you believe does matter!* But equally important is this: *how you live matters to God.* And when the way you are living doesn't match up with what the Bible calls you to, God has a one-word solution—*repent.*

The striking words of Jesus in Revelation say, "Therefore *repent*; or else I am coming to you quickly, and I will make war against them with the sword of My mouth" (Revelation 2:16 NASB).

Now, I admit I have never liked the word *repent.* Images come to mind of a bearded, robed, wild-eyed doomsday prophet walking down the street holding a sign: Repent: The End Is Near!

However, I have come to believe that repentance is one of God's greatest gifts. You're probably thinking, *You've got to be kidding me!* Why do I see repentance as a gift? Because repentance is the opportunity to . . .

- **Get free from your past!** Repentance is God's invitation to let His grace enable you to let go of your past.
- **Change your future!** Repentance is God's invitation to experience His power to change.
- **Break bad habits!** Repentance is God's invitation to stop doing wrong and to start living right.
- **Heal your image of God and your image of yourself!** Repentance is God's invitation to jettison flawed, destructive thinking and to start building your life on His truth and wisdom.
- **Make an impact!** Repentance is God's invitation to stop self-centered living and start giving, serving, and caring.

Repentance is one of the great gifts of God, yet it requires humility, because it starts with saying to God, "I am wrong, You are right, and I will submit." Then a brand-new beginning starts!

5. Unread Bibles

✓ MATTHEW 4:4 NLT

"People do not live by bread alone,
but by every word that comes from the mouth of God."

✗ 1 HALLUCINATIONS 13:16

"In the beginning was the Word, and the Word sat there as an unopened app on your home screen."

Unread Bibles lead to undernourished, underdeveloped Christians.

A pastor told me recently that he didn't know how to take it when a church member said she was leaving. When he asked her why, she said it was because he preached out of the Bible too much.

A recent review about our church on Yelp made me laugh. Someone talked about the great classes, music, and community service opportunities at Bayside, and about how wonderful it was to be with Christians who were not closed-minded or condemning. Then the reviewer wrote what she didn't like: "The one thing I don't like is this. At Bayside, they take the Bible literally. They believe everything in it is true." I'll welcome a review like that any day!

The starting point for *living* well is *thinking* well. Paul wrote to the Roman Christians living in a very worldly city, "Do not conform to the pattern of this world, but be transformed by the renewing of your mind. Then you will be able to test and approve what God's will is—his good, pleasing and perfect will" (Romans 12:2).

The big question for the Romans, and also for us today, is this: How do we live a transformed life while living in a not-at-all transformed world? Where do we find the wisdom, strength, and encouragement to live a God-honoring life? The key to changing your life is to change the way you think.

This verse of Scripture doesn't say, "Transform yourself." You don't transform yourself—you *are* transformed. Your part is just changing what you think about. Then the transformation happens.

All change starts in your thoughts. Scripture says, "As [a person] thinks in his heart, so is he" (Proverbs 23:7 NKJV). The secret of changing your life is to change your thoughts. Then you become *transformed.*

I once had the opportunity to see the Dead Sea Scrolls at the Israel Museum in Jerusalem. I stood inches away from sacred documents thousands of years old. The Bible has stood the test of time even though it has been banned, banished, and burned. The Bible has survived criticism. Theologian Bernard Ramm said, "A thousand times over, the death knell of the Bible has been sounded, the funeral procession formed, the inscription cut on the tombstone, and the committal read. But somehow the corpse never stays put."[6] The Bible's critics have tried to explain away every aspect of the Bible to destroy its authenticity, but the Bible has withstood every attack by its enemies. The Bible is indestructible—so it's too bad almost nobody reads it.

When we are hungry physically, we can eat and become full, so we are no longer hungry. The exact opposite happens with our spiritual lives. The more you worship, the more you want to worship. The more you read the Bible, the more you want to read the Bible.

When we stop reading the Bible, we stop craving the Bible. When we stop going to church every week to worship the God who created us, we develop a smaller and smaller appetite for going to church.

Every week, circumstances and situations conspire to shrink your heart and shrivel your spirit. People are rude to you. People criticize or misjudge you. You face disappointment and worries, and you get bone-tired and fatigued. If you don't nourish your spirit, your heart will grow cold and hard. Your spirit will decay. In old age, you'll become that crotchety, cranky, grumpy, irascible person you never liked. No one wants to turn out like that. You don't have to die before you die.

6. Unresolved Conflicts

✓ MATTHEW 5:23–24

"Therefore, if you are offering your gift at the altar and there remember that your brother or sister has something against you, leave your gift there in front of the altar. First go and be reconciled to them; then come and offer your gift."

✗ 1 HALLUCINATIONS 7:7

"As much as you can, live at peace with all people, and when you are unable, live at a distance."

A couple of weeks ago, while getting ready for work, I thought, *This is going to be a great day!* That was followed by a disagreement with my wife, and thus all the energy drained out of what had looked like a promising day.

We all have conflicts, but unresolved conflicts drain our energy and sap our passion. It's like letting the air out of a tire. Life just goes flat.

Thirty years of working with people have convinced me that the three most damaging emotions that can fill our lives—resentment, jealousy, and anger—will kill every time. They kill relationships, marriages, and the human spirit. Sometimes we're in situations at work or home where there is constant conflict. Sometimes there is nothing we can do about it. How do we keep it from draining our lives? This is the very reason God tells us that forgiveness is so important. This is why God teaches us again and again to forgive other people.

"In your anger," He says, "do not sin. Do not let the sun go down while you are still angry" (Ephesians 4:26).

When we don't forgive, anger and resentment start to control our emotions. And when they control our emotions, they begin to control our lives. We have to let go.

This might be an urban legend, but baseball legend Billy Martin told this story on *Late Night with David Letterman*. Billy Martin was known for altercations during games, engaging in public brawls and getting himself fired. His anger was well chronicled through five decades of play. In his autobiography, he tells about going hunting with teammate Mickey Mantle. Mickey had a friend in Texas who allowed him to hunt on his ranch. Mickey drove up with Billy and went to see his friend.

When they arrived at the gates of the ranch, the friend told Mickey, "Sure, you can come in. But would you do me a favor? I have an old mule that's gone blind and sick. He needs to be put down, but I don't have the heart to do it. Since you've got your gun, would you shoot the mule?"

Mickey said he'd do it. On his way back to the truck, he decided to play a trick on Billy, who himself was known for practical jokes. Mickey acted irate and told Billy that his friend wouldn't let them hunt.

"We drive all the way down here, and he won't let us on his land," Mickey said. "I'll show him. I'm going to go shoot one of his mules."

"You can't do that!" Billy said.

Mickey pulled out his gun and walked down to the barn. He put the mule out of its misery and started walking back to Billy. As he walked, laughing to himself, he heard a couple more shots. He got to the truck and Billy was gone. Billy showed up a minute later.

"Where'd you go?" Mickey asked.

"We'll show that guy," Billy said. "I just killed two of his cows."[7]

Anger is a terrible master. Jesus said not to live with unresolved conflicts.

7. Unused Gifts

✓ LUKE 12:48	✗ 1 HALLUCINATIONS 12:21
"From everyone who has been given much, much will be demanded; and from the one who has been entrusted with much, much more will be asked."	"The eye cannot say to the hand 'I do not need you,' unless of course, your church has plenty of hands. Then just sit and spectate."

God's plan is for you to commit your life to Christ, discover your gifts, spend your life making a maximum impact on your world, and then arrive in heaven, where that great crowd will hear God shout, "Well done!" But it is possible that most American Christians are going to arrive in heaven only to hear, "What were you thinking?"

Scripture is crystal clear. The call of Christ is the call to service. The good news is that every follower of Jesus Christ has one or more spiritual gifts. But then it all goes south. Studies have shown that in the church, a gigantic 80 percent of American Christians can't even tell you what their spiritual gifts *are*.[8] No wonder we live without purpose or passion. We're not being used the way God intended.

In Scripture we read, "Since we have gifts that differ according to the grace given to us, each of us is to exercise them accordingly" (Romans 12:6 NASB). It's our responsibility to seek out our gifts in order to use them.

When I was starting out in ministry, I wanted to do something for God. So I led worship—badly. I kept looking. Then I was invited to speak to some junior high students, and an amazing thing happened: they actually listened! God used that experience to launch me into a life of using my spiritual gifts.

God has that niche for each of us that He wants us to discover.

On Catalina Island at a family camp last summer, I saw a group of people start using some gifts that most of them probably never realized they had. Adults and teenagers had been using a volleyball court with a beautiful view of the ocean all week, until the kids in the camp took it over and absolutely destroyed it. Here's why.

A twelve-year-old kid with special needs had observed from his wheelchair as everyone had fun snorkeling, kayaking, playing volleyball, and more, none of which he was able to do. On the last day, some kids realized they had a gift—the use of their arms and legs—that they could use for a good purpose.

The kids kicked the teenagers off the volleyball court, got shovels, and started rearranging the sand. Others caught on and pitched in until pretty soon they had created an off-road wheelchair X Games track, complete with moguls, bumps, and a jump.

For the next hour, every kid in the camp was laughing, cheering, and chasing the young man in the wheelchair. He buzzed over the moguls and got dumped out of the chair, laughing the whole time. Then he got picked back up and kept going. The whole camp gathered and cheered him on. He had a mile-wide smile, and so did everyone else.

For one hour, that camp was saturated by an emotion that a lukewarm person never experiences—unbridled joy!

Seven years ago, I received a phone call from a lady I knew. She said, "Can you get free immediately? My husband is in trouble and he needs you!"

She said he woke up with his heart beating double time. In the emergency room, the doctors wanted to shock his heart in order to restart it. Her husband was concerned that when they shocked him, he would die.

"He won't let them shock him until you come and pray for him," she said. "They can't proceed without *you*."

I jumped in my car and raced to the hospital. I prayed for him, and the attending nurse asked me to leave. Right then, the doctor walked in and recognized me. He attended Bayside. He asked if I wanted to stay, so I said, "Sure!"

The doctor hooked the man up to the machine, and you could see its power building. The machine had a button the doctor would press to start the shock. When it was ready, the doctor turned and asked if *I* wanted to push the button, so I did.

The man's whole body immediately shook. As I watched the monitor, I saw his heart flatline. Then his heart started working again, with even, rhythmic beats. His heart was reset! That was seven years ago, and his heart is still working fine.

I walked out of the hospital that day and wondered, *Wouldn't it be great if every heart condition could be healed by pushing a button?* What does it take to reset and restart a heart? That's what the next section is about.

PART 3

Meet the Jesus Most People Miss

CHAPTER 7

Christian Zombies

Meet the Jesus Who Wants You Fully Alive

I came that they may have life.
—Jesus, John 10:10 ESV

LAST YEAR, MY DAUGHTERS AND I ATTENDED OPENING DAY for the Los Angeles Dodgers (God's favorite baseball team). We cheered, jumped up and down, high-fived, and hugged one another. And we looked *normal.* American sports fans go absolutely crazy at games. We cry when we lose and cheer when we win, and nobody thinks this behavior is unusual. People say, "There's a *fan*!" But if I went to most churches and did any of that, they'd say (as they ushered me out), "There goes a *fanatic*!"

Passion is a big deal in America. Hollywood movies, soap operas, and thousands of books promote it. Amazon.com features hundreds upon hundreds of books with the word *passion* in the title. Passion is all over the Internet. I Googled "passion" and easily found articles, magazines, and books with titles like these:

- *A Passion for Alligators*
- *A Passion for Artichokes*
- *A Passion for Birds*
- *A Passion for Castles*
- *A Passion for Chocolate*
- *A Passion for Fashion*
- *A Passion for Fly Fishing*
- *A Passion for Flying*
- *A Passion for Gardening*
- *A Passion for Golf* (now we're talking!)
- *A Passion for Hang Gliding*
- *A Passion for Hunting*
- *A Passion for Jazz*

You can even buy books on *A Passion for Mushrooms* (if you were alive in the sixties you remember this), *A Passion for Needlepoint*, *A Passion for Pizza*, *A Passion for Ponies*, *A Passion for Potatoes*, *A Passion for Reading*, and *A Passion for Shoes* (Imelda Marcos's favorite book). If you're feeling especially passionate, you can also purchase the number one bestseller among sauna enthusiasts, *A Passion for Steam*.

It's almost as if we think it's appropriate to get excited, be enthusiastic, and have a passion for anything in life—*as long as it's not God.* And we often are passionate about everything—*except God.*

Jesus was clear about living with passion. A man walked up to Jesus one day and said, in essence, "I'm busy. I don't have time to read the book and missed the movie when it came out. Can you give me the CliffsNotes version of the Bible? Is there a point to the whole thing?"

Jesus responded by giving a summary of the entire Bible. He said, "'You shall love the LORD your God with *all* your heart, with *all* your soul, with *all* your mind, and with *all* your strength.' This is the first commandment. And the second, like it, is this: 'You shall love your neighbor as yourself.' There is no other commandment greater than these" (Mark 12:30–31 NKJV).

You can feel the passion in Jesus' words. The repeated word is *all.* Jesus' summary was defining. He is saying that we are to love God, serve God, love people, and serve people *with passion*! We are to give it *all* we have. No half-hearted commitment will do.

> We are to love God, serve God, love people, and serve people with passion!

Think about this for a minute. What is the greatest sin in the Bible? Some Christians think the greatest sin is being a Democrat. Others think it's being a Republican. Some Christians think the greatest sinners are Oakland Raiders fans. (They may have a point.) Some think getting stoned is the worst sin, while others think it's getting drunk. You might say, "It's the 'scarlet letter,' adultery." Others would say gossip. Some think it's going to church in shorts. The list is endless.

The greatest sin is listed in the third chapter of Revelation, when Jesus said He'd rather have you cold or hot than to be lukewarm. C. S. Lewis wrote, "Christianity is a statement which, if false, is of no importance, and, if true, of infinite importance. The one thing it cannot be is moderately important."[1]

The greatest sin is being disinterested in God and apathetic about His Word.

Perhaps in America we've landed closer to what Salvation Army founder William Booth warned about: "The chief dangers which confront the coming century will be religion without the Holy Ghost, Christianity without Christ, forgiveness without repentance, salvation without regeneration, politics without God, and heaven without hell."[2]

It has never been the smartest, wealthiest, most educated, or most beautiful people who have changed the world. However, the people who have made the biggest difference do have one thing in common—they are always people with passion.

Mother Teresa, Nelson Mandela, Martin Luther King Jr., Florence Nightingale, Billy Graham, Luis Palau, the apostle Paul, King David—they all have one thing in common: they are fueled by passion. At some point they decided, "Life is too short to waste. There are things that matter, and I'm going to give my life to making a difference, to making things happen!"

Nothing great is done without passion. Passion is what . . .

- motivates people to live for great causes,
- drives scientists to find new cures to dreaded diseases,
- equips athletes to break records and get to the Olympics, and
- sustains you in reaching your goals as you go through life.

Passion is the fuel that *energizes* you. It's what makes you feel *alive.* Without passion, your life becomes dull, drab, boring, and routine. The problem is that passion is easy to lose.

Here is a universal equation: *new = passion!*

All new car owners are fired up. The car gets washed every thirty minutes. It gets parked three blocks away from any other car. Nobody else can drive it. That lasts for a while . . . then the new car smell wears off, and the dashboard takes the place of a filing cabinet.

All new parents are fired up. All of their conversations are focused on the baby. They take pictures every minute. That lasts for a while . . . then the third kid comes along and wonders later why there are no pictures of him.

All new marriages are fired up. While they are dating, guys run around to open the car door. That lasts for a while . . . then romance becomes routine and the guy looks at his wife and says, "What's wrong—is your arm broken?"

Everything new is fired up. New restaurants are packed. People stand in lines for hours to buy a new iPhone. New movies sell out.

All new Christians start out this way too. You get passionate when . . .

- you first learn the great truths of the Good News;
- you first learn that every sin you've ever committed has been totally and completely wiped away;

- you first learn that God made you for a purpose, that God wants to use *you,* and that there is deep meaning and significance to your life;
- you first learn that your future is absolutely secure—*forever*! God has promised you a place called heaven that's perfect. Because you've committed your life to Christ, one day you're going to spend eternity with Him.

You get passionate when you first learn those things, and *you want to tell everybody*. That lasts for a while . . . then you slowly run out of gas. Your heart grows cold. Conviction is replaced by complacency. Enjoying God gets replaced by enduring life. After a while, there is no spark, no vision, no excitement, no faith, no enthusiasm, no passion, and no willingness to risk.

You might need to get your passion back. You might need to get your hopes back up. You might need to let go of your past and hear God say to you, *Get back up. I have better days ahead!* You might need to catch a fresh vision from God for your future. More than all that, you may be in danger of wasting the one life you get if you don't ever find your passion and fully live. You *can* get a fire in your heart that will never go out.

The apostle Paul warns us about losing passion with this plea: "Never be lacking in zeal, but keep your spiritual fervor" (Romans 12:11).

The key word there is *keep*! That means it's not automatic.

The good news is this: if you can lose it, then you can recapture it.

The question is *how*.

SIX WAYS TO AVOID BECOMING AN OLD, CRANKY, BORING, UPTIGHT GROWN-UP

Jesus taught and modeled six principles for keeping the fire alive. We've drifted so far from Jesus' life and teaching that *none of these are going to sound familiar.*

1. Jesus Knows You're Better Off *Young*!

JESUS SAID:

"Unless you change and become like little children, you will never enter the kingdom of heaven." (Matthew 18:3)

Cemeteries are full of people who are dead serious about life. Jesus said to the old, respectable, rule-keeping, tradition-bound religious elites of the day these shocking words: *"Unless you change and become like little children . . ."* (Matthew 18:3).

It's true the Bible calls us to "grow up" (1 Peter 2:2) and to "mature" (Colossians 1:28). But maybe we have lost something in the process that God never intended for us to lose. Maybe what we've lost was signaled at the very first Christmas.

The surprising message of Christmas—one that astonished leaders and theologians two thousand years ago and still astonishes today—is this: *God became a baby.* That erases every misconception anyone has ever had about God. Each year at Christmas, we discover how young God is.

In his remarkable book *Orthodoxy*, published in 1908, G. K. Chesterton wrote,

> Because children have abounding vitality, because they are in spirit fierce and free, therefore they want things repeated and unchanged. They always say, "Do it again"; and the grown-up person does it again until he is nearly dead. For grown-up people are not strong enough to exult in monotony. But perhaps God is strong enough to exult in monotony. It is possible that God says every morning, "Do it again" to the sun; and every evening, "Do it again" to the moon.[3]

He is hinting that maybe the sun doesn't just come up each morning. God might be commanding it every single day. And the next morning, He says, "Yesterday was great. Let's see it again! Encore!" Maybe it's not automatic. Maybe God never gets tired of sunrises and sunsets.

Chesterton went on: "It may not be automatic necessity that makes all daisies alike; it may be that God makes every daisy separately, but has never got tired of making them. It may be that He has the eternal appetite of infancy."

Then Chesterton sums it all up with his best one-liner: "for we have sinned and grown old, and our Father is younger than we."[4]

That's what is communicated at Christmas. That's what is signaled in the words of Isaiah, who wrote, "For to us a *child* is born" (9:6). We assume God is older than we are and grouchier than we are and more uptight than we are. But when we get a grip on what was happening at the Incarnation, when we discover *we* are the ones who have "sinned and grown old," we discover that God is younger than we are! He is more alive than we are. He is more creative than we are. He is more full of life and zest than we are.

What we discover at the manger is that we are the old, grouchy ones, and God is the young, delightful One. That is the exact opposite of what most people believe about God and what most Christians believe about spirituality.

The birth of a baby shook up the religious world. Maybe it ought to happen again. Rather than somebody becoming a Christian and then becoming more religious and uptight and judgmental and opinionated and harsh . . .

Maybe it's time we reconnect with the Jesus who wants us to "change and become like little children."

2. Jesus Knows You're Better Off *Dead*!

JESUS SAID:

"Whoever wishes to save his life will lose it; but whoever loses his life for My sake will find it." (Matthew 16:25 NASB)

Jesus is saying in essence, "You're better off dead!"

This is a strange recruitment campaign. Today's marketing gurus would laugh at promising death to get people to join. But today's terrorists don't—they've hijacked a page out of our playbook. The problem is, it's *our* playbook. We just don't follow it.

Today, a cross is a piece of jewelry. We forget that it was an instrument of torture and death. At the time of Christ, more than five hundred Israelites were crucified each day. They were publicly displayed on byways where the rest of the Israelites would have to walk. Scholars suggest that when Jesus said, "Take up [your] cross" (Luke 9:23), He could have been standing near one of those crosses, maybe looking at it. Everybody knew He meant, "Be ready to die."

A life of following Jesus is built on a foundation of dying *to self.*

The issue comes down to *considering* yourself dead. If you will not die to yourself, you can't follow Jesus. But it's not that He won't *let* you follow Him:

- There is a *can't* of permission, which is, "You can't do this because I won't let you."
- Then there is a *can't* of impossibility, which is, "You can't do this because something makes it impossible." For example, training to make the Olympics on an all-Twinkies diet will result in making the team impossible.

The "can't of impossibility" in following Jesus is this: whatever you are refusing to die to will make authentically following Jesus impossible.

We'll never make it if we try to follow two different masters. We're better off obedient.

Sean was one of the wildest guys ever to come through our ministry. A former football player, Sean somehow made it through high school, then partied his way through four years at Sacramento State College. During his high school years, his dad came to Christ. Sean's dad tried to tell him about Jesus, but Sean would have none of it. His dad finally gave up and started praying for him (or *at* him).

During Sean's senior year in college, he ran into a guy he had known in high school. They started talking, and the guy said, "You're not going to believe this, but after high school, I became a Christian." For the first time, Sean was ready. He listened, and the guy led Sean to Christ right there on campus.

Sean's first move was to call his dad. He said, "Dad, are you sitting down?" His dad said, "What now?"

"I want you to know that I've just become a Christian."

Sean's dad, in one of the most memorable moments of a parent's faith walk for his child, said, "Son, call me when you're sober," then hung up. Great response.

Sean's first move was to get into a church (good move), where he heard his first sermon. The topic was Joseph fleeing temptation and running away from Potiphar's wife. Two weeks later, at the end of a date, the girl he was with invited him over to her apartment. He went. She put on music, and they started dancing. In Sean's words, he said, "I was just getting ready to make my move, and then I remembered . . . Joseph! I let go of her, took a step back, and shocked her by saying, 'I'm really sorry, but I gotta go.'"

He walked to the door and put his hand on the doorknob. She said, "You mean to tell me that if I take off all my clothes right now, you will still walk out that door?"

Sean said, "I gotta go *now*!"

He ran down the stairs, jumped into his truck, and on the way out of her parking lot, started shouting for joy because he had just resisted his first temptation.

Self-denial is *not* self-rejection. It is psychologically impossible to surrender to somebody if you do not believe they have your best interest at heart. Self-denial is the process of being weaned off selfish attitudes and sinful appetites that, as it turns out, don't result in better living but do lead to addictive behaviors, empty lives, and broken dreams.

The amazing paradox is this: Dying to self *looks like* it leads to a life of emptiness and loss. But in reality, dying to self leads to a life of joy and freedom. Why?

Dead people aren't stressed.

Dead people aren't enslaved by addictive behaviors.

Dead people aren't weighed down by worry.

Dead people don't abandon wives and kids for younger spouses.

Dead people don't judge, criticize, or condemn.

Dead people are never jealous.

Dead people are able to say no to temptation and walk out of an apartment on their way to a brand-new life.

Somehow dying to sin makes me *more* (not less) alive!

Eugene Peterson, author of *The Message* Bible, wrote, "[Being] confined to the self is a prison, a joy-killing, neurosis-producing, disease-fomenting prison."[5] The ultimate goal of dying to self is not to walk around with the stagnant emptiness that comes when you first begin to deny yourself something you're attached to. The ultimate goal is to arrive at the day when you are "dead to sin but *alive to God*" (Romans 6:11).

By the way, whatever happened to Sean? He is more alive than ever. He has a vibrant marriage and three fantastic kids, and he is pastoring a great church in the San Francisco Bay Area.

Die to yourself. You will never be more alive.

3. Jesus Knows You're Better Off *Dependent*!

JESUS SAID:

"The branch cannot bear fruit of itself unless it abides in the vine, so neither can you unless you abide in Me." (John 15:4 NASB)

When I stop depending on God, I start depending on me. That leads to stress, worry, anxiety, regret, and frustration. Passion is replaced by pressure and panic.

When I was a seminary professor, Jerry and Nancy Reed moved to the community so Jerry could become the professor of evangelism. When he arrived, his presence and grace permeated the seminary in ways I had never seen. Everyone wanted to be *with* him, and everyone wanted to *be* him. His own son met with him once a week to be mentored—by his own *dad.* Amazing! He became a living legend among the community there. I even took one of his courses, just to learn from him. So did my wife. At that point he was in his sixties, yet he was the most alive person on the campus.

I finally asked him, "What is your secret?"

"You're not going to want to hear it," he said.

"No, come on," I said. "You're the most spiritually alive, contagious person here. Everyone, including your own kids, wants your faith. What's your secret?"

"You're not going to want to hear it," he said again. Then he told me. "Twenty-five years ago, my wife and I figured out exactly what we could live on and how much we could give away. And then, on purpose, we gave more money away than we could afford to give away, which forced us to depend on God. Every year since then, we get out on a limb, figuring out where that limb would support us before it would break, and then going a couple of inches more just to depend on God. And every year we have experienced in brand-new ways that we could trust God. I have so many stories of God's grace. I have no idea how anyone has an alive faith until you get in a place where you have to trust God so He can prove Himself."

You're better off dependent. As Jerry told me repeatedly, "God is alive! He proves it every day."

4. Jesus Knows You're Better Off *Connected*!

JESUS SAID:

"Abide in Me, and I in you." (John 15:4 NASB)

Let me ask you a passion-defining question. Has there ever been a time in your life when you were closer to God than you are right now? If the answer is yes, what happened? (By the way, most Christians today answer yes, but the amazing thing is that we don't search for a solution.)

These are clarifying questions to ask yourself:

- Why don't I feel the passion that I used to?
- Why don't I feel the same excitement about my career that I used to?
- Why don't I feel the same enthusiasm about my marriage that I used to?
- Why am I not as close to and on fire for God as I used to be?
- Why does my relationship with Jesus feel so stale . . . or distant . . . or cold?
- Why does so much of my life lack any sense of urgency?

Usually we lack passion because we've *lost connection*. Unplugged appliances don't work. Untended fires soon become nothing more than piles of ashes.

I have never written the following story until now. You will soon see why. A few years ago, because of some amazing connections, I received an invitation to meet the president of the United States in the Oval Office. I was thrilled, but the protocol was unbelievable. They sent letters. The Secret Service contacted me. It was really something. I had just one final question: "What am I supposed to wear?"

The answer was, "Just wear what you normally wear to church."

My wife said, "*That's* not going to happen!"

So I grabbed a suit, made airline reservations, flew across the country, and checked into the closest hotel to the White House on the night before. My friend said to meet him at the front gates at 7:30 a.m. sharp with my identification and to prepare to take a while to get checked in.

I was so excited I couldn't sleep. I closed the heavy drapes on the window, set the alarm on my iPhone for 6:00 a.m., and then started texting everyone: *Tomorrow morning I'm meeting the president in the Oval Office!*

The next morning, my room was pitch-dark when I woke up. My hotel room phone was ringing. My friend said, "Hey! Where are you?"

"Man, I'm still waking up," I said.

"Why aren't you here?"

"What's the problem?" I said. "My alarm hasn't even gone off yet."

"You were supposed to be here at 7:30," he said. "It's 7:35 now."

I looked at my phone—and it was dead! The clock in the hotel room said *7:35*. My heart sank. He was right.

"I can be there in ten minutes," I said. "I'll run across the street."

He said, "I am really sorry. It's too late. You've missed your chance."

It slowly dawned on me. *I've just slept through my one chance to meet the president of the United States in the Oval Office.* I just sat in bed, stunned.

Now let me tell you two things about that story:

One, it's not true. It never happened. I have never received an invitation to meet with the president. (But, Mr. President, if you are reading this book, I'll be happy to accept.)

Two, this same scenario happens to Christians all the time. Every day, every morning, we have the opportunity to meet with Somebody far more important than the president of the United States, and a lot of times we sleep through it. The God of the universe has invited us to get up, to read His Word, to pray, to connect with Him. We actually get to connect with the President of the universe, but many of us sleep through it every morning. No wonder we're so distant, disconnected, dissatisfied, and joyless.

The God of the universe longs to be close to you. You are as close to God as you want to be.

5. Jesus Knows You're Better Off *Future-Focused*!

JESUS SAID:

"No one who puts a hand to the plow and looks back is fit for service in the kingdom of God." (Luke 9:62)

A psychologist once told me, "What a person believes about their future is more important than anything that has happened in their past or anything that is happening in their present."

The only people I know who have sustainable, positive, long-term joy and passion all have one thing in common—they believe God has amazing plans for tomorrow. Why? Future focus creates passion.

That leads to a critical question: Do you have any future dreams? I love being around people who have expectations for their futures. They believe God is alive, the resurrection really happened, God is still going to work, and, better yet, God is going to work *tomorrow*.

When our church was about ten years old, we were constructing our first building. Two months before we moved in, one of the strategic leaders of the church asked me for a tour to see exactly what was happening. We walked through the big construction mess. As we were walking back to my office, he said, "I've got a question for you."

We stopped walking, and he said, "Now that it's built . . . are you going to leave?"

I was shocked. I'd never been asked that question before. I didn't even have to think up an answer. It just spilled out. "Are you kidding me? The first ten years have felt like spring training. In about three or four weeks, it feels like we're throwing out the first pitch. We finally get to do the kind of stuff that we think God has called us to do once this thing is open. We're going to use it as a tool. We have stuff for kids, young people, conferences . . ."

I went on with about fifteen more things that I felt like God was calling us to do. He said, "Good," then got in his car and left. I went back to my office and sat there for a long time. Did I like everything about building the church? Did I like raising money? Did I like the political battles of building *anything* in the State of California? Did I like the weekend we were picketed? Did I like the day that I got sued and the church got sued for building a building? Did I like how much longer it took than we'd planned?

All of those answers were no, but I couldn't imagine leaving, because I believed God had amazing future plans for us. I was tired because building the church was so draining, but when I asked myself if I was more passionate about the ministry than ever, the answer was yes, for one reason—I believed God had future plans for us and had given us the place that made them possible.

Retired advertising executive Whit Hobbs wrote,

> Success is waking up in the morning, whoever you are, wherever you are, however old or young, and bounding out of bed because there's something out there that you love to do, that you believe in, that you're good at—something that's bigger than you are, and you can hardly wait to get at it again today. It's something you'd rather be doing than anything else. You wouldn't give it up for more money, because it means more to you than money. And, hopefully, it's something that makes the world a better place for someone else as well as for you.[6]

6. And Above All . . . Jesus Knows You're *Never* Better Off Self-Absorbed!

JESUS SAID:

"If you wish to be complete, go and sell our possessions and give to the poor, and you will have treasure in heaven; and come, follow Me." (Matthew 19:21 NASB)

Americans should be the happiest people in history. Never have people had more comforts than we do now in America. So why is the suicide rate skyrocketing? Suicide is now the second leading cause of death among young adults ages fifteen to twenty-four.[7] Sales of anti-depressant drugs have gone through the roof.[8] Why? Because people have everything *except* something worth living for. People without purpose will lack passion, because passion and purpose go together. Purpose actually creates passion. The only people I know who are genuinely happy are those people who are giving their lives to make something significant happen.

Contrast the lives of two of the most successful people of the twentieth century.

Starring in more than thirty movies, selling billions of records, loved by millions of fans around the world, and still badly imitated forty years later, Elvis Presley was the first international rock superstar. And, unbelievably, it keeps going. On the twenty-fifth anniversary of his death in 2002, his adoring fans made *ELV1S: 30 #1 Hits* the best-selling album in America.[9] And yet, even with millions of fans and record-breaking sales, Elvis died at age forty-two—and his friends say that he was miserable.

His wife, Priscilla, said in an interview years after his death, "Elvis never came to terms with who he was meant to be, what his purpose in life was. . . . He thought he was here for a reason—maybe to preach, to save, to care for people. That agonizing desire was always with him, and he knew he wasn't fulfilling it. He'd go onstage, and with his adoring fans he wouldn't have to think about it. Elvis hadn't a clue where to begin, where to look. In a sense, he was lost."[10]

Unfulfilled people are always unhappy people.

Contrast that with the life of Nelson Mandela. Suffering from decades of discrimination, persecution, and prison, he experienced horrific life circumstances. But he had a driving purpose that never wavered. Feel the purpose and passion in his words:

- "Leaders must be ready to sacrifice all for the freedom of their people."[11]
- "I hate racial discrimination most intensely and in all its manifestations. I have fought it all my life. I fight it now, and I will do so until the end of my days."[12]
- "Difficulties break some men but make others."[13]
- "I was made, by the law, a criminal, not because of what I had done, but because of what I stood for."[14]
- "We are fighting for a society where people will cease thinking in terms of color."[15]

What kept him going? What gave him strength? What filled him with the kind of passion that frees an entire country? Purpose. In short,

Nelson Mandela was living for a purpose more important than making himself as comfortable as he could be.

The great thing about people who live with purpose, who are connected, and who have future dreams, is that their passion overcomes any obstacle. Pastor and author Max Lucado told a story that illustrates this brilliantly:

> "I have everything I need for joy!" Robert Reed said. . . .
>
> His hands are twisted and his feet are useless. . . .
>
> Robert has cerebral palsy.
>
> The disease keeps him from driving a car, riding a bike, and going for a walk. But it didn't keep him from . . . attending Abilene Christian University . . . .
>
> And Robert's disease didn't prevent him from becoming a missionary in Portugal.
>
> He moved to Lisbon, alone, in 1972. . . .
>
> Within six years he led seventy people to the Lord. . . .
>
> I heard Robert speak recently. . . . I watched people in the audience wipe away tears of admiration. . . . Robert could have asked for sympathy or pity, but. . . . he held his bent hand up in the air and boasted, "I have everything I need for joy."
>
> His shirts are held together by Velcro, but his life is held together by joy.[16]

LEARN TO LIVE WITH PASSION

By far the best way to live with passion is to let the Spirit of God move your heart to unleash compassion.

At our church's annual Thrive Conference, the goal is to inspire everyone to catch a fresh vision and live with passion. Most people arrive at our conference discouraged from whatever circumstances they're in. This year, we wanted to demonstrate the power of encouragement and grace. So, in front of three thousand people, we called a local pizza parlor and ordered one pizza. Then we told the crowd, "Whoever delivers this pizza, we're going to give them a tip they never expected." We passed buckets and told people that if they wanted to tip the delivery person, they could.

> *The best way to live with passion is to let the Spirit of God move your heart to unleash compassion.*

A young woman arrived with our pizza. She walked onstage, and everyone gave her a standing ovation. She was stunned. We found out that her husband had recently left the military and was in school studying to be a teacher. They had moved into the area to take care of an ailing grandparent. Then we gave her our tip. It totaled $3,469. We're pretty sure this breaks the Guinness World Record for pizza tipping.

This young woman started crying. She fell on her knees and said, "No one ever does anything like this for me." I told her that I hoped what we gave would be more than money. I said, "I hope this is a sign for you from God that you matter to Him more than you think and that He has better days ahead for you."

She cried all the way offstage. Three days later, she brought our entire staff cookies (because she could afford them). That tip is changing the life of a phenomenal couple in our community. And it will be a favorite story of three thousand people who learned how simple it is to be driven by passion to live with compassion.

To paraphrase Rabbi Harold Kushner, most people aren't afraid to die—they are afraid to get to the end of their lives and discover they never really lived.

CHAPTER 8

Get Off the Couch

Meet the Jesus Who Calls You to Stop Playing It Safe

Whoever believes in me will do the works I have been doing, and they will do even greater things than these.
—JESUS, JOHN 14:12

THERE IS A NEW IDOL IN AMERICA. IT'S NOT ONE OF THE USUAL suspects—sex, drugs, or materialism. This new idol is so powerful and pervasive that it can dominate your decisions and determine your destiny. People who cave in to it see their dreams discarded, their hearts shrunken, their faith diminished, and their growth stunted. Its victims live with shriveled souls.

What is this idol? The idol of *safety.*

Americans have grown up obeying signs posted everywhere: Safety First! Pastor Scott Dudley preached a sermon that got me thinking about this. Over the last thirty years, we have created the most risk-averse society in history. We are the most seat-belted, bike-helmeted, air-bagged, kneepad-wearing, private-schooled, gluten-freed, hand-sanitized, peanut-avoiding, sunscreen-slathering, hyperinsured, massively medicated, password-protected, valet-parked, security-systemed, inoculated generation in history—and all it has done is make everyone more afraid of *everything*.[1]

I'm not talking about taking risks for risk's sake, but I believe this new safety idol is destroying our faith.

Most Christians don't serve.

Why? *It might not be safe!*

Most Christians don't dream great dreams.

Why? *It might not be safe!*

Most Christians don't share their faith or take a stand.

Why? *It might not be safe!*

Most Christians don't tithe or give sacrificially.

Why? *It might not be safe!*

Most Christians don't break habits, take risks, build relationships, or have adventures . . .

Why? All for one reason:

It might not be safe!

I recently received a thick envelope in the mail. Stamped on the front were bold words:

YOUR INVITATION TO ADVENTURE!

I thought, *Awesome! What's in here? A trip down the Amazon? Hang gliding lessons? A* real *invitation to the Oval Office? A safari in Africa?* Not a chance. I opened the envelope and discovered that my "invitation to adventure" was—wait for it—a packet of coupons for stores at the local mall.

Now, if you're looking for more out of life than a trip to Kmart . . .

. . . if you refuse to believe that the ultimate goal in life is walking slowly up to your grave and falling in safely . . .

. . . if you want more on your tombstone than the phrase, "What a Relief—Nothing Bad Happened" . . .

. . . then this chapter is for you.

FOUR PRICE TAGS OF PLAYING IT SAFE

Let's take a look at the price tags of playing it safe and then listen to what Jesus had to say about dismantling the "safety first" idol.

1. Playing It Safe Limits Our Impact

I am a recovering fear-aholic. If given two options, I will almost always choose the safer one. The results of this kind of lifestyle all came to a head a few years ago.

Two weeks after a major financial campaign we held at our church, I received a phone call from a friend, Don Brewster, who works to save sex-trafficking victims in Cambodia. In two of the areas where we work together, many of the girls are sold into sexual slavery and abused up to seven times per night. Some of these girls are as young as four years old.

So I got this friendly call from Don to give me an update—or so I thought.

"The military general who is over all sex trafficking in our region just met with me," he said. "The general told me, 'Corruption is everywhere.' Then he explained that for the last ten years, each time he's done a raid, the girls and the pimps are already gone because the police are paid off for protection.

"The general would like to start an independent SWAT team. He wants to be sure he can trust the team, so he's going to create a team of Cambodians and some Westerners—all people he can trust. He'll train the SWAT team to do raids and arrests. We've been here for years, Ray, and we're finally going to put some of these terrible abusers of children behind bars."

He went on. "The problem is, this is going to cost a quarter of a million dollars to get started, and we don't have it. The general asked me if I knew anyplace I could get the money. I told him there's a church in Northern California, Bayside, that majors in helping in compassion work like this. So that's why I'm calling. It's going to cost two hundred and fifty thousand dollars just to get started. Can you fund this?"

The timing could not have been worse. The six-week massive "Compassion First" campaign we had just wrapped up had raised money for projects like this already. I'm smart enough to know that most congregations don't like the pastor to talk about money.

"Look," I said, "we just finished a major campaign to raise and give away a ton of money. I'm afraid that if I stand in front of my church and tell them one more time that I need them to give, they'll throw me out. It's just not the right time." (I was thinking, *It's just not safe!*)

I hung up the phone and tried to talk myself out of feeling like a wimp. I had just said no to helping create a task force that would arrest and lock up criminals who were preying on and imprisoning helpless young girls in Cambodia.

If you have ever had God "on your back," you know what the next two days felt like. So I gathered our senior staff and shared with them Don's idea, how it was bad timing for our church, and the wise (read "*safe*"*)* decision I'd made.

I unpacked the whole story. When I finished, they peppered me with questions and opinions. I don't recall exactly what was said, but it felt like this: "Who in their right mind would say no to a once-in-a-lifetime opportunity to create the first effective task force in the history of Cambodia that would lead to real arrests of real child abusers? And what kind of spiritual wimp would have such a hard heart and such a lack of faith to say no to rescuing helpless victims of sex trafficking?" The answer to those questions, of course, was . . . me.

I texted Don before I left the meeting to ask for details and a business plan. He e-mailed it right away. Now, I've seen a lot of proposals and business plans for church and charity work. They usually list needs like, "Bibles, basketballs, food, building supplies." But when Don's plan came, it was a full business plan with one entire page listing things like, "25 bulletproof vests, surveillance equipment, 25 buttonhole cameras with recording equipment . . ."

We said yes and decided to take a shot at raising the funds during our Christmas Eve services. We have about fourteen services, so we set a goal for the entire $250,000. It didn't sound possible, but it sounded right.

As I prepared for Christmas Eve services, I kept thinking, *There's no way our people are going to give $250,000. It won't happen, but at least this offering will get us partway there.*

We raised money at each service. A friend of mine, an artist named David Garibaldi, came onstage and did amazing paintings during our celebration of the girls we could help save. We auctioned those off afterward to bring in even more money. That Christmas Eve, our congregation did not give $250,000. Not even close. They gave $400,000.

As a result, in two cities in Cambodia, for the first time, *everything is changing!* At least once a week now, I get texts updating me on the raids and arrests. Here are a few:

> Hi Ray, the SWAT team just found and arrested a trafficker who had trafficked dozens of girls each week. She's the one who trafficked the girls in the CNN documentary.

> Rescued and providing after-care for two girls trafficked in Thailand for their virginity.

> Conducted our first successful raid on a brothel, rescuing four girls and arresting the manager!

> Rescued and provided after-care for a ten-year-old girl who was gang-raped by five men two nights ago.

> Another successful raid. There was an arrest of a rapist! The first rapist arrested in ten years.

> We have taken in seven Cambodian girls who were trafficked to China. This could lead to the arrest and return of hundreds of Cambodian girls who have been kidnapped and trafficked in China. The abuse they underwent would break your heart, but today they are thriving.

> One more thing, the arrests the team have made are beginning to come to trial now. So far they are three for three on convictions!

> We have 3 girls rescued in China awaiting return to Cambodia, and 21 more on a waiting list. The number of victims will probably reach the thousands.

To date, hundreds of girls have been rescued, and, for the first time, abusers have been put in prison, where they can no longer harm kids. And here's the point: The whole project almost didn't get off the ground. The whole rescue operation almost never happened. For one reason—*me!* I almost caved in to the idol of safety.

How about you? Playing it safe will not only limit your impact but it will also send you down the road to stagnation, unrealized potential, and unfulfilled dreams.

Got any God-honoring risks you are being called to take? The impact you can make explodes the minute you take off the handcuffs of fear and decide to make your life count.

2. Playing It Safe Shrinks Our Faith

One of my favorite friends is pastor and author Francis Chan. At a conference where he was speaking, he called Christians to stop living safe, comfortable lives with no real failures, risks, or struggles.

Francis had a balance beam put onstage. While standing on the beam, he described the desire for security and stability in all of us. He shared his own history. By the time he was sixteen years old, his mother, stepmother, father, aunt, and uncle had all died. That kind of loss creates a desire for a risk-free life of safety and security.

To illustrate the danger of that choice, Francis said, "Imagine you're at the Olympics . . ." Then, instead of doing a risk-filled routine, he just lay down on the beam, wrapped his arms and legs around it, and hugged it. He explained how people respond to instability by refusing to venture out. They say, "I'm just going to have my nice little family. I'm going to homeschool my kids. I'm not going to let them outside because the sun has bad rays."

He went on, "'I don't want to do anything crazy for God. I just want to go to church on Sundays and maybe give like 2 percent, and maybe help in the nursery.' . . . You do this your whole life then you say, 'God, You know what? I would love to die in my sleep and not even feel it and then just go up to heaven.'"

Then he crawled off the balance beam and threw his arms in the air as if he'd just dismounted from a spectacular Olympic performance.

Francis then asked, "Could you imagine watching the Olympics and watching someone do that, then expect a great score? What is the judge supposed to say?"[2]

> I can't find a single verse in Scripture where Jesus says, "Come, follow Me. Play it safe."

Lousy balance beam routine, but great point. Try to turn to a passage, any passage in your Bible, where God calls someone to something safe. Abraham leaves the familiar. Moses goes to Pharaoh. Esther puts her life in danger to persuade the king. David takes on a giant. Joshua crosses a river. Peter gets out of the boat. Jesus goes to the cross.

Authentic faith is developed only when we respond to the call of God and take a risk. That's because, when we take a risk, we learn that God can come through. We learn that God can do what we can't do on our own.

I can't find a single verse in Scripture where Jesus says, "Come, follow Me. Play it safe."

3. Playing It Safe Stunts Our Growth

Some time ago, a dad in our church took me aside. "I'm thinking about letting my fifteen-year-old daughter go on the mission trip to Mexico," he said, "but I have one question. Can you guarantee me it's going to be safe?"

What would you tell him?

For years, we have hauled hundreds of teenagers on an annual mission trip to Mexicali, Mexico. These kids work with the poor, build homes, love children, visit prisons, and do medical care. In the past few years, our kids have built over fifty homes. Yet the short-term trip is unquestionably more life-changing for the teenagers than it is for the people in Mexico.

It was while kids were signing up and everything was getting off the ground that the concerned dad asked me his safety question. I felt his concern, but I believe God has a greater concern.

"No, I can't guarantee complete safety," I said. "But I *can* guarantee you this. It's going to be much safer for your daughter to go to Mexico, learn to trust God, go public about her faith, serve the poor, develop a heart of generosity for other people, and live where she actually has to depend on God, than it ever will be for her to grow up in our community without stretching her faith or learning to take risks, and much safer than following the same routine every day where she thinks she doesn't need God."

The man looked at me in surprise. So I went on, "When your daughter gets into the kind of situation she'll be facing in Mexico, she will deepen her faith, have her values solidified, and possibly fall deeper in love with God. She will be a lot safer doing that than never learning that God is real or how to unleash compassion and take some God-honoring risks."

His daughter went on the trip. She has never recovered—in the best of ways.

The idea that you can insulate your life to the point where you are *guaranteed* total safety is a sham. You can still be taken out in a freak accident. Here are a couple of unexpected accidents you've probably never even considered shielding yourself from.

- In the early ninteenth century in London, a giant vat of beer exploded and a fifteen-foot wall of beer cascaded down the street. Seven people drowned in beer.[3] I know some people would think, *Well, if you gotta go . . .*
- In 1919, in Boston, a giant vat of molasses exploded, and the molasses oozed into the street. It managed to kill twenty-one people. I can hear it now: "Molasses! Walk for your lives!"[4]

Christians stop serving because it might not be safe. They stop tithing and giving because they think it might not be safe for their finances. They stop sharing because it might be embarrassing. They stop risking, they stop asking God what He wants them to do, and they slowly develop an apathetic, boring, "safe" faith.

When you take a risk and God comes through for you, then He becomes real to you. That fires up your heart and starts you on the path to rediscovering a faith that is alive.

4. Playing It Safe Shrivels Our Hearts

If you are a Christ-follower (and are listening for His voice), Jesus is going to challenge your faith by asking you to do what seems impossible . . .

- *I want you to go on a mission trip.* "I can't spend the time, God."
- *I want you to start tithing.* "I can't afford that, God."
- *I want you to go talk to that person about Me.* "I'm afraid of that, God."
- *I want you to ask forgiveness from that person.* "I can't do that, God."
- *I want you to lead a small group Bible study.* "I don't know how, God."
- *I want you to work with junior high students.* "You've got to be kidding!"

Our faith gets tested and stretched only when we respond to Jesus asking us to do something that in our human logic is impossible.

Taking steps of faith is the alternative to the boredom and stagnation that causes most people to wither up and die. Author Gregg Levoy called it the "common cold of the soul."[5]

> To sinful patterns of behavior that never get confronted and changed,
> Abilities and gifts that never get cultivated and deployed—
> Until weeks become months,
> And months turn into years,
> And one day you're looking back on a life of
> Deep, intimate, gut-wrenchingly honest conversations you never had;
> Great bold prayers you never prayed,
> Exhilarating risks you never took,
> Sacrificial gifts you never offered,
> Lives you never touched,
> And you're sitting in a recliner with a shriveled soul,
> And forgotten dreams, and you realize there
> was a world of desperate need,
> And a great God calling you to be part of
> something bigger than yourself—
> You see the person you could have become but did not;
> You never followed your calling.
> You never got out of the boat.[6]

FIVE STEPS TO BREAKING FREE FROM THE IDOL OF SAFETY

Swiss physician, author, and pastoral counselor Paul Tournier wrote, "All of us have vast reservoirs of full potential. But the roads that lead to those reservoirs are guarded by the dragon of fear."[7]

A while back, I had the privilege to take a boat ride across the Sea of Galilee. The weather was warm and the sea was calm. But one night Jesus took Peter on a *real* adventure there. He put the disciples in a boat and sent them ahead of Him to cross this five-mile-wide lake—and then the storm hit. Late at night, hours into the dangerous deluge, they were still laboring to get to the other side. That's when they saw Jesus walking toward them *on the water*.

Matthew recorded Peter's response:

> "Lord, if it's you," Peter replied, "tell me to come to you on the water."
>
> "Come," he said.
>
> Then Peter got down out of the boat, walked on the water and came toward Jesus. (14:28–29)

You also may know the rest of the story. Peter has taken flak for two thousand years for taking his eyes off Jesus and starting to sink. But in my book, he's a hero. Why? The other eleven disciples stayed in the boat and never even gave it a shot. They missed out on their once-in-a-lifetime chance to walk on water. Why? They were playing it safe.

The only way to break the grip of fear is to get out of the boat.

Here are five steps (none of them easy) that will help anyone who takes them dismantle the idol of safety.

1. Stop Saying No to Everything Just Because It's Scary

When Carol and I were living in Northern California many years ago, minding our own business, a few people in a neighboring city, Granite Bay, came to us and said, "Would you be interested in helping to start a church here?" Two copycat teenaged suicides had shaken the community, and these people were hoping we could help start something that would reach teenagers.

Quickly applying the paraphrased verse that says, "Lord, here am I, send someone else," I said, "No."

But I never told them the real reason. *I was afraid!* I was afraid we'd try to start a church and no one would come. Or we'd start it and no helpers would show up. Or we'd start it and I'd be buried setting up the nursery each Sunday in some rented high school. Or we'd have to raise money and build a building. (We did.) And what if we got sued? (We did.) I was afraid of it all.

Instead of admitting my fears to anyone, I just kept saying, "The Lord hath not called his servant Ray to this task."

The people started a prayer meeting to pray for a church to be planted, and I agreed to go pray (only). Twenty-six people attended the first meeting. After prayer, a buddy of mine said, "So, what do you think?"

"This isn't going to happen," I said. "There aren't enough people."

A month later the prayer meeting attendance *skyrocketed* . . . to twenty-eight.

So I agreed to try a test service. I said, "We'll just see if anybody shows up."

We did a test service at the local tennis club. There were 120 chairs set up when I got there, and, thinking only 50 people would come, I took down 40 chairs. I was hoping it would look full when the small group of people showed up. It started raining, so I took down another row of chairs. I still have no explanation as to why 162 people showed up. We put up the chairs and still ran out of room. We ran downstairs and unplugged the NFL game and plugged in our service so people could watch it on a screen.

It was a simple church service. We worshiped, and then I preached. I figured a bunch of people weren't Christians yet, so at the end, I gave a clear invitation and asked them to raise their hands to receive Jesus as Savior and Lord. As half the hands in the room went up I realized that almost 50 percent of the people in the room had just committed their lives to Christ at our very first service. At the end of the service, I announced we'd be back for another service in a month.

The next month, we met in a school. This time, 130 chairs were set up, but I was convinced no more than 80 people would come back, so I took down 50 chairs. Instead, 226 people showed up, and the same thing happened. We worshiped, taught the Bible, and gave an invitation, and people became Christians.

After that service, I flew to Chicago for a prayer summit with thousands of leaders. The second night, the direction of my life changed. I was in a late-night, *long* prayer meeting. After about two hours and running out of things to pray for, I decided to ask God to give that group in Granite Bay a pastor (because it sure wasn't going to be me).

This has never happened to me before or since. But the minute I started praying that God would give Bayside a pastor, God, as clear as crystal, told me to read the book of Acts, chapter 18. I read these words: "The Lord spoke to Paul in a vision: 'Do not be afraid'" (v. 9). For the first time in my life, I felt the *direct* call of God.

I walked out of that prayer meeting at midnight, went to my hotel room, and called my wife to find out whether or not I had heard from God. (Husbands know what I'm talking about.) I will never forget her response. Carol started crying on the phone. "I knew God was telling us to do this," she said. "I was just waiting for God to make it obvious to you."

Carol and I told the core group that they were stuck with us. The explosion that continues to this day has been unlike anything I've ever seen. People have come to Christ by the thousands. Kids, teenagers, adults—even relatives we've prayed for twenty years to come to Christ came to Him in our church.

Other than my salvation, my wife, and my kids, pastoring Bayside Church has been the best thing that has ever happened to me. The past twenty years of my life have been by far the best twenty years of my life. But I almost missed the best thing God would ever do with me, for one reason—*fear.*

Fear is the darkroom where negatives develop. Fear will cause you to miss the best thing God wants to do with you.

Reading this, you may be feeling that God is asking you to do something, give something, serve somewhere, or launch something, and you're a little afraid to do it. You just might be on the first day of the best twenty-year run of your life.

2. Start Praying Some Dangerous Prayers

The most dangerous prayer you will ever pray is, "Thy will be done." Jesus prayed this prayer. You and I need to learn how to pray dangerous prayers more often. Once we pray it, we need to start listening for the call of God in our lives and then act on what God tells us.

Pastor John Ortberg tells a story in his great book *If You Want to Walk on Water, You've Got to Get Out of the Boat* about a guy named Doug Coe. Doug works in Washington, DC, and has a ministry where he disciples and does Bible studies with businesspeople.

> Bob, an insurance salesman. . . . became a Christian and began to meet with Doug to learn about his new faith.
>
> One day, Bob came in all excited about a statement in the Bible where Jesus says, "Ask whatever you will in my name and you shall receive it."
>
> "Is that really true?" Bob demanded.
>
> Doug explained, "Well, it's not a blank check. . . . But yes—it really is true. Jesus really does answer prayer." . . .
>
> "All right. I'll pray for Kenya."
>
> "Do you know anyone in Kenya?" Doug asked.
>
> "No." . . .
>
> Doug . . . challenged Bob to pray every day for six months for Kenya. If Bob would do that and nothing extraordinary happened, Doug would pay him five hundred dollars. But if something remarkable did happen, Bob would pay Doug five hundred dollars. . . .
>
> Bob began to pray, and for a long while nothing happened. Then

one night he was at a dinner in Washington. . . . One woman said she helped run an orphanage in Kenya—the largest of its kind. . . .

Bob roared to life. . . .

"You're obviously very interested in my country," the woman said to Bob, overwhelmed by his sudden barrage of questions. "You've been to Kenya before?"

"No." . . .

She asked Bob if he would like to come visit Kenya. . . .

When Bob arrived in Kenya, he was appalled by the poverty and the lack of basic health care. . . . He began to write to large pharmaceutical companies, describing to them the vast need he had seen. . . .

This orphanage received more than a million dollars' worth of medical supplies.

The woman called Bob up and said, "Bob, this is amazing! We've had the most phenomenal gifts because of the letters you wrote. We would like to fly you back over and have a big party. Will you come?"

So Bob flew back to Kenya. While he was there, the president of Kenya came to the celebration . . . and offered to take Bob on a tour of Nairobi. . . . In the course of the tour, they saw a prison. Bob asked about a group of prisoners there.

"They're political prisoners," he was told.

"That's a bad idea," Bob said brightly. "You should let them out."

Bob finished the tour and flew back home. Sometime later, Bob received a phone call from the State Department of the United States Government: . . .

"Were you recently in Kenya?"

"Yes."

"Did you make any statements to the president about political prisoners?"

"Yes."

"What did you say?"

"I told him he should let them out."

The State Department official explained that the department had

> been working for years to get the release of those political prisoners, to no avail. . . . But now the prisoners had been released, and the State Department was told it had been largely because of . . . Bob.[8]

All that happened because one guy connected to a living Savior and started believing He answered prayer. One guy started believing God is not dead and is not done working in our lives—through our lives—in the world. One guy dared to pray a dangerous prayer and then act on the answers God gave him.

3. Get Out Your Wallet

Gratitude is one of the healthiest human emotions. Maybe that's why the apostle Paul said, "God loves a cheerful giver" (2 Corinthians 9:7). Somehow joy and giving are connected.

This runs counter to the prevailing American opinion that having more will make us more happy or more fulfilled. If a lifestyle of acquisition and affluence led to a happy life, Howard Hughes would have had a ball. As described by pastor and author Bill Hybels:

> All he ever really wanted in life was more. He wanted more money, so he parlayed inherited wealth into a billion-dollar pile of assets. He wanted more fame, so he broke into the Hollywood scene and soon became a filmmaker and star. He wanted more sensual pleasures, so he paid handsome sums to indulge his every sexual urge. He wanted more thrills, so he designed, built, and piloted the fastest aircraft in the world. He wanted more power, so he secretly dealt political favors so skillfully that two U.S. presidents became his pawns.
>
> All he ever wanted was more. He was absolutely convinced that more would bring him true satisfaction. Unfortunately, history shows otherwise. . . .
>
> He concluded his life emaciated; colorless; sunken chest; fingernails in grotesque, inches-long corkscrews; rotting, black teeth; tumors; innumerable needle marks from his drug addiction.

> Howard Hughes died believing the myth of more. He died a billionaire junkie, insane by all reasonable standards.[9]

Giving breaks the grip of materialism in life. That may explain why sacrificial generosity was one of Jesus' themes and became the lifestyle of the early church. The first church was barely up and running when it was described this way: "They began selling their property and possessions and were sharing them with all, as anyone might have need" (Acts 2:45 NASB).

Generosity is riskier but also far more fulfilling.

Last year, during one of Bayside's Compassion First generosity campaigns, we called everyone to give sacrificially so we could raise two million dollars. Our goal was to give it away to fund twenty-five different compassion projects in the region and around the world. We gave the kids banks to raise their money. We gave high school kids cans of Pringles to empty and then stash them with cash. Their goal? We asked them to raise fifty thousand dollars to launch a child-survival program with Compassion International in Kenya.

Many church members took sacrificial giving seriously for the first time. The first family that came to talk to me after we launched the campaign had received Christ in our church just three weeks earlier. "We figured out how we're going to sacrifice," they said.

"How's that?" I asked.

"We've decided to stop drinking and smoking for the next three years. We're going to give all our alcohol and cigarette money to the church for three solid years!" (What they didn't know was that living like that could become *permanent.*)

The seniors in the church were just as eager, as you can see from an incredible couple I'll call Jim and Cheryl. One day Cheryl came up to me at church with tears in her eyes. She said, "My husband is amazing."

When a wife says that, it always stops me dead in my tracks. I encouraged her to explain.

"We've been praying about how to give sacrificially. He's getting ready to retire, but he came to me and said he'd been praying about it. He asked me how I felt about him working for two more years instead of retiring as scheduled. He said we could give everything he earned for his last two years to build the kingdom of God."

She punctuated how she felt with this statement: "They don't make men like this anymore, do they?"

Teenagers got involved in learning to sacrifice. One family met together and the father said they were too tight financially to do anything. "I don't think we'll participate," he told his family, "but we can serve."

His fifteen-year-old daughter spoke up. "What if we sacrifice?"

If you haven't been around any fifteen-year-olds lately, then you wouldn't know that they all look alike—all you see is the tops of their heads. They are glued to their phones. But this young teen had caught the vision to help others. She put her iPhone on the table and said, "What if I gave up my phone for three years? Will that help?"

"Well, your phone bill would probably pay for the whole campaign," her dad joked.

"Okay, I'll do it," she said, pushing the phone across the table. The dad's dropped jaw had not yet closed when she looked him in the eye and added, "Now, what are you and Mom going to do?"

The parents had saved to purchase a new car, but decided they would try to make their car last for another three years. They pooled everything they could and cut everywhere possible. Over the next three years, the family that thought they had nothing to give managed to give eighteen thousand dollars to Compassion First projects.

Even the kids got involved. And God rewarded their sacrifice in surprising ways that they would never forget. My secretary is one of those born-happy people, so I was surprised when she came into my office one day with tears streaming down her face. She was holding a big brown-paper sack. "You're not going to believe this," she said.

I could see some crumpled dollar bills on the top of the bag, and below them were coins. There was a note at the top of the sack, so I picked it up. There, in a child's scrawl, was this message:

Dear Pastor Ray,

We really really really wanted to go to Disneyland, but we really think the Compassion First stuff is better. Here is all our money.

—Courtney and Micha, ages 5 and 7

We brought our staff into the office, and everyone was choked up as we passed around the letter. The next Sunday, I wanted to share the kids' note, so I showed a PowerPoint slide for the whole church to see. As God would have it, that Sunday, a senior executive from Disney was in town and visited our church. He called my secretary the next week and gave a scholarship for the entire family to spend a full week at Disney and the Disneyland Hotel. Those kids were ecstatic, running around the house trying to figure out what else they could give!

I'm not promising that if you pass up a trip to Disney to give the money to your church that you'll end up with a week at the Disneyland Hotel. But I am saying that when you start giving and living and developing a heart of sacrificial generosity, you will find that you have come fully alive!

4. Stop Watching—Try Living!

My friend Paul Carroll was a field reporter for the *Wall Street Journal.* He intentionally set out to *live life* rather than merely watch and report on others living it. Great decision. It has given him some unforgettable experiences.

Once, he became a crewman on a sailboat, the forty-two-foot *Philadelphia*, which crossed the North Atlantic from Belgium in a race celebrating the two hundredth anniversary of the US Constitution. The only experience he'd had with boats before was something like canoeing to Tom Sawyer Island at Disneyland.

At the beginning of the race, a spectator craft collided with their boat, which required half a day to repair. The inconvenience seemed major to the crew until they were out on the open seas and encountered worse problems. Seventy-foot waves pounded them while sixty-five-knot winds raged. Paul watched as gigantic walls of water rushed toward them, and he wondered if they would break over the boat or if their craft would survive, only to drop straight down on the other side. One night the whole crew thought the ship would break apart, but they survived to see the morning. After three thousand miles, they pulled down a third-place finish.

Another time, Paul was stationed in Mexico City. Again, wanting to be involved instead of only watching, he decided to find a matador who would teach him to bullfight. Perhaps fortunately, no one would teach him. It seems the matadors have a code of ethics that doesn't include allowing foreigners in tights to make their profession look foolish.

The closest most of us are going to come to anything like this is watching a video. Imagine the impact on America if every one of the roughly two hundred million self-professed Christians in America *for one week* took all the time normally spent in front of the television or online, got out of our homes, and served the community. It would make national news—so when we turned on the news, we would be watching ourselves making an impact.

Many Christians will listen to a sermon about getting out of the boat and then go home and spend the next six hours in the top-selling chair in America—the La-Z-Boy. Think about the number of Americans sitting on their couches day after day. We consume, on average, five hours of television every day.[10] Instead of watching reality TV, try *living* some reality!

More than a decade ago, I spoke at a massive youth rally in Seattle. While there, I met one of the most effective youth workers I've ever been around. He was also a successful businessman. I was talking to him and his wife between sessions and got curious. I said, "How did you get connected to teenagers?"

He looked at his wife and said, "You tell him."

She said, "He was becoming a couch potato. He'd come home from work and sit on the couch and watch television until it was time for bed. I kept watching him do this and finally got fed up with his sedentary lifestyle. On a Monday, I called Young Life and donated my husband."

We had a good laugh, and she explained more. "I asked when their next meeting was, and told them he'd be there to help. At first, he didn't want to do it. I told him, 'I donated you and told them you'd show up.' He showed up that next Monday and found out that teenagers liked him. So he started working with the teenagers in the schools. Then we started opening up our home to teenagers."

The year I talked to that couple, his impact on the teenagers was so great that the high school students dedicated their annual yearbook to him.

Bestselling Christian author Philip Yancey, describing an idea originated by G. K. Chesterton, wrote that we need "a new kind of prophet, not like the prophets of old who reminded people that they were going to die, but one who reminded them that they are not dead yet."[11]

Get in motion and start living. And, as much as possible, get in motion to serve others.

5. Realize What's at Stake

The four most depressing words in the English language are these: *It's just too late.* For Moses, it looked like it was.

Moses killed a guy trying to do God's work his own way. He ended up a fugitive hiding out in the wilderness, a runaway murderer, an escaped felon—a has-been.

Thinking he was washed up, Moses saw God in a burning bush, heard the call, and eventually went back to Egypt. After a ten-round prizefight, Pharaoh let the Israelites start marching out, only to run straight into the banks of the Red Sea. They were trapped. So Moses stopped going forward and prayed.

I love what happened next, because it's the only time in the Bible that I can find God telling somebody to stop praying. God said to Moses, "Why do you cry to me? Tell the people of Israel to go forward" (Exodus 14:15 ESV).

God said not to stand still or move sideways but to go forward. He said, "Raise your staff and stretch out your hand over the sea to divide the water so that the Israelites can go through the sea on dry ground" (Exodus 14:16).

Moses stretched out his hand over the sea, and all that night God drove the sea back. The next morning, the Israelites were able to walk over on dry ground, with a wall of water on the right and left. The Egyptians pursued, so all Pharaoh's horses and chariots followed them into the sea. Then God told Moses to stretch his hand over the water again—and the entire Egyptian army had to learn to tread water.

Think about it. Moses' best moments in life began when he finally said yes to God. In other words . . .

- when Moses finally stopped saying no,
- when he finally stopped making excuses,
- when he finally stopped being overcome with fear and discouragement,
- when he finally stopped thinking, *It's just too late*,
- when he finally stopped saying, "I'm too old," and, "I've messed up too much,"
- when he finally stopped being driven by his insecurities,
- when he finally said yes, obeyed God, took a risky step with God, and moved forward . . .

. . . look at what happened!

The minute Moses said yes to God, he experienced the unlikely but commanding performance before Pharaoh.

After he said yes, two million people were freed from hundreds of years of slavery.

After he said yes, he watched the Red Sea part and two million people escape through on dry land.

After he said yes, he received the Ten Commandments, wrote the first five books of the Bible, and experienced the miracle of the manna, Mount Sinai, the promised land, the glory of God . . .

The best years of Moses' life happened only after saying yes! None of these experiences would have happened had Moses not stopped wallowing in self-pity and finally started to say yes to God.

> When you say yes to God, incredible things happen.

When you say yes to God, incredible things happen.

On the other hand, nothing much happens to people who always say no.

So which are you going to be?

You want adventure? You want a sense of purpose? Say yes, and then hang on for the ride of your life.

CHAPTER 9

Nothing Great Ever *Just* Happens

Meet the Jesus Who Wants to Work Through You

Greater love has no one than this: to lay down one's life for one's friends.

—Jesus, John 15:13

YEARS AGO I WROTE A BOOK CALLED *MAKING SUNDAY SCHOOL Come Alive* and included a story about one paralyzed guy, four friends, Jesus, and one (ex-) youth pastor. This story, which might be greatly embellished, is about a youth pastor in Florida who got creative teaching a story from Mark's gospel about Jesus. At the church where the youth pastor served, a large room in one wing was about to be remodeled. The youth pastor talked to the builders, then scheduled his junior high Sunday school class in that room the week before the remodel was to begin.

With everything in place, the youth pastor started reading the kids the second chapter of Mark.

"A few days later, when Jesus again entered Capernaum, the people heard that he had come home. They gathered in such large numbers that there was no

room left, not even outside the door, and he preached the word to them. Some men came, bringing to him a paralyzed man, carried by four of them."

The kids heard footsteps on the roof as he read. Undaunted, the youth pastor kept reading.

"Since they could not get him to Jesus because of the crowd, they made an opening in the roof above Jesus by digging through it."

Then kids heard an explosion of noise as a chainsaw started up right above them. The noise increased as the builders conspiring with the youth pastor started cutting a hole in the roof. Ceiling tiles fell. Dust and debris filled the room as the shocked kids fled to the sides.

The youth pastor ignored the commotion and kept reading.

"And then lowered the mat the man was lying on."

Then the four workers lowered a guy on a stretcher right in front of the youth pastor. Who just kept reading . . .

"When Jesus saw their faith, he said to the paralyzed man, 'Son, your sins are forgiven.'"

The youth pastor paused, looked at the guy on the stretcher, and said, "Son, your sins are forgiven." Then he kept reading.

"Now some teachers of the law were sitting there, thinking to themselves, 'Why does this fellow talk like that? He's blaspheming! Who can forgive sins but God alone?'

"Immediately Jesus knew in his spirit that this was what they were thinking in their hearts, and he said to them, 'Why are you thinking these things? Which is easier: to say to this paralyzed man, "Your sins are forgiven," or to say, "Get up, take your mat and walk"? But I want you to know that the Son of Man has authority on earth to forgive sins.' So he said to the man, 'I tell you, get up, take your mat and go home.' He got up, took his mat and walked out in full view of them all."

The youth pastor looked again at the man who had been lowered into the room and said, "Rise, take up your mat, and walk." The guy leaped up, ran around the room, and high-fived the shocked kids. Then, as his friends on the roof celebrated, he ran out of the room.

Then the youth pastor finished:

"This amazed everyone and they praised God, saying, 'We have never seen anything like this!'"

The young people had never seen anything like it either. Of course, that youth pastor is still looking for a new church, but the kids will never forget Mark 2. Neither should you, because it raises a life-changing question. Here it is:

Is it possible to *trigger a miracle* in the life of someone you care about?

All of us have people we love and want great things for . . .

- Moms and dads want to see their kids have lives that honor God.
- Wives and husbands want to see God transform a spouse.
- We have good friends, relatives, neighbors, and business associates . . . and for the people we love most, our desire is to see God do great things in their lives.

So my question is this:

Is it possible to *take steps of faith* that actually lead to God changing lives?

Now, before you discard this chapter, notice I didn't say, "Is it possible to *make* the miracle happen?"

And . . .

I'm not selling holy water from the Jordan River.

I don't own any prayer cloths dunked in the Sea of Galilee.

So let me ask one more time: For the people you love most, is it possible to *take steps of faith* that actually lead to God changing lives? I believe the answer is yes, because . . .

. . . that is *exactly* what happened in the second chapter of Mark.

The man's friends didn't do the miracle (that is God's job alone). But it was their *faith*, their *expectation*, their *actions*, and their *willingness not to quit* that triggered the miracle in the life of this man.

I believe that anyone willing to take the same steps two thousand years later can see the same kinds of things happen in the lives of people they care about.

FIVE STEPS TO R-A-I-S-E YOUR FAITH

Is there someone you deeply care about, in whose life you'd like to see a miracle happen? Maybe you want to see God do something in the life of your spouse, your children, your parents, your friends, your neighbors, or your relatives.

I once taught the Mark 2 principles to a roomful of people. A mom who heard me had a son who had lost his faith, walked away from God, and declared to his family that he was now an atheist. The mom felt understandably discouraged and helpless. She wrote the five following specific points and taped them up inside her closet. She determined she would keep repeating the five steps over and over until God worked in the life of her son. It did take a long while. (Kids are never easy.) It took time, but today her son *is* walking with God—and, to her surprise, he married a really cool Christian woman. They are all thrilled. She has a right to be thrilled. She refused to give up on her son. She refused to give in to discouragement and hopelessness. As a result she got to experience the thrill of taking steps that, over time, helped trigger a miracle. How does that happen?

Please understand that these five steps are not magic, but they sure beat giving in or giving up. Here they are with a simple way of remembering them—R.A.I.S.E.

1. Raise Your Expectations

What impresses God?

Think about that for a minute. What could possibly impress God? Is LeBron James impressed watching a bunch of third-graders shooting hoops on a playground? Would you take a baby gift to Kate Middleton and hope to impress the royal parents?

If you're God, what could ever impress you? The only thing I've ever found in Scripture is this: "When Jesus saw their faith" (Mark 2:5). Jesus was moved by the faith of the paralyzed man's four friends. It was their faith that led to actions that triggered a miracle.

You will never lift anybody up until you start to believe that God has not stopped working in the lives of people. The four friends *expected* Jesus to work in the life of their friend, so they brought him to Jesus. If you quit *expecting* God to show up and work, don't be surprised when that happens.

They somehow knew if they could just get the guy in a room with Jesus, three things would happen. Their friend would

- hear Christ's words,
- receive Christ's forgiveness,
- experience Christ's power,

    . . . and never be the same.

By the way, that's a great definition of a church service—*hear* the Word of God; *receive* God's forgiveness and a brand-new start; *experience* His power; and leave changed by the Word of God, the grace of God, and the power of God.

You will never raise people to higher levels until your faith raises your expectations.

The best example I've seen for this recently is a poverty-stricken pastor in Korea who, like many of the people in our church, sponsors kids through Compassion International. The difference is this: He is so poor that in his spare time he shines shoes to support the *seven* kids he is sponsoring. And because he is convinced that God wants to break the cycle of poverty in the lives of these kids, every single day he looks at their pictures and prays *great expectation prayers* for what "his kids" can become:

You will never raise people to higher levels until your faith raises your expectations.

- For Luis in Ecuador to become a doctor.
- For Ikenshia in El Salvador to become a leader in her country.
- For Zenabou in Burkina Faso to be a lawmaker.

- For Eric in Kenya to become a great politician.
- For Jesus in Peru to become a pastor.
- For Zharick in Colombia to become Miss Colombia.
- For Joel in Bolivia to become a general in the army.

Believe that God is ready to work in people. Someone asked me about the church where I pastor. I said it's like an In-N-Out Burger. He said, "I love that place." (Who doesn't?) Then he asked, "What do you mean?"

In-N-Out Burger has a simple menu. They've never changed. Twenty years ago, when we started Bayside, we had a simple menu. We worship God and teach the Bible. We've never changed.

In our very first service, I gave a crystal clear invitation to receive Christ. A sea of hands went up, indicating those who had prayed and committed their lives to Christ. That was twenty years ago, and ever since, people have made commitments to Christ in almost every service, every week. We finally started a table called "I Raised My Hand." People who want to know more about Christ and to receive Him as Savior and Lord can come to the table, talk to someone, and pick up a book. (I'll mail you one, if you want. Just e-mail Ray@RayJohnston.com.)

For a six-week series called "For Atheists Only," we put up a second table called "I'm Thinking About Raising My Hand."

We said, "Those of you who raised your hand and received Christ, go to that table. Those of you who are thinking about raising your hand, there's a bunch of smart people who will answer questions at this other table." People flooded both tables in every service for six weeks.

A visiting pastor once asked me, "You actually *expect* people are going to become Christians in every service, don't you?"

I said, "Absolutely. If the day ever came when people did not respond, I would be shocked. There's a spiritual principle at work. My experience tells me that you usually don't get what you deserve—*you get what you expect.*"

Jesus "saw their faith." What does He see when He looks at you?

2. Anticipate Obstacles

Why are we shocked when life's not easy? When plans are going really well, Christians will often say, "God is really in this." But when things are not going well, we assume that God is not going to work. I love what these four friends did. Their first attempt was a complete disaster. Blocked by the crowd (a first-century traffic jam), they were unable to reach Jesus. They failed. *It is exactly at this point most of us go wrong.*

Notice what the friends did *not* do. They *didn't* respond how I usually respond when things don't go well:

- They didn't become cynical.
- They didn't blame all the people in their way.
- They didn't tell their friend, "Well, it just must not be your day."
- They didn't let obstacles derail them.
- They didn't lose faith.
- Above all, they didn't give in to discouragement.
- And above that—*they didn't give up!*

Most of us will try something until it gets hard—then we quit. Effective people don't stop when they run into obstacles. The great missionary to China from the 1800s, J. Hudson Taylor, said, "I have found that there are three stages in every great work of God: first, it is impossible, then it is difficult, then it is done."[1]

About a hundred years after Hudson Taylor, Pastor Rick Warren said, "There is no such thing as opportunity without opposition."[2] Chuck Swindoll said, "Opposition is to be expected when God's will is carried out."[3]

Sometimes you have to just *stay at it!* This profound statement, often attributed to Calvin Coolidge, urges us to press on: "Nothing in this world can take the place of persistence. Talent will not; nothing is more common than unsuccessful men with talent. Genius will not; unrewarded genius is almost a proverb. Education will not; the world is full of educated derelicts. Persistence and determination are omnipotent."[4]

- Without overcoming obstacles, you can't get or keep a job.
- Without overcoming obstacles, you can't buy a house.
- Without overcoming obstacles, you can't get married.
- Without overcoming obstacles, you can't stay married.
- Without overcoming obstacles, you can't get a driver's license.
- Without overcoming obstacles, you can't build a career.
- Without overcoming obstacles, you can't build a church.

On a cold, drizzly Sunday morning, I drove up to our church. Back then, we were still meeting at a high school. We were building our first church home, and, as with almost everything built in California, opposition developed. Pulling up, I was shocked to see anti-Bayside protesters picketing our worship services. They even came with ammunition—anti-Bayside literature. I had never seen anything like this. But my next thought was, *God never said it would be easy. But He did say He would be with us.*

Then I started thinking about how we are commanded to love our enemies. It was a cold morning, so we brought out hot coffee and doughnuts to the protestors. The drizzle turned to a light rain, so our team went outside and gave them umbrellas. But then it started raining harder. We said if they wanted to leave we'd be willing to stuff their materials into every single program for the rest of the services that morning so their team could go home and get warm.

They were unrelenting. One of the protestors told me it would be a cold day in hell before we got that church built. Three years later, there must have been a dramatic temperature drop in hell, because we gathered for the first time in our new building. The best part of that day was when one of my team came to me and said, "A guy outside wants to meet you."

I went outside and met a guy who made my day when he said, "I was one of the opponents. I didn't want this church here because I live nearby. But I was so impressed by how you treated us. So, if it's okay with you, I'd like to attend here because I like being able to walk to church."

I shook his hand and said, "Welcome to Bayside! You're the reason we built this church!" A lot of former opponents are with us now, including one who now serves on our land development team.

The problem is this: we assume that God is not working when we don't experience instant success.

In the face of opposition, press on, because God might have even bigger purposes for the obstacles. Scan the Bible. Watch people's lives. Almost everything great that ever gets developed happens not on the mountaintops but in the valleys of life.

Think about it:

- Character is developed in the valleys of life.
- Compassion is developed in the valleys of life.
- Depth is developed in the valleys of life.
- Integrity is developed in the valleys of life.
- Commitment to a marriage is tested and developed in the valleys of life.
- Almost everything worth having is developed in the valleys of life.

A little-appreciated mark of spiritual maturity is when you're able to *stay positive under pressure.* When we hit valleys, it might be a sign that God is actually at work—even if it doesn't look like it. As my friend Sherwood Carthen used to say, "Christians, stop whining. We are not 'under attack.' We are the ones 'on the attack!'"

3. Increase Contact

There is no impact without contact. The closer you are to people, the greater your potential for impacting their lives.

In our culture, contact is on the way out. America is rapidly becoming a high-tech/low-touch culture. There was a day when Americans relaxed on their front porches. Now we have garage door openers so we can get into our houses without having to look at or talk to anyone. There was a day when people sat in living rooms and actually *talked.* Now we watch TV or text every time we sit down. We had a bunch of teenagers in our living room recently. We confiscated their cell phones, forcing them to have real conversations. Our culture is removing interpersonal connection from America, which is developing an isolated, disconnected culture.

Those four friends did the opposite. They *attached* themselves to their friend and *stayed* connected. When they wanted to see Jesus work in his life, the first step they took was this: they increased contact.

Jesus connected with real people. Especially the people He wasn't *supposed* to be connected to. Jesus went after Levi, an "unspiritual," "unclean" tax collector (Luke 5:27–28). Levi met Jesus, experienced grace, and discovered, to his surprise, that Jesus accepted and loved him. That connection changed his life.

What did Levi do in response? He said, "I've got a bunch of friends just like me. And maybe the same thing can happen to them. I'm going to throw a party! I'll invite Jesus, and then I'll fill the party with my friends." (His friends were corrupt tax collectors, notorious cheaters, and despised traitors.) It looks like Levi—like the four guys—was thinking, *If I can just get 'em in the same room as Jesus, who knows what could happen?*

Think about the religious climate at the time. Jesus would never meet with these friends of Levi, right? It would ruin His credibility. It would trash His reputation. It would damage His ministry. But that's exactly what Jesus did.

Levi loved his friends so passionately that he connected them to Jesus. The party was a smash hit, with a huge crowd meeting Jesus. Afterward, everyone was thrilled—except the religious elite. The Pharisees and teachers of the law complained to the disciples, "Why do you eat and drink with tax collectors and sinners?" (Luke 5:30).

Jesus ate and drank with the people who needed Him most. People who felt rejected and condemned by the religious elites of the day flocked to Jesus and were never the same.

We put a sign in front of our church one Christmas that said:

Nobody's perfect.
Everyone's welcome.
Anything's possible.

To have *impact*, you have to increase *contact*.

4. Start Lifting People Up (Instead of Putting People Down)

Before sunrise on the morning of July 16, 1945, the darkness in the sky over New Mexico lit up. Starting with a brilliant flash, the first test of a nuclear bomb sent an atomic fireball thirty thousand feet into the sky. Because of the intense heat, all that was left of the blast site at ground zero was green radioactive glass. The heat had even melted the sand.

Twenty-one days later, that power was harnessed in a bomb called Little Boy, put in a B-29 bomber named *Enola Gay*, flown toward Japan, and dropped on Hiroshima. Robert Lewis, the copilot of the *Enola Gay*, wrote in his journal, "My God, what have we done?"[5] And the pilots flew on in stunned silence.

Six years later a building in Arco, Idaho, lit up with that same nuclear power. There was no mushroom cloud, no explosion, no sand-melting heat, no sky bright as day. Nuclear energy in the form of electricity came from the same reactions—just a little different arrangement. Today about one-fifth of our electricity that warms homes and lights cities comes from that kind of power.

Amazing. Pastor Chris Brown pointed out that the exact same uranium, the exact same chemical process, can absolutely destroy a city, wreck lives, and cause instant death, pain, and sorrow—or it can bring light and life and generate power for hospitals and homes.[6]

That is exactly what James talks about in his third chapter: "With the tongue we praise our Lord and Father, and with it we curse human beings, who have been made in God's likeness. Out of the same mouth come praise and cursing. My brothers and sisters, this should not be" (vv. 9–10).

James is saying that some people have character without compassion. Critical, condescending, cocky, conceited people push others down instead of lifting them up. Something in them refuses to affirm and lift other people.

Fundamentally, everybody has one life to live. With that life, you are going to destroy people by putting them down or brighten people's lives by lifting them up.

You want to see God start working in someone's life—start lifting them up! The four friends of the paralyzed man were constantly lifting him up. That morning, they lifted him up and carried him. It didn't work. He didn't get to Jesus. So they lifted him up higher.

People never get lifted to a higher level by people who put them down. The Bible is filled with people lifting up other people.

Barnabas lifted a future leader, Paul, and we have the Christian faith, the New Testament, and our church because of that.

Nehemiah lifted a wall and forever changed the course of an entire city and the nation it represented.

Joseph lifted a nation and saved an entire generation from starvation.

Four guys lifted a hurting friend and triggered a miracle that still inspires people two thousand years later.

The best use of your life is to let God use you to lift people up.

5. Expect God to Work

God is more ready to work in the lives of people than we think He is.

Did it amaze people when Jesus healed the four men's friend? Yes! Did it amaze the four friends? No!

It didn't amaze them, because the four friends expected God to work. It did amaze the crowd, because although they went to see what Jesus would do, they didn't expect Him to do *that*.

Become convinced that God wants to work in the lives of people around you. Become convinced God is just as powerful today as He ever was.

C. S. Lewis eloquently explained why we should care for those around us:

> There are no *ordinary* people. You have never talked to a mere mortal. Nations, cultures, art, civilisations—these are mortal, and their life is to ours as the life of a gnat. But it is immortals whom we joke with, work with, marry, snub, and exploit—immortal horrors or everlasting splendours. . . . Next to the Blessed Sacrament itself, your neighbour is the holiest object presented to your senses.[7]

I was at the Focus on the Family headquarters in Colorado recently. At a staff gathering, one team member told about how her husband passed away a few years ago. When she visited his grave, she saw a man in the cemetery sobbing because his wife had recently died. She went over and asked if she could pray for him. He told her, "I'm just so lonely." Thanksgiving was coming up, so she invited him to come to her house. He went to dinner, and that started a connection for him to Jesus. She started inviting people every year. This Thanksgiving, she has twenty-eight people coming. She just invites them and expects that when she does, Jesus will start to meet their needs. What a hero.

WE WILL BELIEVE GOD *CAN*; CAN WE BELIEVE GOD *WILL*?

Who is changed in the presence of Jesus? Everyone. When you care enough to take someone into the presence of Jesus, every person can leave totally forgiven and set free.

Dave Roever is a great speaker and evangelist. He was horribly disfigured when an explosion in the Vietnam War burned over 37 percent of his body, which was considered fatal in that day. Dave was transferred to a burn unit with other mangled warriors. One day, officials told the burn victim in the bed next to Dave that the victim's wife would be coming to see him.

> *When you care enough to take someone into the presence of Jesus, every person can leave totally forgiven and set free.*

The day came and Dave heard footsteps coming down the hall. Then he heard the man's wife gasp in horror. Dave looked over and watched as she slipped off her wedding ring and placed it on the man's chest. She turned on her heel and left. Within a few weeks, Dave's roommate was dead.

Then came the inevitable day when the doctors told Dave that his wife would be coming to see him for the first time since he'd been burned. Dave steeled himself for his wife's reaction.

Again, he heard footsteps coming down the hall. Dave's wife appeared at the door. The way he tells it, he watched her eyes as she scanned him from head to toe. Then, without a word, she bent over and kissed his face where his lips should have been.

Finally she spoke. "Dave, I love you. I will always love you. Welcome home, Davey."

Dave was hospitalized for a year and two months. And now he speaks all over the country about the power of the unconditional love of God.[8]

That's the kind of power unleashed when you decide to let your expectations soar, take a few steps of faith, and RAISE people up!

CHAPTER 10

Stop Thinking You Don't Matter

Meet the Jesus Who Redefines Greatness

Whoever wants to become great among
you must be your servant.
—Jesus, Matthew 20:26

AMERICAN CHURCHES HAVE DEVELOPED A *CULTURE OF SPIRITUAL intimidation.*

How bad is it?

- I know business leaders running large companies who are afraid to join a Bible study (much less lead one).
- I know public speakers who are afraid to open a meeting in prayer.
- I know university professors who are afraid to teach a Sunday school class.
- I know world-class coaches who are afraid to teach a meeting of teenagers.
- I know event planners who are afraid to serve Communion.

Somehow, we have developed a culture in which the majority of our people are convinced they don't know enough or aren't spiritual enough for God to use them.

How in the world did this happen? Simple. *Spiritual intimidation.*

My first spiritually intimidating experience came the first time I attended a church service. I knew no words to the songs. I had never seen an offering envelope. And I will never forget the pastor saying, "Turn in your Bibles"—I thought he meant to pass them in—"to the book of Hebrews." In a flash, everyone on my whole row was there. Fifteen minutes later, I stumbled across the right page and I was *sure* the whole row noticed. Then I began to realize that church people spoke a whole new language. The church people were *saints* who had been *predestined* . . . *sanctified* . . . and *glorified* because of *substitutionary atonement* and *propitiation.* They *extended the right hand of fellowship,* sang *here I raise mine Ebenezer,* and wrapped up by singing something called the *doxology.*

Then I noticed robe-wearing pastors quoting a lot of Greek and Hebrew words in their sermons. That, of course, had the effect of communicating to all of us who did not know Greek and Hebrew that we couldn't possibly study or teach the Bible accurately.

And serving? Don't even think about it. I was unqualified, unfit, and unspiritual, and the only thing I was absolutely certain about was that it was going to take years before I fit into this brave new world, learned all the language and customs, and finally became someone God could start using.

This culture of elitist spiritual intimidation runs counter to everything in the New Testament.

What did Jesus and the disciple Peter have in common? They didn't have advanced theological degrees or seminary degrees of any kind. Jesus and Peter spoke in plain language to normal people. Jesus empowered others instead of intimidating them. Jesus' approach to people was as a liberator, not a conqueror. Rather than intimidating, Jesus inspired!

> *Every Christian is called. Every Christian is gifted. If you are a Christ-follower, then you are called to serve!*

The fact is, *every* Christian is called. *Every* Christian is gifted. If you are a Christ-follower, then you are called to serve!

Jesus drove this home in chapter 6 of Mark's gospel. The disciples and five thousand of their closest friends had been listening to Jesus all day. It was getting late. Everyone was exhausted and baked by the sun. The disciples could hear the people's stomachs growling. They were worried the people would start growling at them. Worse, it seemed Jesus was oblivious to the situation. The disciples' anxiety level rose to the point they went to Jesus and said, in essence, "It's late, this place is deserted, the people are hungry, and it's just not safe. Send these starving people home" (Mark 6:35–36).

Jesus then shocked the disciples by saying, "*You* give them something to eat" (v. 37).

With no resources, the disciples replied something like, "You have got to be kidding. You are going to delegate this to *us*? We have no food, and McDonald's won't be invented for two thousand years. What do you expect us to do? We're broke fishermen! We don't have what it takes!"

Jesus said, basically, "Well, what *do* you have?" (v. 38).

As the old radio commentator Paul Harvey would say, "And now for the rest of the story"—which involved stealing a kid's lunch box, sushi and bread for everyone, five thousand people full, baskets of leftovers, and twelve stunned disciples.

Jesus was trying to get something through to those disciples and all of us who would come after them.

Stop being intimidated by what you don't have.
Stop thinking you don't have what it takes!
Stop thinking you don't matter.
Start serving!

LIFE IS TOO SHORT TO WASTE

Ever feel like Timothy? He was young, insecure, overwhelmed, tired, and in way over his head. The fire had gone out. From all indications, Timothy had lost it. Worn down and worn out, he lost his passion, his confidence, his vision, and his nerve.

I know what that feels like, and likely so do you. The fire for making a difference gets replaced by apathetic indifference. I stop caring, because it's easier not to care. I stop believing that God wants to do anything significant through me, because it's safer not to believe. I stop serving, because it takes less effort not to serve. Paul wrote these words to this young, insecure, over-his-head Christ-follower: "Fan into flame the gift of God, which is in you" (2 Timothy 1:6).

He is saying to Timothy (and maybe to you and me), "I want you to get your fire back. You need to get your hopes back up. Don't waste the one life you get to live."

SEVEN WAYS TO REDISCOVER A FRESH VISION FROM GOD

Paul wrote to Timothy to inspire him to ask one question:

How do you rediscover a fresh vision from God for life and service?

Glad you asked. Let's get at it.

1. Realize What's at Stake

What's at stake? *Everything!*

Dr. James Stuart, professor of New Testament at the University of Edinburgh, said, "The threat to Christianity is not atheism, materialism, or communism. The greatest threat to Christianity is Christians who are trying to sneak into heaven incognito without ever having shared their faith."[1]

Napoleon Bonaparte famously said, "China is a sleeping giant. Let her sleep, for when she wakes she will move the world."[2] When I read this for the first time, I thought of the American church. The American church is a sleeping giant, and *if it ever wakes up*, it will shake the world. Currently America has 350,000 congregations.[3] Imagine what would happen if churches and Christians ever wake up . . .

The American church is a sleeping giant, and if it ever wakes up, it will shake the world.

2. Stop Being a Spectator

College Football Hall of Fame coach Bud Wilkinson popularized a description of the spectator sport of American football: "Twenty-two boys on the field badly in need of rest being watched by 40,000 people in the stands badly in need of exercise."[4]

I heard that and thought, *What a great description of the American church!* A few people (*badly in need of rest*) frantically run around, while the vast majority of people (*badly in need of exercise*) sit in the stands and watch.

American culture is a *spectator culture.* We watch movies. We watch television. We don't play sports; we watch sports. We go to school and watch teachers teach. And to live our faith, we go to church and watch preachers preach. The number one need in American Christianity today may be to move Christ-followers from being apathetic spectators to passion-filled participants.

3. Stop Thinking Everything Is Impossible

George Dantzig was a student at the University of California, Berkeley. One day he arrived late to Jerzy Neyman's graduate-level statistics class. Written on the board were two equations that George assumed was the class homework assignment. He copied them down.

A few days later, George handed his assignment to Professor Neyman.

"I'm sorry for taking so long to complete the work," George said. "The proofs seemed harder than usual."

"Just throw it on my desk," Dr. Neyman said. George hesitated to throw the difficult assignment on Neyman's messy desk because he was sure it would be lost in the stacks of papers.

Six weeks later, George and his wife were awakened on a Sunday morning by Dr. Neyman banging on their door. George opened the door and Dr. Neyman rushed in, his hands filled with papers.

"I've just written an introduction to one of your papers!" the professor said. "Read it so I can send it out right away for publication!"

George soon realized his mistake. What Dr. Neyman had written on the board was not homework, but *two unsolvable problems.* They were two famous unproved statistical theorems, and George had just solved them with written proofs. George was awarded the US Medal of Science in 1975 for his work.[5]

Imagine if George had been on time for class and heard that the problems on the board were unsolvable. He may not even have written them down. Even if he did, he may not have kept trying to solve the problems when he noticed they were difficult. If he had been like most people, he probably wouldn't have even *tried.*

Turn to the chapter in the Bible where God calls anyone to something *easy.* Don't bother looking. That chapter doesn't exist. David was called to fight a giant-sized problem. Joshua was called to a military maneuver with impossible odds. Nehemiah was called to rebuild a wall that for ninety-two years had proved impossible to build.

Jesus has plans for us that are bigger than we think. Do you ever think God can't use you? Think again.

- Moses was a stutterer, but God used him to speak.
- David's armor didn't fit, but God used him to defeat the giant.
- John Mark abandoned Paul, but God used him anyway.
- Hosea's wife was a prostitute, but God used her.
- Jacob was a liar, but God used him.
- Solomon was rich, but God used him.
- Abraham was old, but God used him.
- Samson had long hair, but God used him (and his hair!).
- Timothy was young and insecure, but God used him.
- Peter was impetuous, but God used him.

- Paul was a murderer, but God used him.
- Jonah ran from God, but God used him.
- Gideon and Thomas both doubted, but God used them.
- Jeremiah was depressed and suicidal, but God used him.
- Elijah was burned out, but God used him.
- John the Baptist was a loudmouth, but God used him.
- Martha was a worrywart, but God used her.
- Lazarus was *dead,* and God still used him!

As leadership writer Max Depree said, "Never insult someone by calling them to an easy job."[6] God never does.

4. Start Living *for* Something

I live in California, where it seems *everyone* is trying to figure out how to live longer. That's a great goal. However, we all know people who live long and *miserable* lives. It's not how *long* you live that matters. It's *how* you live that matters!

Jesus said, "What good is it for someone to gain the whole world, yet forfeit their soul?" (Mark 8:36). Studies show the average American will live for 28,708 days.[7] The sum of those days is your life. And every single one of those days is going to be exchanged for something. Which means this: *every person gives his or her life for something!*

Some people give their lives away for a career. Forty years later they get a gold watch. (Or thirty-nine years later, they get downsized before they can secure their pension.) Some people give their lives to attain power, popularity, or possessions. Some people give their lives away to get rich. (However, the one who dies with the most toys—*still dies.*)

Author James Emory White paints a picture of what this type of life could be like:

> We allow the movement of God on the surface of our spirits to become lost amid the stones the world tosses thoughtlessly into our lives. As a result, we lose the vision God could give us of our world and our place

> in it. Too quickly, and often without struggle, we trade making history with making money, substitute building a life with building a career and sacrifice living for God with living for the weekend. We forgo significance for the sake of success and pursue the superficiality of title and degree, house and car, rank and portfolio over a life lived large. We become saved, but not seized; delivered but not driven.[8]

The Bible urges us to "live a life worthy of the *calling* you have received" (Ephesians 4:1). We only get one shot at life. You and I are going to give our lives for something. The question each of us must ask ourselves is this:

Is what I am giving my life to actually worth it?

5. Redefine Greatness

Some people think greatness is connections and influence.

Some people think greatness is power and possessions.

Some people think greatness is fame and fortune.

But God has a whole different definition. Jesus redefined greatness. He said, "Many who are first will be last, and many who are last will be first" (Matthew 19:30).

God says whoever wants to be great must be a servant of others. Jesus said, "Anyone who wants to be first must be the very last, and the servant of all" (Mark 9:35). Until we learn to serve, we stay in spiritual kindergarten.

Again Jesus said, "The Son of Man did not come to be served, but to serve, and to give his life as a ransom for many" (Matthew 20:28).

Two words best define the Christian life: *serve* and *give*. That's what Jesus did. He came "to *serve*" and "to *give*."

Greatness and service go together. Great teachers serve students. Great salespeople serve customers. Great leaders serve followers. Great managers serve employees. The key to being great in anything is serving.

Last year I drove to San Francisco Airport, wrapped my arms around my daughter Christy, and nervously watched her board a plane to fly to Kenya. She had come home from college and asked (announced) if she could spend her summer working in an orphanage for children with special needs in a slum in Kenya. We spent the summer getting letters like this:

> Dear Mom and Dad,
>
> Going abroad independently has been a blessing and a challenge, figuring out every aspect of the trip: down to the details of what we are going to be doing that day, what we are going to be eating for the next meal, etc. But in this freedom I've found that God has gone before me and knows exactly what I'll be doing, so worrying about it is trivial. He's also brought incredible opportunities just for the fact that we were available. I want to tell you about a few of those opportunities.
>
> We just returned to the orphanage after a shorter day of teaching. We grabbed one of the 10-year-old orphans, Martin, out of the school here (oops, reason #453 I shouldn't be a teacher), and meandered down the road to Shimo, the local slum. We asked if he had any friends here, in which he responded by taking us to a small 12x15 mud hut, which housed Mercy, a mother of 6 children. All 7 of them live in this tiny place. We asked Martin to ask where she slept, and she pulled apart a curtain where wooden slats were laid, indented and smooth from use. We asked her if there was anything we could get for her, and she requested a mattress and food. And then we were able to pray for her and her family. It broke my heart to see their living conditions, but what astonished me more was the pride and welcoming spirit Mercy had as she ushered us inside. That was Tuesday. We went into town and bought a mattress and food today for her. Upon arrival, she grabbed the mattress and threw it above her head and started jumping up and down, laughing with delight. It was like she had won the lottery. We'll continue to visit Mercy and her family, and hopefully provide them with shoes. We are going back into Shimo today with Martin to find another family to help. (This wouldn't be possible without you, by the way.)

Today, we were also able to go to District Hospital. We found a woman around my age lying underneath a couple blankets with a badly wounded leg. I asked for her name and she said Jane, but very quietly and reserved. Sylvia explained to me that her husband had beaten her and she had been in here for three days so far. Jane let me pray for her, and I was just overcome with sorrow. The rest of the room was very receptive of our treats and prayers. One lady even pulled out her x-rays for us to look at. Ha ha. We are going to return back to the hospital early next week.

It's been a great week, and I look forward to the two weeks to come. I am thankful for your prayers and couldn't be more excited to see you all in a couple weeks!

Love,
Christy

I have *never* been prouder of my daughter. Seeing your child love God and serve people—what in the world could be better? And that is *exactly* how your heavenly Father feels about you when He sees you give your life in service to others.

It's time to redefine greatness in your life. What are you doing in service for others? Whether you realize it or not, although you may claim to be a Christian and have all the doctrine down, you're not an authentic Christian until you learn to serve others and give your life away.

6. Realize God Created Everything (*Including You*) to Be Used

During a recent power outage at my house, I was prepared. About three years earlier, I'd bought a new flashlight, put brand-new batteries in it, and stored it in the laundry room. I had never needed it, but I knew exactly where it was. When the lights went out, I felt like a very well-prepared dad. I announced, "Hold on, I've got this."

I got out the still-brand-new, never-been-used flashlight and turned it on. And . . . nothing happened. That was strange, because it had never been used. The flashlight was new. The batteries were new. I started unscrewing the top and heard a grinding noise. I opened it and rusty flakes started flying everywhere. The batteries were totally corroded.

Batteries are made to be used. So are people. Human beings are made to serve a purpose, and when we're not serving other people, we get corroded and rotten on the inside. And that stops the light of God from shining through us.

Everything was created to be used. We were created to be used by God. We were gifted to be used by God. We were designed to be used by God. When we're not, we end up filled with toxic emotions. Maybe that's why as so many people get older, they get less fun to be around.

After you become a Christian, you're going to end up in heaven, so why doesn't God just take you right then? Why are you still here? It's because He has something for you to do. And that is your calling, your mission, your purpose. And that will keep you happier and *healthier* than any other pursuit.

7. Someday Is *Today*

The very first response to Jesus from the disciples was this: "*Immediately* they left their nets and followed Him" (Mark 1:18 NASB). The Bible is filled with stories of Jesus calling people to follow and serve Him *now*. Jesus said to come *now*.

A guy once asked Jesus about how to be a Christian. Jesus said to him, "'Follow me.' But he replied, 'Lord, first let me go and bury my father'" (Luke 9:59). The word "but" contradicts the word "Lord." You cannot call Jesus "Lord," and then say, "me first." Jesus was basically saying four words: *If not now, when?*

An unused gift equals a wasted life. You don't have a day to waste before you put your gift to use. Some people delay choosing to follow Christ . . .

- . . . because they *choose comfort over growth.* "But first let me get financially independent." Jesus said, "Any of you who does not forsake . . . all that he has cannot be My disciple" (Luke 14:33 AMP).

- . . . because of *fear.* "Lord I'll live for You, but first assure me that I will be a success." Scripture states, "Fear of man is a dangerous trap" (Proverbs 29:25 TLB).
- . . . because of *indecision.* They stall out. "But first let me figure out exactly what I'm going to do." James tells us that "a double-minded man [is] unstable in all his ways" (James 1:8 NASB).
- . . . because they're *lazy.* The proverb teaches that "a lazy fellow has trouble all through life" (Proverbs 15:19 TLB).
- . . . because they're *commitment-phobic*, which is why there was a sign on a Hollywood jewelry store that said "We rent wedding rings." Let's admit it: some people won't make a commitment to anything—a church, a club, a country, a career, a marriage, a friend, or even a family. But the psalmist writes, "Commit your way to the LORD" (Psalm 37:5).
- . . . because they think they're *not qualified.* "But first let me get it all figured out." Paul writes, "[Jesus] told me, 'My power is strongest when you are weak.' So I will brag even more about my weaknesses in order that Christ's power will live in me" (2 Corinthians 12:9 GW).
- . . . because they got too *busy.* Jesus clearly said, "But seek first His kingdom and His righteousness, and all these things will be added to you" (Matthew 6:33 NASB).

Some people underestimate the paralyzing power of procrastination. Procrastination will fill your life with regret, rob you of relationships, and steal your opportunity for success. Procrastination is a self-defeating spiral that takes your life in one direction—downhill.

Procrastination could lead you to end up like Pharaoh at the time of Moses in ancient Egypt. He said, "Who is the LORD, that I should obey him?" (Exodus 5:2). God, being God, of course, overheard this and gave Pharaoh ten audiovisual presentations called plagues. Pharaoh's answer to everything was always "tomorrow." The result—one more night with the frogs . . . Finally, his army was annihilated.

Someone once said, "Procrastination is my sin. It only brings me sorrow. In fact, I'm going to change my ways. It will probably happen tomorrow."

CHAPTER 11

Stop Running on Empty

Meet the Jesus Who Says, "Come to Me!"

Apart from me you can do nothing.
—Jesus, John 15:5

THE UNIQUENESS OF CHRISTIANITY IS ROOTED IN THE UNIQUENESS of Jesus Christ. He is unlike any other religious leader who ever walked the planet. Listen to the difference between what other religious leaders say and what Jesus said:

- Other religious leaders say, "Follow me and I will show you how to find the truth." Jesus said, *"I am the truth."*
- Other religious leaders say, "Follow me and I'll show you the way to salvation." Jesus said, *"I am the way to eternal life."*
- Other religious leaders say, "Follow me and I'll show you how you can become enlightened." Jesus said, *"I am the light of the world."*
- Other religious leaders say, "Follow me and I'll show you many doors that lead to God." Jesus said, *"I am the door."*

- Other religious leaders say, "Follow me and I'll show you how you can find spiritual nourishment." Jesus said, *"I am the bread of life."*

But the most startling thing Jesus said was His stunning three-word invitation to *all* people at all times, *"Come to me"* (Matthew 11:28).

Notice He didn't say, "Come to religion," "Come to rituals and rules," "Come to catechism," "Come to confirmation," or "Come to liturgy." All those things may be fine and good, but they are *not* the main thing. The main thing is this: *"Come to me."* Jesus' primary invitation is to a *relationship*! When we miss this, we end up going through the motions and miss the life-giving relationship that is the heart of the Christian faith.

"Daaad . . . !" The child's plaintive cry came from the back of the church, *loud.* I knew immediately it was my son Mark. When he was four years old, I decided it would be fun to take him to a conference where I was speaking. We had a blast, but as the weekend went on, he went into overload. He was with me as I spoke on Friday night . . . and Saturday morning . . . and Saturday afternoon. And on Saturday night, I was in front of a sea of people speaking again. By that time, Mark was worn out.

So, right in the middle of my message, Mark cried out, "Daaad . . . !" I knew immediately who it was. I stopped speaking and said, "Yes, son?"

He called over the crowd, "Dad, I'm lonely." A collective "Awwww" came from the people.

Then he said, "Can I come up and be with you?"

I knew that if I said no, the people were going to look at me and think, *I'm not listening to this guy—he doesn't even like his own son.* On the other hand, if I said yes, it was going to wreck my message midway through it. The choice was easy. I said, "Come on up."

Like the moment the bride comes down the aisle, people's heads turned and watched Mark as he walked down the center aisle, lower lip thrust out, whimpering. Down the long aisle, up the platform stairs, and across the stage he came until he reached me and wrapped his arms around my legs.

I reached down and picked him up, thinking I was going to finish this episode in some nice way and get back to the message. But I made a strategic mistake. I hugged him to my chest, and his mouth landed right next to my lapel microphone. He started saying, "I'm sad, Dad . . . I'm lonely . . . I miss Mom . . . Let's get out of here!"

My mind scrambled to come up with a plan. Maybe I could say something comforting to him, then try to buy ten minutes so I could rush through the end of the message. I said, "Son, is there anything you need?"

He pulled himself up closer, squeezed his arms tight around my neck, spilling tears down the front of my shirt. With the whole conference listening, he said right into the lapel microphone, "Yes, Dad, there's something I need. *I need you, Dad.*"

Time froze. It was at that moment that I got it. It occurred to me that Mark had said exactly what God wants all of us to say. Forgetting the end of the message, I walked to the edge of the stage, with my son in my arms, and said, "Ladies and gentlemen," I said, "I just need to ask you, *when was the last time you did this with your heavenly Father?* When was the last time you threw yourself into the arms of God and knew you were loved, knew you were forgiven, knew you were cared for, and knew that you were in the palm of His hands, because you knew the arms of your heavenly Father were wrapped around you?"

Churches are packed with people who are distant and disconnected from God. Ever felt like this? "I am going through the motions, but my heart feels icy cold." "My faith feels dead." "My prayers feel anemic." "I'm losing battles I can't afford to lose,

> At some point, every Christian grows tired of being spiritual but feeling miserable.

because I feel powerless to resist temptation." "I feel nothing of the presence and power of God."

We bounce between numb and overwhelmed. At some point, every Christian grows tired of being spiritual but feeling miserable.

THREE THINGS THAT ARE KILLING YOUR SPIRITUAL LIFE

How do you find God when you are dry? How do you draw near when you are disconnected? How do you rediscover the passion, the warmth, the joy, the power, the presence that is *promised* in a relationship with Jesus but is experienced by so few?

The first step is identifying the cause: *What is killing my spiritual life?*

1. Ceremonial Christianity (Going through the Motions)

A friend of mine, Rene Schlaepfer, pastors an outstanding church in Santa Cruz, California, that is more than one hundred years old. The church was relocated once, but the "new" worship center needed to be remodeled some years ago. The question was what to do with pews that seated fifteen hundred people. Figuring that's what Craigslist is for, they advertised "Free Pews to Good Home. You Pick Them Up."

A Russian church nearby took the offer and sent several burly Russian guys to pick up the pews. After two minutes of small talk, the men got to work dismantling, removing, and loading the pews. They worked like crazy all day, but the pews were so heavy that it took more time than they thought it would.

Rene is a great guy, so he offered, "Can I get you guys hotel rooms for the night?"

One of the men said in broken English, "No! When we are getting tired, we put pews together in, how you say—*casket*?" He motioned that they would wedge two fronts together to make a two-sided bed out of them.

As Rene related the story, I thought, *Sleeping in pews! Every pastor sees that every weekend!* Then it hit me what a great metaphor it is for what our spiritual lives can become. *The pews that used to be life-giving can easily turn into caskets.*

Ceremonial Christianity is not just about liturgy and stained glass. It's about going through the motions. And getting close to Jesus is not as simple as following the one-two-three of someone else's Christianity. That can lead to legalism, not the kind of authentic closeness that Jesus wants to have with you.

Imagine that you walk into a room that has a big common area with a sound system. One guy is listening to a song and starts getting into the music. He's moving his head, tapping his feet, and sometimes clapping to the rhythm. He closes his eyes and has a big smile on his face. He isn't even thinking about his reaction to this favorite tune. He's just responding to the music he loves.

Now let's say that someone with a hearing impairment comes into that room. He doesn't notice that the music is on. He can't even hear it. But he sees this other guy smiling and laughing, and he thinks, *Now that guy looks like he's having a great time. I'll do that too.* So he starts imitating the guy, making the same motions and plastering a smile on his face. He's thinking, *This isn't very fun. In fact it's kind of boring. But maybe it'll get fun if I keep doing it.* He doesn't hear the music—he just repeats the motions.

Now a third guy walks into the room and sees two guys doing exactly the same thing. But one guy is loving life and listening to the music, and the other guy is just going through the motions.

When we substitute rituals, religion, and rules in place of relationships, we end up tone-deaf to the love and grace of God.

Jesus said, "These people honor me with their lips, *but their hearts are far from me*" (Matthew 15:8).

2. Distractions

Corrie ten Boom, who hid Jews from the Nazis and paid for it by being imprisoned in death camps that cost her family members their lives, is one of the greatest Christian leaders of the last century. She became an accomplished speaker, sharing her faith far and wide. One of her favorite illustrations involved a prop flashlight that wouldn't turn on:

> "Look, I have with me a flashlight which does not light. I open it and pull out a piece of rag labeled 'pride.' Then others labeled 'worry,' 'discouragement,' 'inferiority,' also 'adultery' and 'dishonesty.' Finally a yellow one stamped 'hatred.' All these in besides the batteries—small wonder the flashlight did not work."[1]

Effective people are effective because they commit to habits that ineffective people simply won't commit to.

Each of those rags represented a distraction—second-class things that we put in first-class positions. Distractions waste your time, sap your energy, dampen your spirit, and derail you spiritually.

Jesus compared distractions to soil filled with thorns and weeds (Luke 8:7, 14). How much effort does it take to grow weeds in a garden? Zero. When I neglect my lawn, weeds grow. When I neglect my marriage, weeds grow. When I neglect my kids, weeds grow. When I neglect my relationship with God, weeds grow.

What do you do with weeds? You rip them out. Uproot them. Eliminate them. Think pesticides . . . RoundUp . . . Whatever it takes! Get rid of them.

Jesus is saying to use any means necessary to eliminate the weeds that distract you from connecting and walking with God.

Why? *Because an overcrowded life ends up being an unproductive life.*

This message is no small matter, because if you miss it, you waste your life.

3. Superficial Commitment

We launched Bayside Church twenty years ago. I have been amazed by the stunning ways lives have changed. I have seen God change marriages, transform character, and liberate people from self-destructive habits. Self-centered people have learned to serve. Greedy people have become sacrificial givers. Harsh people have become kinder. It has been astonishing how thousands of lives have changed.

I have also been amazed by the lives that *haven't* changed. We have people who were grouchy, negative, and condemning when they came—and they are just as grouchy, negative, and condemning as they were before. We have people a decade or two later who are no happier or healthier than they were before. Some are just as toxic, angry, or critical as ever.

What's the difference between people who grow and thrive and people who remain stuck and miserable? In other words, how does *transformation* happen?

Looking at two decades of transformation, or nontransformation, I have come to believe that one of the greatest barriers to spiritual growth, life change, and spiritual maturity is *superficial commitment.*

Twenty years ago, I heard Rick Warren ask a question that I have never forgotten: "Why are some people more effective than other people?"[2] Great question. Why do some get more out of life than others? Why do some people flourish while others fall? Why do some fly while others never get off the ground? Why do some people enjoy God and people and life while others endure the whole thing?

The same question can be asked relationally. Why do some people have better relationships? Why do some people cultivate friendships while others remain isolated and lonely?

The same question can be asked of families. Why do some parents get more out of parenting? Why do some marriages thrive while others fizzle and die out?

Take it into the spiritual realm. Why do some Christians have an alive, thriving faith while so many possess a lifeless faith? Why do some believers have more joy, peace, and answered prayers? What's the secret? Is God playing favorites?

Let me give you the point in a sentence:

Effective people are effective because they commit to habits that ineffective people simply won't commit to.

How do you develop depth?

How do you develop character?

How do you put down roots?

How do you come alive and stay alive?

How do you recapture the joy, passion, and power?

We grow, develop, and thrive only by *making* and *keeping* spiritual commitments.

THREE LIFE-CHANGING SPIRITUAL COMMITMENTS

I want to give you three life-changing spiritual commitments that have shaped the lives of every thriving Christian in history. These three commitments will help you pursue a lasting, loving relationship with Christ. They have shaped my life, faith, and relationships for decades. These are essential for spiritual health!

1. Take Worship Seriously

Never underestimate the power of worship. Carol and I have enjoyed the sunshine of California for years, and we finally decided a couple of years ago to harness it (insanely high energy bills had something to do with this decision). We had solar panels installed on the roof of our house, and, in no time, our electric bills dropped to almost nothing.

I was so thrilled about it that one sunny day I just stood in my driveway and looked at those panels. I thought, *You know what those panels are doing? Nothing! They're sitting on the roof doing nothing! They're not active. They aren't stressed. They aren't frantically working. They are just sitting still, soaking up the rays of the sun. And because they are still and soaking in the light, they are generating power.*

That is one of the reasons we worship. There is something about setting aside one day each week and carving out time to sit in the presence of God and soak up His light. Somehow, worshiping with God's people in God's presence generates power that can't be manufactured any other way.

Now you may say, "Wait a second. I can worship God in nature. I can worship God privately. I can worship God by myself at the beach or in the mountains." All of that is true, and I hope you do. But a unique power is unleashed when Christians gather together to worship.

Jesus put it this way: "For where two or three are gathered together in my name, there am I in the midst of them" (Matthew 18:20 KJV).

The early church modeled it this way: "They devoted themselves to the apostles' teaching and to fellowship, to the breaking of bread and to prayer" (Acts 2:42).

The writer of Hebrews puts it like this: "And let us consider how we may spur one another on toward love and good deeds, *not giving up meeting together, as some are in the habit of doing*, but encouraging one another—and all the more as you see the Day approaching" (Hebrews 10:24–25).

The current lone-ranger, church-avoiding, worship-neglecting, isolated, it's-all-about-me Christianity is *not* biblical faith. However vocal people may be about their theology, if they are not connected with other believers to worship, then they are not living authentic Christianity.

An epidemic is happening in American Christianity. American Christians have stopped going to church. Weekly worship has dropped to levels that would have been unimaginable anytime in Christian history. A recent study of church attendance in America had to broadly define "a regular attendee" as "someone who shows up at least three out of eight weeks."[3]

This means that the pattern for American Christians is to gather to worship God once every three weeks! And that means, out of 8,760 hours given to us each year, most American Christians will spend less than eighteen of those hours gathered in worship.

No wonder Christians are so weak. So anemic. So shallow, disconnected, and ineffective.

Why does that matter? The Bible is packed with illustrations of the life-changing power unleashed when we worship.

The prophet Isaiah writing to a nation recovering from the loss of a popular leader said, "Those who *hope* in the LORD [present tense] *will renew* their strength [future tense]. They *will soar* on wings like eagles; they *will run* and not grow weary, they *will walk* and not be faint" (Isaiah 40:31).

If you will worship, *your future will be different.*

- You'll have strength you don't have now.
- You'll have energy you don't have now.
- You'll have a resistance to discouragement you don't have now.
- You'll grow to heights you don't have now.

It's been that way throughout the entire Bible.

It is in worship that God . . .

- . . . *rekindles your hope,* as He did for Isaiah: "In the year that King Uzziah died, I saw the Lord" (Isaiah 6:1).
- . . . *renews your confidence,* as He did for David: "I sought the Lord, and he answered me; he delivered me from all my fears" (Psalm 34:4).
- . . . *restores your perspective,* as He also did for David: "When I tried to understand all this, it troubled me deeply till I entered the sanctuary of God; then I understood their final destiny" (Psalm 73:16–17).
- . . . *restores your joy,* as He did for Nehemiah: "Nehemiah said, . . . 'Do not grieve, for the joy of the Lord is your strength'" (Nehemiah 8:10).
- . . . *releases your anxieties,* as He did for Jehoshaphat, who was pressured from all sides: "After this, the Moabites and Ammonites with some of the Meunites came to wage war against Jehoshaphat. . . . 'For we have no power to face this vast army that is attacking us. We do not know what to do, but our eyes are on you'" (2 Chronicles 20:1, 12).
- . . . *reconnects you with Himself,* as He did for James: "Come near to God and he will come near to you" (James 4:8).
- . . . *re-enlists your service,* as He did for Isaiah: "Then I heard the

voice of the Lord saying, 'Whom shall I send? And who will go for us?' And I said, 'Here am I. Send me!'" (Isaiah 6:8).

The pattern of the early Christians was to set aside time every week to worship. Jesus said, "God is spirit, and his worshipers must worship in the Spirit and in truth" (John 4:24). The writer of Hebrews wrote that God "is a rewarder of those who diligently seek Him" (11:6 NKJV).

Worship is exhilarating, inspiring, and encouraging—*sometimes*!

But what do we do when it isn't? Why show up when we don't feel like it? Why keep doing it when we get nothing out of it? Because the real reason we gather to worship is this: *God is worthy of our worship!*

We worship a Savior who did exactly that: He saved. Jesus' hands were pierced, and He was mangled on a cross so that all of us in His family could have a future we could never have without Him.

And *that* is why we gather to worship!

2. Recharge Your Spiritual Batteries

Christian educator and author Henrietta Mears has inspired me for the last thirty years. I have read everything she wrote. Billy Graham called her "one of the greatest Christians I have ever known."[4] Bill Bright and his wife moved in with her to start Campus Crusade for Christ. Rich Halverson, Senate chaplain and pastor of Hollywood Presbyterian, was one of her students. She started Gospel Light, Forest Home Christian Conference Center, and the largest college conference in the country during a season when women were discouraged from doing any of these things—and she was unmarried. When someone asked her why she didn't marry, she said, "The Apostle Paul didn't wait around."[5]

What fueled her?

She occasionally invested in an extended "God time." That is more than a quick quiet time or a church service. It is more similar to the types of festival days they celebrated in the Old Testament. It is giving God a few hours—or a couple of days—to help us catch a fresh vision for our lives and futures. The power of that can be life changing.

Henrietta was in college when she was entrusted with a large Sunday school class. One night she awoke feeling restless and determined never to fail the Lord again. She got out of bed and wrote ten rules that she would live by for the rest of her life.

Here they are:

1. I will win the personal allegiance of every student in my Sunday school class to the Lord and Master by talking, writing, and prayer.
2. I will not think my work over when my pupil has made his decision for Christ.
3. I will see that he finds a definite place in some specific task.
4. I will bring Christianity out of the unreal into everyday life.
5. I will seek to help each one discover the will of God, because the Master can use every talent.
6. I will instill a divine discontent into the mind of everyone who can do more than he is doing.
7. I will make it easy for anyone to come to me with the deepest experiences of his inner life.
8. I will keep the cross of Christ central in the Christian life.
9. I will pray as I have never prayed before for wisdom and power.
10. I will spend and be spent in this battle.[6]

These "rules" have shaped my adult life. What was the root? Henrietta Mears decided she would spend time to reconnect with God, and He connected with her.

Our church hosts a conference every year called Thrive. We have three goals: *recharge* your spiritual batteries, *renew* your love for Christ, and *refocus* on God's vision for the future. Each year, the Thrive Conference sells out a couple of months in advance. We have massive worship times, speakers, comedians, and lots of inspiration.

One year during the conference, I was walking across the courtyard and a pastor grabbed me. He had tears in his eyes and said, "I just want to thank you for starting this conference." I asked him why. His reply made it all worthwhile. He said, "I bring forty people with me each year, but the real reason I want to say thanks is this—this is where I meet God every year."

We all need places where we meet God.

I tell our church every year, going to church is like taking a drink of water. Coming to an event like Thrive is like standing under Niagara Falls for three days.

3. Unleash the Bible into Your Life

Never underestimate the power of opening your Bible.

I love where I live, *but* if Carol and I were called to go pastor in a beach town (say, in Maui) it would take a lot to leave where I am—like maybe fifteen minutes to pack swim trunks and find a flight. I don't think that is going to happen, but if it ever came down to giving one final sermon to my family and friends at Bayside, I know exactly what I'd say.

My message would sound trite and unoriginal, because it's a really simple thought. Yet I'd say it because it's the single most important thing I could ever teach anyone to do. Why is this one thing so important?

This one thing will do all this for you:

- Increase stability
- Decrease anxiety
- Draw you closer to God
- Help you resist temptation
- Help you make wise decisions
- Enable God to use you
- Increase your influence in every relationship you have
- Give you a solid foundation in a shaky world
- Restore your hope when you are discouraged

- Comfort you when life falls apart
- Renew your relationship to God when you have strayed

For parents, it is the ultimate training guide.

For marriages, it is the best marriage manual ever written.

For people looking for direction, it is the best guidance ever written.

Here's the sermon in a sentence:

Read your Bible (and do what it says).

In case those reasons are still not enough, here are a few more.

FIVE REASONS TO CONNECT WITH YOUR BIBLE

1. Connecting with Your Bible Prevents Self-Destructive Decisions

The headline read, "'Death by GPS' in Desert." A twenty-eight-year-old nurse had taken her eleven-year-old son and their dachshund on a camping trip. Packing Pop Tarts, cheese sandwiches, and bottled water, Alicia Sanchez drove from their Las Vegas home into Death Valley National Park on a Saturday morning.

The last her family heard from her, she was fixing a flat tire. She fixed the flat then followed the GPS device in her car into the desert, landing in what officials called one of the most isolated areas you could ever find.

The GPS's route apparently led her Jeep off track, and it sank into the sand. It wouldn't move. She and her son walked for miles searching for help. She climbed a large peak nearby to try to get a cell phone signal, all to no avail.

Five days after setting out, Alicia's son died. Finally, Alicia lay down next to her Jeep and prepared to die too. She was done. That Wednesday, when she didn't arrive at work for her scheduled shift, family members called police and rangers, who started searching.

They found her and the dog, dehydrated but alive. Her lifeless son was in the front seat.

"She turned down a wrong road," Ranger Amber Nattrass said.

"It's what I'm beginning to call 'death by GPS,'" said Death Valley wilderness coordinator Charlie Callagan. "People are renting vehicles with GPS and they have no idea how it works and they are willing to trust the GPS to lead them into the middle of nowhere."[7]

When we are navigating life, direction matters. This may be why Jesus called His followers to build their lives on the words, wisdom, and direction of God. If we don't, it leads to disaster.

"There is a way which seems right to a man, but its end is the way of death" (Proverbs 14:12 NASB).

Jesus was crystal clear. There is only one reliable GPS for life, and it's God's Word.

2. Connecting With Your Bible Will Strengthen Your Character

Developing God-honoring character, standing up to temptation, and raising G-rated kids is tougher these days. Why? Because—let's admit it—we are living in an X-rated world.

A story I heard recently tells it all. Two five-year-olds were sitting on the porch. One said to the other, "The other day I saw a condom on the patio." The other one said, "What's a patio?" Values are not a given anymore. And the pressure is increasing.

A friend of mine who is a youth pastor did a series on love, sex, and dating. At the end of the four-week series, a girl raised her hand and said, "I know the Bible says not to have sex, but we have condoms today, so it's different."

The youth pastor looked at her and said, "It's like buying a car or leasing a car. If you buy a car you take care of it, but if you lease a car you might trash it because you can turn it in."

The girl raised her hand again and said, "What if you lease with an option to buy?"

That's the world we live in. The problem is this: *sin fascinates then assassinates.* The Bible protects us against assassination.

"I have hidden your word in my heart that I might not sin against you" (Psalm 119:11).

3. Connecting with Your Bible Will Give You Direction

Did you ever get "paralysis by analysis"? It's like the guy who goes to a psychiatrist. The doctor says, "Are you indecisive?"

The guy says, "Yes and no."

The doctor says, "What do you mean by that?"

The guy says, "Well, I used to be, but now I'm not sure!"

People try all kinds of systems to get divine direction—astrology, numerology, metaphysical books, and more. Americans bought over two million Ouija boards the first year they were sold.[8] One person said, "Gideon laid a fleece to find God's will, but a lot of people are getting fleeced to find God's will."

God's will is found in God's Word. That's why the Word calls us to renew our minds (Romans 12:2), which we do by reading God's Word. Most of God's will has already been revealed. As we read His Word, He speaks to us.

A pastor friend of mine, David Allen, said, "When you open your Bible, God opens His mouth. When you shut your Bible, God shuts His mouth."[9]

God's will never contradicts God's Word. When people say they have an "impression," my first reaction is, "What does the Bible say about it?" False ideas and religions get started when somebody gets an "impression" that isn't anchored in Scripture. In fact, the Bible says that even if an angel comes and tells you some new revelation, if it's contrary to what's in the Bible, don't accept it. It's not God's will (Galatians 1:8).

People will say, "I feel this is God's will for my life." "I feel it's right!" "Look how the circumstances all worked out." But it will never be right if it's not based on the bedrock of Scripture, because God's will never contradicts His Word.

Many Christians today are confused about God's will because they don't know His Word. In a confused world, God's Word will give you direction. "Open my eyes that I may see wonderful things in your law" (Psalm 119:18).

Every major decision I have made—what to do with my life, the decision to marry Carol (a great call!), the decision to launch Bayside—was made while spending time with God in His Word.

God's Word will provide the kind of direction that will lead to a lifetime of fulfillment instead of regret.

4. Connecting with Your Bible Develops Authentic Faith

Some years ago, I heard Bill Hybels tell a story to lead off a sermon series that later became his book, *Honest to God?* He said he was speaking at a conference and was backstage before the program started. There in the green room, he saw the worship leader, conference organizer, and program committee chair all screaming in a knock-down, drag-out fight. Then someone yelled it was time to start, and they walked onstage, arm in arm in seeming unity, and told the people what a great evening they were all going to have together.

In Bill's words, "That was my initiation into the world of inauthentic Christianity."[10]

It seems there is an epidemic of people of faith living without the faith they claim. Two primary attitudes are fueling this movement.

1. "I'm a Christian, but I'm going to believe what I want." This is what I call "Cafeteria Christianity." We've invented a faith where, instead of opening the Bible and choosing to believe the whole thing, people are taking their tray through the Bible and picking up what they want to believe, then leaving the rest. This has led to the adoption of all kinds of toxic beliefs.

In this brand of Christianity, people mix biblical truth with their own ideas. They take Christianity and say, "I like this, but I'm going to believe this other stuff as well."

This was going on in the early church. A lot of New Testament books—Colossians, Ephesians, 1 John, and others—were written to correct a defective view of Jesus Christ and the Christian faith. In their search for God's will, these early Christians fell into all kinds of false beliefs. Similarly, today, people will say, "I'm a Christian, but I read my horoscope." "I'm a Christian, but I go to a palm reader." "I'm a Christian, but I go to séances." "I'm a Christian, but I don't believe everything the Bible says."

2. *"I'm a Christian, but I'm going to live how I want."* These people will say they like Jesus, but they don't want to restrict themselves to following what He says.

The desire to choose how we want to live, regardless of what Scripture says, has led to the adoption of all kinds of destructive lifestyles. These people say, "I like what the Bible says about *this*, so I will live it out . . . but I don't like *that*, so I'll ignore it." So, for example, they might obey something the Bible says about serving the poor but won't take seriously what the Bible says about sexuality. They wear the label "Christian" but refuse to let it affect the way they live, who they date, how they raise their kids, how they treat their enemies.

The starting point for developing spiritual maturity is to accept the Bible as your final authority—not culture, media, Hollywood, tradition, some well-meaning Christian, or your own feelings.

Everyone has a UCV, whether you know it or not. That is your Ultimate Core Value. Your UCV determines the decisions you will make. When there are two options, you'll gravitate in the direction your UCV sends you. If my Ultimate Core Value is "fun," and there are two options, I'll automatically choose the fun one. If my UCV is "safety" and one option has risk, I'll automatically run to the other.

Your UCV will determine your decisions and the direction of your life. The problem is this: Many Christians have received Jesus but have not made following His will their Ultimate Core Value. And if you don't make the authority of the Bible your UCV, then you're going to have problems following Jesus, getting close to Jesus, and listening to Jesus. The first thing every Christian has to do is to let Jesus replace whatever their Ultimate Core Value is with a commitment to the unchanging core values found in Scripture. Why? Because, if the Bible claims to be God's

Word, then the starting point for authentic Christian living is this—I have to accept the authority of the Bible.

Jesus put it this way: "Why do you call me, 'Lord, Lord,' and do not do what I say?" (Luke 6:46).

I'm still looking for the first person I can find who will say, "I read my Bible and did what it said. Bad decision. What a disaster." But I have had thousands of conversations with regret-filled people who disregarded God's instructions and are suffering the consequences.

5. Connecting with Your Bible Restores Your Life (Like Nothing Else)

In the Bible, every time God spoke, something got created. God spoke, "Let there be light"—*wham*! Light was created (Genesis 1:3). God spoke the world into existence.

When God speaks, something always gets created.

That carries over to the New Testament. Jesus spoke, and Lazarus came back to life. Jesus spoke, and people were healed. Jesus spoke, and discouraged people found encouragement. Jesus spoke, and a thief found a way into heaven. When Jesus speaks, life, health, joy, or something gets created.

Even today, when God speaks, something gets created. That's why we're encouraged to read the Bible.

- When we're discouraged, we read the Bible and hope gets created.
- When we're afraid, we read the Bible and confidence gets created.
- When we're confused, we read the Bible and direction gets created.
- When we're down, we read the Bible and inspiration gets created.

The Bible wasn't written to satisfy your curiosity. It was written to change your life. But if you don't crack it open, nothing ever happens.

One day about a year ago, I was feeling pretty down. I was writing the book *Hope Quotient* and probably needed to read it to myself that day. It was as if my hopes had sunk so low I felt like giving up. But instead of wallowing in it (my normal pattern), this is what I did.

I drove around town and found a little restaurant that looked deserted. I took my Bible and walked to the back and started reading. Words started jumping off the page. As I read and prayed, I got choked up. I quietly told God everything that had me feeling down. As I kept reading, I started crying harder.

The waitress kept coming by to check on my coffee, which I never drank, and would say, "Are you okay?" "Is there anything I can get you?"

I kept crying, talking to God, and reading bits of my Bible for about an hour. I started getting my eyes off myself and back on God. One promise in Scripture after another started lifting my spirit. Then I started getting original thoughts, fresh ideas, and a whole new perspective. I jotted down notes for the other half hour that I sat in that booth, then generously tipped the kind waitress and shot out of my seat.

I walked into that diner filled with the toxic emotions of fear, anxiety, and discouragement. Ninety minutes later, I walked out a whole different person. During that time, I became absolutely convinced that God was bigger than my circumstances and that He was not done working in and through my life. The circumstances hadn't changed. They didn't need to. What needed to change was . . . me.

What made that huge difference? And how do you also get that kind of perspective? How can you effect that kind of change in your own life?

Read the Bible. Then do what it says.

ABOVE ALL ELSE—JESUS IS CONNECTED TO *YOU*

When our kids were young, we lived in Chicago. It is a great city—Wrigley Field, Michigan Avenue at Christmas, great pizza, and some of the busiest streets in the world. Every time I crossed a street with any of our kids, I would grip their tiny hands and say, "Hold on tight to Daddy's hand." My kids would squeeze my hand as hard as they could. But I *never* depended on their grasp to keep them secure. Even if they tried to let go, there was no way I was going to lose connection. They were secure because I loved them too much to let them disconnect.

You can count on this. Jesus is connected to *you*. It is the power of Jesus' grasp on us—not our grip on God—that keeps us safe and connected.

- Christ Jesus has laid hold of you (Philippians 3:12). Or more exactly, Christ has a grip on you!
- Nothing can separate you from the love of God that is in Christ Jesus your Lord (Romans 8:39). Even yourself!
- He will never leave you nor forsake you (Hebrews 13:5).

Jesus said, "I give them eternal life, and they shall never perish; no one will snatch them out of my hand. My Father, who has given them to me, is greater than all; no one can snatch them out of my Father's hand" (John 10:28–29).

These same hands that created the universe, that shaped everything in all of creation, that flung the stars into space, have now taken hold of your hand! And when you belong to Him, He will not let go.

CHAPTER 12

"I Love Jesus—I Just Can't Stand Church"

Meet the Jesus Who Still Believes in the Church

I will build my church, and the gates of
hell shall not prevail against it.
—Jesus, Matthew 16:18 ESV

I KNOW THIS IS GOING TO BE POLITICALLY INCORRECT. I KNOW that these days it's trendy to bash the church. And I also know that new books come out every week with titles like *Help! I Hate Church, Death by Church, Loving God When You Don't Love the Church*, and my favorite, *101 Things to Do During a Dull Sermon.*

So I know it's politically incorrect. And it may be because I grew up a million miles away from the faith. But I have a confession to make, and here it is:

I love the Christian church.

Now, before you throw this book away, let me tell you why:

- It was the Christian church that introduced me to Jesus when I was an atheist.
- It was the Christian church that didn't excommunicate me when I talked one of its members right into agnosticism. (This does not look good on the pastor's résumé.)
- It was the Christian church that tolerated me asking nonstop questions for six straight months.
- It was the Christian church that healed my image of God.
- It was the Christian church that healed my image of myself.
- It was the Christian church that challenged me to take Jesus seriously.
- It was the Christian church that challenged me to grow.
- It was the Christian church that taught me the Bible and discipled me.
- It was the Christian church that taught me to serve and to give.
- It was the Christian church that helped me discover my gifts and my life mission.
- It was the Christian church that let me try stuff, fail completely, and keep on trying.
- It is the Christian church that has helped me raise four kids, all of whom met Christ in the church, had their gifts developed in the church, and now serve in some capacity of the church.
- It was the Christian church that let me lead worship *one time*.
- It was the Christian church that helped me figure out that I should *never, ever, ever* lead worship again.
- It was also the Christian church that healed my image of marriage . . . and that needed healing! In my family tree, going back 150 years, *everybody* is divorced. My wife and I recently celebrated thirty-one years of marriage. That means I now have the longest-running marriage in the entire history of my family.

So when a critic says, "I don't think the church makes that much of a difference," all I do is take out my family tree. In my life, Jesus and His church broke 150 years of negative past patterns.

> *When the Christian church gets it right . . . it is the most powerful force for God and for good on this worn planet.*

I can't imagine where my life would be without the Christian church. I don't know what I would be. I don't know where I would be. I don't know where my family would be. I'll be in heaven forever because some people at a Christian church had the guts to reach me for Jesus when I was an arrogant atheist.

When the Christian church gets it right—and, we've admitted, a lot of times it doesn't—it is the most powerful force for God and for good on this worn planet.

Because when the Christian church gets it right . . .

- Communities are transformed.
- Marriages are healed.
- Lost people have their lives and eternal destinies changed.
- The poor are helped and lifted.
- Racial barriers are blown away.

The church today and the church right after Christ, the early church, don't look much alike. Most churches today are so allergic to the leading of the Holy Spirit that nothing new ever starts.

SIX THINGS EARLY CHRIST-FOLLOWERS MAJORED IN

What fueled the expansion of the early church? Here are six things early Christ-followers majored in that we have got to get back.

1. They Believed God Uses Everyone

The life and impact of the early church exploded because the church was filled with servants.

On the other hand, our churches today are filled with spectators. This might be one of the things keeping the American church stagnant.

The early church changed the world without many resources. It had *one* resource—its people. They all served.

These first Christians did not have financial backing. They did not have great buildings. They did not have organizational structures. They did not have denominational support. They did not have lighting systems, microphones, video capability, or seminary training.

They did not have a stable economy, and neither do we. They didn't have favorable government conditions, and neither do we. They didn't have supportive media, and neither do we. They were basically eleven or so people who had just come off a season of failure, and they were very discouraged.

What they did have—*impact*. Why?

They had impact because everyone was a player, not a spectator. That seems like the opposite of the American church.

Peter, Paul, Barnabas, James, Stephen, Philip, Lydia, Priscilla, and Aquila were some of the early Christian leaders, out of a number that started with only 120 people total. But they went to thirty-two countries, fifty-four cities, nine islands, and to the superpower of that day, Rome.

They were all-in.

When Carol and I went to Europe, we visited St. Peter's, St. John the Divine's, and St. Paul's. But when I read the New Testament, it looks like nobody would have built anything to honor those guys. They would be shocked to see what was named for them. Why? They were ordinary people—just like most of us. Peter's mouth was always open, and his foot was always in it. Then he chopped off someone's ear with his sword. Thomas couldn't be hired by anyone. They'd say, "This is going to be great," and he'd say, "I doubt it." The other disciples were always arguing about who was going to be the greatest.

The problem with the statues we build to these guys is that we can easily believe, "God can't use me because I'm not one of those statue-type people." But when you read the New Testament, you see they weren't like that.

Scripture says, "When they saw the courage of Peter and John and realized that *they were unschooled, ordinary men*, they were astonished and they took note that these men had been with Jesus" (Acts 4:13).

I met with World War II hero Louis Zamperini in his home two years before he died. He said it this way:

> Take the greatest religious guys in the Bible. Noah? He failed God. Lot? He failed God. And the person that was the apple of God's eye was David and he failed God like nobody, but he repented. And that's what God wants is repentance and to come back to Him. So you're not alone. The greatest religious guys in the Bible all failed God. And He took them back in because of repentance.[1]

We live in a celebrity age now. We have celebrity artists, celebrity actors, and even celebrity pastors. One prominent pastor told me, "I'm the Lord's anointed one." I said, "No, you're not—you're *one* of the anointed ones. If you have a thousand people in your church, you have a thousand anointed ones!"

If you're reading this and you doubt that God can use you—and if you haven't gotten it yet—this ought to be good news: God uses everyone.

2. They Lived to Unleash Compassion

I call it my second conversion. I met with a group of pastors in Southern California for two days of study and prayer—and I have never recovered. I have never been the same. Our church has never been the same.

What happened?

In this study, we were reading the second chapter of Acts. Three phrases *jumped out.*

- "They sold property and possessions to give to anyone who had need" (Acts 2:45).
- "Every day they continued to meet together in the temple courts. They broke bread in their homes and ate together with glad and sincere hearts, praising God and *enjoying the favor of all the people*" (Acts 2:46–47).
- "And the Lord added to their number daily those who were being saved" (Acts 2:47).

We discussed in that study how the early church started with *good deeds*, which led to *good will*, which created openness to the *good news*.

Acts 2:45–47

"They sold property and possessions to give to anyone who had need . . ."	GOOD DEEDS
" . . . praising God and enjoying the favor of all the people . . ."	GOOD WILL
" . . . and the Lord added to their number daily those who were being saved."	GOOD NEWS

1. The early Christians began with *good deeds*. They decided to sell stuff in order to take care of other people.
2. That led to *good will*. Then they enjoyed the favor of all the people. The people had good will toward the Christians. That is not happening in America.
3. Because *good deeds* led to *good will*, it created an openness to the *good news* that we're not seeing now.

I sat there in that study, stunned. Here I was, with advanced theological degrees and thirty years of pastoring experience, and yet I was finally understanding a passage of Scripture that was telling me I was doing ministry backward.

Our church, and almost every other American church I knew, was trying to deliver *good news* without *good deeds*, so there was *no good will*.

I went home and called our outreach pastor and said, "We are absolutely going to wreck our church—in Jesus' name."

Then I called our whole staff together. "I just had a second conversion," I announced to them. "My first conversion was to Christ. And my second conversion is to compassion."

Then we went to the congregation. I said, "Now, I'm warning you in advance. We're going to read this passage. We're going to pray it. We're going to teach it. And we're all going to live it."

Nothing has ever been the same.

We had conducted two capital campaigns to build our buildings, and we kept all the money to ourselves. We started a new capital campaign and decided to give half of the money away to compassion projects. Everyone told us we were nuts. Every consultant said, "People will not give capital dollars if you're going to siphon some off and give it away."

"If that's true, then that's crazy," I told one consultant. "Christians are going to be known as the people who have great buildings and shrunken hearts."

As I write, we've now conducted three capital campaigns with compassion as our first goal. We give the money away to the compassion projects first, as our first goal, and then we raise the capital needed for the life of the church, and our needs are more than met. (And I'm sending those consultants a copy of this book!)

I spoke at a capital campaign at an enormous church in one of the wealthiest zip codes in the country, to help them raise some funds. When I turned down the driveway, I was overwhelmed by the beauty of their campus, which was a backdrop to their drop-dead gorgeous buildings. They were doing an eighty-million-dollar campaign—to make their already gorgeous buildings even more gorgeous. Not one dime was being raised and given to the poor, to the hurting, or to the needy.

We have to be called to unleash compassion. Our church is in the process of letting God flip everything around.

Every year a team of people from Bayside travels to Nairobi, Kenya, to partner with a courageous church in one of the toughest locations in the world. This church is the center of compassion for the whole community. This heroic church has taken responsibility for caring for over three hundred local kids. They care for, educate, support, and train up these kids, who had been locked *into* the vicious cycle of poverty and locked *out of* all opportunities for education and a future. In other words, this church is the center for *good deeds* in that community. The result was that they had tremendous *good will.*

A couple of years ago, when war broke out in the area, gangs ran wild and torched the whole neighborhood. Everyone hid in their houses, except the mothers of the children who were served by that church. They ran into the street and headed toward the church building. They surrounded the church and yelled at the rioters, telling them they better not dare touch the church. Everything in that area was torched—except the church. Not only had good works resulted in good will, but the good news was preached, and the people who received it were willing to defend it.

Our church has been trying to follow their example. Once, we decided to shut down the whole church for a weekend and send ten thousand people into the community to do good works. By this time, I'd been alerted to many problems in the inner-city schools. They had broken windows, no playgrounds or landscaping, and worse. So we made a list of places we could go and started calling school principals to see how we could serve.

That first year, some of the schools we called refused to allow us to help. They said, "All you want to do is preach."

The weekend of ministering to the community was such a success that we keep doing it each year. Last year, one of the area school districts that had previously refused to allow us on campus actually called *us*. "Are you doing that again this year?" the administrator asked. "We'd love for you to send a team to every one of our campuses."

The question is this: *What do you want your church to be known for?*

Do you want people to identify you as going to the "large church in the wealthy area," or the "church with the big cross," or the "church that has the big Christmas show each year"? Or would you want people to identify your church as "the church that actually cares about the community"?

A great goal for every church would be to unleash so much compassion that if you tried to shut the doors of your church, the community outcry would be so great they wouldn't let you close.

3. They Exchanged Self-Centered Living for Sacrificial Giving

I heard a story about a statue of Jesus in a church in South Africa that provides an unusual reminder. During the days of apartheid, the church was raided and the statue toppled. The hands of the statue broke off. The church leaders determined to put the statue back up exactly the way it was. They said, "This will remind us to be His hands to the world around us."

Imagine the impact on our country if overnight every single Christ-follower made this decision: *from now on, I am going to live for things that are more important than pleasing myself!*

The Bible is packed with the sacrificial generosity of the early Christians. They apparently actually acted on what Jesus said and put Christlike generosity to work. I'm adding emphasis here so you can see what they did:

> All the believers were one in heart and mind. No one claimed that any of their possessions was their own, but they shared everything they had. With great power the apostles continued to testify to the resurrection of the Lord Jesus. And God's grace was so powerfully at work in them all that there were no needy persons among them. For from time to time those who owned land or houses sold them, brought the money from the sales and put it at the apostles' feet, and it was distributed to anyone who had need.
>
> Joseph, a Levite from Cyprus, whom the apostles called Barnabas

(which means "son of encouragement"), *sold a field he owned and brought the money and put it at the apostles' feet.* (Acts 4:32–37)

Jesus talked more about money than about heaven and hell combined. He said, "Sell what you have and give to the poor" (Matthew 19:21 NKJV). We have become theological gymnasts to try to get Jesus not to say what He actually said.

Nothing great happens by accident. Starting with the example of Jesus, *all expansion of the kingdom of God is the result of somebody's sacrifice.*

Don Brewster is the guy from our area who got involved in bringing relief to abused children worldwide. After going to Cambodia in 2005, he and his wife, Bridget, sold their house, gave up their careers, and moved to Cambodia to rescue girls entrapped in sex trafficking.

In one city where Don chose to work, 100 percent of the girls were trafficked. There was no escaping it. The trouble is so bad that CNN did a one-hour special about it, hosted by actress Mira Sorvino. The world wouldn't have known if not for the sacrifice of Don's family.

The people from our church decided to sacrifice as well. Long before we raised that special Christmas offering, we built a home for the girls Don and Bridget were rescuing in Cambodia. Then some business people got involved, including the owner of the apparel chain Apricot Lane. He dreamed of doing more than just rescuing these young girls—he wanted to give them a hope and a future. So he created a business for them and sells their goods in his stores. He then took it a step further by adopting one of the young Cambodian women who had been brought to the United States to testify against a pedophile. His adopted daughter is now thriving in her faith and is in her second year at a Christian college.

One main benefit comes to any person or church that moves into sacrificial giving mode: generous people are *always* happier. The word *miser* is the root of the word *miserable.* Maybe Jesus was more right than we realize when He said, "It is more blessed to give than to receive" (Acts 20:35).

American Christians and churches will be ineffective and joyless until we wake up and get this right! We are called to go beyond tipping—even beyond tithing. We have to be called to sacrificial giving, and only then will we experience the joy of giving and the blessing of changing lives and communities!

Still think living for yourself brings joy? Let me ask you a question—when was the last time you met a self-centered, happy person? They don't exist.

4. They Were Passionate for the Last and the Least

Who are the least and the last to come into the kingdom? Jesus is specific about them.

The "least" are *not* people who are less valuable or important. They *are* people who are often forgotten. Jesus ended a parable saying, "I tell you the truth, just as you did it for one of the least of these brothers or sisters of mine, you did it for me" (Matthew 25:40 NET).

Recently, my staff and I became aware of how inadequate our church was in ministering to the kids and adults in our community who had special needs. When we realized we had missed "the least of these," we set aside budget and manpower to retrofit our facilities to expand the ministry to include them.

Six months after we started, I was walking through the church courtyard when a woman came up to me and burst into tears. She grabbed me and hugged me and wouldn't let go. Finally she composed herself enough to talk.

"I just want to thank you," she said. "Our son has special needs and is really noisy. Our old church asked us never to bring him back and never to put him in a class again. I'm raising him alone because my husband couldn't stand the nonstop pressure and left us. You have no idea what it means to be the mom of a special needs kid and to have a place where he's wanted."

"Absolutely Jesus wants him," I said, "And we want him. Every kid matters to God, and every kid ought to matter to us."

Once we had the facilities, we adjusted the church calendar as well.

We started a club one Friday night a month for teenagers with special needs. One day my son, who is a worship leader, told me he was going to lead worship at the club. I thought I'd go watch and support him. But I had no idea what a treat I was in for.

I walked into the room, and it was total pandemonium. My kid was onstage with his band, leading worship for sixteen kids. Half the kids were sitting in front of the stage. One kid in a wheelchair was parked right down front and waving his arms, screeching with the music, lost in worshiping God. Half the kids were in their own worlds in one way or another. One girl was running back and forth, from wall to wall. Through the whole worship time, she never stopped expressing her exuberance through running.

The room where they hold the club has no stained glass, no organ, nothing breakable. Just a band, some kids with special needs, and Jesus. As I watched, I thought about all the worship coming up later that weekend in churches across the world. There would be a beautiful Mass at St. Peter's Basilica, a pipe organ number at Notre-Dame, maybe seventeen services at amazing megachurches. But I don't think there was any worship service on the planet that God was more pleased with than the disorganized chaos I watched that night.

"The least of these" might also be junior high kids. Of all the joys of youth one can reminisce about, nobody ever wants to go back to junior high. Our youth leaders do a junior high-only event called Vertigo several times each year. It is a wild, loud, crazy night of mayhem (did I mention *loud*?) that almost destroys our building every time. About two hundred volunteers serve at the event and every junior high kid in town is invited. We usually have about fourteen hundred kids come.

Vertigo has become so popular that a few years ago, when it landed on the same day as a local dance, the school had to cancel the dance because only five kids bought tickets. Everyone else was going to Vertigo. Now that school calls our church to synchronize their calendar with Vertigo.

At the last Vertigo, 278 junior high kids stood up to receive Christ and got on a follow-up program as well.

5. They Were Passionate About People Far from God

A West Coast meeting changed the course of my life. A denominational board had invited West Coast pastors to meet with church-planting expert Bob Logan. Bob was tasked with helping to figure out how to plant more churches on the West Coast to increase market share in the churches there. The meeting started at eight thirty. At nine o'clock, Bob stood up, put his briefcase on the desk, started packing everything into it, then snapped it shut and announced, "I'm leaving."

They were all shocked. The room got tense. The leader presiding over the meeting protested, "You can't leave! We hired you for the whole day."

"I'll refund your money," Bob said, picking up the last of his things.

"But why are you leaving?" the leader asked.

"Here's the deal," Bob said. "You want to plant churches just so the denomination looks better. In my opinion, *you have lost your love for lost people.* I recommend you get down on your knees and ask God to forgive you for losing your heart for people far from God. Ask Him to give you a heart for the communities on the West Coast. Ask Him to give you a passion for those who are far away from God. When He gives you *that*, give me a call and I'll come back. Maybe then God can get something done."

> We have to care about people who are far away from God.

To their credit, the leadership stopped the meeting right then. Bob stayed. They all got down on their knees and turned the meeting into a prayer meeting. One year later, the church I pastor today started as a result of that prayer meeting. Seldom do I drive to my church without thinking, *This place was started by people who had lost their love for lost people but were willing to repent and get it back.*

We have to care about people who are far away from God.

A congregation in Maryland recaptured their heart for lost people and tasked a leadership team with coming up with a plan. The team had a meeting to discuss only one question: "Is there a group of people in our community that no church is targeting for Jesus?"

No one could think of a specific group until somebody wise-cracked, "Sure, smokers! I know of no church in our community that has as its mission statement, 'We exist to reach people who smoke.'"

After they laughed, the team all agreed it wasn't a bad idea. To which the smart-mouth added, "If we're going to do it, let's do it now! They're probably going to heaven or hell faster than any of us anyway, so we better be fast about it."

The team agreed to two things. One, they would reach people who smoked. Two, they would make the smokers feel welcome. That led to a couple of problems. The first was how to reach smokers. They ended up buying tens of thousands of packs of matches and imprinted them with, "God loves you and so do we," along with their church address. Then the congregation fanned out to every bar and restaurant to give the packs out for free. The second problem was what to do with the smokers—who came to church in droves, by the way. So the congregation put ashtrays outside the church.

The campaign was an enormous success. Smokers who would normally not have attended church became Christ-followers.

6. They Were Called to a Full Commitment to Both Grace and Truth

Scan the whole Bible and you will see that everything hinges on the twin theological foundations of grace and truth.

In John's gospel, chapter 1, he wrote, "The Word became flesh and made his dwelling among us. We have seen his glory, the glory of the one and only Son, who came from the Father, full of *grace* and *truth*" (v. 14). Jesus came with grace and truth. Both are essential. Every page you turn in Scripture, you read about grace and truth—the love of God and the Word of God.

The problem today is that most Christians major in one and minor in the other. Whole churches and denominations have thrown out truth but kept grace. And whole churches and denominations have thrown out grace but kept truth.

Jesus was the perfect example of commitment to both grace and truth. Jesus said to the woman caught in adultery, "Neither do I condemn you; go and sin no more" (John 8:11 NKJV). Notice that "Neither do I condemn you" is *grace*. "Go and sin no more" is *truth*. Perfect balance.

Have you ever been in a church that had one but not the other? In other words, have you ever been in a Bible-believing church that beat everyone up when they made mistakes? That's probably so common that almost every Christian has or has heard a horror story.

On the other hand, have you ever been to a church that loves everybody and says everyone is okay and nothing's wrong, because they've thrown out the clear-cut teaching in the Bible?

When we loosen our grip on truth, people no longer have a solid foundation to stand on. When we lose our grip on grace, we become toxic Pharisees.

The most exciting thing about representing Jesus in a polarized culture is holding on to both grace and truth. Making a 100 percent commitment to both the truth and grace of God is like hooking together two live wires—sparks fly and the power flows. When you commit to holding both grace and truth, you might get shot at from both fringes, but you will be in the center of the will of God—and following in the footsteps of Jesus. In this new era of Christianity, it is exciting to hold on to biblical truth with one hand, and hold the hand of every person with the other—and never let go.

A WORD FOR DISCONNECTED CHRISTIANS

Christians are called to be believers, but we're also called to be *belongers*. You will never be the type of believer God wants you to be until you get rooted in a local church.

When I was a bachelor, I had the gift of killing houseplants. Plants need water. Without water, they don't have a future. Imagine that you are a plant. You get put into a pot, and you get food and water. One week later, you get yanked out of that pot, and you get food and water. Every single week for twelve weeks, you get put into a different pot, and you get food and water. After twelve weeks, you, the plant, are going to die. Why? Not because you didn't get food and water, but because you weren't in one place long enough to put down roots, get nourishment, and really grow.

That is exactly what is going on in most people's church experience today. People are church shopping and hopping, going from one church to another to another. One reason there is so much shallow Christianity is that people are not staying in one church long enough to put down deep roots and get nourishment and really grow. There are God-honoring, grace-and-truth-filled churches in almost every community. If you're not connected to one, it's time to find one, sink down roots, and let God use that group of believers to strengthen and challenge your faith.

The success or failure of your life is largely determined by the equipment you use. You wouldn't try to fly across the Pacific with a hang glider. You wouldn't try to hit a baseball without a bat. You wouldn't try to fight a forest fire with a squirt gun. You have to use the right equipment.

God has created a piece of equipment for you to use: the church. Without it you'll never be what you could be. But recommending the church comes with a warning: you're never going to find the "perfect church." What you will find, however, is a church that is loaded with benefits.

A WORD FOR DISCOURAGED CHRISTIANS

When the Christian church gets it right, showing people the real Jesus and letting His light shine, there is no more powerful force on planet Earth for God, for good, or for changing lives. Christians invented hospitals, schools, universities, democracy, charity, and human rights. We advanced art, architecture, music, and many important notions, such as the rule of law.

American society today is based on the Christian ideals of individual responsibility, hard work, charity, compassion, humility, self-sacrifice, love, pride in working for the common good, and honoring social obligations to one another, to our families, and to our communities. It was British prime minister David Cameron who synthesized that list and went on to say about his own nation: "We are a Christian country. And we should not be afraid to say so."[2]

The notion of tolerance, which is widely trumpeted today as if it is something *against* Christians, was built into the fabric of American society *by* Christians so that people could exercise the power of choice written about in Scripture—the freedom to choose their own method of worship.

These are the results that follow the real Jesus.

Human Rights

Being made in God's image, with a dignity making each individual unique and worthy, is the very basis of human rights.[3]

Christians headed the movements to combat human rights abuses such as infanticide, gladiatorial combat in the Roman Empire, slavery, child labor, and many others. Christians in the United States and England led their respective movements to abolish the slave trade and banish slavery. The Wesleyan denomination was initially formed with the sole objective to fight slavery. In the United States, Christians in the North saved runaway slaves, printed thousands of newsletters to raise awareness of the injustice of slavery, and created pressure to abolish slavery that spread across the country. Likewise, the civil rights movement of the 1950s came out of the African American church.

Relief Work

Christians have been at the forefront of caring for the poor, which was a very unpopular notion in the Roman world when Christianity originated. Onc of the first commands to the early church was to care for others, and it is the very reason that deacons were established (Acts 6:1).

Most immigrants to America were processed through Ellis Island, where Christians fed and clothed the destitute and ministered to the sick. The Salvation Army, formed in 1865 to reach the poor and homeless, is today one of the largest providers of relief in every disaster that occurs in the United States. The Salvation Army got there faster and fed more people in the aftermath of Hurricane Katrina than the federal government.

Women

The dignity of women was elevated when Christ spoke openly to women, enjoyed women's friendship, and took time to bless and heal them. The apostle Paul continued this when he publicly acknowledged the women who were some of the first church leaders and supporters of the faith.[4]

Still today, American culture holds to the ideal of a husband sacrificially loving his wife, which was nonexistent before the dawn of Christendom.

Labor

Unlike Greco-Romans, Christians saw labor as honorable, dignified, a calling, and deserving of a fair wage.[5] The work ethic that certain countries, such as America, are known for didn't just happen and isn't a worldwide value. Christians infused the Western world with a value for work.

Education

Mandatory education for all children was first championed by Martin Luther.[6] Most of the great colleges and universities in the world began as Christian colleges, including Harvard, Yale, Princeton, and Dartmouth. The Christian church started almost all of the first 182 colleges and universities in America.[7]

Language and Literature

Christian missionaries codified and preserved the languages in much of the world, particularly for cultures that formerly had no written language. Hundreds of languages were not written until Christian Bible translators learned the languages and devised writing for them. When

Martin Luther translated the Bible into German, he had to choose which dialect to use. The German he chose is the German language we know today.

Christians have led the world in literature. Christian faith motivated and inspired classic works by Augustine, John Bunyan, Dostoevsky, Tolstoy, Pascal, Solzhenitsyn, Dickens, Milton, Defoe, Tennyson, Tolkien, C. S. Lewis, and many more.[8]

Art and Music

Christian faith inspired musical works by Bach, Handel, Mendelssohn, Beethoven, Mozart, and many others, and great works of art by da Vinci, Michelangelo, Raphael, Rembrandt, and more. A Yale professor wrote, "The victory of Jesus Christ over the gods of Greece and Rome in the fourth century did not, as both friend and foe might have expected, bring about the demise of religious art; on the contrary, it was responsible over the next fifteen centuries for a massive and magnificent outpouring of creativity that is probably without parallel in the entire history of art."[9]

Science

Copernicus, Kepler, Galileo, Pascal, Descartes, Newton, Kelvin, Mendel, and Boyle were all devout Christians. Father Steno, a priest, is the father of modern geology. The Basilica of San Petronio was for many years the most sophisticated solar observatory in the world. Jesuits helped contribute to the development of clocks, barometers, microscopes, and telescopes. They theorized about things like human flight, the moon and tides, and blood circulation. For more than five centuries, no institution funded and supported the sciences more than the Christian church.[10]

Physical and Spiritual Health

How would the church benefit you if you joined today? Studies show religious believers are far less likely than nonbelievers to experience many societal and physical ills.[11] People who do not attend church are four times more likely to commit suicide than frequent church attenders.[12]

The "importance of religion" is the single best predictor of not abusing drugs or alcohol. One survey of fourteen thousand youths found substance abuse varied in direct proportion to strength of religious commitment.[13]

High levels of faith boost psychological health and the ability to deal with stress and decrease psychological distress, depression, and the negative effects of stress.[14] There is also a positive association between religious faith and physical health.[15] Male churchgoers have a 60 percent lower risk of heart disease. Women churchgoers have only half the risk of dying from heart disease or emphysema.[16] Men who consider religion to be "very important" have far lower blood pressure and far reduced risk of cardiovascular disease.[17] Women with a strong religious faith recover from surgery far more quickly than nonbelievers.[18]

A major study found that church attendance predicted marital satisfaction better than any other variable.[19] A massive study found that "very religious women" report greater happiness and satisfaction with marital sex than either moderately religious or nonreligious women.[20]

People committed to religious faith have much higher levels of personal happiness and psychological well-being than atheists or agnostics.[21] In a Gallup survey, people who said, "My religious faith is the most important influence in my life," were *twice* as likely as others to describe themselves as "very happy."[22]

When the church gets it right, the community is never the same, the world is never the same, and people are never the same.

CHAPTER 13

Share Your Faith Without Embarrassing God

Meet the Jesus Who Is a Magnet for Sinners

For the Son of Man came to seek and to save the lost.

—Jesus, Luke 19:10

WHEN OUR SON MARK WAS FOUR YEARS OLD, CAROL AND I lost him. It was the longest twenty minutes of our lives. We were taking Mark and his brother Scott on a return flight home to Chicago. Our plane landed at O'Hare and parked at United Terminal C (which seems about five miles from the main terminal). We jostled off the plane with the crowd—and within seconds, it seemed, Carol turned around and said in a concerned voice, "Where's Mark?"

That started the Parent Game where you say back and forth to each other, "I thought he was with *you*!" For maybe two minutes, we were sure he would turn up when the next tall person got out of the way, but then frustration gave way to sheer terror. We'd lost our son in the busiest airport in the world.

Carol rushed to the United Airlines counter to ask for help. I tore through the airport to the entrance of the terminal. Every scary story I'd ever heard about kids getting kidnapped, disguised, and walked past their parents was going through my mind. With my heart pounding, I watched every little kid in the crowds of people, ready to tackle anyone with a boy who looked like mine. Then it dawned on me that there wasn't only one exit—there were thirty-eight gates! Sure that my son was on his way to Madagascar, I raced back to find Carol.

In the meantime, Carol had cut to the front of the service desk line and gave the staff the color of Mark's eyes, shoes, hair, and clothes. They were awesome. Immediately, they announced a code over the loudspeaker. As I was running, it looked like every door flew open in that terminal. Airline personnel, mechanics, flight attendants, and government employees flooded into the terminal, leaving their jobs for this higher priority, then fanned out in every direction, all doing one thing—looking for our lost son.

Still feeling terrified, I said to Carol, "We gotta keep looking." Right then, I turned, and at the other end of the terminal I saw the best sight I've ever seen. Two United Airlines flight attendants were walking with this little blond-haired, brown-eyed kid between them. One was holding each hand.

As he got to me, I thought, *He's gonna be really shaken up.* Carol and I, with tears of relief, held him. I said, "Son, are you okay?"

Mark said, "Dad! You oughtta see this plane down there! It's amazing. Come on! I'll show it to you!"

As we walked out of the terminal that day, hand in hand, I was overwhelmed by two thoughts that I've never forgotten.

First, my son was lost and in danger, but he had no clue he was lost and no idea he was in danger. Doesn't that describe the world around us? People who have never come to Christ are lost, but they have no clue they are lost and no idea of the danger they are in from being lost.

The second was this sober realization. I didn't find my own son. Other people heard he was lost, stopped what they were doing, searched for him, then took him by the hand and walked him into the arms of a very grateful father.

As I stood in the terminal, unable to hold back tears, all I could say to those flight attendants was, "Thank you, thank you, thank you."

Now, fast-forward into eternity. One day you will walk into heaven, and I believe Jesus will be there with His arms wrapped around all the people who—because of your love, care, and concern—are there with Him. I believe He will be filled with gratitude, saying, "Thank you, thank you, thank you."

He'll say, "You stopped what you were doing. You made something a higher priority. You cared enough to take action. You took these people by the hand and walked them into the arms of a very grateful Father."

That's evangelism.

SO WHAT'S THE PROBLEM?

American Christians and non-Christians have at least one thing in common—they're both uptight about evangelism.

Look at what Jesus said:

- "Follow Me, and I will make you become fishers of men" (Mark 1:17 NASB).
- "Jesus answered them, 'It is not the healthy who need a doctor, but the sick. I have not come to call the righteous, but sinners to repentance'" (Luke 5:31–32).

These are great verses of Scripture. The problem is that almost every American church and every American Christian ignores them. Why?

Evangelism is not in the DNA of the American church—*and it never has been.* Most Protestant churches in America were started by people fleeing religious persecution, coming to America, and starting churches *for themselves.* I am convinced that five hundred years later, the average American church is still a group of people whose primary concern is *themselves*. Amazing!

> What would happen if Jesus started a church today and put a sign out front that said, "I'm here to seek and to save the lost"?

Things have gone so far south that in some scenarios evangelism is considered politically incorrect. When a church actually *does* start reaching their community and leading people to Christ, then other Christians who couldn't care less about evangelism start labeling those churches as shallow—because the focus is on saving others instead of growing deeper themselves.

What would happen if Jesus started a church today and put a sign out front that said, "I'm here to seek and to save the lost"? (His words, not mine—see Luke 19:10). What would happen? I am convinced that many Christians in the community would criticize His church. They would say things like, "Whatever you do, don't go to Jesus' church. It's one of those *shallow* churches." I could hear the persuasion intensify. Someone would eventually say, "Don't go to Jesus' church. He's too shallow. He preaches only the gospel, not deep theological truths. We're deeper than Jesus."

WHAT EVANGELISM IS *NOT*

Maybe the problem is that we have a warped idea of what evangelism is. Last year I was speaking in a Southern town and was so surprised by a sign on a church door that I made a U-turn and took a picture. In big, bold letters, the sign proclaimed:

THE WAGES OF SIN IS DEATH.

How welcoming is that? I wanted to tell the church, "If you're going to show part of a scripture, at least for the sake of our Lord, *put the whole verse on the door*: 'The wages of sin is death, *but the gift of God is eternal life in Christ Jesus our Lord*'" (Romans 6:23).

Here are a few of the misconceptions about what evangelism is and isn't:

- Evangelism is not a high-pressure sales job.
- Evangelism is not condemnation and guilt. Jesus said He came *not* to condemn the world (John 3:17).
- Evangelism is not arguing people into the faith.
- Evangelism is not only the pastor's job.
- Evangelism is not an exclusive spiritual gift. Paul wrote to Timothy, who did not have the gift of evangelism (he had the gift of pastoring), and told him to "do the work of an evangelist" (2 Timothy 4:5). In other words, regardless of your gifts, get out and *do it*!
- Evangelism is not done only by people who have all the answers.
- Evangelism is not a crusade or event.
- Evangelism is not preaching thundering, guilt-inducing sermons.
- Evangelism is not hanging out a sign to give people "bad news."

WHAT EVANGELISM *IS*

Evangelism is simply helping someone move one step closer to Jesus. It is giving people who are in eternal danger the invitation to come home.

Remember the story of *Apollo 13*? The spacecraft was to make America's third lunar landing, but flight director Gene Kranz ordered the mission aborted when an oxygen tank exploded, setting in action a catastrophic series of events. As power, heat, water, and air depleted in space, the crew on the ground had to figure out how the astronauts could create an air purifier using items onboard the spacecraft. The day after the crew returned home safely, President Nixon stopped in Houston to give the entire team the Presidential Medal of Freedom, the nation's highest civilian award. (Scriptwriters later immortalized the attitude expressed by flight controller Jerry Bostick in the famous phrase, "Failure is not an option.")[1]

Think of the lengths hundreds of people went to in order to get three guys home. Then think of the lengths God went to in order to get you and me home. *If we care, those are the lengths we will go to in order to get other people home.*

THREE REASONS WE SHOULD EVANGELIZE

Jesus said, "As the Father has sent me, I am sending you" (John 20:21). If you let it, that one verse can change your life. Here is God's plan: first, He sent His Son, and then He sent *you*!

1. Life Is Too Short Not to Fish

Evangelism is our primary purpose. That's a strong statement, but Jesus was crystal clear about this. He said:

- "For the Son of Man came to seek and to save the lost" (Luke 19:10).
- "It is not the healthy who need a doctor, but the sick. I have not come to call the righteous, but sinners" (Mark 2:17).
- "Go out to the highways and hedges and compel people to come in" (Luke 14:23 ESV).

Our purpose isn't to build a business, make a million dollars, or retire early. If that happens, great. But that isn't our primary purpose. The problem is when we get so consumed building our own kingdoms that the real kingdom—the kingdom of God—gets neglected.

How fired up should we be about this? "The Lord . . . is patient with you, not wanting anyone to perish, but everyone to come to repentance" (2 Peter 3:9). God isn't nearly as nonchalant about people as we are. Every individual is *important* because every individual is *eternal.*

2. Lost People Matter to God (and Ought to Matter to Us)

Jesus called us to a "Great Commission" five different times in five different ways. He said:

- "Therefore go and make disciples of all nations, baptizing them in the name of the Father and of the Son and of the Holy Spirit, and teaching them to obey everything I have commanded you" (Matthew 28:19–20).
- "You are to go into all the world and preach the Good News to *everyone, everywhere*" (Mark 16:15 TLB).
- "This message of salvation should be taken from Jerusalem to all the nations: There is forgiveness of sins for all who turn to me" (Luke 24:47 TLB).
- "As the Father has sent me, I am sending you" (John 20:21).
- "You will receive power when the Holy Spirit comes on you; and you will be my witnesses in Jerusalem, and in all Judea and Samaria, and to the ends of the earth" (Acts 1:8).

Doing what Jesus said is not optional. Either we obey Him or we're disobedient to Him. If we had the cure for earthly diseases like cancer, AIDS, or Ebola, we'd be eager to share it, and perhaps it would be criminal not to. When we have the answer to an eternal disease, we have to share it.

Here's the test to know whether you have completed your mission or not: Are you still alive? If you're alive, then your mission is not over!

God has never made a person He didn't love. Loving people demands that we move beyond our comfort zones. We are called to reach out to people with different backgrounds, different education levels, different languages, and different politics. God tells us to reach out and says our love is proved by our actions.

One day, the famous Catholic bishop Fulton Sheen was in a leper colony in Africa. He was repulsed by open, cankerous sores on the skin of everybody lying there in the dirt. He said:

> I brought with me 500 silver crucifixes, intending to give one to each of the lepers—this symbol of the Lord's Redemption. The first one who came to meet me had his left arm eaten off at the elbow by the

> disease. He put out his right hand and it was the most foul, noisome mass of corruption I ever saw. I held the silver crucifix above it, and *dropped it*. It was swallowed up in that volcano of leprosy.
>
> All of a sudden there were 501 lepers in that camp; I was the 501st because I had taken that symbol of God's identification with man and refused to identify myself with someone who was a thousand times better on the inside than I. Then it came over me the awful thing I had done. I dug my fingers into his leprosy, took out the crucifix and pressed it into his hand. And so on, for all the other 499 lepers. From that moment on I learned to love them.[2]

Jesus said, "Let me assure you that no one has ever given up anything . . . for love of me and to tell others the Good News, who won't be given back, a hundred times over" (Mark 10:29–30 TLB).

3. Lost People Are More Open Than We Think

People assume that others aren't interested in spiritual issues. Nothing could be further from the truth. Every poll says Americans are more interested in spiritual things today than ever before. Out of every ten Americans, eight would be willing to go to church—if someone would only invite them.[3]

There has never been a problem with the harvest—only with the harvesters. Jesus gave a prayer request to the church: "Then he said to his disciples, 'The harvest is plentiful but the workers are few. Ask the Lord of the harvest, therefore, to send workers into his harvest field'" (Matthew 9:37–38).

The problem for two thousand years has been the number of harvesters. We need to be like a wallpaper hanger in our area who is in high demand because he's just that good. When he finishes a job, he'll say to the owner, "Now you've seen my side job. Let me take five minutes to tell you about my real job." Then he tells them about the love of Jesus Christ.

JESUS SAID, "YOU WILL BE MY WITNESSES"—NOT MY PROSECUTORS

Evangelism is simply sharing good news.

Jesus said, "You will be my witnesses" (Acts 1:8). He didn't say, "You will be my prosecuting attorney." "You will be my defender." "You will be my slick salesperson." He simply said, "You get to be a witness of really great news."

John Ortberg once spoke at our annual Thrive Conference and gave a great analogy. He said to imagine you are at a stoplight in your 1971 Ford Pinto with smoke pouring out of the exhaust. Someone pulls up next to you in a shiny new Lamborghini—750 horsepower, top speed of 220 mph—that sells for a cool half million. The owner looks over and feels compassion for you and the piece of junk you're driving. He gets out of his car, comes over to yours, knocks on your window, and says, "I've got a deal for you. I will trade you my brand-new Lamborghini for your 1971 Pinto right on the spot."

Who wouldn't take this deal?

God looks down and sees our pathetic Pinto-like condition and feels compassion for us. He offers us an exchange. He says, "I'll exchange the life of my Son for yours, and His perfection for your imperfection. Want to trade?"

Or imagine that Bill Gates calls you because he's heard about the unsuccessful hot dog stand you own that's about to be repossessed. Gates says, "The board just met, and we've decided to offer you Microsoft in exchange for your hot dog business."

If you were offered a deal like that, you'd take it!

The deal God offers every single human being is much, much better than either of these. For one thing, what good is that Lamborghini when you're dead? (And there's no way Microsoft Windows will be in heaven—we'll all have Macs.)

The good news is too important not to share!

God's deal for us is too good not to share. Because of Christ . . .

- you can know God.
- you can receive complete forgiveness.
- you can let go of guilt.
- you can receive eternal life.
- you can live with God's power.
- you can live with God's purpose.
- you can experience hope.
- you can experience real peace.
- you can experience God's presence.
- you can overcome fear.
- you can overcome discouragement.
- you can trust God's promises.
- you can develop a confident faith.
- you can discover you matter to God.

Who in their right mind would pass up all *that*?

THREE WAYS TO SHARE YOUR FAITH WITHOUT TURNING EVERYONE OFF

Years ago, I was asked to be the second speaker at a conference of teenagers. The band rocked the packed house. The crowd was on their feet. The comedians were hilarious. Then the first speaker got up and absolutely destroyed the momentum of the evening with three simple words. She had the attention of over a thousand teenagers and said, "Now, young people . . ." A groan broke out. I watched those kids completely tune out—*instantly*. The problem is this: she thought her words were turning the teenagers on, when in fact, she turned them all off. How often do the harsh words, stupid gimmicks, and manipulative tactics designed to attract people to our faith instead send them running away?

From my first days trying to tell people about Jesus, up until today—whether it's sharing the gospel in a coffee shop or to thousands of people in a stadium—this is what I've learned.

1. Don't Be Intimidated

Hearing star-studded testimonies in church can be intimidating. It's often discouraging to the rest of us when we hear a dramatic story about how God used someone. Testimonies usually sound something like this: The guy was flying back from a trip to New York. He started talking to the person next to him on the flight about God. Pretty soon, five more people joined the conversation. The flight attendant started crying and received Christ on the spot. The plane hit bumpy air. The flight attendant gave the microphone over, and the guy led every passenger on the plane to Christ. As they landed, the pilot got on the loudspeaker, renounced atheism, and professed faith.

Someone listens to this and thinks, *Man, I can't do that! I'm scared to death even to open my Bible on a flight because someone might see it and ask me a question!*[4]

Ever felt like you don't have a clue what to say? Eloquence is often overrated and sometimes not that helpful. Paul was brilliant in Athens, and nothing happened (Acts 17:16–19:1). He was weak in Corinth, and God showed up (1 Corinthians 2:1–5).

So many evangelism training programs give you six weeks of instruction on a three-ring, eighty-page training manual that has every answer, every argument, every refutation, the theistic evidence for intelligent design, plus laws and amendments—and on and on . . .

Try this: put the notebook away and just buy someone dinner. How does evangelism actually happen for most people? Most people are influenced by those they are closest to, and usually someone simply invites them to church.

Jesus told His followers, "Go everywhere in the world, and tell the Good News to everyone" (Mark 16:15 NCV). Who was Jesus addressing? Leaders? Missionaries or pastors? No, Jesus was talking to normal followers. He said, "Follow Me, and I will make you fishers of men" (Matthew 4:19 NASB).

The point isn't to be brilliant. The point is to get started. If we're not fishing, we're not following.

2. "Come and See" Is More Effective Than "Shut Up and Listen"

Singer Amy Grant once told a great story while receiving an award. She said her nieces and nephews went with her to the beach, and they had never seen the ocean before. She gathered them at the top of the little rise before the ocean and said, "Now you get to meet the beach!" Then they held hands together and ran over the hill. The kids saw the ocean and went crazy, running, splashing, and high-fiving.[5]

What a great picture. Evangelism is the incredible privilege to introduce people to the ocean of the love of God that many times they've never seen and didn't even know existed.

"Philip found Nathanael and told him, 'We have found the one Moses wrote about . . . Jesus of Nazareth, the son of Joseph'" (John 1:45). Philip was doing "come and see" evangelism. He wanted Nathanael to get in the presence of Jesus. One key of evangelism is to get people in a situation where God can work in their lives. "Go out into the country lanes and behind the hedges," Jesus said, "and urge anyone you find to come, so that the house will be full" (Luke 14:23 NLT).

I was the first guy in my neighborhood to connect with Jesus. I was clueless, but I had a deep conviction that the guys I grew up with needed the same thing. God worked (in spite of me). When my best friend met Jesus, we teamed up, and every single guy on the blocks where I grew up ended up meeting Christ in the next two years. We kept dragging them to church. I didn't argue with anyone. I didn't know enough answers to have an argument. I just kept saying, "Hey, I'm going to this awesome church. Come with me."

Then a couple of years later, a well-meaning Christian told me we weren't commanded to take people to church—we were commanded to lead people to Christ. So I took an evangelism seminar, and for the next three years, I didn't lead anybody to Christ.

Then I read, "By this everyone will know that you are my disciples, if you love one another" (John 13:35). I thought, *How can they see that love if they're not around Christians?* So I went back to bringing people to church, and people I knew started becoming Christians again. It's not either/or, but both/and. Witness all you want but also bring them to church. "Come and see" is always more effective than "shut up and listen."

Last year, I took my daughters with me to Nordstrom because they thought I needed a nonembarrassing shirt to wear for Christmas Eve services. There was a waiting area where ladies were waiting for guys in the dressing room. A mom was there waiting on her teenage son. We started joking with her. While I was trying on shirts, my daughters chatted with her more. I came out and asked if she shopped there often, but she said she was new to the area. "Listen, that's great," I said, "because we go to a church for people who don't like church, and we have unbelievable Christmas Eve services. Here are a couple of 'You're Invited' cards if you and your son want to come."

The first service was that night. After the meeting, someone came to me and said, "There are a couple of people with 'You're Invited' cards and they want to see you." I went out and saw that lady and her son. They had both come to church, met Christ, and were at the follow-up table to get plugged in to their new Christian family.

The last thing that lady needed in the store was a sermon (or clothing advice from me). What she did need was an invitation so she could bring her son to church and discover they both mattered to God more than they ever thought. God can work even in a Nordstrom department store!

3. Remember We're Called to Win People, Not Arguments

We have to share our faith, but we don't have to get into arguments or try to win debates. By arguing, you won't win anyone and will only frustrate those you're talking to!

The bottom line is that God has reconciled us, which means He has exchanged for us. He has exchanged our failure for His forgiveness. He has exchanged our guilt for His grace. He has exchanged our imperfection for His perfection. That's what people need to know.

GET READY—GOD MIGHT ACTUALLY WANT TO USE *YOU*

K-LOVE, a contemporary Christian radio network, recently built the best recording studio in Northern California. When I spoke at their dedication, I had the opportunity to talk to an engineer they had flown in to build the studio. He said, "My crew and I have never done a job at a place like this before."

He said that one morning when they walked in, the radio station's entire staff had come in early to cook and serve them breakfast. He said, "I'm going back home, but I'm sad. This is the first time I've ever felt like I was leaving family because of finishing a job."

I don't have a clue where that guy is spiritually, but he is a whole lot more impressed with Jesus and the people who follow Him after spending a couple of months working alongside the *positive, encouraging* people at K-LOVE.

"Be ready at all times to answer anyone who asks you to explain the hope you have in you" (1 Peter 3:15 GNT).

GET YOUR FIRE BACK! PASSION COMMUNICATES IN ANY GENERATION

Azusa Pacific University has some fragments of the Dead Sea Scrolls and other treasured documents from throughout church history. One of my favorite things out of that collection is a letter written from Charles Spurgeon. More than one hundred years later, you can still feel his passion. He wrote:

O Lord bless this letter.

My Dear Arthur Layzell,

I was a little while ago at a meeting for prayer where a large number of ministers were gathered together. The subject of prayer was "our children." It soon brought the tears to my eyes to hear those good fathers pleading with God for their sons & daughters. As they went on entreating the Lord to save their families, my heart seemed ready to burst with strong desire that it might be even so. Then I thought I will write to those sons & daughters, to remind them of their parents' prayers.

Dear Arthur, you are highly privileged in having parents who pray for you. Your name is known in the courts of heaven. Your case has been laid before the throne of God.

Do you not pray for yourself? If you do not do so, why not? If other people value your soul, can it be right for you to neglect it? All the entreaties and wrestlings of your father will not save you if you never seek the Lord yourself. You know this.

You do not intend to cause grief to dear mother and father but you do. So long as you are not saved, they can never rest. However obedient and sweet and kind you may be, they will never feel happy about you until you believe in the Lord Jesus Christ to find everlasting salvation.

Think of this. Remember how much you have already sinned and none can wash you but Jesus. When you grow up you may become very sinful and none can change your nature and make you holy but the Lord Jesus, through his Spirit.

You need what father and mother seek for you, and you need it *now*. Why not seek it at once? I heard a father pray, "Lord save our children, and save them young." It is never too soon to be saved; never too soon to be happy; never too soon to be holy. Jesus loves to receive the very young ones.

> You cannot save yourself, but the great Lord Jesus can save you. Ask him to do it. He that asketh receiveth. Then trust in Jesus to save you. He can do it, for he died and rose again that whosoever believeth in Him might not perish, but have everlasting life. Come & tell Jesus you have sinned; seek forgiveness; trust in Him for it & be sure that you are saved.
>
> Then imitate our Lord. Be at home what Jesus was at Nazareth. Yours will be a happy home, and dear Father and Mother will feel that the dearest wish of their hearts has been granted them.
>
> I pray you to think of heaven & hell, for in one of those places you will live for ever. Meet me in heaven! Meet me at once at the mercy-seat. Run upstairs and pray to the great Father, through Jesus Christ.
>
> Yours very lovingly,
> C.H. Spurgeon[6]

I know a businessman who told me he has two goals in life. He said, "One, I want to go to heaven when I die. Two, I want to take as many people with me as possible."

The question we have to ask ourselves is, *When I get to heaven, is anybody going to say thank you, thank you, thank you to me because I told them the Good News?* The most dangerous prayer you can pray is, "God, use me."

NO ONE IS EVER BEYOND GOD'S REACH

My mother and I had a great relationship. She lived her entire life apart from Christ. Mom worked until she was seventy-eight years old, and we talked two or three times a week for years. Every time I called her office, the receptionist would always ask, "May I tell her who's calling?" I would always answer "Bill Clinton" or "Michael Jordan" or "Justin Timberlake"—whoever was in the news, someone different each time. That receptionist never caught on. She would say, "Okay, Mr. Sinatra," then connect me to my mom, saying, "There's a Mr. Sinatra on the phone for you."

Mom and I would usually talk for thirty minutes, laughing most of the time, followed by me telling her I loved her. I did love her. She battled back from cancer, twice. But one day I heard she was on her way to the hospital again. In no time, I was on a flight to see her. Seven days later, Mom died.

Four days before her passing, while I was sitting at her bedside, I said, "Mom, I want to talk to you about God." For the first time, she didn't stop me.

"Here's what I want to tell you," I said. "The first person to go to heaven with Jesus never went to church. He was not a religious guy at all. He was just a thief who was hanging on the cross. But he did say, 'Lord, remember me when You come into Your kingdom.' Mom, it doesn't matter if you never went to church or if you lived a good enough life. All that matters is to believe in your heart that Jesus is real and that He died for you, and to confess that with your mouth by praying a prayer with me right now. Will you repeat after me?"

Mom smiled, and right there, after all those years, she received Christ. Four days later, she closed her eyes for the last time.

On the Sunday after Mom's memorial service, I was feeling pretty sad. During the worship service, I felt like God whispered to my heart, *It's okay, I've got My arm around your mom right now. She's in good hands.*

Anything in our lives that doesn't have eternal impact will be eternally out of date. As a friend of mine says, "There are only two things you can't do in heaven. One is lead people to Christ. Two is sin." Which one do you think God has left you on earth to major in?

Great question.

No one is ever too far away from God to receive Christ.

You may have read through this entire book and just realized you're in the same place as my mom. There is a difference between knowing about someone and knowing them personally. A lot of people have read the Bible, but they've never met the Author. I know a lot about LeBron

James, but I've never met him. I know a lot about Jack Nicklaus, but we've never met personally.

Knowing *about* Jesus is not enough. We need to meet Him. It's so simple to meet Him that people miss it all the time. The way you start a relationship with Jesus is by receiving Him through prayer. If you've never taken that step, then the following prayer may help:

> *Dear God, thank You for sending Your Son, Jesus Christ, into the world. I believe Jesus is who He said He was and proved it by rising from death. I want to get to know You personally. Thank You, Jesus, for dying for me so that I could be forgiven and freed from my past. Please forgive me for all of those sins and come into my life. I receive You as my Lord and Savior. Help me to follow You for the rest of my life. Thank You for Your free gift of eternal life. Amen.*

If you prayed that prayer, I want to welcome you to the greatest adventure of your life. To help you get started with a solid foundation, e-mail me at Ray@RayJohnston.com and I'll send you the same free resources that we give to everyone at Bayside who decides to become a Christ-follower. A relationship with God is real and possible, regardless of anything that has ever happened before in your life or anything you have ever heard—because Jesus is not only dying to *know* you; He literally died *for* you.

No one is ever too far away from God to receive Christ.

Read This Last

STILL DOUBTING GOD CAN USE *YOU*?

Years ago, I resigned a job as a senior pastor in Southern California and became a youth pastor in Marin County, California. At the time, Marin County was the third wealthiest county in America. The church I went to had many of the wealthy people and their teenagers attending. You can imagine what they were like.

I walked into the first youth meeting and realized that I was looking at the richest, best-looking, logo-wearing, Porsche-driving, Princeton-bound, spring-skiing, apathetic bunch of church brats I'd ever encountered. (You know the type.)

I decided then and there I was going to get them into mission and service if it killed me. It nearly did. I asked them what they did during spring break, and before they could answer, I gave them a thirty-minute manipulative pitch motivating them to sign up for an Easter week of service in Mexico. I then said, "All right. Who's going with me?"

Eighteen teenagers later, I had eighteen nos. Their reasons for not going ranged from their traditional spring skiing in Vail and Aspen and Tahoe to one girl who said, "Oh, during Easter I fly to Paris and shop!" (Don't we all?)

It took six months of motivating, but by April, I had thirty-eight kids pretty much handcuffed and on their way to Mexico.

They have never recovered.

One of the first things they saw as we drove into the village were four teenage guys laying a friend down on the side of the road who had no arms and no legs—four amputations.

They saw families living in cardboard shacks, and hungry kids wearing rags with their ribs sticking out. For the first time, they got a firsthand view of what it was to earn less than sixty bucks per month and try to raise a family.

We drove an hour down a dirt road looking for our assigned church. The plan was to find the church, worship with them, then team up and bring the love of Christ by serving the community.

Finally, at the end of another dirt road, we saw our destination church and realized at once that something was terribly wrong—there was no church! The church had been burned down. There were four charred walls, a burned roof, and, as we pulled to a stop, I had thirty-eight teenagers looking at me saying, "Way to go, Ray."

Thinking the same thing, I got out and walked up to survey the charred building, but I realized we were not alone. There was a service going on! Looking through one of the burned-out windows, I saw this young, tough-looking pastor preaching his heart out to nine very discouraged-looking people sitting on salvaged benches. I thought, *Should we go in? Should we stay out?* Something had obviously gone wrong with the trip organizer's communication. But we had just driven a thousand miles to be with these people. So I walked back to the bus and said, "Let's go in."

Now, this had to seem surreal for the little church. Because in the middle of Nowhere, Mexico, right in the middle of the pastor's sermon, thirty-eight Marin County teenagers filed into the back of the church.

The pastor was so shocked, he stopped his sermon and said, "*Qué pasa?*" which means, "What are you yuppies doing here?"

One of our kids spoke a little . . . Spanglish. "We're Christians," he said. "We're from America, and we're here to help and serve in any way we can."

I could see the pastor getting emotional. He told us that the church had been damaged six months ago. (We found out later that a gang in the village had burned down the building.) He said, "For six months we have been praying that God would send help. We had given up hope that help would ever arrive, but now *here you are*."

Our kids were shocked. The tiny congregation had prayed. We showed up. Every youth group has a loud-mouthed kid, and ours blurted out, "Hey! We're an *answer to prayer*!"

They actually were! Back home, they caused prayer—but here, they were the answer to prayer.

At a team meeting the day after the kids saw the wrecked roof, they decided to rebuild it. Without any prompting, they grabbed a sombrero and took their own offering. They even asked me to take pictures of them taking the offering, so they could prove to their parents they gave away money.

Three days later, our teenagers, working side by side with the locals, had finished the roof, repainted the church, and installed new windows. The church transformation was remarkable. The transformation of the teenagers was even more remarkable.

We had brought carloads of attractive Marin County high school girls, some of whom had never even seen *dirt*. They brought suitcases loaded with hair dryers and curling irons (I forgot to tell them there would be no electricity). Three days into the trip, they had given up trying to look good and spent the days rolling in the dirt with these amazing village kids. Those teenagers got filthy from head to foot, but they were never more attractive than they were that week. Why? There is a spark, a radiance, an energy in the eyes of people who are living for purposes greater than just looking good.

During the day, the kids served the community, built homes for the poor, and led day camps for the kids in the area, and at night we held meetings where we showed the JESUS film projected on a big sheet. The kids led the music and taught the Bible, and by the end of the week, the roof wasn't even needed—that dirt road was so packed with people coming to see what was happening that we had to move the meetings outside.

Their clothes weren't the only things that got ruined on that trip. Those kids went home wrecked. They got connected to God. They got connected to each other. Then they crossed the line and started living to give and to serve and to do something great with their lives.

But the kids weren't the only ones wrecked. That youth group wrecked our affluent congregation in the best of ways. The youth group exploded, and the next year eighty-six kids signed up for the trip. That created a transportation problem. We couldn't get all the kids to Mexico. So one Sunday morning I got up in front of Marin County's wealthiest church and said, "We're taking eighty-six teenagers to Mexico. *We need to borrow your cars.*"

And . . . nothing happened. They had BMWs—which is short for Basic Marin Wheels—and they were not about to loan those.

The next week, a friend named Al said he'd make the announcement. Before he went onstage, he turned to me and said, "I hope they packed their bags. I'm taking them on a guilt trip."

Al stood up and delivered my all-time favorite church line: "Did you hear the rumor about our church? The adults in our church are willing to send their *kids*, but not their *cars*, to Mexico!"

Grand slam. The parents were practically throwing their keys on the stage. Eighteen vehicles were provided on that one Sunday. One guy donated a four-door Mercedes Benz, which, of course, I drove . . . in order to protect it. The church and those students were never the same.

As long as I live, I will never forget being at the end of a dirt road in Nowhere, Mexico, with thirty-eight teenagers taking a risk and serving God for the first time. Why? Because those kids taught me this:

The second you wake up . . .

The second you get out of your comfort zone . . .

The second you stop being intimidated . . .

The second you let go of fear . . .

The second you actually start serving, and start giving and start caring . . .

. . . here is what happens. You wake up and discover:

You have become the answer to somebody else's prayer!

My question is this. Why would you want to live any other way?

Acknowledgments

THE JESUS PROJECT STARTED YEARS AGO WITH A PASSION TO "reintroduce the American church to Jesus." That became the theme of our Thrive Conference and our family of churches. It also ignited a passion to write a book that could be used by individuals, groups, and churches to reintroduce people to the passion, grace, truth, vision, freedom, and power that are only unleashed when people are connected to Jesus.

None of this happens without the following people . . .

To my cowriter, Joann Cole Webster: I love working with people with passion. Thank you for bringing vision and energy to this project.

To Rick Nash: Being possibly the only Harvard and Dallas Theological Seminary grad in the world, you continue to provide what I would expect from that combination: great theology and brilliance. Like everything I do in this arena, without you, this project doesn't get far.

To Rick Christian and Bryan Norman at Alive Communications: I love the way you both honor God and inspire people.

To Debbie Wickwire: For your class, ideas, brilliance, and patience, I can only say thank you. This book is better because of you.

To Darlene Anderson: You remember everything, serve everyone, and are a joy to work with. Without you . . . Well, I don't even want to think about it!

To my executive assistant, Donna Bostwick: Carol and I are honored to have you in our lives. If you didn't do what you do, there would be no way we could do what God has called us to. Thank you for keeping the universe and me running.

To my four kids—Mark, Scott, Christy, and Leslie: I will be forever grateful you turned to Jesus at an early age and have committed yourselves to walking with Him now as adults. No dad ever had it better, and I am prouder of you than you will ever know! Keep living like Jesus (and turning out like Mom)!

And to my wife, Carol: You are the most Christlike person I know.

Notes

Read This First

1. Adapted from Donald Kraybill, *The Upside-Down Kingdom* (Harrisonburg, VA: Herald Press, 2011), 13.

Read This Second

1. Pew Research Center, "America's Changing Religious Landscape," May 12, 2015, http://www.pewforum.org/2015/05/12/americas-changing-religious-landscape/.
2. Steve McSwain, "Why Nobody Wants to Go to Church Anymore," *Huffington Post*, updated January 23, 2014, http://www.huffingtonpost.com/steve-mcswain/why-nobody-wants-to-go-to_b_4086016.html.

Chapter 2: Seven Lost Decades

1. Malcolm Logan, "Dumped On: The Messy Truth about Love Canal, NY," My American Odyssey, October 19, 2012, http://myamericanodyssey.com/dumped-on-the-messy-truth-about-love-canal-ny/. See also Eckhardt Beck, "The Love Canal Tragedy," *EPA Journal*, January 1979, http://www2.epa.gov/aboutepa/love-canal-tragedy.

2. Brian Stelter, "Ownership of TV Sets Falls in U.S.," *New York Times*, May 3, 2011, http://www.nytimes.com/2011/05/03/business/media/03television.html?_r=0.
3. Nielsen, "A Look Across Media: The Cross-Platform Report Q3 2013," December 3, 2013, http://www.nielsen.com/us/en/insights/reports/2013/a-look-across-media-the-cross-platform-report-q3–2013.html.
4. "Better TV Means Better Kids," www.EducationNews.org, March 11, 2013, http://www.educationnews.org/parenting/better-tv-better-kids/.
5. Ibid.
6. Quentin J. Schultze, Roy M. Anker, James D. Bratt, William D. Romanowski, John W. Worst, and Lambert Zuidervaart, *Dancing in the Dark: Youth, Popular Culture, and the Electronic Media* (Grand Rapids: Eerdmans, 1991), 1–13, 38–39, 56–57, 77–79, 89, 199, 203; William D. Romanowski, *Eyes Wide Open: Looking for God in Popular Culture*, rev. ed. (Grand Rapids: Baker, 2007), 150, 178.
7. Rob Nagel, ed., "The 1970s: An Overview," *UXL American Decades*, vol. 8: 1970–1979 (Detroit: UXL, 2003), xxi–xxiii.
8. Andy Serwer, "The '00s: Goodbye (at Last) to the Decade from Hell," *Time*, November 24, 2009, http://content.time.com/time/magazine/article/0,9171,1942973,00.html.
9. Kenneth Raposa, "Have Americans Lost Faith in the 'American Dream'?", *Forbes*, November 15, 2011, http://www.forbes.com/sites/kenrapoza/2011/11/15/have-americans-lost-faith-in-the-american-dream/.

Chapter 3: Building on a Cracked Foundation

1. Paul Berman, "The Philosopher of Islamic Terror," *New York Times*, March 23, 2003, http://www.nytimes.com/2003/03/23/magazine/the-philosopher-of-islamic-terror.html?pagewanted=all.
2. Linda and Charlie Bloom, "The Price of Success," *Psychology Today*, April 24, 2012, http://www.psychologytoday.com/blog/stronger-the-broken-places/201204/the-price-success.
3. Christopher Lasch, *The Culture of Narcissism: American Life in an Age of Diminishing Expectations* (New York: W. W. Norton, 1991).
4. "A Biblical Worldview Has a Radical Effect on a Person's Life," Barna Group, December 1, 2003, https://www.barna.org/barna-update/article/5-barna-update/131-a-biblical-worldview-has-a-radical-effect-on-a-persons-life#.VW0Qb-sk_ww.

5. Ibid.
6. Cao Li, "Building Collapse Kills One Worker in Shanghai," *China Daily*, June 27, 2009, http://www.chinadaily.com.cn/china/2009–06/27/content_8330067.htm.
7. Santa Cruz Public Library, "Loma Prieta Earthquake, 1989: Facts and Statistics," http://scplweb.santacruzpl.org/history/disaster/89quake.shtml; "October 17, 1989 Loma Prieta Earthquake," USGS, October 15, 2014, http://earthquake.usgs.gov/regional/nca/1989/.
8. Julia Glick, "Mother Who Cut Off Baby's Arms Acquitted by Reason of Insanity," *Boston Globe*, April 8, 2006, http://www.boston.com/news/nation/articles/2006/04/08/mother_who_cut_off_babys_arms_acquitted_by_reason_of_insanity/.
9. Paul Vitz, *Faith of the Fatherless: The Psychology of Atheism* (San Francisco: Ignatius Press, 2013).
10. Dallas Willard, unpublished talk, cited in Mike Erre, *Why the Bible Matters: Rediscovering Its Significance in an Age of Suspicion* (Eugene, OR: Harvest House, 2010), 129.

Chapter 4: "I'm a Non-Christian, Just Like Most Christians"

1. James Dobson, *Coming Home: Timeless Wisdom for Families* (Wheaton, IL: Tyndale, 1998), 122.
2. Bill Maher, "Bill Maher: The Hypocrisy of Evangelical Christians," May 15, 2001, https://www.youtube.com/watch?v=Ao_PdmERD_U.
3. "Americans Love Jesus, Lincoln, and Themselves" (press release), Public Policy Polling, November 17, 2011, http://www.publicpolicypolling.com/pdf/2011/PPP_Release_US_1117424.pdf.
4. Nikki Schwab, "Poll: Gay People More Popular Than Evangelicals," *U.S. News and World Report*, March 27, 2014, http://www.usnews.com/news/blogs/washington-whispers/2014/03/27/poll-gay-people-more-popular-than-evangelicals.
5. Sheldon Vanauken, *A Severe Mercy* (New York: HaperCollins, 1977), 85.
6. H. L. Mencken, *A Book of Burlesques* (1920), quoted in H. L. Mencken, *A Mencken Chrestomathy: His Own Selection of His Choicest Writing* (New York: Vintage, 1982), 624.
7. Dan McGrath, "Bart of Darkness," *The Simpsons*, season 6, episode 1, directed by Jim Reardon, aired September 4, 1994.

8. Frank Viola, "Shocking Beliefs of John Calvin," Patheos, April 8, 2015, http://www.patheos.com/blogs/frankviola/shockingbeliefsofjohncalvin/.
9. Charles Stanley, *Living the Extraordinary Life: Nine Principles to Discover It* (Nashville: Thomas Nelson, 2008), 23–24; emphasis added.

Chapter 5: Fed Up with Church

1. Edwin Louis Cole, *Real Man* (Pittsburgh: Resolute Books, 2013), 39.
2. Jon Meacham, "The End of Christian America," *Newsweek*, April 3, 2009, http://www.newsweek.com/meacham-end-christian-america-77125.
3. Thom Rainer, "13 Issues for Churches in 2013," *Church Leaders*, December 31, 2012, http://www.churchleaders.com/pastors/pastor-articles/164787-thom-rainer-13-issues-churches-2013.html?p=1.
4. Pew Research Center, "Nones on the Rise," *Pew Research Center's Religions and Public Life Project*, October 9, 2012, http://www.pewforum.org/2012/10/09/nones-on-the-rise/; Barry A. Kosmin, Egon Mayer, Ariela Keysar, "American Religious Identification Survey," CUNY Graduate Center, http://www.gc.cuny.edu/CUNY_GC/media/CUNY-Graduate-Center/PDF/ARIS/ARIS-PDF-version.pdf.
5. Kelly Shattuck, "7 Startling Facts: An Up Close Look at Church Attendance in America," Church Leaders, 2014, http://www.churchleaders.com/pastors/pastor-articles/139575-7-startling-facts-an-up-close-look-at-church-attendance-in-america.html.
6. Ibid.
7. Ibid.
8. Ibid.
9. Jon Meacham, "The End of Christian America."

Chapter 6: Lukewarm and Loving It!

1. Chad Walsh, *Early Christians of the 21*st *Century* (New York: Harper and Brothers, 1950), 11; emphasis added.
2. William Willimon, *Pulpit Resource*, September 10, 1995.
3. C. S. Lewis, *The Weight of Glory* (1949; repr. New York: HarperOne, 2001), 26.
4. R. Albert Mohler, "Moralistic Therapeutic Deism—The New American Religion," *Christian Post*, April 18, 2005, http://www.christianpost.com/news/moralistic-therapeutic-deism-the-new-american-religion-6266/.
5. Christian Smith with Melina Lundquist Denton, *Soul Searching: The*

Religious and Spiritual Lives of American Teenagers (New York: Oxford University Press, 2009), 118ff.

6. Bernard L. Ramm, *Protestant Christian Evidences: A Textbook of the Evidences of the Truthfulness of the Christian Faith for Conservative Protestants* (Chicago: Moody, 1953), 232–33.
7. Billy Martin, interviewed by David Letterman, *Late Night with David Letterman,* December 4, 1985, https://www.youtube.com/watch?v =CgzZcfGro8g; Billy Martin and Peter Golenbock, *Number 1* (New York: Random House, 1981), 162–63.
8. Charles Schwartz, *Natural Church Development: A Guide to Eight Essential Qualities of Healthy Churches* (Carol Stream, IL: ChurchSmart, 1996), 54.

Chapter 7: Christian Zombies

1. C. S. Lewis, *God in the Dock* (1970; repr. Grand Rapids: Eerdmans, 2014), 102.
2. "William Booth," Salvation Army, http://www1.usw.salvationarmy.org/usw /www_usw_torrance2.nsf/vw-sublinks/FCD98CD6A8BFB1B68825771 D00178DE1?openDocument.
3. G. K. Chesterton, *Orthodoxy* (1908; repr. Chicago: Moody, 2009), 92.
4. Ibid.
5. Eugene H. Peterson, *Where Your Treasure Is: Psalms that Summon You From Self to Community* (1985; repr. Grand Rapids: Eerdmans, 1993), 12.
6. Whit Hobbs, *I Love Advertising* (New York: Adweek Books, 1985), 14–15.
7. "Suicide Facts," Suicide Awareness Voices of Education, http://www.save .org/index.cfm?fuseaction=home.viewPage&page_id=705D5DF4-055B -F1EC-3F66462866FCB4E6.
8. Peter Wehrwein, "Astounding Increase in Antidepressant Use by Americans," Harvard Health Publications, Harvard Medical School, October 20, 2011, http://www.health.harvard.edu/blog/astounding -increase-in-antidepressant-use-by-americans-201110203624.
9. Gary Trust, "Elvis Presley's Billboard Chart Records," Billboard, January 8, 2013, https://www.billboard.com/articles/columns/chart-beat/1481559 /elvis-presleys-billboard-chart-records.
10. Dotson Rader, "'There Had to Be Something More Out There,'" *Parade,* February 9, 1997, 7, http://www.newspapers.com/newspage/9474010/.
11. Nelson Mandela, *Notes to the Future: Words of Wisdom* (New York: Atria Books, 2012), 26.

12. Nelson Mandela, *Long Walk to Freedom: The Autobiography of Nelson Mandela* (New York: Little, Brown, and Company, 2008), 326.
13. Nelson Mandela, *Notes to the Future,* 96.
14. Ibid., 6.
15. Ibid., 11.
16. Max Lucado. *The Applause of Heaven* (Nashville: Thomas Nelson, 2008), 7.

Chapter 8: Get Off the Couch

1. Thank you, Pastor Scott Dudley, for getting me started on this list!
2. Francis Chan, "Challenge 2006," July 2006, https://www.youtube.com/watch?v=LA_uwWPE61Q.
3. Oliver Hong, "The London Beer Flood," *Atlas Obscura,* http://www.atlasobscura.com/places/site-london-beer-flood.
4. Dylan Thuras, "Morbid Monday: Sweet Death," *Atlas Obscura,* March 19, 2012, http://www.atlasobscura.com/articles/morbid-monday-sweet-death.
5. Gregg Michael Levoy, *Callings: Finding and Following an Authentic Life* (New York: Harmony, 1998), 9.
6. Gregg Levoy, quoted in John Ortberg, *If You Want to Walk on Water, You've Got to Get Out of the Boat*, DVD edition (Grand Rapids: Zondervan, 2005), 34–35.
7. Paul Tournier, quoted in Keith Miller and Bruce Larson, *The Edge of Adventure* (Waco, TX: Word, 1976), 180.
8. John Ortberg, *If You Want to Walk on Water, You've Got to Get Out of the Boat*, 90–93.
9. Bill Hybels, *Leadership Journal* 10, no. 3 (Summer 1989): 38.
10. David Hinckley, "Average American Watches 5 Hours of TV Per Day, Report Shows," *New York Daily News,* March 5, 2014, http://www.nydailynews.com/life-style/average-american-watches-5-hours-tv-day-article-1.1711954.
11. Philip Yancey, *Soul Survivor: How Thirteen Unlikely Mentors Helped My Faith Survive the Church* (Colorado Springs: WaterBrook, 2003), 59.

Chapter 9: Nothing Great Ever *Just* Happens

1. Leslie T. Lyall, *A Passion for the Impossible: The Continuing Story of the Mission Hudson Taylor Began* (London: OMF Books, 1965), 5.
2. Rick Warren, *How a Leader Handles Opposition: Nehemiah*, part 6, http://www.isom.vnsalvation.com/Resources%20English/SaddleBack%20

Resources/Nehemiah/225006_HOW_A_LEADER_HANDLES_OPPOSITION.PDF.

3. Charles R. Swindoll, *Hand Me Another Brick*, rev. ed (Nashville: Thomas Nelson, 1998), 43.
4. Amity Shlaes, *Coolidge* (New York: Harper Perennial, 2013), 5.
5. Newsweek Staff, "My God . . . What Have We Done?", *Newsweek,* July 23, 1995, http://www.newsweek.com/my-god-what-have-we-done-184696.
6. Chris Brown, "Sexual Purity Is For Prudes and Losers" (sermon), Bayside Church, Granite Bay, CA, February 6, 2011.
7. C. S. Lewis, *The Weight of Glory* (1949; repr. New York: HarperOne, 2001), 46.
8. Dave Roever with Kathy Koch, *Scarred* (Roever Communication, 2015). © 2015 by Roever Communication, P.O. Box 136130, Ft. Worth, TX 76136.

Chapter 10: Stop Thinking You Don't Matter

1. Quoted in Kenneth Boa, *Conformed to His Image: Biblical and Practical Approaches to Spiritual Formation* (Grand Rapids: Zondervan, 2001), 374.
2. Blago Kirov, *Napoleon Bonaparte: Quotes and Facts* (Charleston, SC: CreateSpace, 2015), 22.
3. "Fast Facts about American Religion," Hartford Institute for Religion Research, http://hirr.hartsem.edu/research/fastfacts/fast_facts.html#numcong.
4. Barry Popik, "Football is 22 people on the field who need rest and 22,000 people in the stands who need exercise," *The Big Apple,* June 22, 2014, http://www.barrypopik.com/index.php/new_york_city/entry/football_is_22_people_on_the_field.
5. Albers, Donald J. and Constance Reid, "An Interview of George B. Dantzig: The Father of Linear Programming," *College Mathematics Journal* 17, no. 4 (1986): 293–314.
6. Quoted in John Ortberg and Sherry Harney, *Pursuing Spiritual Authenticity: Life Changing Words from The Prophets* (Grand Rapids: Zondervan, 2004), 37.
7. In 2011, the life expectancy in the United States was estimated by the World Bank to be 78.6 years (http://data.worldbank.org/indicator/SP.DYN.LE00.IN/countries/US—XS?display=graph), or 28,708 days.
8. James Emory White, *Serious Times: Making Your Life Matter in an Urgent Day* (Downers Grove, IL: InterVarsity, 2005), 12.

Chapter 11: Stop Running on Empty

1. Corrie ten Boom, *Not Good if Detached* (1957; repr. as e-book, Christian Literature Crusade, 2012), chapt. 29.
2. Rick Warren, "The 3 Spiritual Habits of Effective People," part 2 of *Building My Character Through Commitment* sermon series, http://www.saddlebackresources.com/products/the-3-spiritual-habits-of-effective-people-1.
3. Kelly Shattuck, "7 Startling Facts: An Up Close Look at Church Attendance in America," Church Leaders, http://www.churchleaders.com/pastors/pastor-articles/139575–7-startling-facts-an-up-close-look-at-church-attendance-in-america.html/1.
4. Barbara Hudson Powers, *The Henrietta Mears Story* (Old Tappan, NJ: Fleming H. Revell, 1957), introduction by Billy Graham, http://ccel.us/mears.toc.html.
5. Marcus Brotherton, *"Teacher": The Henrietta Mears Story* (Regal Books, 2006), 51–52.
6. Earl Roe, ed., *Dream Big: The Henrietta Mears Story* (New York: Regal, 1990), 359–61.
7. Tom Knudson, "'Death by GPS' in Desert," *The Sacramento Bee,* January 30, 2011, http://www.sacbee.com/2011/01/30/3362727/death-by-gps-in-desert.html#storylink=cpy.
8. Linda Rodriguez McRobbie, "The Strange and Mysterious History of the Ouija Board," Smithsonian.com, October 27, 2013, http://www.smithsonianmag.com/history/the-strange-and-mysterious-history-of-the-ouija-board-5860627/?all&no-ist.
9. David Allen, quoted in Rick Warren, "How to Discover God's Will: Grace: The Truth That Transforms," part 28, http://albany-umc-oh.org/AUMCEdu_files/2011BothBible&Sermons/BibleStudyArchives2011PDF's/Bible%20-%20Romans%2028.pdf.
10. Bill Hybels, *Honest to God? Becoming an Authentic Christian* (Grand Rapids: Zondervan, 1992), 11.

Chapter 12: "I Love Jesus—I Just Can't Stand Church"

1. To see Louis speak, visit www.RayJohnston.com/LZVideo.
2. David Cameron, "King James Bible Speech," December 16, 2011, Christ Church Cathedral, Oxford, England, https://www.gov.uk/government/news/prime-ministers-king-james-bible-speech.

3. Jonathan Hill, *What Has Christianity Ever Done for Us?: How It Shaped the Modern World* (Downers Grove, IL: InterVarsity, 2005).
4. Alvin J. Schmidt, *How Christianity Changed the World* (Grand Rapids: Zondervan, 2004), 120.
5. Ibid., 214.
6. Murray N. Rothbard, *Education: Free and Compulsory* (repr. Auburn, AL: Ludwig von Mises Institute, 1999), 20.
7. Daniel J. Boorstin, *The Americans: The National Experience* (New York: Random House, 1965), 153–57.
8. E. Calvin Beisner, *Answers for Atheists, Agnostics, and Other Thoughtful Skeptics: Dialogs About Christian Faith and Life*, (Boston: G.K. Hall, 1994), 137.
9. Jaroslav Pelikan, *Jesus Through the Centuries: His Place in the History of Culture* (n.p.: Yale University, 1999), 83.
10. Matt Walsh, "Christianity Has Done More for Science Than Atheism Ever Could," The Matt Walsh Blog, September 13, 2013, http://thematt walshblog.com/2013/09/13/christianity-has-done-more-for-science-than-atheism-ever-could/#sW25XAsqfBrZUx3Y.99.
11. A summary of these studies can be found in David B. Larson, *The Forgotten Factor in Physical and Mental Health: What Does the Research Show?* (Washington, DC: National Institute for Healthcare Research, 1994).
12. G. W. Comstock and K. B. Partridge, "Church Attendance and Health," *Journal of Chronic Disease* 25, no. 12 (December 1972): 665–72.
13. R. B. Loch and R. H. Hughes, "Religion And Youth Substance Abuse," *Journal of Religion and Health* 24, no. 3 (1985): 723–27.
14. David B. Larson, *The Forgotten Factor in Physical and Mental Health,* 76–81.
15. J. S. Levin and P. L. Schiller, "Is There a Religious Factor in Health?" *Journal of Religion and Health* 26, No. 1 (1989): 9–35.
16. Comstock and Partridge, "Church Attendance and Health," 665–72.
17. D. B. Larson, et. al, "The Impact of Religion on Men's Blood Pressure", *Journal of Religion and Health,* 28, no. 4 (December 1989): 265–78.
18. P. Pressman, J. S. Lyons, D. B. Larson, and J. J. Strain, "Religious Belief, Depression, and Ambulation Status," *American Journal of Psychiatry* 147, no. 6 (1990): 758–60.
19. N. D. Glenn and C. N. Weaver, "A Multivariate, Multi-Survey Study of Marital Happiness, *Journal of Marriage and the Family* 40 (1978): 269–82.

20. Carol Tavris and Susan Sadd, *The Redbook Report on Female Sexuality* (New York: Delacorte, 1977).
21. David Myers, "Pursuing Happiness," *Psychology Today,* July-August 1993, 32–38.
22. Ibid.

Chapter 13: Share Your Faith Without Embarrassing God

1. Gene Kranz, *Failure Is Not an Option: Mission Control From Mercury to Apollo 13 and Beyond* (New York: Simon and Schuster, 2009), 309–37.
2. Fulton J. Sheen, *Treasure in Clay: The Autobiography of Fulton J. Sheen* (New York: Image, 1982), 127.
3. Thom S. Rainer, *The Unchurched Next Door: Understanding Faith Stages as Keys to Sharing Your Faith* (Grand Rapids: Zondervan, 2003), 24–25.
4. Thanks for this mythical illustration from my good friend Chris Brown.
5. Amy Grant, *Mosaic: Pieces of My Life So Far* (New York: Three Rivers Press, 2008), 10.
6. Arnold A. Dallimore, *Spurgeon: A New Biography* (Carlisle, PA: Banner of Truth, 1985), 224–25.

About the Author

Ray Johnston HAS A RICH, VARIED BACKGROUND AS A professor, speaker, writer, and founder of Thrive Communications and the Thrive Leadership Conference. Author of the bestselling book *The Hope Quotient*, he is the founding pastor of Bayside Church, one of the largest churches in the United States, with more than twelve thousand people. Ray has spoken to more than four million people over the last ten years and served on the board of trustees at Azusa Pacific University, his alma mater. Ray and his wife, Carol, have four children.

Date Due

MY 10 '9[illegible]	[illegible]		
	AP 27 '0[illegible]		
FE 16 '93			
MY 28 '93			
JA 7 '94			
AG 8 '9[illegible]			
[illegible]			
[illegible]			
AP 29 '99			
AG 3 '00			
AG 9 '01			

HT
975
C8

Curtin, Philip D

The Atlantic slave trade; a census, by Philip D. Curtin. Madison, University of Wisconsin Press, 1969.

xix, 338 p. maps. 22cm.

Bibliography: p. 299-311.

1. Slave-trade--History. I. Title.

THE ATLANTIC SLAVE TRADE

THE ATLANTIC SLAVE TRADE *A Census*

BY PHILIP D. CURTIN

THE UNIVERSITY OF WISCONSIN PRESS
Madison, Milwaukee, and London

Published 1969
THE UNIVERSITY OF WISCONSIN PRESS
Box 1379, Madison, Wisconsin 53701
The University of Wisconsin Press, Ltd.
27–29 Whitfield Street, London, W. 1

Printings 1969, 1970
Printed in the United States of America
ISBN 0–299–05400–4; LC 69–17325

CONTENTS

LIST OF ILLUSTRATIONS

LIST OF TABLES

PREFACE

The history of the Atlantic slave trade, like that of New-World slavery as a whole, is an aspect of history where revision is long overdue. The reasons are, or should be, obvious enough. The Western historical tradition until recent decades was thoroughly ethnocentric and ill-adapted to the investigation of other societies—still less to considering historical processes that involved two or more societies. The slave trade was a commercial system to recruit forced workers in one society and transport them to another with a vastly different culture. Both Africans and Europeans participated in the trade, and both societies were deeply influenced by it; but Western involvement had certain peculiarities that have left their mark on later historiography. The European metropolis imported very few slaves for its own use. Instead, it controlled the shipping and created the economic policies that governed both the "plantations" and the maritime leg of the trade. The traditional national histories of European states therefore tend to view the slave trade as something peripheral to their own social and political development. This same parochial tradition of ethnocentric national history was transplanted to the Americas. There too, historians tended not to see the slave trade as a whole, but to concentrate on the one segment that brought workers to their own particular region. Even within their national sector, historians have too often regarded the Afro-American community created by the trade as an alien body on the periphery of national life.

In fact, the institutions of the slave trade were common to the Atlantic community as a whole. One important line of revision is therefore the search for whole institutions and whole processes, seen in the large and separate from the mere national subdivisions. Several works in this spirit have appeared recently, and more are on the way. A few historians are beginning a genuinely comparative study of the social and economic history of New-World slavery, while others are penetrating the African branch of the trade—the movement of slaves within Africa until they were finally sold to the Europeans on the coast.

This book shares some of these revisionist attitudes. It too is set in an Atlantic perspective, but it seeks to explore old knowledge, not to present new information. Its central aim is to bring together bits and pieces of incommensurate information already published, and to do this for only one aspect of the trade—the measurable number of people brought across the Atlantic. How many? When? From what parts of Africa? To what destinations in the New World?

It may seem that the quantitative dimensions of the slave trade are either unknowable, or else well enough known. The literature is full of estimates that seem to agree as to the range of possibility —the common range being fifteen to twenty-five million slaves landed in the Americas during the whole course of the trade. In fact, this range of estimates is a heritage from the nineteenth century, from a period when the history of Africa and tropical America was only beginning to be explored. Since then, hundreds of new monographs have appeared, but the old synthesis lives on—uncorrected by the new knowledge.

This gap between monograph and synthesis can be explained. In part at least, it came about because some areas of knowledge were neglected, perhaps rightfully so, in the recent effort of historians and other social scientists to correct the ethnocentric tradition of the past. In Latin American and African studies, historians came to realize about twenty years ago that our basic data were inadequate. At about the same time, the university world began to recognize African and Latin American studies. The second of these two tendencies produced an external demand for more research-oriented professional specialists. The first produced an internal demand for new research, better data, and especially for field research. Where the "library thesis" was once quite common, major universities today rarely grant the Ph.D. in African or Latin American studies unless the candidate has spent a respectable amount of research time in Africa or Latin America. This is as it should be. The library thesis was not the best beginning for a professional career. The second or third book is the appropriate place for synthesis.

But here is the trap. The young scholar is lured away from synthesis in depth by another kind of pressure. The discovery of the wider world beyond the United States and Europe has created a demand for textbooks, broad summaries, collections of readings, and collections of documents. As the publishing industry rushes in to fill the gap, young scholars and old find themselves inveigled by contract-waving publishers' representatives, promising lucrative returns for a quick summary of the field. This too is perfectly legitimate and necessary to the task of spreading the new knowledge created by the new research.

The problem comes when the pressures for more research and more textbooks are combined. A gap appears between the two kinds of work. Basic research is designed to produce a small and discrete contribution to knowledge. The writer of a text or a broad work of synthesis has the task of summarizing and presenting the new knowledge in its broader context. But even the best standards of the craft do not require him to rearrange the building blocks of monographic research in order to produce a new synthesis at every point. As a result, many important historical problems remain—too broad in scope for monographic research, yet too narrow for detailed treatment in a broad work of synthesis, in a textbook, or in the classroom.

This book is an attempt at this intermediate level of synthesis. It is therefore written with an implicit set of rules that are neither those of monographic research, nor yet those of a survey. Historical standards for monographic research require the author to examine every existing authority on the problem at hand, and every archival collection where part of the answer may be found. This has not been done. The rulebook followed here sets another standard. I have surveyed the literature on the slave trade, but not exhaustively. Where the authorities on some regional aspect of the trade have arrived at a consensus, and that consensus appears to be reasonable in the light of other evidence, I have let it stand. Where no consensus exists, or a gap occurs in a series of estimates, I have tried to construct new estimates. But these stop short of true research standards. I have not tried to go beyond the printed sources, nor into the relevant archives, even when they are known to contain important additional data. The task is conceived as that of building with the bricks that exist, not in making new ones. This often requires the manipulation of existing data in search of commensurates. In doing this, I have tried to show the steps that lead from existing data to the new synthesis. Not everyone will agree with all the assumptions that go into the process, nor with all the forms of calculation that have been used. But this book is not intended to be a definitive study, only a point of departure that will be modified in time as new research produces new data, and harder data worthy of more sophisticated forms of calculation. It will have served its purpose if it challenges others to correct and complete its findings.

This point is of the greatest importance in interpreting any of the data that follow. One danger in stating numbers is to find them quoted later on with a degree of certitude that was never intended. This is particularly true when percentages are carried to tenths of 1 per cent, whereas in fact the hoped-for range of accuracy may be plus or minus 20 per cent of actuality. Let it be said at the outset, then, that most of the quantities that follow are wrong. They are not intended to be precise as given, only approximations where a result falling within 20 per cent of actuality is a "right" answer—that is, a successful result, given the quality of the underlying data. It should also be understood that some estimates will not even reach that standard of accuracy. They are given only as the most probable figures at the present state of knowledge. These considerations have made it convenient to round out most quantities to the nearest one hundred, including data taken from other authors.

All of this may seem to imply estimates of limited value on account of their limited accuracy. For many historical purposes, greater accuracy is not required, and some of the most significant implications of this quantitative study would follow from figures still less accurate than these. Their principal value is not, in any case, the absolute number, an abstraction nearly meaningless in isolation. It is, instead, the comparative values, making it possible to measure one branch of the slave trade against another.

Some readers may miss the sense of moral outrage traditional in histories of the trade. This book will have very little to say about the evils of the slave trade, still less in trying to assign retrospective blame to the individuals or groups who were responsible. This omission in no way implies that the slave trade was morally neutral; it clearly was not. The evils of the trade, however, can be taken for granted as a point long since proven beyond dispute.

I should like to thank many friends and colleagues for their assistance—Norman Ryder for his answers to many problems in demography, Allen Bogue for his suggestions on quantitative method, Franklin Knight for setting me right on aspects of the nineteenth-century slave trade to Cuba, and most of all Anne Curtin for her rigorous criticism. I owe much to the facilities of the University of Wisconsin and to those who operate them. The Memorial Library, the Social Science Research Institute, the Cartographic Laboratory, and the Computing Center have been especially helpful. Much of the financial burden has also been borne by the Program in Comparative Tropical History, through funds made available by the Carnegie Corporation of New York, and by the Graduate Research Committee, with funds voted by the State Legislature of Wisconsin. None of these institutions or individuals, however, can be held responsible for my errors.

PHILIP D. CURTIN

Blue Mounds, Wisconsin
August 21, 1969

THE ATLANTIC SLAVE TRADE

CHAPTER I

THE SLAVE TRADE AND THE NUMBERS GAME: A REVIEW OF THE LITERATURE

Now that many historians are trying to make history into a social science—at a time when the social sciences themselves are becoming more quantitative—one way to gauge the state of historical scholarship is to examine the way historians have dealt with an important quantitative problem. The rise and fall of the Atlantic slave trade poses just such a problem. The impact of the slave trade on African societies is a crucial problem for African historiography. For the Americas, both North and South, Africans who came by way of the slave trade were the most numerous Old-World immigrants before the late eighteenth century. Today, their descendants are the largest racial minority in many countries. Even for European history, the South Atlantic System —as a complex economic organism centered on the production in the Americas of tropical staples for consumption in Europe, and grown by the labor of Africans—was a crucial factor in European competition for overseas empire in the seventeenth and eighteenth centuries. A wide range of historical specialists are therefore concerned with quantitative aspects of the slave trade, and their treatment of it is not encouraging.

The principal secondary authorities and the principal textbooks are, indeed, in remarkable agreement on the general magnitude of the trade. Most begin with the statement that little is known about the subject, pass on to the suggestion that it may be impossible to make an accurate numerical estimate, and then make an estimate. The style is exemplified by Basil Davidson's *Black Mother*, the best recent general history of the slave trade.

> First of all, what were the round numbers involved in this forced emigration to which the African-European trade gave rise, beginning in the fifteenth century and ending in the nineteenth? The short answer is that nobody knows or ever will know: either the necessary records are missing or they were never made. The best one can do is to construct an estimate from confused and incomplete data.
>
> . . . For the grand total of slaves landed alive in the lands across the Atlantic an eminent student of population statistics, Kuczynski, came to the conclusion that fifteen millions might be "rather a conservative figure." Other writers have accepted this figure, though as a minimum: some have believed it was much higher than this.[1]

Roland Oliver and J. D. Fage in their *Short History of Africa,* the most widely-read history of Africa to appear so far, are less concerned to express their uncertainty, and they too come to a total estimate in the vicinity of fifteen million slaves landed. They go a step farther, however, and subdivide the total by centuries. (See Table 1.)[2]

The total is again given as a minimum, and it is clearly derived from R. R. Kuczynski. Indeed, Professor Fage gave the same break-down in his *Introduction to the History of West Africa* and in his *Ghana,* where the citation of Kuczynski is explicit. The estimate is repeated by so many other recent authorities that it can be taken as the dominant statement of present-day historiography. Some writers cite Kuczynski directly. Others, like Robert Rotberg in his *Political History of Tropical Africa,* strengthen the case by citing both Kuczynski and a second author who derived his data from Kuczynski. Rotberg, however, improved on his authorities by raising the total to "at least twenty-five million slaves," an increase of two-thirds, apparently based on the general assurance that the fifteen-million figure was

1. B. Davidson, *Black Mother* (London, 1961), p. 89.
2. R. Oliver and J. D. Fage, *A Short History of Africa* (London, 1962), p. 120.

TABLE 1

A COMMONLY FOUND ESTIMATE OF SLAVES LANDED IN THE AMERICAS, BY CENTURY

Up to 1600	900,000
Seventeenth century	2,750,000
Eighteenth century	7,000,000
Nineteenth century	4,000,000
Total	14,650,000

Source: R. R. Kuczynski, *Population Movements* (Oxford, 1936), p. 12.

likely to be on the low side. Another alternative, chosen by D. B. Davis for his Pulitzer-Prize-winning *Problem of Slavery in Western Culture,* is not to bother with Kuczynski (who wrote, after all, more than thirty years ago), but to go directly to a recent authority—in this case to the words of Basil Davidson quoted above.[3]

Since Kuczynski is at the center of this web of citations, quotations, and amplifications, it is important to see just how he went about calculating his now-famous estimates. The crucial passage in *Population Movements* does indeed present a general estimate of fifteen million or more slaves landed in the Americas, and it includes the distribution by centuries indicated in Table 1. But Kuczynski himself shows no evidence of having made any

3. Among recent works accepting the Kuczynski estimates are: J. D. Fage, *Introduction to the History of West Africa* (Cambridge, 1955), pp. 59, 82–84; J. D. Fage, *Ghana: A Historical Interpretation* (Madison, 1959), pp. 46, 100–101; W. Zelinsky, "The Historical Geography of the Negro Population of Latin America," *Journal of Negro History,* 34:158–59 (1949); J. D. Hargreaves, *West Africa: The Former French States* (Englewood Cliffs, N.J., 1967), p. 36; D. B. Davis, *The Problem of Slavery in Western Culture* (Ithaca, 1966), p. 9; R. I. Rotberg, *A Political History of Tropical Africa* (New York, 1965), p. 152; D. P. Mannix and M. Cowley, *Black Cargoes: A History of the Atlantic Slave Trade, 1518–1865* (New York, 1962), pp. 32, 71; R. O. Collins, ed., *Problems in African History* (Englewood Cliffs, N.J., 1968), p. 351. S. Mintz reviewing S. Elkins' *Slavery,* in the *American Anthropologist,* 63:579–87 (1961), indicates ten to twenty million as the total number of slaves *exported* from Africa, which suggests eight to sixteen million imported.

calculation on his own. He merely found these estimates to be the most acceptable of those made by earlier authorities, and the particular authority he cited is none other than W. E. B. Du Bois.[4]

Du Bois was, indeed, an eminent authority on Negro history, but Kuczynski's citation does *not* lead back to one of his works based on historical research. It leads instead to a paper on "The Negro Race in the United States of America," delivered to a semi-scholarly congress in London in 1911—a curious place to publish something as important as an original, overall estimate of the Atlantic slave trade—and in fact the paper contains no such thing. Du Bois's only mention of the subject in the place cited was these two sentences: "The exact number of slaves imported is not known. Dunbar estimates that nearly 900,000 came to America in the sixteenth century, 2,750,000 in the seventeenth, 7,000,000 in the eighteenth, and over 4,000,000 in the nineteenth, perhaps 15,000,000 in all."[5]

The real authority, then, is neither Kuczynski nor Du Bois, but Dunbar. Though Du Bois's offhand statement was not supported by footnotes or bibliography, the author in question was Edward E. Dunbar, an American publicist of the 1860's. During the early part of 1861, he was responsible for a serial called *The Mexican Papers,* devoted to furthering the cause of President Juárez of Mexico and of the Liberal Party in that country. The Liberals had just won the War of the Reform against their domestic opponents, but they were hard pressed by European creditors and threatened with possible military intervention—a threat that shortly materialized in the Maximilian affair. Dunbar's principal task was to enlist American sympathy, and if possible American diplomatic intervention, in support of Juárez' cause. But Dunbar was a liberal, by implication an anti-slavery man in American politics, and he published *The Mexican Papers* during the last

4. R. R. Kuczynski, *Population Movements,* pp. 8–17.

5. W. E. B. Du Bois, "The Negro Race in the United States of America," *Papers on Inter-Racial Problems Communicated to the First Universal Races Congress* (London, 1911), p. 349.

months of America's drift into civil war. It was therefore natural that he should write an article called "History of the Rise and Decline of Commercial Slavery in America, with Reference to the Future of Mexico," and it was there that he published a set of estimates of the slave trade through time (Table 2).[6] He remarked that these were only his own estimates, and he made the further reservation (so often repeated by his successors) that they were probably on the low side.

TABLE 2

DUNBAR'S ESTIMATES OF SLAVE IMPORTS INTO THE AMERICAS

1500–25	12,500
1525–50	125,000
1550–1600	750,000
1600–50	1,000,000
1650–1700	1,750,000
1700–50	3,000,000
1750–1800	4,000,000
1800–50	3,250,000
Total	13,887,500

Source: Edward E. Dunbar, "Commercial Slavery," pp. 269–70.

The total is not quite the same as that in Table 1. Du Bois rounded out the inconvenient figure of 887,500 for the sixteenth century to a neater 900,000. He also rounded out the nineteenth-century figure to 4,000,000, adding three-quarters of a million in the process. He can be excused for a small increase, since the slave trade had not yet ended when Dunbar wrote, but this dual "rounding out" produced a 5-per-cent increase; and this was passed along to his successors—Dunbar to Du Bois to Kuczynski to Fage to Davidson to Davis.

The sequence is an impressive tower of authority, though it also suggests that even the best historians may be unduly credulous when they see a footnote to an illustrious predecessor. Basil

6. *The Mexican Papers,* 1:269–70 (No. 5, April, 1861).

Davidson should have identified the original author as "an obscure American publicist," rather than "an eminent student of population statistics," but the *ad hominem* fallacy is present in either case. Dunbar's obscurity is no evidence that he was wrong; nor does Kuczynski's use of Dunbar's estimates make them correct. The estimates were guesses, but they were guesses educated by a knowledge of the historical literature. They earned the approval of later generations who were in a position to be still better informed. Even though no one along the way made a careful effort to calculate the size of the trade from empirical evidence, the Dunbar estimates nevertheless represent a kind of consensus.

One reason for the easy acceptance of these figures is a weight of authority and tradition, derived from a number of partial estimates that were repeated down through the historical literature in much the same way Dunbar's figures and other myths are repeated by one authority after another. The partial figures have been reprinted with varying degrees of certitude. One of the most tenuous statements is found in Sir Reginald Coupland's *British Anti-Slavery Movement.*

> An authoritative calculation made more than a century ago fixed the total slaves imported into the English colonies in America and the West Indies between 1680 and 1786 at 2,130,000. Guesses at the total for all European colonies have gone as high as 40,000,000. But if half or less than that figure be accepted, and if it be remembered that the European Slave Trade was to continue in full volume till past the middle of the nineteenth century, that an incalculable multitude must be added for the Arab Slave Trade, that it was . . . [and so on].[7]

This is hardly a direct statement—much less a considered estimate—but Coupland seems to suggest a total in the vicinity of twenty millions. The only evidence brought forward is the unidentified "authoritative calculation," but the source is prominent enough to be easily spotted. It was Bryan Edwards of

7. R. Coupland, *The British Anti-Slavery Movement* (London, 1964), p. 21. The work was first published in 1933.

Jamaica, writing in the late 1780's, and his figure was indeed a calculation and not a mere guess.[8] But it was a weak calculation at best. Edwards began with the slave trade of the seventeenth century, estimating British exports from Africa between 1680 and 1700 on the basis of the pamphlet literature attacking and defending the Royal African Company. This yielded an estimate of 300,000 slaves exported from Africa by British merchants. As a second step, he took the actual records of Jamaican imports between 1700 and 1786—records that no longer survive in exactly that form he used—giving a total of 610,000 slaves imported into Jamaica. Then, from his general sense of the importance of Jamaica in the British Caribbean, he multiplied this figure by three to obtain an estimate of the total British slave trade. Coupland apparently based his own overall estimate on a second multiplier assumption, that the British slave trade would be about one fifth of the whole. In short, his figure of 20 million slaves landed rests on the evidence of Jamaican imports over 87 years, plus the estimate that this would be one-fifteenth of the whole Atlantic slave trade. A projection of this kind is no more valid than its multiplier: Coupland's guess is therefore no better than Dunbar's.

Bryan Edwards' estimate of the British slave trade has itself had a long and curious life in the historical literature. It was used in part by George Bancroft in his classic *History of the United States,* but Bancroft came to a different general conclusion. He assessed the British-carried imports into the French, Spanish, and British West Indies plus the continental North American colonies at nearly three million over the period 1675–1776.[9] This estimate was revived in turn by W. E. H. Lecky, who cited Bancroft and referred to him as a "distinguished modern historian."[10] Both Eric Williams and E. D. Morel

8. B. Edwards, *The History, Civil and Commercial, of the British Colonies in the West Indies,* 2nd ed., 2 vols. (London, 1793–94), 2:55.

9. G. Bancroft, *The History of the United States of America . . . ,* 3rd ed., 3 vols. (New York, 1892), 2:277.

10. W. E. H. Lecky, *A History of England in the Eighteenth Century,* 7 vols. (London, 1892–1920), 2:243–44.

in turn picked up the figure from Lecky,[11] but Morel slipped the dates by ten years, making the estimate of three millions cover the years 1666–1766 and failing to mention the fact that it did not include the Spanish or French mainland colonies in South America. Morel's version, which he claimed was derived from "the most reliable authors," was in turn picked up by Melville J. Herskovits, Morel's error included. The result was a second line of authority—Edwards to Bancroft to Lecky to Morel to Herskovits.[12]

With each author, new partial estimates were added, some giving the imports of a particular colony over a number of years, others giving an estimate of imports into the whole of the New World for a limited period. Many of these, including Edwards' estimates, were repeated in Frank Tannenbaum's *Slave and Citizen,* where they were joined by other, similar estimates of Latin American origin. Tannenbaum intended these figures to give an impression, nothing more, but he barely hinted at a total estimate as well. Citing *O Brasil* by J. P. Oliveira Martins, he wrote: "Another author suggests a total of 20,000,000 exported from all Africa for the entire period. Again an exaggeration? But by how much? Even a conservative estimate would hardly cut this figure in half."[13]

In short, the range of partial estimates suggests a total not far different from that of the Dunbar-Du Bois-Kuczynski-Fage-Davidson sequence, even though the historians of the Bancroft-Lecky-Morel-Williams-Herskovits-Tannenbaum school were apparently ignorant of the rival tradition. It was inevitable that the two should someday meet, and they did so with D. B. Davis's

11. E. Williams, "The Golden Age of the Slave System in Britain," *Journal of Negro History,* 25:60–106 (1940); E. D. Morel, *The Black Man's Burden* (London, 1920), p. 19.

12. M. J. Herskovits, "Social History of the Negro," in *Handbook of Social Psychology* (Worcester, Mass., 1935), pp. 235–36. Herskovits apparently became conscious of the unreliability of these estimates, since he dropped them when he published *The Myth of the Negro Past* in 1941.

13. F. Tannenbaum, *Slave and Citizen: The Negro in the Americas* (New York, 1946), pp. 29–32.

Problem of Slavery in Western Culture. Davis picked up both traditions in their latest version, citing Davidson and Tannenbaum. The result was mutually reinforcing. Even though Davidson's statement on quantities was most tentative, and Tannenbaum's was hardly a suggestion, Davis (on the authority of the two together) stated bluntly: "For three centuries the principal maritime powers competed with one another in the lucrative slave trade, and carried at least fifteen million Africans to the New World."[14]

As for Oliveira Martins, his work was first published in 1880, with augmentations by others in successive editions, of which the sixth appeared in 1953. In that edition total slave imports into the Americas are given as 20,000,000—a figure derived by the familiar technique of using a partial estimate plus a multiplier. In this case, the estimate was 5,000,000 slaves imported into Brazil, a figure drawn from a mid-nineteenth-century encyclopedia and then multiplied by four.[15]

The literature of the slave trade, then, carries a broad impression that total slave imports into the Americas came to something like fifteen to twenty million. But, on closer examination, the vast consensus turns out to be nothing but a vast inertia, as historians have copied over and over again the flimsy results of unsubstantial guesswork. The passage of time brought little or no change. Instead, the hesitant guesses of the last century have been passed off as hard data.

There are, of course, exceptions. Pierre Chaunu published an offhand comment in 1964, that the Brazilian slave imports over the whole period of the trade were 40 per cent of the total.[16] The calculations of Chapter 2 below make it 38 per cent. In addition, Chaunu accepts a figure for the total Brazilian slave trade which

14. Davis, *Slavery,* p. 9.

15. J. P. Oliveira Martins, *O Brasil e as colonias portuguezas* (Lisbon, 1953), p. 59.

16. P. Chaunu, "Pour une 'geopolitique' de l'espace américain," in R. Konetzke and H. Kellenbenz, eds., *Jahrbuch für Geschichte von Staat, Wirtschaft, und Gesellschaft Lateinamerikas* (Cologne, 1964), 1:16.

yields an estimate for the whole Atlantic slave trade in the vicinity of 8,000,000—about half of the traditional figure, and probably more accurate.

Another exception is Donald Wiedner's *History of Africa South of the Sahara.* He came to his own total estimate by reference to the Negro population of the New World in about 1860. By assuming that one-third to one-half of the New-World Negroes at that time were American-born, while the remainder were born in Africa, he projected total imports in the range of 3.5 to 5.5 million.[17] His further estimates of numbers imported into particular countries, however, were out of line with the monographic research of recent decades, being especially low for Brazil and the West Indies. The new approach was welcome, but the demography was weak, the data were insufficient, and Wiedner himself no longer supports such a low estimate.

The surprising fact here is that Wiedner's book was virtually alone, among recent English-language general works on African history or on the history of the slave trade, in trying to go beyond the repetition of nineteenth-century guesswork. Yet monographic studies have appeared over the decades, each adding a little more to our potential knowledge—and the sum of all monographs adding nothing at all, apparently, to the actual knowledge represented in the textbooks and general works.

Curiously enough, the only twentieth-century attempt to add up piecemeal estimates occurs in a work as far off the mainstream of slave-trade history as Dunbar's *Mexican Papers* was. This calculation forms a long chapter in Noel Deerr's *History of Sugar,* and its fortunes in later literature were dramatically different from those of Dunbar's essay.[18] While Dunbar's figures were canonized by generations of repetition, Deerr's were completely neglected: they are not mentioned in any of the later general histories of the slave trade or of Africa. For that matter,

17. D. L. Wiedner, *A History of Africa South of the Sahara* (New York, 1962), p. 67.

18. N. Deerr, *The History of Sugar,* 2 vols. (London, 1949–50), 2:259–88.

Deerr was apparently unaware of the Dunbar-Du Bois-Kuczynski estimates, though he used some of the scatter of partial figures of the kind published by Tannenbaum. It is therefore interesting that his independently-based total was only 14 per cent lower than the more famous, if less carefully calculated, tradition that goes back to Dunbar.

TABLE 3

DEERR'S ESTIMATES OF SLAVE IMPORTS INTO THE AMERICAS

Old-World traffic (Madeira, Canaries, São Thomé, southern Europe)	200,000
Spanish America, asiento period (to c. 1750)	450,000
Spanish America, post-asiento period	550,000
Portuguese America	3,325,000
English islands (including Guiana and Honduras)	1,900,000
English mainland of North America	1,500,000
US imports, 1776–1808	420,000
Illicit US imports, 1809–61	1,000,000
French New-World territories	1,650,000
French imports to Mauritius and Réunion	450,000
Dutch Guianas and Dutch West Indies	900,000
Danish West Indies	75,000
Total	12,420,000
Total Atlantic slave trade	11,970,000

Source: Data from Deerr, *History of Sugar*, 2:284.

Perhaps the principal lesson is that historians are too sharply divided between the standards required for monographic research and those required of historical synthesis. The range of estimates in the general historical literature, from Wiedner's 3.5 million minimum to Rotberg's 25 million, is a telling demonstration of the communication gap between the monograph and the textbook. But history is not necessarily a body of non-cumulative knowledge, nor is the overall total the only important dimension of the slave trade. Historians have, in fact, explored many facets of the trade during the past century, and the quantitative aspects of their work add up to an impressive and many-dimensional outline.

CHAPTER 2

DISTRIBUTION IN SPACE: THE HISPANIC TRADE

The Hispanic nations of the Iberian peninsula were the first to begin the slave trade, and the last to quit. In the fifteenth and sixteenth centuries, the Spanish and Portuguese carried the rudimentary institutions of the South Atlantic System from the Mediterranean to the Atlantic Islands, then to Santo Domingo and Brazil. In the seventeenth and eighteenth centuries, the Dutch, English, and French dominated the slave trade, but, in the nineteenth century, Brazil and Cuba accounted for the vast majority of slaves imported—and by that time the northern powers had made their own slave trade effectively illegal. The long duration of this trade to Brazil and Spanish America greatly complicates the problem of estimating the total imports, and the earliest phases provide very uncertain evidence.

A point of departure is nevertheless available in Noel Deerr's set of estimates. They are the only detailed, overall estimates anywhere in the historical literature; and, though some are simply guesses, most are calculated estimates, and the basis of the calculation is explained. In addition, Deerr used most of the available methods for calculating the size of the trade from diverse evidence.

The most obvious and direct kind of evidence is a systematic record of the slaves imported through a particular port or into a given colony over a period of years. Such evidence exists, but only for a small fraction of the total slave trade. Equivalent direct evidence of exports from Africa is still more rare.

Shipping records are still another form of direct evidence. Many European and American ports preserved long series of records covering the destinations and cargoes of their ships. Still other European records are concerned with the number of slaves authorized or contracted for in order to supply the colonies.

Where direct evidence is missing or faulty, several forms of indirect evidence are available. The slave population of an American colony is clearly related to the number of slaves imported in the past. Population estimates and even genuine census data are usually available in the literature, at least for the last two centuries of the slave trade. If they are carefully used, they can be of great value. The number of slaves imported was also closely related to economic productivity. Especially in colonies that practiced sugar monoculture, annual time-series of sugar production can be used to measure the probable level of the slave trade.

Similar indirect evidence of slaves exported from Africa is less common, but it is at least theoretically possible to construct estimates of exports *from* Africa by reference to the European exports *to* Africa, where the value of these exports, the price of slaves, and the value of non-slave exports from Africa are all known.

The most valuable records, whether direct or indirect, are time-series over a period of years, since the slave trade was always subject to great annual variation. Although the literature contains a very large number of short-term records, covering periods from a few months to a few years, this short-term evidence has only a limited value. Unless it can be carefully controlled in the light of other qualitative evidence, it may be more misleading than otherwise.

Alongside the actual records (which claim, at least, to be based on a genuine count) a number of contemporaneous estimates are also available. Ships' captains, travellers, officials and supercargoes stationed in Africa, or merchants generally knowledgeable about the state of the trade would often produce a figure indicating the size of the trade they knew about. As quantitative evidence, the value of these opinions is extremely uneven. In some instances, an estimate—say, of the annual average export of slaves from a particular African port—was based on actual records that are now lost. In another case, an equivalent figure could be nothing but a shot in the dark. The men-on-the-spot, furthermore, tended to inflate the export figures from their own part of Africa. They looked to future prospects rather than present reality, or they hoped to persuade the home authorities to send more trade goods, more personnel, or a bigger defense force. When contemporaneous estimates deal with larger aggregates, such as the whole British or French slave trade of a particular period, the same caution applies. Some officials had records that no longer exist. Some merchants were in a position to assess the whole trade along several thousand miles of African coastline, but many were not.

Any general set of quantitative estimates of the slave trade must necessarily use all of these forms of evidence. As a result, some estimates will necessarily be stronger than others. Others must rest on the weakest kind of evidence for lack of anything better.

Old World Traffic

For his estimated imports into Europe—including Sicily, Portugal, Spain, and Italy—Deerr began with the often-quoted statement of Cadamosto, that, in 1458–60, 700 or 800 slaves were exported annually from the African coast to Europe. We have no way of knowing whether or not these were average years, but we also have no other way of knowing what the level of the trade may have been. Taking Cadamosto's figure as an annual average that might well have held good for the whole of 1450–1500, Deerr came to an estimate of 35,000 slaves imported into Europe during that period.[1] Others have guessed at an equivalent figure

1. Deerr, *History of Sugar,* 2:283.

as high as 100,000, but this estimate included exports to the Atlantic Islands as well as to Europe itself.[2]

A scattering of other evidence similar to Cadamosto's report is available for the late fifteenth and early sixteenth centuries. The Lisbon customs house reported a flow of 442 slaves a year into Lisbon alone over the period 1486–93. Again, in 1511–13, an annual average import of 506 slaves has been reported for Portugal. These samples are congruent with still another report that the *Guiné de Cabo Verde*, as the region from Senegal to Sierra Leone was then called, exported 988 slaves a year from 1513 through 1515. The higher annual figure in this case is accounted for by the fact that Guiné de Cabo Verde was the principal exporting region at the time, and its exports served the Atlantic Islands and the Spanish Caribbean as well as Europe.[3]

These samples suggest that the European import rate of 700 or more a year was not sustained. Five hundred a year seems more likely for the second half of the fifteenth century, and that rate could be continued into the early sixteenth century, though it apparently declined as the American demand for slaves increased. It therefore seems reasonable to lower Deerr's estimate to a total of 50,000 slaves for Europe during the whole course of the slave trade, imported at a decreasing rate through the sixteenth century and into the seventeenth.[4]

For Madeira, Deerr used another form of calculation, projecting the number of slaves imported by reference to the slave imports of another territory where they are better known. In this

2. A. Luttrell, "Slavery and Slaving in the Portuguese Atlantic (to about 1500)" in C. Fyfe, ed., "The Transatlantic Slave Trade from West Africa" (Centre of African Studies, University of Edinburgh, 1965, mimeo.), p. 68.

3. J. L. de Azevedo, *Epocas de Portugal económico* (Lisbon, 1929), pp. 69, 75; J. Melo Barreto, *História da Guiné 1418–1918* (Lisbon, 1938), p. 74.

4. For seventeenth-century imports into Europe, see M. J. de La Courbe, *Premier voyage du sieur de La Courbe fait à la coste d'Afrique en 1685* (Paris, 1913), p. 59; A. Ly, *La Compagnie du Sénégal* (Paris, 1958), pp. 153–54.

case, he showed that Madeira had a flourishing sugar industry for about the same period of time as Nevis did, and Madeira's peak sugar production was comparable to that of Nevis. He therefore guessed that the total number of slaves imported should have been about the same as the number imported into Nevis—or 50,000 for the whole period of the trade, a guess made intentionally generous to allow for a small import into the Azores and Cape Verde Islands as well.[5]

While sugar production or slave population of a "sugar colony" should bear some relationship to the rate of slave imports, that relationship is far from uniform. The crux of the problem is the actual demographic structure of the slave population, and this structure is rarely known. The age and sex distributions of creole slaves, born in the colony, were normally different from those of the imported slaves, who tended to be young people with a high ratio of male to female. The proportion of African-born in the population, and the length of their residence, would therefore come into the picture. Furthermore, imported slaves were migrants. They were therefore subject to the epidemiological factors that affect all people who move from one disease environment to another. Most important immunities to disease are acquired in childhood. To move into a new disease environment as an adult normally exacts some price in higher rates of morbidity and mortality among the immigrants. The mortality of migration might be very high, as it was among Europeans who went as traders to the West African coast, or it could be quite low if the range of diseases in the new environment was similar to that of the old country.[6]

In short, the rate of slave imports is related to slave population, but only as one variable among many. When it can be established that the other variables were nearly constant, then

5. Deerr, *History of Sugar,* 2:283.

6. See P. D. Curtin, "Epidemiology and the Slave Trade," *Political Science Quarterly,* 83:190–216 (1968) where this point is made in greater detail.

calculation by analogy—like that between Madeira and Nevis—should be valid. With Madeira and Nevis, however, the disease environments were not closely comparable, and Madeira attracted a large population from Europe as well as from Africa. Its sugar production would therefore not depend exclusively on the size of the labor supply of African origin. These considerations suggest that Deerr's estimate is too high. Perhaps 25,000 slaves for Madeira, Cape Verde Islands, and the Canaries over the whole period of the slave trade would be closer, but this can be nothing but a guess.

TABLE 4

REVISED ESTIMATES OF OLD-WORLD SLAVE IMPORTS

Europe	50,000
Atlantic Islands	25,000
São Thomé	100,000
Total	175,000

Source: See text, pp. 17–21.

The position of São Thomé was also *sui generis*. Its disease environment was probably similar to that of the neighboring African mainland. It became an important sugar colony early in the sixteenth century, and it served the Portuguese as an entrepôt for the slave trade to Brazil. Many of the fragmentary references to slaves exported from Africa to São Thomé therefore include re-exports destined for the Americas. It seems clear that the greatest part of São Thomé's retained imports came during the sixteenth century, though the island was still importing about 200 slaves a year in the mid-seventeenth.[7] Deerr's estimate was 100,000 slaves imported during the whole period of the trade, and this figure is not contradicted by the published literature

7. A. F. C. Ryder, "Dutch Trade on the Nigerian Coast during the Seventeenth Century," *Journal of the Historical Society of Nigeria,* 3:206 (1965).

concerning the island.[8] It can therefore be accepted as uncertain but plausible, and the general set of revisions concerning the Old-World traffic shares this uncertainty. (See Table 4.)

Slave Imports into Spanish America

Spanish America poses another set of problems, and a small error could be important, simply because this trade was a larger part of the whole. During most of the long centuries of the slave trade, Spain carried few slaves under her own flag. After trying unsuccessfully in the sixteenth century to break the Portuguese hold on the Africa trade, she reverted to a system of licenses or *asientos,* issued mainly to foreign firms. An asiento gave the foreign shipper permission to infringe the Spanish national monopoly over the trade of the American viceroyalties, in return for an obligation to carry a stipulated number of slaves to specified destinations over the period of the contract. One source for calculating imports into Spanish America is therefore the series of asientos, which appear to be completely recorded from 1595 to 1773, even though all asientos were not equally precise in the terms they laid down.

Furthermore, an asiento's stipulations cannot be accepted literally. The asiento was considered a great commercial prize, but not for the sake of profits to be made on the slave trade. Quality standards and duty payments required by the Spanish government were too stiff to allow a high profit on slaves alone. The *asientista* counted far more on the opportunity for illicit sales of other goods to Spanish America in return for silver. Richard Pares, one of the most authoritative economic historians of the Caribbean, has doubted that any of the series of asientistas actually made a profit from the slave trade. Few, if any, actually fulfilled the delivery stipulations of the contract. Their economic advantage was in pretending to carry more slaves than they actually did, leaving room to fill out the cargo with other goods.

8. See F. Mauro, *Le Portugal et l'Atlantique au xviie siècle (1570–1670): Etude économique* (Paris, 1960), pp. 178–79, 185–86, 190–91.

For this reason, delivery figures are likely to be inflated through the corruption of American customs-house officers, even though the official returns (where they exist) show that deliveries were not up to the contract stipulation.[9] A calculation of Spanish American slave imports based on a simple addition of the quantities mentioned by each asiento in turn would therefore give a greatly inflated figure.

On the other hand, certain factors work in the opposite direction. Most asiento contracts gave the quantities to be delivered in *piezas de India,* not individual slaves. A pieza de India was a measure of potential labor, not of individuals. For a slave to qualify as a pieza, he had to be a young adult male meeting certain specifications as to size, physical condition, and health. The very young, the old, and females were defined for commercial purposes as fractional parts of a pieza de India. This measure was convenient for Spanish imperial economic planning, where the need was a given amount of labor power, not a given number of individuals. For the historian, however, it means that the number of individuals delivered will always be greater than the number of piezas recorded. Market conditions in Africa made it impossible to buy only the prime slaves and leave all the rest, but the extent of the difference varied greatly with time and place. The definition of a pieza and its fractional values also changed. The asiento of the Portuguese Cacheu Company in 1693, for example, provided for an annual delivery in Spanish America of 4,000 slaves, so distributed in sex, age, and condition as to make up 2,500 piezas de India.[10] This implied the expectation that the number of individuals was 60 per cent greater than the number of piezas. In this case, though, it made little differ-

9. R. Pares, *War and Trade in the West Indies 1739–1763* (Oxford, 1936), esp. p. 10; H. and P. Chaunu, *Séville et l'Atlantique (1504–1650)*, 8 vols. (Paris, 1955–60), 6:42. See also the older works on the diplomacy of the asientos: J. A. Saco, *Historia de la esclavitud de la raza africana en el Nuevo Mundo y en especial en los países américo-hispanos,* new ed., 4 vols. (Havana, 1938); G. Scelle, *La Traite négrière aux Indes de Castille* . . . 2 vols. (Paris, 1906).

10. Scelle, *La Traite négrière,* 2:26–27.

ence: the company failed to meet either standard of delivery. At other times, the relationship between piezas and individuals was much closer. One cargo brought into Cartagena by the South Sea Company in 1715, for example, contained 174 individuals, assessed as 166¾ piezas, the number of individuals exceeding the number of piezas by only 4.3 per cent.[11]

A second cause for overestimation in using asiento data is the known existence of a considerable smuggling trade. While it was to the advantage of the official asientista to deliver fewer slaves than required, the unfilled demand created a market for smuggled slaves that met no quality standards and paid no duties. This part of the slave trade to Spanish America was apparently very profitable in most periods, but extremely difficult to estimate.

In spite of these uncertainties, the asiento figures have a considerable value, not as a record of the number of slaves delivered but as a rationally conceived estimate of manpower requirements. In this sense, they are not unlike the production targets in a modern planned economy. If the Spanish officials were correct (and they had access to information that is now lost), their estimates of demand might not be far from the actual imports, though chronic complaints of a labor shortage suggest that the demand estimated in piezas de India was likely to have been met only in terms of individual slaves delivered, if that. The total contractual obligations in piezas de India can therefore be accepted as a rough estimate of individuals actually delivered in the Americas. One recent authority calculated the number of slaves allowed by the asientos from 1595 to 1640 at 132,574, and a second gives a total of 516,114 for 1641–1773. The contracts from 1595 to 1773 therefore come to 648,688 slaves, or an annual average of 2,882 for 1595–1640 and 3,880 for 1641–1773.[12]

11. J. F. King, "Negro Slavery in the Viceroyalty of New Granada" (unpublished Ph.D. thesis, University of California, 1939), p. 94.

12. G. Aguirre Beltrán, *La población negra de México, 1519–1810* (Mexico, D.F., 1946), p. 220; R. Mellafe, *La esclavitud en Hispanoamérica* (Buenos Aires, 1964), pp. 58–60.

The husband-and-wife team of Pierre and Hugette Chaunu found in their monumental study of the Seville trade that licenses were issued for 263 ships between 1551 and 1595, with an average allowance of 138 piezas per ship.[13] To this recorded total of 36,294 piezas for 1551–95 (810 annual average), it might be appropriate to add 500 slaves a year for the period 1521–50—the total of 15,000 being intentionally large in order to account for the trickle that entered the Spanish American possessions before 1521, and for some between 1551 and 1595 that might have escaped the Chaunu net. We are therefore left with the figures in Table 5, representing the Spanish American slave imports between 1521 and 1773. (The double set of estimates for 1595 is unavoidable in the data as found in the literature, but the degree of error introduced is not significant.)

This total of 700,000 is notably higher than Deerr's estimate of 450,000 for the slave trade to Spanish America in the asiento period—and Deerr considers that period to extend up to 1789, presumably because certain aspects of the Spanish slave trade were still controlled during the latter part of the eighteenth century.[14] The figure may, indeed, be a little on the high side,

13. Chaunu, *Séville et l'Atlantique,* Table 188, 6:402–3 and text 6:41–42. Mellafe also gave a count of the number of slaves provided for by the asientos of 1551–1640, his total being "approximately 100,000 slaves," but Aguirre's count has the appearance of greater precision and is therefore taken instead. Mellafe, in addition, used the Chaunu data, giving the total number of ships permitted as 1,207 totaling about 142,426 *toneladas,* which he evaluates at a total import of 350,000 slaves of all ages and both sexes. These totals differ from those in Table 22, because Mellafe failed to correct for the errors of addition in the original Chaunu table (*Séville et l'Atlantique,* 6:402–3, Table 188). He also apparently converted from toneladas to slaves at the rate of 2.4 slaves per tonelada, while the Chaunus pointed out that the contracts themselves allowed approximately 1.2 piezas per tonelada. (1:310–13). The conversion from piezas to individuals by doubling is not acceptable, but Mellafe's count for the asientos of 1641–1773 has been accepted. Mellafe gives this datum as "Negroes imported" though it appears from the context to be the number of piezas authorized. Mellafe's own estimate of Spanish American slave imports for this period is much higher (Mellafe, *Esclavitud,* p. 59).

14. Deerr, *History of Sugar,* 2:281.

TABLE 5

ESTIMATES OF SPANISH-AMERICAN SLAVE IMPORTS, 1521–1773

	No.	Annual average
1521–50	15,000	500
1551–95	36,300	810
1595–1640	132,600	2,880
1641–1773	516,100	3,880
Total	700,000	2,770

Source: See text, pp. 21–25.

since its origin is an administrative estimate of demand; and that demand may not have been filled at certain periods. It is accepted nevertheless as the best approximation available.

The period after 1773 is more complex. Some Spanish-flag slavers entered the trade, and partial asientos were occasionally signed for the supply of particular colonies by either foreign or Spanish firms. The progressive opening of *commercio libre* for the Spanish empire, moreover, did not imply free entry for foreign ships, only a slackening of control over Spanish shipping. Smuggling therefore continued, but the series of general asientos stopped—and with it one convenient basis for estimating the level of slave imports.

Some other evidence is, however, available. The British slave trade of the eighteenth century normally carried more slaves than the British colonies needed. The Spanish were allowed to come to Jamaica and some other English colonies to buy slaves —legally in Jamaican, but not in Spanish, law. Being legal, these re-exports were recorded, and the records have survived for most of the eighteenth century. With interpolations, a time-series can be completed for the whole of 1701–1807, and these estimates appear in Table 6.

Most of these slaves were re-exported to Spanish America, and the Jamaican re-exports can be taken as a rough guide to the probable number of slaves diverted from the British slave trade to the Spanish colonies in the Caribbean, northern South America, and Middle America. The Spanish may well have bought

TABLE 6

SLAVE RE-EXPORTS FROM JAMAICA, 1701–1807

1701–10		8,800
*1701	350	
1702–10	8,450	
1711–20		24,900
1721–30		33,200
1731–40		27,000
1741–50		14,500
1751–60		11,100
1761–70		9,900
1771–80		14,900
1771–73	2,400	
1774–75	4,100	
*1776–80	8,400	
1781–90		17,900
*1781–88	13,500	
1789–90	4,400	
1791–1800		26,200
1791–98	21,100	
*1799–1800	5,100	
*1801–7		17,800
Total		206,200

* Estimate

Source: Calculated from data of R. B. Le Page, "An Historical Introduction to Jamaican Creole," in R. B. Le Page, ed., *Jamaican Creole* (London, 1960), pp. 81–82.

slaves from the British elsewhere, but it seems a fair guess that these other sources were about equal to the Jamaican re-exports to non-Spanish colonies. The numbers going elsewhere were probably small in any case. Jamaica was much the most convenient entrepôt for the Spanish, while the French islands, which also brought slaves from the British, tended to patronize the eastern entrepôts on Dominica and the Bahamas.

A second key to the Spanish American slave imports of this period comes from the Plata basin. Elena F. S. de Studer has made an intensive study of the slave traffic into ports on the Rio de la Plata—ports which served not merely the present-day Argentina and Uruguay, but also the more distant markets of Bolivia, and even Chile and Peru. The recorded imports for 1742–1806 were at an annual average of 399 slaves, a rate which yields an estimate of 13,566 slaves imported legally for 1774–1807.[15] In addition, Sra. Studer allowed 50 per cent additional for contraband imports, or a total of about 20,300. Taken together with the Jamaican re-exports of the period, the result is a "known" total of about 94,700 slaves entering the Spanish empire by these two routes in the period 1774–1807.

But what of other sources of supply? A few slaves were carried to the Spanish colonies by French slavers. The Dutch and Danes and North Americans, to say nothing of the Spanish themselves, were also in the slave trade. It is tempting to resort to a speculative multiplier, guessing that these diverse sources might have accounted for half the Spanish slave imports of 1774–1807. If this were accurate, the total Spanish imports for the period would have been about 200,000 slaves.

One way of checking this kind of guess is to look at estimates of the slave imports into each individual Spanish territory. The viceroyalty of La Plata is already covered by the Studer figures. The slave trade to Mexico had virtually ceased by this time.[16] Brito Figueroa, who has recently published estimates of slave imports into Venezuela, allowed an annual average of 705 a year for the whole of the eighteenth century. Since it is known that the Venezuelan economy developed more rapidly in the second half of the century than in the first, this might be raised to 1,000 a year from 1774 through 1799, or at least 26,000. In addition, Brito Figueroa calculated imports of 2,343 for the period 1800–10—to the end of Venezuelan slave imports. A total esti-

15. E. F. S. de Studer, *La trata de negros en el Río de la Plata durante el siglo xviii* (Buenos Aires, 1958), p. 325.

16. G. Aguirre Beltrán, "The Slave Trade in Mexico," *Hispanic American Historical Review*, 24:412–31 (1944), estimates that no more than 20,000 were imported from the beginning of the eighteenth century to legal abolition of the trade in 1817.

mate for Venezuelan imports after 1774 would therefore be about 30,000.[17]

The remainder of the Spanish Caribbean poses more serious problems. Population data, giving the breakdown into white, colored, and slaves, are available for each colony at various dates in the eighteenth century, but no reliable annual return of slaves imported has yet been published for any of them. Thus, while a calculation from analogy might be possible here—as it was not between Madeira and Nevis—the necessary data are not available.

They are available for some of the English colonies during this period, but the English colonies were "sugar islands," with intense exploitation of the land, high ratios of African-born to total slave population, and high ratios of men to women among the slaves. These conditions, which were common to all regions of sugar cultivation, tended to produce an excess of deaths over births among the slave population. This net natural decrease varied from less than 10 per thousand per annum, to as high as 40 per thousand per annum, and it was normally balanced by continuous slave imports from Africa. This in turn caused the situation to persist, since the African-born suffered from higher rates of morbidity and mortality than the creoles did, and the imported slaves had a sex ratio unfavorable to a high gross birth rate. As a general tendency, the higher the proportion of African-born in any slave population, the lower its rate of natural increase—or, as was more often the case, the higher its rate of natural decrease.[18]

The phenomenon of a naturally decreasing population was nearly universal in northeast Brazil and the Caribbean sugar

17. F. Brito Figueroa, *La estructura económica de Venezuela colonial* (Caracas, 1963), pp. 137–38.

18. For the general trends of West Indian and Brazilian slave demography see M. Goulart, *Escravidão africana no Brasil* (São Paulo, 1950), pp. 155–56; G. W. Roberts, *The Population of Jamaica* (Cambridge, 1957); D. Lowenthal, "The Population of Barbados," *Social and Economic Studies*, 6:445–501 (December, 1957).

colonies, but it was not universal in the Americas as a whole. In other physical and social environments, slave populations could grow by natural increase. The most striking contrast existed between the British mainland colonies and the British Caribbean. As early as 1826, Humboldt was struck by the rapid increase of slave populations in the southern United States, compared to the natural decrease that was still the rule for most of the Caribbean.[19]

Naturally increasing slave populations are also found in parts of Latin America during the eighteenth century. While northeastern Brazil had high rates of natural decrease, and even Minas Gerais as late as 1821 had a rate of natural decrease at 22 per thousand per annum for mulatto slaves and 40 per thousand for slaves of unmixed African descent, other parts of Brazil had naturally growing slave populations. São Paulo had achieved this condition by the early nineteenth century, and even Maranhão in the tropical north had a natural growth rate of 6 per thousand as early as 1779. The contrast is even more striking in inland Argentina. An estate near Córdoba preserved records of births and deaths over the whole period 1754–92. The size of the slave population was not recorded, but the number of births was more than twice the number of deaths.[20]

In the sugar colonies themselves, demographic history tended to fall into a regular pattern over time. With the initial settlement, or the initial entry into the South Atlantic System with its dependence on slave labor from Africa, the ratio of slave imports to population was very high. Then, as the island or colony reached full production, the total slave population began to level off. Slave imports continued, but only enough to make up the

19. A. von Humboldt, *Personal Narrative of Travels to the Equinoctial Regions of the New Continent . . . 1799–1804,* 7 vols. (London, 1814–29), 7:150–52.

20. Goulart, *Escravidão,* pp. 155–56; N. Coelho de Senna, *Africanos no Brasil* (Belo Horizonte, 1938), p. 64; C. Gazón Maceda and J. W. Dorflinger, "Esclavos y mulatos en un dominio rural del siglo XVIII en Córdoba," *Revista de la Universidad Nacional de Córdoba,* 2 (2nd ser.):627–40 (1961).

deficit between deaths and births. Over time, the proportion of American-born slaves increased; the deficit diminished and then disappeared. Barbados reached this point by about 1810, Jamaica by the 1840's. From this point on, even without further input of imported slaves, the population began to grow, slowly at first and then more rapidly. By the end of the nineteenth century, the earlier underpopulation of Barbados and Jamaica had changed to a chronic overpopulation that still persists.[21]

By now, the problem of estimating the slave imports into Spanish America should be clear. Was New Granada of the late eighteenth century like Jamaica, or like Argentina? The part of the viceroyalty that was to become Venezuela had a plantation component, and Brito Figueroa's estimates appear to be acceptable. The rest of the viceroyalty (the present-day republics of Colombia, Panama, and Ecuador) presents another problem. Placer gold mining in Colombia depended on the slave trade much as a plantation sector would have done, but the mulatto population of Colombia was 40 to 50 per cent of the total by 1800.[22] This suggests a growing African-derived population in one sector and a naturally decreasing slave population in another.

A guess is called for, and it must be highly uncertain. Using Venezuela as a guide, an import of 30,000 for Colombia, Panama, and Ecuador, plus re-exports southward to Peru and Chile, seems reasonable for the period 1773–1810. A final and even more uncertain guess at 5,000 for Central America, allowing for a trickle into Mexico as well, would complete the accounting for the Spanish mainland colonies.

The island colonies—Cuba, Puerto Rico, and the Spanish part of Hispaniola—were a backwater of the Spanish empire up to the middle of the eighteenth century. They had few settlers of any kind, and their slave populations were a small part of the

21. See Roberts, *Population of Jamaica,* and Lowenthal, "The Population of Barbados," *passim.*

22. T. Lynn Smith, "The Racial Composition of the Population of Colombia," *Journal of Inter-American Studies,* 8:215 (1966).

total. Comparatively large numbers were free settlers of partial African descent. Given the fact that the slave trade to these islands had been gradual over several centuries, both the slave populations and the free black populations probably attained natural growth by the mid-eighteenth century. The mulatto population certainly did. Then, beginning in Cuba in the 1760's and in Puerto Rico somewhat later, these islands finally entered the South Atlantic System and developed a plantation sector worked largely by newly-imported slaves from Africa. As the plantation sector grew, it changed the demographic pattern of the islands. For this sector at least, a naturally declining slave population appeared, and the demographic pattern, like the economic pattern, came to resemble that of Jamaica or Saint Domingue a century earlier.[23] Although Spanish Santo Domingo missed the new phase on account of the anarchy and warfare that spread from French Saint Domingue after the great slave revolt of 1791, Cuba and Puerto Rico began to import slaves in greatly increased numbers at the precise period when the slave trade to continental Spanish America showed signs of tapering off.

The Cuban slave trade of this period from 1774 through 1807 was investigated by Baron von Humboldt, one of the first scholars to take a serious interest in historical demography. H. H. S. Aimes used Humboldt's work for his own annual estimates covering the period up to 1819.[24] This set of estimates put Cuban slave imports at 119,000 for the period 1774–1807.

Although no equivalent estimates are available for Puerto Rico, slave imports into that island can be projected by analogy to the Cuban experience. Unlike Deerr's attempted analogy of Nevis and Madeira, the demographic, epidemiologic, and social patterns of the two Spanish Caribbean islands proceeded with a

23. S. Mintz, "Labor and Sugar in Puerto Rico and in Jamaica, 1800–1850," *Comparative Studies in Society and History,* 1:273–80 (1959); Humboldt, *Equinoctial Regions,* vol. 7; H. H. S. Aimes, *A History of Slavery in Cuba, 1511 to 1868* (New York, 1907); L. M. Díaz Soler, *Historia de la esclavitud en Puerto Rico, 1493–1890,* 2nd ed. (Rio Piedras, 1965).

24. Aimes, *Slavery in Cuba,* p. 269.

common rhythm in the late eighteenth and early nineteenth centuries, as indicated in Table 7 and Fig. 1.[25] (The figure is plotted on a semi-logarithmic scale, where the angle of the curve is proportional to percentage changes, regardless of the absolute level of the two populations.)

Cuban slave imports of 1774–1816 must account both for the growth of the Cuban slave population from 1774 to 1817 and for any deficit caused by an excess of deaths over births.[26] In this instance, the actual rate of growth for the Cuban slave population was 3.5 per cent per year. With slave imports over the whole period amounting to 176,800, the implied rate of net natural decrease is 0.5 per cent a year (a low rate for the Caribbean at that period, and one that supports the possibility that natural growth had taken place before the 1760's).

In Puerto Rico over the period 1765–1811, the actual rate of increase among the slave population was 2.7 per cent per annum. If demographic conditions followed the pattern of Cuba in 1774–1816, Puerto Rican slave imports would have been large enough to account for this rate of increase combined with an annual net natural decrease of 0.5 per cent among the slaves. On

25. Reports of slave populations at various dates are not always in perfect agreement, and the Cuban census of 1846 has been set aside as suspect by Cuban scholars. When the date of census is indicated by year only, it is assumed that census data apply to January 1 of the year indicated.

26. In mathematical terms, where r equals the annual rate of growth, m the annual rate of immigration, and i the annual rate of natural increase (or decrease if negative), $r = i + m$.

If it is known that a population has increased in size from N_o to N_t in t years, then the average rate of growth, r, is given by:

$$e^{rt} = \frac{N_t}{N_0}, \text{ or by } r = \frac{1}{t}\log_e\left(\frac{N_t}{N_0}\right).$$

Where the size of the population at the beginning and end of the period of time is known, and where the rate of growth, r, and rate of immigration, m, are also known, the relationship simplifies to give the average annual number of immigrants, T, so that: $T = \frac{m}{r}\left(N_t - N_0\right)$. Or, where T is known, but i or m is unknown:

$$m = \frac{Tr}{N_t - N_0}.$$

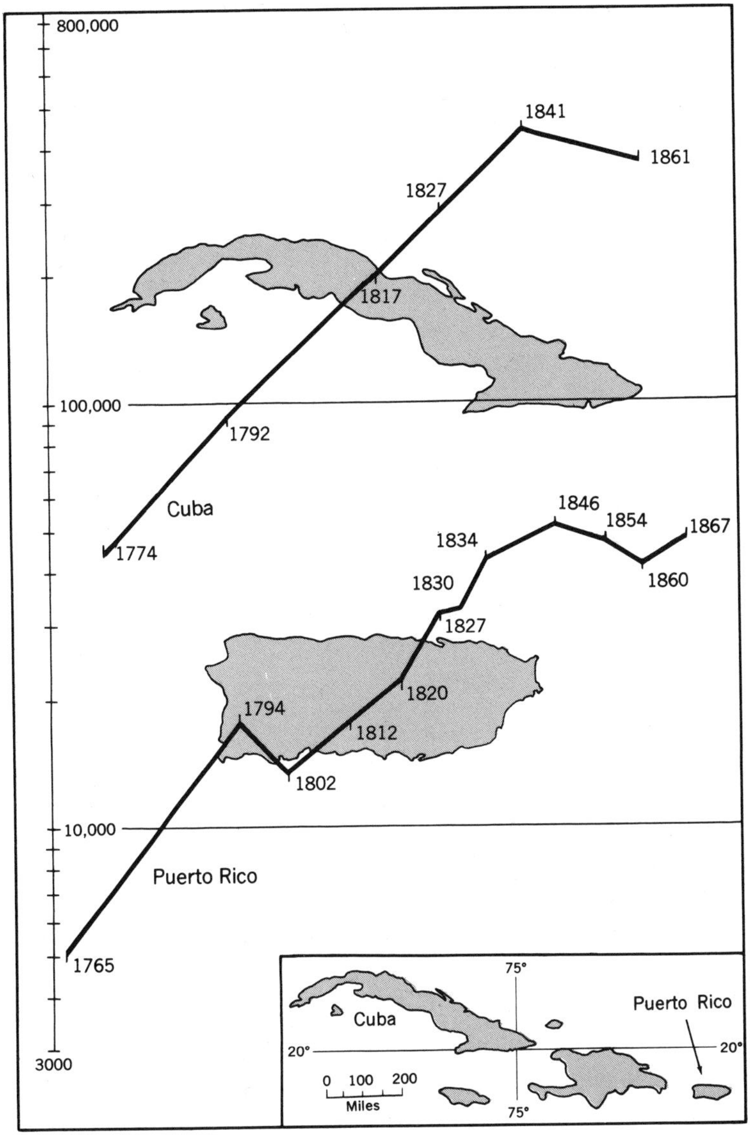

Fig. 1. Slave populations of Cuba and Puerto Rico, 1765–1867. Fig. by UW Cartographic Lab. Data from Table 7.

TABLE 7

THE SLAVE POPULATIONS OF CUBA AND PUERTO RICO, 1765–1867

Place and date	Slave population	Rate of increase p. a. over period indicated (%)
Cuba		
1774	44,300	3.5 (1774–1816)
1792	85,900	3.7 (1774–91)
1817	199,100	3.4 (1792–1816)
1827	286,900	3.7 (1817–26)
1841	436,500	3.0 (1827–40)
1861	367,400	−0.9 (1841–60)
Puerto Rico		
1765	5,000	2.7 (1765–1811)
1794	17,500	4.3 (1765–93)
1802	13,300	−3.4 (1794–1801)
1812	17,500	
1820	21,700	2.7 (1802–19)
1827	31,900	
1830	32,200	3.9 (1820–29)
1834	41,800	
1846	51,300	2.9 (1830–45)
1854	46,900	
1860	41,700	−1.5 (1846–59)
1867	47,000	1.7 (1860–66)

Source: Population data from Aimes, *Slavery in Cuba*, pp. 37–89; Díaz Soler, *Esclavitud in Puerto Rico, passim;* Deerr, *History of Sugar*, 2:280; R. Guerra y Sanchez and others, *Historia de la nacíon cubana* (10 vols., Havana, 1952), 4:170–71.

these assumptions, Puerto Rico would have imported 14,800 slaves over the period 1765–1811. In fact, these imports probably fell within a still narrower period of time. Puerto Rican plantation development began somewhat later than the Cuban development of the 1760's, and the population data indicate that the Puerto Rican slave population fell steeply during part of the Napoleonic wars, indicating that very few slave ships arrived. The figure of 14,800 slaves imported can therefore stand roughly for the total Puerto Rican imports of 1774–1807.

Santo Domingo, on the other hand, is not susceptible to this kind of calculation. No comparable Caribbean society has ade-

TABLE 8

ESTIMATED SLAVE IMPORTS INTO SPANISH AMERICA, 1774–1807, BY AREA

La Plata basin	20,300
Mexico and Central America	5,000
Venezuela	30,000
Colombia, including Panama and re-exports to Chile and Peru	30,000
Cuba	119,000
Puerto Rico	14,800
Santo Domingo	6,000
Total	225,100

Source: See text, pp. 26–35.

quate data on slave imports and population. Population guesses for Santo Domingo itself vary greatly, though the most reliable appears to be that of Moreau de Saint Méry, which put the slave population of 1790 at about 15,000.[27] A guess at slave imports in 1774–1807 might come to 6,000. The general total of these estimates is shown on Table 8.

Rough as this total estimate must necessarily be, its suggested level of 225,100 slaves imported into Spanish America between 1774–1807 is reasonably close to the first estimate of 200,000 based on the level of Jamaican re-exports and the recorded flows into the Plata basin. The estimated total of Table 8 is almost 13 per cent higher than this figure; but with data as weak as this, a discrepancy of only 13 per cent is welcome, though it also suggests that the estimates of Table 8 may possibly be on the high side.

The total given in Table 8 is nevertheless accepted as the more likely figure for 1774–1807. Combined with estimates to 1773 (Table 5), it yields a total Spanish American slave import of 925,100 for the whole period of the trade up to 1807. For most of Spanish America, the Napoleonic Wars, the abolition of the British slave trade, and the wars of independence marked the

27. M. L. E. Moreau de Saint-Méry, *Descripción de la parte española de Santo Domingo* (Santo Domingo, 1944; originally published 1796), p. 82.

effective end of the slave trade at about that date. After 1807, significant slave flows into Spanish America went only to Cuba and Puerto Rico. The estimate of 925,100 is therefore a general figure for the Spanish-American colonial period, and it agrees with other estimates based on other data. Brito Figueroa, for example, put the total Spanish-American imports at one million slaves up to 1810.[28] Deerr's estimate, however, was somewhat lower, since he allowed one million slaves for the whole period of the trade, including the nineteenth-century imports into Puerto Rico and Cuba.

The final period of the slave trade to Spanish America is, indeed, one of the most controversial of all. For most times and places in the history of the trade, a single time-series claiming to be an authentic record of imports is rare. For nineteenth-century Cuba, however, overlapping estimates abound. H. H. S. Aimes produced an annual series of estimates from 1790 to 1865. This series drew partly on Humboldt's work, and it closely follows the official customs house figures for the period 1791–1820. It can therefore be accepted as reasonable for that period.[29]

For the period after 1821 Aimes's series continues (see Table 9, col. 1), based on a variety of different data. He used the reported changes in slave population between census dates, assuming that the existing slave population would add 1,800 to 2,000 to the population by natural increase each year. He further checked these estimates against the reports of British diplomatic representatives and against earlier calculations made by José Antonio Saco, principally from newspaper announcements in the *Diario de la Habana*. Finally, he modified his estimates according to the

28. Brito Figueroa, *Venezuela colonial*, pp. 137–38.

29. Aimes, *Slavery in Cuba*, p. 269. J. Bandinel, *Some Account of the Trade in Slaves from Africa* (London, 1842), pp. 284–86, on the other hand, has claimed that the customs house figures should be doubled on account of illicit trade. Illicit trade may have existed, but no evidence is available to show its level. For that matter, Bandinel's fondness for doubling recorded figures and making liberal allowances for the unknown is one source of the highly inflated estimates he made throughout his book, many of which have been innocently adopted by later historians.

changing price of slaves.[30] But for all the apparent care, Aimes's estimates cannot be accepted. He did not publish the actual calculations, nor explain how the different factors were weighted. His assumption of a naturally increasing slave population is unrealistic, and the estimates themselves appear to be more and more dubious with each passing decade after the 1820's.

It was precisely in the 1830's and onward that the Cuban slave trade received the greatest international publicity, especially in Great Britain, where it lay at the heart of a prolonged controversy over the effectiveness of the British navy's effort to stop the trade on the high seas. The number of slaves arriving in Cuba was therefore widely discussed; but publicists and Parliamentarians sought to attack and defend, not merely to illuminate. British official publications, however, contain at least four different time-series of slave imports into Cuba, partly overlapping and presenting their data on different bases.

One list was published in the Parliamentary sessional papers for 1845. This was apparently a compilation of the raw data available to the Foreign Office. It listed more than 2,000 ships known by the Foreign Office to have landed slaves in the Americas over the years 1817–43. It named the ship in most cases, with the number of slaves landed, point of origin in Africa, and other information. It was published without tabulation or analysis, but it listed some 254 ships landing slaves in Cuba, for a total of 86,814 slaves. This figure can be taken as a minimum for the Cuban slave imports of the period concerned.[31] (See Table 9, col. 2.)

A second set of estimates was published by the Foreign Office in 1848 (Table 9, col. 3), and it is an interesting example of the way Foreign Office personnel used their quantitative data. This time, the total estimates were far higher than those shown in the sample of 1845. They covered slave exports from Africa back to

30. Aimes, *Slavery in Cuba,* pp. 244–49.
31. *Parliamentary Papers* (cited hereafter as PP), 1845, xlix (73), pp. 593–633.

1798, losses in transit, and the imports of the Spanish and Portuguese colonies listed separately. For the period 1798–1839, these data were presented as quinquennial annual averages, followed by an annual series for the years 1840–47. Unlike the Aimes figures or the 1845 sample, they lump together the Cuban and Puerto Rican slave imports as a single total.[32]

This set of estimates was not a routine statistical return. It was designed specifically for the Parliamentary Select Committee on the Slave Trade, which was considering whether or not the government's anti-slave-trade policy should be continued. The Foreign Office was deeply committed to that policy, and to the anti-slavery blockade then under attack in Parliament. The strongest case for the blockade would be to show large totals for the slave trade of the 1820's and 1830's and greatly reduced figures for the 1840's.

The third official British series was also presented to the Committee on the Slave Trade (see Table 9, col. 4). Its central focus was an annual list of the number of slaves captured by British cruisers over the period 1836–47, but it also gave estimated annual imports into Havana and vicinity over the same years.[33] In this case, the political purpose was quite different from that of the Foreign Office. Where the Foreign Office sought to show that the slave trade was decreasing through British efforts, these figures showed that the navy was less effective in the late 1840's than it had been a few years earlier. The Cuban import figures, however, were not very different from those of the Foreign Office for 1836–47, the difference being accounted for by the imports of Puerto Rico and minor Cuban ports. Its political purpose was served, however, if readers could be led to the natural assumption that illegal imports would avoid the capital city—that Havana figures were therefore the tip of a very large iceberg.

32. PP, 1847–48, xxii (623), p. 8.

33. The table has been frequently reprinted, for example in H. J. Matson, *Remarks on the Slave Trade and African Squadron* (London, 1848), p. 7 and J. H. Rose, "The Royal Navy and the Suppression of the West African Slave Trade," *Mariner's Mirror,* 22:64 (1936).

TABLE 9A

NINETEENTH-CENTURY CUBA: SOME ESTIMATES OF SLAVE IMPORTS AT SELECTED PERIODS

	(1)	(2)	(3)	(4)	(5)
Period	Aimes	Foreign Office sample, 1845	Foreign Office estimates, 1848 (both Cuba and Puerto Rico)	British official estimate for Havana and vicinity only	Foreign Office estimates, 1865
1821–30	49,915	22,742	396,000	—	—
1831–40	93,189	42,556	319,470	—	—
1836–40	52,939	33,953	130,470	57,916	—
1841–47	16,200	—	37,557	27,492	—
1848	1,950	—	—	—	—
1849–50	6,000	—	—	—	11,800
1851–60	28,100	—	—	—	123,332
1861–64	4,600	—	—	—	49,532

Source: Calculated from the data of Aimes, *Slavery in Cuba*, p. 269; PP, 1845, xlix (73), pp. 593–633; PP, 1847–48, xxii (623), p. 8; PP, 1865, v (412); H. J. Matson, *Remarks on the Slave Trade*. See text, pp. 36–39.

The fourth British series of Cuban import estimates applied to a later period. It was prepared for the Parliamentary Committee on West Africa in 1865, and it gave an annual series for the Cuban slave trade of 1849–64 (see Table 9A, col. 5).[34] For some years of the early 1850's, these figures are clearly educated guesses, rounded out to the nearest thousand. In the later 1850's, however, they correspond to the official Spanish figures in years where the Spanish government in Cuba was itself making a serious, though unsuccessful, effort to control the trade.[35]

Close estimates of the actual number of slaves imported into Cuba between 1821 and 1865 can only be made after detailed archival study and cross-checking, and no such studies have yet

34. PP, 1865, v (412).

35. Personal communication from Prof. Franklin Knight, State University of New York, Stony Brook, based on his forthcoming study of Cuban slavery in the nineteenth century.

TABLE 9B

NINETEENTH-CENTURY CUBA: ACCEPTED ESTIMATES OF SLAVE IMPORTS SUBDIVIDED ACCORDING TO CENSUS DATES

Period	No. imported	Annual average	Source of data	Implied annual rate of net natural decrease (%)
1801–7	46,000	6,570	Aimes	—
1808–16	57,800	6,420	Aimes	—
1817–26	103,500	10,350	Aimes	0.7
1827–40	176,500	12,610	Saco, based on ann. average est. for 1835–39	0.5
1841–47	33,800	4,830	F.O. estimate 1848, adjusted for Cuban imports only	—
1848	2,000	2,000	Aimes	—
1849–50	11,800	5,900	F.O. estimate 1865	—
1851–60	123,300	12,330	F.O. estimate 1865	3.0 (1841–60)
1861–64	49,500	12,380	F.O. estimate 1865	—
1865	12,000	—	Sheer guesswork	
Total	616,200	9,480		
Total (1808–65)	570,200			

been made. The discrepancies in the five available time-series of Table 9A can, however, be adjusted to some degree by checking against Cuban census data and demographic expectations. Some parts of some series, for example, are clearly implausible. Cuban censuses of 1817 and 1827 indicate the annual growth rate of the slave population. The Foreign Office estimates of 1848 were presumably prepared under the direction of James Bandinel. If they are combined with his estimates for 1817–20, published elsewhere,[36] the Cuban slave imports of 1817–26 come to 366,178. Given an annual growth rate of only 3.7 per cent, Bandinel's estimates could only be correct if the annual rate of net natural

36. Bandinel, *Trade in Slaves,* pp. 284–86.

decrease among the slave population were 11.7 per cent. This is not only far higher than the rates of natural decrease commonly found in the Caribbean; it is higher than the Cuban rates for periods immediately preceding and following this one. The figures in col. 3 can therefore be set aside as wildly implausible.

Aimes's estimates for 1817–26 can also be tested in the same way: the implied rate of annual net natural decrease would be 0.7 per cent. Given an annual growth rate of 3.7 per cent and a sex ratio among the slave population of 1,671 males to one thousand females in 1817, rising to 1,768 in 1827,[37] this rate of net natural decrease is a little lower than might be anticipated. On the other hand, it is not impossible. Jamaica, for example, appears to have had a rate of net natural decrease of 1.2 per cent in 1703–21, when the growth rate of the Jamaican slave population was a nearly-equivalent 3.0 per cent. But Jamaican rates of net natural decrease were generally higher than this during the eighteenth century.[38] Aimes's estimates to 1826 can be accepted, but with suspicion that they may be lower than actuality.

The next intercensal period, 1827–40, poses a more difficult problem. In this case, Aimes's figures imply an annual natural *increase* of 0.6 per cent among the Cuban slaves, even though the growth rate remained at 3.0 per cent and the sex ratio rose to 1,823 males per thousand females by 1841. They are therefore unacceptably low. But the Foreign Office estimates of 1848 are

37. From Cuban census data reprinted in Deerr, *History of Sugar,* 2:280. In this context, the sex ratio is used as a rough indication of the proportion of African-born slaves in the total slave population, since the slave cargoes at this period contained between two and five males for each female, while creole slaves can be assumed to have been approximately half male and half female. It is known that high proportions of African-born slaves meant high rates of natural decrease, partly because the African-born slaves had higher rates of mortality than the native-born. High rates of morbidity may also have kept down the fertility rate among the African-born. But each slave cargo, with virtually all of its women of childbearing age, could possibly have an initial birth rate much higher than that of a native-born population with a more even sex ratio but also with a more normal age distribution.

38. See table in G. W. Roberts, *Population of Jamaica,* p. 36.

unacceptably high, indicating a net natural decrease at the rate of 5.7 per cent per year. It is therefore necessary to examine the other time-series, incomplete as they are. The British figures for Havana and vicinity are higher than Aimes's and lower than the Foreign Office estimates of 1848. They therefore appear to be in an appropriate range, and they look like actual records—not mere estimates. But they are only for Havana. Fortunately, they can be checked against still another set of estimates, not included in Table 9. J. A. Saco produced import estimates for the whole island in the years 1835–39—a total of 63,053 slaves landed, based on the books of the Lonja Mercantil and published information from the *Diario de la Habana.*[39] This figure is congruent with the British reports for Havana alone. It is therefore an acceptable possibility, and its annual average is a reasonable indication of the possible annual average Cuban imports for the whole of 1827–40. (See Table 9B.) This estimate derived from Saco implies an approximate annual rate of net natural decrease at 0.5 per cent—nearly the same as the annual rate suggested by Aimes's estimates for 1817–26. The estimate is therefore taken as a reasonable guess, though again perhaps on the low side.

For the next census period, 1841–60, the alternative time-series are in better accord. The Foreign Office estimates of 1848, so suspicious for earlier periods, now begin to look like real records. The annual figures for 1841–47 come to a total of 37,557 for Puerto Rico and Cuba together. Since Puerto Rico had about 10 per cent of the population of the Spanish Caribbean, that much can be deducted to arrive at a figure for Cuba alone. The resulting figure of 33,800 appears to be in line with the British data for Havana alone, and to differ only slightly from the total of known slave ships published in 1845. It is therefore accepted. For 1848, Aimes gives the only estimate in any of the series. It appears to be plausible, and its acceptance will make little difference in the long-run totals. From 1849 to 1860, a very wide

39. Aimes, *Slavery in Cuba,* p. 245.

discrepancy appears between Aimes's estimates and those of the Foreign Office. In this case, the Foreign Office figures are preferred—partly because Aimes's figures are only rounded-out estimates for this period, and partly because their demographic implications are implausible.

By skipping from one time-series to another, it is possible in this way to arrive at a preferred series of Cuban slave imports from the census of 1841 to that of 1861. The total of 170,900 slaves landed may appear to be high in the face of an actual decline in Cuban slave population between these two dates. The annual rate of net natural decrease implied by this estimate is, indeed, 3.0 per cent—high, but not beyond the experience of other Caribbean slave populations, and the 1850's was a decade of population loss throughout the Caribbean on account of the great cholera epidemic.

For the final period of the Cuban slave trade, 1861–65, the Foreign Office figures again appear to be acceptable, though they end with 1864 and the trade itself ended only gradually over the next few years. The final estimate for 1865 is therefore intentionally higher than the probable level of the trade for that year alone. The total Cuban imports estimated for 1801–65 are therefore intended to represent the entire Cuban slave trade from Africa during the nineteenth century.

Although these estimates for Cuba are weak in many respects, they are some guide to the imports of Puerto Rico as well. Puerto Rico and Cuba showed markedly similar slave-population curves (Fig. 1). It can therefore be assumed that Puerto Rican slave imports during any intercensal period can be estimated from the rate of growth among the slave population (Table 7), adjusted according to the rate of net natural decrease estimated for Cuba at an equivalent period. For the period 1860–65, matching Cuban census data are not available, but an estimate can be constructed by assuming that Puerto Rico's rate of import per capita of slave population in 1860 would be equal to Cuba's rate of import per capita of slave population in 1861. The result of these calculations is shown in Table 10.

TABLE 10

ESTIMATED PUERTO RICAN SLAVE IMPORTS, 1801–65

Period	No. imported	Annual average	Based on Cuban rate of net natural decrease (%)
1801	nil	nil	—
1802–19	10,400	580	0.7
1820–29	11,900	1,190	0.5
1830–45	22,600	1,410	0.5
1846–59	9,800	700	3.0
1860–65	5,600	930	
Total	60,300	940	
Total (1808–65)	56,900		

Source: Calculated from the data shown on Tables 7 and 9. See text, p. 43.

If these estimates are correct, the total slave imports into Spanish America were in the vicinity of 1,552,000 over the whole period of the slave trade. Some of the estimates on which this figure is based are geographical import estimates, while others are flow estimates for the whole trade to the Spanish empire over a period of time. One way of simultaneously checking the result and establishing the possible pattern of geographical distribution within Spanish America is to set these estimates against those that appear in the literature for particular countries. The calculations for Cuba and Puerto Rico have been given.[40] Authorities on regional history have produced import estimates for Mexico at 200,000 during the whole of the slave trade, and for Venezuela at 121,000.[41] For the Plata basin, we have the import estimates

40. That is, for Cuba: to 1773, 13,100 (Aimes, *Slavery in Cuba*, p. 269); 1774–1807, 119,000 (from Table 8); 1808–65, 568,500 (from Table 9). For Puerto Rico: to 1773, 5,000 (estimate based on slave-population data in Table 7); 1774–1807, 14,900 (from Table 8); 1808–65, 59,600 (from Table 10).

41. Aguirre Beltrán, "Slave Trade in Mexico," p. 431; Brito Figueroa, *Venezuela colonial*, pp. 137–38. See also J. Roncal, "The Negro Race in Mexico," *Hispanic American Historical Review*, 24:530–40 (1944).

worked out by Elena de Studer, which are roughly equivalent to imports into the present Argentina, Uruguay, Paraguay, and Bolivia.[42] A more problematic estimate for Peru is reported by Deerr.[43] For Chile, Rolando Mellafe estimated 2,000 slaves imported between 1555 and 1615, and this can serve as the basis for a speculative overall estimate of about 6,000.[44]

These partial estimates by geographical region are shown in Table 11. Together they add up to 1,301,000 slaves imported and cover all important regions—except Santo Domingo, Colombia, Panama, Ecuador, and Central America. If the balance of 251,000 that remains after this figure is subtracted from the overall total estimate of 1,552,000 can fit comfortably into these countries, the broad accuracy of the estimates would be confirmed. Santo Domingo can be dealt with by an educated guess, based on the general level of economic development there in the sixteenth and seventeenth centuries. It was more important than either Cuba or Puerto Rico in those early centuries, but its slave imports were cut off sharply in the 1790's. It might therefore be allowed 30,000.

The northwest corner of South America is a more difficult region to deal with at the present state of knowledge. Cartagena was a very important entrepôt in the Spanish slave trade of the sixteenth and seventeenth centuries. Panama served as the trans-shipment point to the Pacific coast of South America, and the dominant racial strain all along that coast south to the Gulf

42. Studer, *Trata de negros,* pp. 100, 112, 284, 325.

43. From Garland, *La industria azucarera en el Perú* (Lima, 1914), p. 51, quoted in Deerr, *History of Sugar,* 2:266. The figure is reasonably consonant with the reported slave population of Peru, given as 40,336 slaves and 41,256 free colored people in about 1791, and as 17,000 slaves at the time of emancipation in 1854. See E. Romero, *Historia económica del Perú* (Buenos Aires, 1949), p. 166; W. Stewart, *Chinese Bondage in Peru* (Durham, N.C., 1951), p. 5; F. Romero, "The Slave Trade and the Negro in South America," *Hispanic American Historical Review,* 24:377–78 (1944).

44. R. Mellafe, *La introducción de la esclavitud negra en Chile* (Santiago de Chile, 1959), p. 196.

TABLE 11

ESTIMATED GEOGRAPHICAL DISTRIBUTION OF SLAVE IMPORTS INTO SPANISH AMERICA DURING THE ENTIRE PERIOD OF THE SLAVE TRADE

Based on new calculations or those found in the historical literature	
Cuba	702,000
Puerto Rico	77,000
Mexico	200,000
Venezuela	121,000
Peru	95,000
La Plata and Bolivia	100,000
Chile	6,000
Subtotal	1,301,000
Based on rough estimates	
Santo Domingo	30,000
Colombia, Panama, and Ecuador	200,000
Central America	21,000
Total	1,552,000

Source: See text, pp. 44–47.

of Guayaquil is African. Furthermore, the placer gold mines of western New Granada were worked mainly by African slaves, and the gold camps are known to have had an extremely high ratio of men to women. This implies a very high rate of net natural decrease and thus a high ratio of imports to surviving slave populations. The population of unmixed African descent in New Granada in 1810 is estimated at 72,270, but the proportion of mulattos to the total population was already 50 per cent by 1800. This suggests that the population of African descent contained a high proportion of creoles, which means that it may well have been growing by natural increase. This supposition is further supported by the fact that the Negro population of Colombia has remained at about the same percentage of the total since the latter part of the eighteenth century.[45] Taking the combination

45. T. L. Smith, "The Racial Composition of the Population of Colombia," p. 215.

of high wastage in the mining camps and comparatively early development of natural growth, and having the import estimates for Mexico and Venezuela for comparison, an overall figure of 200,000 for Colombia, Ecuador, and Panama might be a reasonable guess.

This leaves a balance of 21,000 for Central America. The number may be a little high, but it is not drastically out of line with the Mexican figure, with qualitative impressions, or with the later population of African descent. The result of this cross-check of asiento-based estimates against geographical import estimates is therefore quite satisfactory, but it should not breed false confidence. Even the best of the estimates in Table 11 can hardly be expected to be closer to actuality than plus or minus 20 per cent. Those that involve more guesswork can be considered satisfactory if they are within 50 per cent of the actual figure.

The Slave Trade to Brazil

The slave trade to Brazil has received a great deal of attention from historians, but it continues to pose some difficult problems. The Portuguese imperial bureaucracy was not so tightly organized as that of Spain, and the slave trade was not so closely controlled. Archival data are therefore fewer to begin with, and in Brazil they are scattered among the half-dozen principal ports of entry. Since the trade was open to Brazilian as well as Portuguese shipping most of the time, metropolitan sources tend to be weak, though the Portuguese posts in Angola have produced longer time-series of slave exports than any other part of the African coast.

Like the historical work on the slave trade elsewhere, the range of estimates for total Brazilian slave imports is extremely wide, with some of the older and more offhand guesses running as high as 50 million slaves for the whole period of the trade. The passage of time, however, has tended to lower the estimates and finally to bring about substantial agreement. Calógeras, for example, put the total imports at 15 million. Pedro Calmon reduced this to 6–8 million by the time the fifth edition of his

História de civilização brasileira was published.[46] Edward Dunbar paid special attention to the Brazilian trade in making his famous estimates in 1861, and his guess was an overall Brazilian import of 5,750,000.[47] By 1937, Roberto Simonsen had brought the figure down to 3,500,000, and it has stayed in this vicinity ever since, with very few exceptions.[48]

The height of Brazilian slave-trade research and publication, however, came in the 1940's. It began with Luís Vianna Filho's study of the Bahia trade, which dealt not merely with the quantities imported but also with the sources of slaves in Africa. Then came a series of additional contributions, as historians built on the work of others. In 1941, Affonso de E. Taunay brought together a great deal of data then in the literature and made his own general estimate of 3,600,000 slaves imported. This was followed by the work of the Portuguese historian Correia Lopes, with new numerical data from Angolan sources. In 1949, Alfredo Gomes published still another summary, and in 1950 Mauricio Goulart reconsidered the whole body of recent contributions and came to the conclusion that the total number of slaves imported into Brazil was between 3,500,000 and 3,600,000.[49] Nor was this the final word on the slave trade to Brazil. In 1968, Pierre Verger added still more to our detailed knowledge of the Bahian slave trade, this time from an Atlantic rather than a purely American perspective.[50]

46. See A. Gomes, "Achegas para a história do trafico africano no Brasil—Aspectos numéricos," *IV Congresso de Historia Nacional, 21–28 Abril de 1949* (Rio de Janeiro, 1950), pp. 29–30.

47. Dunbar, "Commercial Slavery," p. 240.

48. R. Simonsen, *História econômica do Brasil 1500–1820* (São Paulo, 1937), pp. 196, 208.

49. L. Vianna Filho, "O trabalho do engenho e a reaccão do índio. Establecimento de escravatura africana," *Congresso do Mundo Portugues,* 10:12–29 (1940); A. de E. Taunay, *Subsídios para a história do trafico africano no Brasil* (São Paulo, 1941); E. Correia Lopes, *A escravatura* (Lisbon, 1944); A. Gomes, "Tráfico africano no Brasil"; M. Goulart, *Escravidão africana no Brasil.*

50. P. Verger, *Flux et reflux de la traite des nègres entre le golfe de Benin et Bahia de Todos os Santos du 17ᵉ et 18ᵉ siècles* (The Hague, 1968). A

For present purposes, the figure of 3,646,800 is accepted as the total estimate for the slave trade to Brazil, mainly because it is the sum of the estimates by time period of Mauro and Goulart. It is not necessarily any more accurate than any other estimate in that vicinity, and it may well be higher than the actual figure; but the evidence now available tells little about the amount of downward revision that may be required. Deerr's figure of 3,325,000 is therefore equally possible, though even the discovery of new evidence or more accurate statistical inference is hardly likely to reduce it far below three million.

---

quantitative appendix to this book was published separately as "Mouvement de navires entre Bahia et la Golfe de Benin (xviie–xixe siècles)," *Revue française d'histoire d'outre-mer,* 55:1–36 (1968).

CHAPTER 3

DISTRIBUTION IN SPACE: THE COLONIES OF THE NORTH EUROPEANS

The demographic history of the English, French, Danish, and Dutch colonies in tropical America was markedly different from that of the Spanish and Portuguese. Not that one group were Nordic and Protestant while the other were Latin and Catholic; the crucial difference was a matter of timing. The Spanish and Portuguese experimented with the South Atlantic System for nearly two centuries before the north Europeans began to move into their preserve. When the northerners did move in the early seventeenth century, they found in northeast Brazil a model they could follow. Within a century the Dutch, then the English and French, adopted the model, planted it in the Caribbean, and carried it to new extremes of specialization. They depended almost entirely on Africa for their labor force, and the African laborers were concentrated intensively in one form of enterprise —plantation agriculture, without the diversity provided in Latin America by separate sectors of mining, ranching, or small-scale industry. Even the plantation regime was concentrated on sugar cane, with only small quantities of coffee, cotton, or indigo as a sideline.

This "perfection" of the South Atlantic System in the eighteenth-century Caribbean made that time and that place the core of the system, with Jamaica and Saint Domingue as ideal types of what the System could mean, when carried to the furthest extremes. In this sense, the late-blooming cotton plantations of the southern United States were a pale reflection of the System in its most extreme form, just as the early sugar estates of Santo Domingo or Brazil can be seen, in retrospect at least, as steps toward the kind of society and economy that was to arise in the eighteenth-century Antilles.

The dimensions of the slave trade to the French and British West Indies therefore have a peculiar kind of importance. Historical literature has touched on this area extensively, if in a piecemeal fashion, and, even though the records of the Dutch West India Companies are still to be mined, some estimates are possible.

The British West Indies

Deerr's estimate that the British West Indies imported nearly two million slaves over the whole period of the trade was a consolidation of import estimates for individual colonies or groups of colonies, as shown in Table 12.

Of these totals, Jamaica and Barbados are the most solidly based on archival records, even though neither island preserved a year-by-year record of slave imports for the whole period of the trade. For Jamaica, the principal published record is a report drawn up by Stephen Fuller, the agent for Jamaica in 1778. It gives the annual imports and re-exports of slaves from 1702 through 1775, for a total net import of 353,200 during that

Table 12
Deerr's Slave-Import Estimates for the British West Indies

Jamaica	650,000
Barbados	350,000
Leeward Islands	450,000
Ceded and conquered islands	400,000
Miscellaneous small possessions	50,000
Total	1,900,000

Source: Deerr, *History of Sugar*, 2:281–82.

period. In addition, Bryan Edwards gave the figure of 610,000 for all the slaves imported into Jamaica between 1700 and 1786, which he claimed to be based on actual returns that were in his possession at the time of writing (c. 1790). As a West India merchant and one-time member of the Jamaican House of Assembly, Edwards might well have had access to records of this kind.

These two sets of import figures (from Fuller and Edwards respectively) have been re-examined recently by R. B. Le Page, who added new estimates of Jamaican slave imports in the late seventeenth century.[1] These were based partly on K. G. Davies' work with the records of the Royal African Company, and partly on contemporaneous estimates of the numbers landed by interlopers or private traders. The estimated total import for 1655–1702 came to 88,000—only 7 per cent higher than Deerr's calculations for the period to 1701. From 1702 to 1776, Edwards' and Fuller's figures are not in serious disagreement. Then, from 1776 onward, Le Page used Bryan Edwards' data, supplemented by partial returns and qualitative assessments in the primary literature. He ended with a total estimate of Jamaican net imports at no less than 736,000, nor more than 759,000.[2] On present evidence this is as close as anyone is likely to come to the actual figure, and it is accepted here at 747,500, the mean between Le Page's minimum and maximum. In comparison with other estimates available for Cuba or Brazil, the Jamaican totals are very soundly based. Taken in conjunction with population data, they can be used to assess the probable imports into other Caribbean colonies as well.

The time-series of slave imports for Barbados are similar to those for Jamaica. F. W. Pitman compiled the basic data for 1708–35 and 1747–66 from the treasurer's account of the island preserved in the Public Record Office, London, and these annual

1. Fuller's original report to the Board of Trade, 30 January 1778, is in the Public Record Office, London, C. O. 137/28. See Le Page, "Jamaican Creole," pp. 73, 80–83.

2. Le Page, "Jamaican Creole," p. 74.

figures have been used by most of his successors, including Deerr.[3]

For the late seventeenth century, the records of the Royal African Company are a help, and they show 26,245 slaves delivered to Barbados in the years 1673–89.[4] Something must also be added for the interlopers, English ships which illegally infringed the Company's monopoly of the English slave trade. Their importance is hard to assess, but the Company found that 29 per cent of all English ships landing slaves in the British West Indies during 1679–82 were interlopers. If they held the same share of imports into Barbados alone, and over a somewhat longer period of time, total deliveries to Barbados over 1673–89 would have amounted to 36,700 slaves.[5]

Direct evidence is missing for the Barbados imports of 1690–97 but private slave trade became legal in 1698 and official returns of both Company and private imports to Barbados are available from the end of June 1698 to December 1707. They show 34,583 slaves imported in 9.5 years[6]—or 3,640 a year, allowing an estimate of 36,400 for the ten years 1698–1707. The gap remains in the records for 1690–97, but it can be filled by interpolation. If it is assumed that the annual average import for these years might well have been near the mean of the annual averages for 1673–89 and 1698–1707, the result is an estimated annual import of 2,910, or total Barbados imports for 1690–97 at 23,300 slaves.

A second gap in the Barbados record occurs in the period 1736–46, but this can be filled in a similar manner by taking the mean of the annual averages for the six years immediately preceding and the six years immediately following the period of missing data. The result is an annual average of 2,455, or a total for 1736–46 of 27,000. With these interpolations and projections,

3. F. W. Pitman, *The Development of the British West Indies 1700–1763* (New Haven, 1917), p. 32; Deerr, *History of Sugar,* 2:278, which contains some mistakes in addition, made in the process of consolidating Pitman's data.

4. K. G. Davies, *The Royal African Company* (London, 1957), p. 363.

5. Davies, *Royal African Company,* pp. 113 ff.

6. Davies, *Royal African Company,* p. 143.

TABLE 13

ESTIMATED SLAVE IMPORTS INTO BARBADOS, 1640–1807

Years	Total imported	Annual average
*1640–44	6,500	1,300
*1645–72	56,800	2,030
1673–89	37,000	2,180
1690–97	23,300	2,910
1698–1707	36,400	3,640
1708–29	71,700	3,260
1730–35	13,700	2,280
1736–46	27,000	2,460
1747–52	15,800	2,630
1753–66	46,900	3,350
*1767–1807	51,900	1,270
Total	387,000	2,300

* Projections based on partial data. Other estimates are either recorded figures or interpolations from recorded data.

Sources: Pitman, *British West Indies*, p. 72; Davies, *Royal African Company*, p. 363; plus interpolations. See text, pp. 53–61.

the record of Barbados slave imports is complete for the whole period from 1673 to 1766. (See Table 13.)

For Barbados, this leaves the more serious problems of estimating for the years before 1673, and for those after 1766. Up to 1663, the slave trade to Barbados was practically a Dutch monopoly, and the Dutch records have not yet been investigated. As a result, we have little more than spot estimates, with their expected low level of reliability. In 1663, for example, the Company of Royal Adventurers Trading to Africa was founded. In that and the following year, it managed to deliver about 1,200 slaves a year to Barbados.[7] Another spot estimate suggests an import level of about 1,000 a year in 1645.[8]

7. V. T. Harlow, *A History of Barbados 1625–1685* (Oxford, 1926), p. 313.

8. Harlow, *Barbados*, p. 44.

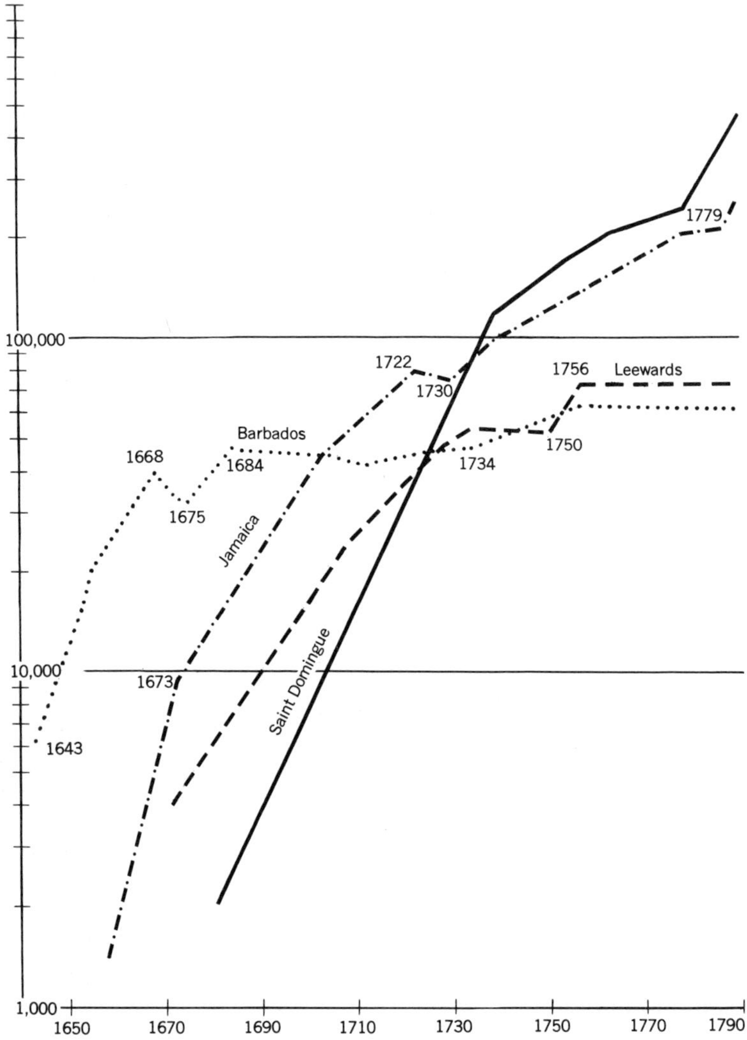

Fig. 2. Slave populations in the Caribbean, 1650–1790. Fig. by UW Cartographic Lab. Data from Tables 14 and 19.

Something more, however, can be done with Barbadian slave population figures and a careful comparison to similar data from Jamaica, combined with Le Page's calculations of Jamaican slave imports before 1701. As Table 14 and Fig. 2 indicate, the slave populations of Barbados and Jamaica rose at a similar rate in the seventeenth century, but Jamaica's development lagged behind that of Barbados by twenty-five to thirty years. Since the serious development of the plantation system in Jamaica began in the late 1660's, while that of Barbados began about 1640, the general course of economic and demographic history in Jamaica over 1673–1702 should be roughly comparable to that of Barbados over 1645–72. The slave imports of Barbados should therefore be calculable by analogy to the later and better known imports into Jamaica.

These calculations, however, are faulted to an uncertain extent by inter-island migration. This problem, indeed, has a bearing on all the calculations of slave imports by region or colony. Slaves were re-exported regularly from the colonies of the major shipping nations, such as Portugal, Britain, or the Netherlands. In addition, planters often moved with their slaves from one colony to another. This pattern was especially prevalent in the first phase of settlement. Jamaica, for example, was first settled from Barbados—not directly from England and Africa. As the fortunes of war transferred Caribbean territory from one country to another, planters tended to move as refugees and often with their slaves. One group of British planters and nearly a thousand slaves, for example, moved from Surinam to Jamaica in 1675.[9] Again, after the American Revolution, loyalists moved to the Bahamas and other parts of the British West Indies, and they brought their slaves with them. In the early nineteenth century, after the British slave trade had legally ended, other British planters moved slaves to the new planting frontiers of Trinidad and British Guiana.

9. Le Page, "Jamaican Creole," p. 17.

It is virtually impossible to allow for these movements, or to be certain of their demographic consequences. While it is known that Barbados was a major center for dispersion to other islands in both the seventeenth and eighteenth centuries, and the size of the movement can sometimes be estimated, its impact on population in the supplying and receiving areas is indeterminate. Barbados, for example, supplied about one-third of all slaves imported into Jamaica between 1655 and 1674, the proportion dropping to a quarter between 1675 and 1688, and then to about 5 per cent between 1689 and 1701.[10] At these rates, about 16,000 slaves moved from the eastern Caribbean to Jamaica between 1655 and 1701. During this same period, Le Page allowed for an estimate of about 4,000 slaves re-exported from Jamaica, mainly to the Spanish possessions.

At first sight, this net import of 12,000 slaves into Jamaica from the eastern Caribbean might seem, for the purpose of estimating Jamaican slave imports, to be no different from importing slaves directly from Africa. If, however, a planter leaving Barbados for Jamaica chose creole slaves, the younger women, and brought roughly equal numbers of men and women, he removed part of Barbados' capacity to renew its population by internal growth and transferred this capacity to Jamaica. This would mean in turn that Jamaica's progress toward "maturity" or self-sufficiency in terms of slave population would be accelerated, while Barbadian progress in the same direction would be retarded. The extent to which planters removed "seasoned" and creole slaves from Barbados is unknown—hence the indeterminacy.

In spite of this uncertainty, the recorded slave population of Jamaica can be combined with Le Page's estimates of Jamaican slave imports to calculate the annual rate of net natural decrease among Jamaican slaves over the period 1673–1702 as 6.7 per cent.[11] If the assumption of demographic similarity between

10. Patterson, *Sociology of Slavery,* pp. 134–35.

11. The Jamaican population increased from 9,500 in 1673 to 45,000 in 1703 (the date of census on estimate being assumed to be January 1st in both cases, and population totals rounded to the nearest hundred). Follow-

TABLE 14

REPORTED SLAVE POPULATIONS OF BARBADOS, JAMAICA, AND THE BRITISH LEEWARD ISLANDS

Barbados		Jamaica		Leeward Islands	
1643	6,000	*1658*	1,400	*1672*	4,200
1645	5,700	*1673*	9,500	*1707*	23,000
1655	20,000	*1703*	45,000	*1720*	36,000
1668	40,000	*1722*	80,000	*1729*	48,600
1673	33,200	*1730*	74,500	*1734*	54,200
1675	32,500	*1734*	86,500	*1756*	70,600
1680	38,400	*1739*	99,200	*1774*	81,300
1684	46,500	*1746*	112,400	*1787*	73,900
1712	42,000	*1754*	130,000	*1807*	73,800
1734	46,400	*1762*	146,500	*1834*	51,300
1757	63,600	*1768*	166,900		
1786	62,100	*1775*	190,000		
1792	64,300	*1778*	205,300		
1809	69,400	*1787*	210,900		
1834	82,000	*1789*	250,000		
		1808	324,000		

Sources: Deerr, *History of Sugar*, 2:278–79; Harlow, *Barbados*, p. 339; Roberts, *Population of Jamaica*, p. 36; Le Page, "Jamaican Creole," p. 74; B. Edwards, *West Indies*, 1:224.

Jamaica of 1673–1702 and Barbados of 1645–72 is valid, then Barbados should have had a similar rate of net natural decrease. In fact, Barbadian population rose from 5,700 in 1645 to 33,200 in 1673, an annual growth rate of 6.3 per cent. To sustain this rate in the face of a net natural decrease of 6.7 per cent per year would have required slave imports totalling 56,800 over 1645–72, an annual average of 2,030.

---

ing the formula used in Ch. 2 in connection with Cuban-Puerto Rican comparisons, the annual rate of growth was about 5.2 per cent. During this same period, Jamaican slave imports were an estimated 81,500—a total made up of Le Page's estimate of 80,000 for 1674–1701, plus recorded net imports of 516 for 1702 and a guess at 1,000 for 1673. ("Jamaican Creole," pp. 70–71, 80.) Following these same formulae, the annual rate of immigration in Jamaica was 11.9 per cent and the rate of annual net natural decrease was 6.7 per cent.

The period before 1645 is harder to deal with. While it is possible to calculate the number of imports required each year to meet a given rate of net natural decrease, the rate of net natural decrease for a slave population in its initial years is not known. One solution is simply to guess that the number of slaves required to produce a slave population of 5,700 by 1645 would be slightly higher than the size of the population—say 6,500.

The other problem period for the slave trade to Barbados comes after 1766, when the island's demographic pattern was altogether different. By that time, Barbados was a maturing plantation society where slave population was no longer increasing and slave imports were necessary only to offset the natural decrease. Barbadian slave population reached one plateau of stability from the 1680's into the 1730's. Then, after further increase, slave population again stabilized from the 1750's until well into the nineteenth century.[12] As time passed, the proportion of African-born decreased, the sex ratio lowered toward an equality of men to women, and the excess of deaths over births diminished. By about 1805–10, Barbados reached a point where births and deaths were nearly equal.[13]

Though the demographic pattern is clear enough, no continuous record of slave imports has been published for the period after 1766—neither for Barbados nor for an equivalent phase in the demographic life of any other sugar colony. A number of ways remain for estimating Barbados' slave imports of 1766 to 1807 from the scattered data that exist. One solution, though not an acceptable one, was attempted by Deerr, who simply assumed that the annual average slave imports would continue throughout the eighteenth century at the levels current in mid-century. This method gave Deerr an estimate of 74,000, which is certainly far too high.

Another method is to use the recorded imports, even though

12. Pitman, *British West Indies*, p. 373, indicates a slave population of 69,870 in 1753 and a Negro population of 69,132 in 1812.

13. Roberts, *Population of Jamaica*, pp. 40–41; Lowenthal, "Population of Barbados"; Harlow, *Barbados*, p. 339.

these records exist for only seven out of the forty-one years between 1767 and the abolition of the trade in 1807. These show an annual average of 362 for 1784–88 and 1,022 for 1802–3.[14] If the general annual average of these years is applied to the whole period 1767–1807, the result would be an estimate of 22,600—surely far too low.

A third possibility is to interpolate from the seven known years in order to find estimates for the missing periods, 1767–83, 1789–1801, and 1804–7. If the annual average for each unknown period is taken to be the mean of the annual averages of adjacent known periods, if the annual average for 1736–66 is taken as a base line representative of the mid-eighteenth century, and if the annual average for 1802–3 is continued through 1807, this method yields an estimate of 44,500 for the whole of 1767–1807.

Finally, it could simply be assumed that slave imports fell from their mid-century level of 2,890 for 1736–66 to zero by 1807, in a flat curve. On this assumption, the annual average for the whole of 1767–1807 would be half of the base for 1736–66, or 1,445, and the total imports for 1767–1807 would be 59,200. There is little to choose between these last two estimates, but the figure of 54,000 can be accepted as a reasonable compromise.

For the Leeward Islands—Antigua, Montserrat, St. Kitts, and Nevis—the slave import records are even more scarce and uncertain than they are for Barbados. Import records for the four major islands are available for less than twenty years out of more than a century and a half during which they imported slaves. Deerr's solution was to compare the slave population of the Leewards with those of Barbados in 1734 and 1757.[15] Since the slave population of the Leewards was higher than that of Barbados, he guessed that the slave imports must also have been larger. But this was not necessarily the case: as Fig. 2 indicates, the slave population of the Leewards came in time to exceed that of Barbados, but the Leewards' period of rapid initial growth

14. Deerr, *History of Sugar*, 2:278.
15. Deerr, *History of Sugar*, 2:281.

TABLE 15

LEEWARD ISLANDS: ESTIMATED SLAVE IMPORTS AND RATES OF GROWTH AMONG THE SLAVE POPULATION

Years	Slaves imported	Annual average	Annual growth rate of slave population (%)	Assumed annual rate of net natural decrease (%)	Precedent
To 1671	7,000	—	—	—	—
1672–1706	44,800	1,280	4.9	6.7	Jamaica (1673–1702)
1707–33	43,100	1,600	3.2	1.2	Jamaica (1703–24)
1734–1807	251,100	3,440	0.4	5.0	Barbados (1684–1756)
Total	346,000	2,490 (1672–1807)			

Sources: Based on data from Tables 13 and 14; Le Page, "Jamaican Creole," pp. 70–71. See text, pp. 61–64.

lagged behind that of Barbados by about forty years. The Leewards therefore passed through a shorter period of sustained slave imports.

A more carefully constructed estimate of slave imports into the Leeward Islands can be made by taking one period at a time. But the period before the 1670's eludes all calculation. The Dutch were dominant at sea in the Caribbean and the principal carriers of the slave trade. Therefore, English or French shipping records are no use. In addition, the Leeward Islands were partly occupied by the French and partly by the English, and the European metropolis shifted frequently through wartime capture. The only possibility is a sheer guess, that it might well have taken 7,000 slaves or so under these conditions to arrive at a slave population of 3,200 by 1672.

The next phase of development, 1672–1706, is similar to the initial phase of development in Jamaica in both timing and rate of growth among the slave population. The Jamaican data for 1673–1702, already used for Barbadian calculations, again seem to be appropriate. Between 1672 and 1707, the slave population of the Leewards increased from 4,200 to 23,000, an annual rate of 4.9 per cent. If net natural decrease were at the Jamaican rate of 6.7 per cent per annum, 44,800 slaves would have been required during the period 1672–1706. After 1707, slave population in the Leewards grew more slowly, but the change ran parallel to a slower rate of growth and predictable decline in the rate of natural decrease on Jamaica as well. The development of the Leewards over 1707–33 thus appears similar to the Jamaican pattern of 1703–21, when the annual increase was only 3.0 per cent and the natural decrease dropped to 1.2 per cent per year. If this same rate of natural decrease is assumed for the Leewards over 1707–33, the number of slaves needed to produce the actual growth rate of 3.2 per cent would have been 43,100, or 1,600 per annum.

The 1730's mark a sharp change in the growth pattern of the Leewards' slave population. The islands then entered a period of comparative stability, similar to the Barbadian pattern of the 1680's onward. In fact, the growth rate of the Leewards over the 74 years 1734–1807 was 0.4 per cent per annum, exactly the same rate as that of Barbados over an equivalent period from 1684 to 1756. Though the slave population in Barbados was now increasing rapidly, the period was marked by a substantial rate of natural decrease, as slaves brought in during the period of rapid growth began to age and die without leaving equivalent numbers of children to take their places. If the Barbadian rate of decrease at 5.0 per cent per year is applied to the Leewards for the period 1734–1807, the number of slaves required to produce the actual population of 1808 would have been 251,100 or an annual average of 3,440.

These estimates, summarized in Table 15, are reasonably consonant with the recorded slave imports into the Leeward Islands. In 1674–86, for example, the Royal African Company delivered an annual average of 552.[16] Since interlopers are thought to have

16. C. S. S. Higham, *The Development of the Leeward Islands under the Restoration, 1660–1688* (Cambridge, 1921), p. 154.

done about the same, the implied level of 1,100 slaves a year is as close as might be expected to the calculated level of 1,280. Slave imports for the major islands of the Leeward group are again recorded for most of the 1720's, and the general annual average was 3,010. This figure, twice the calculated annual average of 1,600 for the period 1707–33, seems at first sight to contradict the calculation, but the two are actually in reasonable agreement. The form of calculation is consciously made over a long term of years in order to avoid the great short-run variation of slave imports into any part of the Caribbean. In estimating 1,600 slaves a year over 1707–33, followed by 3,440 slaves a year over 1734–1807, there is no implication that the rate of imports jumped sharply in the mid-1730's. If the Leewards followed the demographic trend of Barbados, imports should have been climbing during the 1720's to a peak in perhaps the 1760's or 1770's, after which they would have dropped gradually. This expectation is further borne out by Pitman's estimate of 3,750 slaves a year imported between 1720 and 1755;[17] it should be higher than the long-term figure of 3,440 a year from 1734 to 1807, and it is.

Deerr's category of "ceded and conquered islands" is a mixed bag of small islands whose only common characteristic may be their demographic diversity. St. Vincent, St. Lucia, Dominica, and Tobago were known together in the early eighteenth century as the "neutral islands," but even this was a misnomer. They were never neutral in wartime—only "neutral" in the fact that neither England nor France formally laid claim to them during the first half of the century. Even then, Dominica and St. Vincent were thought to belong to the Carib Amerindians, while St. Lucia and Tobago had a mixed and shifting population of escaped slaves, French or English settlers, woodcutters, and other transients. By this time, the Caribs had survived their initial exposure to European disease. Many had intermarried with shipwrecked Africans to produce the Black Caribs, who numbered

17. Pitman, *British West Indies,* pp. 76–77.

TABLE 16

REPORTED SLAVE POPULATIONS OF THE SMALLER TERRITORIES IN THE BRITISH WEST INDIES

Grenada		St. Vincent		Dominica		Trinidad		Tobago	
1700	500	*1763*	3,400	*1763*	5,900	*1797*	10,000	*1776*	10,800
1753	12,000	*1764*	7,400	*1766*	8,500	*1800*	15,800	*1787*	10,500
1771	26,200	*1787*	11,900	*1773*	18,800	*1802*	19,700	*1805*	14,900
1779	35,000	*1805*	16,500	*1780*	12,700	*1811*	21,100	*1834*	11,600
1785	23,900	*1834*	22,300	*1787*	15,000	*1834*	20,700		
1788	26,800			*1805*	22,100				
1834	23,600			*1834*	14,200				

St. Lucia		Virgin Islands		Bermuda		Bahamas		British Honduras	
1776	10,800	*1756*	6,100	*1773*	2,200	*1787*	2,200	*1834*	1,900
1834	13,300	*1787*	9,000	*1787*	4,900	*1834*	10,100		
		1834	5,100	*1834*	4,000				

Sources: Deerr, *History of Sugar*, 2:279; Edwards, *West Indies*, 1:376, 460, 462, 470; 2:2; A. Burns, *History of the British West Indies* (London, 1954), p. 629. In cases of conflicting data, Edwards and Burns have been preferred to Deerr. Data for 1834 are slave compensation figures at the time of emancipation.

about one thousand on St. Vincent in the mid-eighteenth century. European settlement, though not the establishment of numerous plantations, had long since been common on both Tobago and Dominica—and the settlers, mostly French, took some slaves with them. Up to 1750, however, the population of African descent must have been small. As a practical matter, it can be taken as already incorporated in the import estimates for Martinique and Barbados, the mutually antagonistic bases for European activity in the neutral islands.[18]

When England acquired the four neutral islands in 1763, they and Grenada came to be known as the "ceded islands," though Grenada's earlier history had been quite different. Unlike the others, Grenada had been a "sugar island" of sorts, with a

18. See R. Pares, *War and Trade in the West Indies, 1739–1763* (Oxford, 1936), pp. 194–216; Edwards, *West Indies*, 1:351–419.

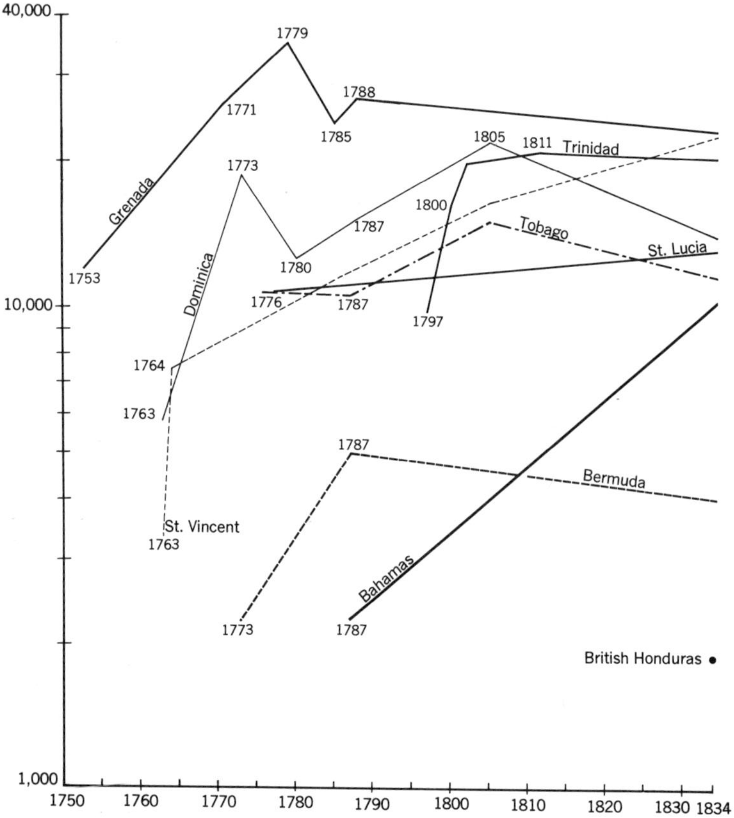

Fig. 3. Slave populations of the smaller British West Indian colonies. Fig. by UW Cartographic Lab. Data from Table 16.

significant slave population reported at almost 12,000 in 1750. Its economy reached a peak of activity in the 1770's and then began to decline.[19]

Trinidad is still another exception. After remaining a half-forgotten corner of the Spanish empire until nearly the end of the eighteenth century, it was captured by the British in 1797 and annexed in 1802. With that, it entered into the main stream of

19. Edwards, *West Indies,* 1:379–80.

the South Atlantic System for the first time, with a small planting boom and a consequent rise in slave population.

For all six of these islands, data are so scarce in the published literature that estimates of slave imports before the eighteenth century are virtually impossible. Estimates for this early period may also be unnecessary. Without a high ratio of slave imports to total population, the assumption of a net natural decrease is improbable, and these populations were all small in any case. They also responded very drastically to political changes. As Fig. 3 indicates, the slave populations of St. Vincent and Dominica went up extremely rapidly after British annexation in 1763. It was a simple matter to move slaves over from nearby British colonies to take advantage of the newly acquired territory. This is why it is safer to ignore the initial black population of the four neutral islands on the assumption that they and their ancestors have already been counted as immigrants into one of the other colonies in the eastern Caribbean.

This provides a base population of about 20,000 for the four neutral islands at the time of their annexation in 1763. It also presents another example of the double-counting problem, since many of the slaves imported both before and after 1763 were surely re-exported from another colony. The most likely source was Barbados, and this is precisely the period, from the 1760's onward, for which Barbadian slave import and export records are lacking.

If my suspicion is correct, that many of the slaves imported into the neutral islands before 1763 were actually re-exported from Barbados, then the rate of net natural decrease calculated for Barbados in that period actually represents an excess of deaths *plus* emigrants over births. This weakness would not affect the import estimates for Barbados, but it would tend to inflate those for the Leeward Islands which are partly based on Barbadian records for 1684–1756. The Leeward Island estimates are nevertheless left as they are, on the assumption that re-exports from Barbados were not large—but with a warning as well. The problem of double counting recurs in many other and

TABLE 17

POSSIBLE SLAVE IMPORTS INTO THE WINDWARD ISLANDS, TRINIDAD, AND TOBAGO

The "neutral islands"*		
All four islands, 1763–79	32,100	
Dominica, 1780–1807	8,000	
St. Lucia, St. Vincent, & Tobago, 1780–1807	30,000	
Total, 1763–1807		70,100
Grenada		
To 1752	10,000	
1753–78	39,700	
1779–84	nil	
1785–1807	17,300	
Total to 1807		67,000
Trinidad		
To 1796	10,000	
1797–1807	12,400	
Total to 1807		22,400
Total, all islands		159,500

* Dominica, St. Lucia, St. Vincent, Tobago.
Source: Population data from Table 16. See text, pp. 64–71, and Fig. 3.

unpredictable ways. The rush of slaves into Trinidad after its capture by Britain, for example, may have come in large measure from other islands. Among the ceded islands themselves, the opportunities for transferring slaves from one island to another were so great that little more than a word of warning is possible.

The population history of Dominica, Tobago, St. Lucia, and St. Vincent has a remarkably similar character from the 1780's to 1834 (see Fig. 3), but slave-import estimates are more seriously damaged by sheer lack of data, or even reasonable analogies, than they are by the double-counting problem. They can hardly be more than a guess, though the guess can be made more acceptable by taking account of the recorded rates of population growth and some possible rate of net natural decrease. The slave population of the four neutral islands, for example, increased from about 20,000 in 1763 to about 42,000 in 1780. This represents an annual increase at the rate of 4.4 per cent. A rate of net natural decrease at 2 per cent a year is at least possible in the light of rapid population growth, and at this rate it would have required 32,100 slaves imported to produce the population level of 1780. But this kind of calculation must be understood to have a much lower probable accuracy than the similar calculations made in the cases of Barbados, the Leewards, or Puerto Rico. The neutral islands were only on the fringes of the plantation regime. An assumed net natural decrease at 2 per cent is only a median between possibilities as high as 4 per cent and as low as zero.

In certain cases, calculation from demographic analogy has no meaning at all. On Dominica, for example, the population shifted irregularly, as might be expected from the fact that its principal economic function in the late eighteenth century was to act as an entrepôt for the illicit British slave trade to Guadeloupe and Martinique. The high population figure for 1805, therefore, is likely to reflect the disturbed wartime conditions on the two neighboring islands and have nothing at all to do with the net number of immigrants. Dominica may have had a self-sustaining population of permanently resident slaves from as early as the 1770's, or it might have added more than 10,000 between 1780 and 1807. A guess of 8,000 as the net imports of that period fills a blank space with a possible figure, but that is all.

The other three neutral islands show a more even rate of growth in the slave population between 1780 and 1807. St. Lucia grew at only 0.4 per cent per year from 1776–1834, which could have been mainly natural increase or could represent a more rapid increase in the slave population to about 1808, followed by a decline. St. Vincent and Tobago increased more rapidly and at nearly the same rate in the two islands, their combined slave populations rising from about 21,000 in 1780 to about 33,000 in

1808. This increase represents a growth rate of 1.6 per cent per year, hardly possible in conditions of that period by natural increase alone. Still, the slave populations of the three islands *could* have increased by taking re-exports from other islands like Barbados. In this case, their net imports from Africa would have to be counted as zero. Or, with other assumptions, they might have imported slaves continuously from Africa and sustained a net natural decrease as high as 5 per cent per year. In this case, their net imports from Africa over the period 1780–1807 *could* have been as high as 50,000. A guess at 30,000 simply marks a point within this range of uncertainty.

Grenada, though more closely integrated with the plantation system, is almost as difficult a case when it comes to accurate estimates of the number of slaves imported. Census data are available quite frequently between 1753 and 1788, but not for other periods. (See Table 16 and Fig. 3.) One problem is to account for the numbers required to produce about 12,000 slaves in 1753. A large proportion of these were simply re-exports from Martinique and Guadeloupe. Virtually all imports might have been through such indirect channels. At least 15,000 slaves would probably have been needed, whatever the source, and perhaps 10,000 of these can be counted as coming directly from Africa.

The period of sustained growth from 1753 to 1779 is easier to deal with. The slave population grew at the rate of 4.1 per cent a year, a rate close to the pattern on other sugar islands. Precedent suggests that a rate of net natural decrease might have been in the neighborhood of 3 per cent per year. At that rate, the number of immigrants needed to achieve the population of 35,000 by 1779 would have been 39,700. But from 1779 through 1784, slave imports must have been negligible. Then from 1785, the Grenadine population appears to have been relatively stable at about 25,000 slaves. If the assumed rate of net natural decrease is continued at 3 per cent per annum, the immigration necessary to sustain the population would also be stable at about 750 slaves a year, or 17,300 over the period 1785–1807.

TABLE 18

REVISED ESTIMATES OF SLAVE IMPORTS INTO THE BRITISH WEST INDIES

Region	Deerr	Revised
Jamaica	650,000	747,500
Barbados	350,000	387,000
Leeward Islands	450,000	346,000
Ceded and conquered islands	400,000	159,500
Miscellaneous small possessions	50,000	25,000
Total	1,900,000	1,665,000

Sources: Deerr, *History of Sugar*, 2:281–82; Le Page, "Jamaican Creole," p. 74; Tables 13, 15, 17.

Trinidad is the final anomaly in this group. Its population spurted very rapidly after British seizure in 1797, jumping from about 10,000 to about 20,000 in 1808. The growth rate over these 11 years was therefore 6.3 per cent a year and the newly imported slaves must have had a net natural decrease even higher than the 2 per cent assumed in other calculations. On the other hand, the existing slave population can be taken as at least self-sustaining and perhaps growing naturally at a slow rate. Thus, while a net natural decrease of at least 3 per cent per year was possible for the newly arrived, only 1.5 per cent per year is a likely mean for the whole of the Trinidadian slave population. The number of newly imported slaves required to raise the slave population to 20,000 in 1808 would therefore be about 12,400 over 1797–1807. Trinidadian slave imports over the whole period of the trade can therefore be set at 23,300 on the assumption that 10,000 imported at a slow rate during the Spanish period would be sufficient to produce a population of that size by 1797.

Deerr also allowed 50,000 for "miscellaneous small possessions," mentioning specifically the Bahamas, Bermuda, and British Honduras (British Guiana being estimated along with Surinam). This is very generous indeed, since these colonies and the British Virgin Islands were almost entirely non-planting areas and therefore lacked the intense economic push that would bring in large drafts of slaves and consequent natural decrease. Indeed, the total slave imports over the whole period of the trade would probably not exceed the slave population remaining when the trade ended. Given the fact that all four colonies together were paid slave compensation for only 21,148 slaves at the time of emancipation, an allowance of 25,000 slaves imported seems sufficient. The revision of Deerr's estimates for the British West Indies is therefore as shown in Table 18.

The United States

Slave imports into the United States pose fewer problems than those of the West Indies. Historical statistics are better than those for most other American territories. The regular decennial census began in 1791, and the Bureau of the Census has assembled and published a useful compendium of earlier data.[20] Partly as a result, historians of the United States have tended to be in substantial agreement as to the number of slaves imported in the seventeenth and eighteenth centuries, and this consensus goes back more than a century. George Bancroft in 1840 guessed at 530,000 slaves imported up to the American Revolution. As early as 1853, H. C. Carey published a book-length study of the North American slave trade, in which he estimated some 263,500 as the number of slaves imported into the thirteen colonies by 1790, and more recent authorities still place the total slave imports for that period in the range of 250,000 to 300,000.[21] The mean of this range can therefore be taken as reasonably accurate, and Carey's further estimate of 70,000 for the period 1791–1807 would complete the period of the legal slave trade at a total in the vicinity of 345,000.[22]

20. United States, Bureau of the Census, *Historical Statistics of the United States, Colonial Times to 1957* (Washington, 1960).

21. For a review of the earlier estimates see L. C. Gray, *History of Agriculture in the Southern United States to 1860* (2 vols., Washington, 1933). See also H. C. Carey, *The Slave Trade, Domestic and Foreign* (Philadelphia, 1872; first published 1853), p. 18; J. Potter, "The Growth of Population in America, 1700–1860," in D. V. Glass and D. E. C. Eversley, eds., *Population in History: Essays in Historical Demography* (Chicago, 1965), p. 641.

22. Carey, *The Slave Trade*, p. 18.

By contrast, Deerr's estimates for the thirteen colonies are very much higher than this. He paid no attention to the American historians, working instead by analogy to the slave imports into Jamaica and Saint Domingue. Since the slave population of the United States in 1789 was roughly equal to the combined slave populations of the two Caribbean territories, he assumed that North American imports must have been equivalent. He therefore came to an estimate of 1,500,000, rather than 275,000. Deerr was clearly wrong in this case. His error serves to underline the fact that slave population data can sometimes be a very bad indicator of the numbers imported, and it points up one of the most striking contrasts in New-World demographic history.

Rather than sustaining the regular excess of deaths over births typical of tropical America, the North American colonies developed a pattern of natural growth among the slaves. It is hard to know how early this pattern appeared, but it was certainly present by the early eighteenth century—at least outside South Carolina. By the end of the eighteenth century, North American slave populations were growing at nearly the same rate as that of the settler populations from Europe. By the early nineteenth century, Humboldt noticed this contrast to the Caribbean pattern, and other demographers have occasionally remarked on it.[23] It is therefore all the more curious that historians have neglected it almost completely, even though it has an obvious and important bearing on such recent historical problems as the comparative history of slavery in the New World. Nor have demographic historians yet produced a complete or satisfactory explanation of the phenomenon.

Historians disagree about the extent of the slave trade to the United States after 1808. From the formal abolition of the trade to the beginning of the Civil War in 1861, it is certain that *some* slaves were imported. Anti-slave-trade legislation was very badly enforced, and some historians have argued that non-enforcement automatically implied a high level of imports. W. E. B. Du Bois

23. Humboldt, *Equinoctial Regions,* 7:150–52; Kuczynski, *Population Movements,* p. 15.

estimated a total import of 250,000 during this period, and others have suggested a figure around 270,000.[24] Deerr, on the other hand, placed the figure at 1,000,000,[25] which is impossibly high, and the direction of recent scholarship has been to reduce the estimate even below the level of the Du Bois figure. It appears that historians in the past have been deceived by the large number of slave ships outfitted in American ports. The ships were certainly built, and they certainly carried slaves, but they were more likely to take them to Cuba or Brazil than to the United States. Warren S. Howard's study of *American Slavery and the Federal Law* (1963) points out that rumors of slave landings were often false. For the 1850's, indeed, the shipping available was simply not enough to carry the number of slaves found in the older estimates.[26] Other historians have argued that a high and regular import of slaves would surely have been noticed—that abolitionists would have called attention to an obvious or substantial number of Africans working American plantations. This kind of evidence has simply not come to light, and Potter's demographic survey (1965) concluded that, whatever the number of illegal imports during this period, it was too small to influence the demography of the Afro-American population.[27] Since many more men than women were shipped from Africa in the illegal slave trade, substantial imports would have influenced the sex ratio of the North American slave population. Yet, the census of 1861 actually shows the number of Negro women slightly exceeding the number of Negro men in the United States.

The evidence seems strong enough to reduce the older estimates drastically, but by how much? Only a shot in the dark is possible: a figure of perhaps 1,000 a year is not unreasonable,

24. Gray, *History of Agriculture,* 2:648–49.

25. Deerr, *History of Sugar,* 2:282.

26. W. S. Howard, *American Slavers and the Federal Law, 1837–1862* (Berkeley, 1963), esp. pp. 142–54, 255–57; P. Duignan and C. Clendenen, *The United States and the African Slave Trade 1619–1862* (Stanford, 1963), pp. 19, 36.

27. Potter, "Population in America, 1700–1860," p. 30.

including the slave trade to Texas before it joined the union. This would give a total estimate of 54,000 for 1808–61, and the total estimate for slave imports into English North America (still excluding Louisiana in the French and Spanish periods) would therefore be 399,000.

The French West Indies

For the French West Indies, even the partial and sometimes dubious import data of the kind available for Barbados and Jamaica are not found in the historical literature. They may be available in the archives, but, even if they were, they would be suspect. At most periods, the slave trade to the French Antilles was supposed to be reserved to French shipping. In fact, the French slave trade rarely met the demands of the French islands, and the deficit was made up illegally by buying slaves from the North Americans, British, Danes, and Dutch. On the other hand, the French administration called for relatively frequent reports of slave population. These records have nothing like the accuracy of a modern census, but they provide a useful clue to the possible movement of the slave trade. (See Table 19 and Fig. 4.)

The most important of the French colonies was Saint Domingue, and Saint Domingue in the 1780's was perhaps the pinnacle of achievement for the South Atlantic System as a whole. It was then regarded as one of the most valuable of all the European overseas colonies, and the slave imports for 1788–89 are reported at an annual average of 30,172,[28] which must have been between one-third and one-half of the entire Atlantic slave trade of those years.

The closest parallel to the general course of development in Saint Domingue was the neighboring island of Jamaica. The striking similarity in growth rate is clearly shown on Fig. 4 but the parallel extends broadly to the whole social and economic history of the two colonies in the eighteenth century. Deerr therefore based his estimated slave imports for Saint Domingue

28. Deerr, *History of Sugar*, 2:280.

directly on those for Jamaica. Since the plantation regime in Saint Domingue was abruptly cut off by the great slave revolt late in 1791, he assumed that the slave populations of the two

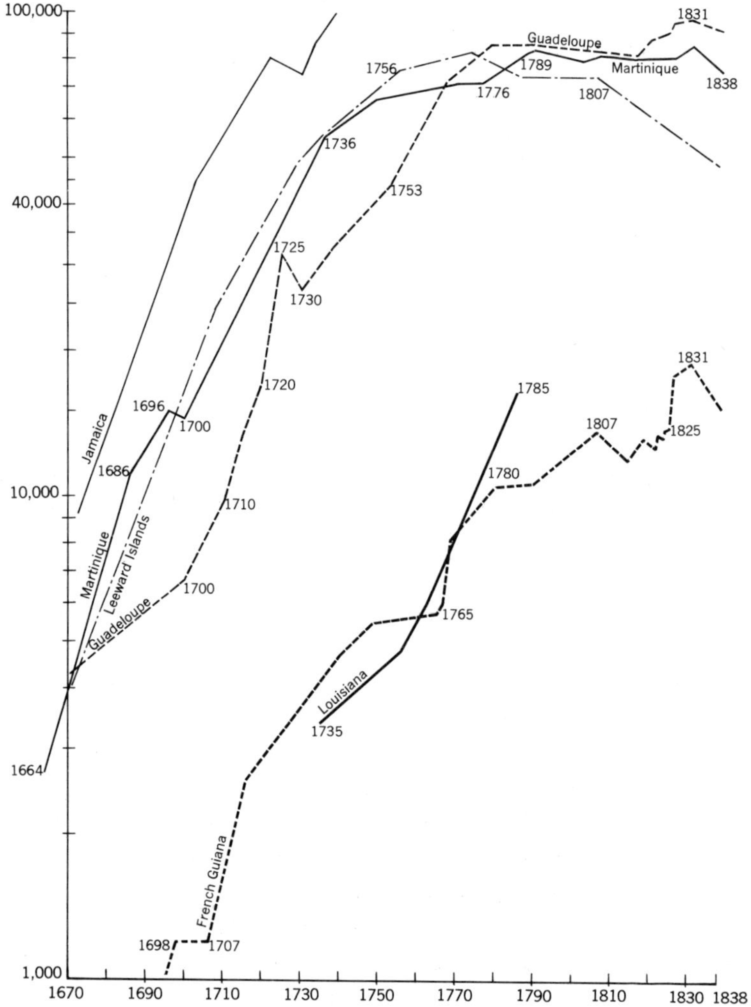

Fig. 4. Slave populations of the French West Indies, 1670–1838. Fig. by UW Cartographic Lab. Data from Table 19.

islands as of 1789 would be proportional to the total slave imports. This yielded an estimate of 820,000 slaves imported into Saint Domingue during the whole period of the slave trade.[29] This figure, however, was based on Deerr's estimate of Jamaican slave imports—a lower figure than the more thorough estimate made by Le Page, which has been used here. If, indeed, Deerr's method of calculation is applied to Le Page's data for Jamaica, the estimate would be more than 1,000,000.

But Jamaica also differed from Saint Domingue: Jamaican development began about twenty years before that of Saint Domingue, and Saint Domingue grew at a considerably faster rate than Jamaica did. Deerr's estimate can therefore be revised by a more careful examination of the parallels between the two islands. As Fig. 4 indicates, the growth of slave population on Saint Domingue falls into three distinct phases—rapid growth from about 1680 to 1739, slower growth (parallel to the rates prevalent on Jamaica) from 1739 to 1778, then very rapid growth during the 1780's. If the annual rate of growth in each of these three periods is taken in conjunction with the rate of annual net natural decrease in Jamaica at an equivalent period in that island's development, it is possible to calculate the number of slave imports necessary to produce the reported increases in slave population.[30] (See Table 20.) The result is within striking distance of Deerr's estimate, and the annual average of 26,100 for 1779–90 is consonant with the reported import rate of about 30,000 in 1788–89, since imports were concentrated in the peacetime years after 1783.

A similar technique can be used to estimate the slave imports into the smaller French colonies, though with a good deal less confidence. As Fig. 4 indicates, the general pattern of growth on both Martinique and Guadeloupe was vaguely similar to that of

29. Deerr, *History of Sugar,* 2:282.

30. The Jamaican data used for making these calculations were taken from Le Page, "Jamaican Creole," pp. 74 and 81, and the population data for Saint Domingue are those compiled in Table 19. The figure for slave imports into Saint Domingue through 1680 is sheer guesswork.

Table 19

Slave Populations of the French Caribbean

Martinique		Guadeloupe		French Guiana		Saint Domingue		Louisiana	
1664	2,700	1671	4,300	1695	1,000	1681	2,000	1735	3,400
1686	11,100	1700	6,700	1698	1,400	1739	117,400	1756	4,700
1696	15,000	1710	9,700	1707	1,400	1754	172,200	1763	6,000
1700	14,600	1715	13,300	1716	2,500	1764	206,000	1785	16,500
1736	55,700	1720	17,200	1740	4,700	1777	240,000		
1751	65,900	1725	31,500	1749	5,500	1779	249,100		
1767	70,600	1730	26,800	1765	5,700	1789	452,000		
1770	71,100	1739	33,400	1769	8,000	1791	480,000		
1776	71,300	1753	40,400	1780	10,500				
1784	78,600	1767	71,800	1789	10,700				
1788	83,400	1772	78,000	1807	13,500				
1789	83,400	1774	80,000	1814	12,100				
1790	84,000	1777	84,100	1819	13,300				
1802	79,800	1779	85,300	1820	13,200				
1807	81,700	1788	85,500	1821	12,800				
1816	80,800	1816	81,700	1822	13,500				
1826	81,100	1817	81,200	1823	13,200				
1831	86,300	1818	82,300	1824	13,700				
1832	82,900	1819	85,400	1825	14,000				
1833	79,800	1820	88,400	1826	18,200				
1834	78,200	1821	88,000	1827	18,900				
1835	78,100	1822	89,500	1831	19,100				
1836	77,500	1823	90,400	1832	18,200				
1837	76,000	1824	91,400	1833	17,600				
1838	76,500	1826	96,400	1834	17,100				
		1831	97,300	1835	16,900				
		1832	99,500	1836	16,600				
		1833	99,000	1837	16,100				
		1834	96,700	1838	15,800				
		1835	96,300						
		1836	95,600						
		1837	94,600						
		1838	93,300						

Sources: A. Moreau de Jonnès, *Recherches statistiques sur l'esclavage colonial et sur les moyens de le supprimer* (Paris, 1842); Deerr, *History of Sugar*, 2:281; L. Peytraud, *L'Esclavage aux Antilles françaises avant 1789* (Paris, 1897), p. 136; M. L. E. Moreau de Saint-Méry, *Description . . . de la partie française de l'isle Saint-Domingue*, 3 vols. (Paris, 1958), 1:28; Gray, *History of Agriculture*, 1:335.

TABLE 20

ESTIMATED SLAVE IMPORTS INTO SAINT DOMINGUE TO 1791

				Calculation based on Jamaican precedent	
Years	Slaves imported	Annual average	Growth rate of slave population (%)	Period	Rate of natural decrease (%)
*To 1680	4,000	—	—	—	—
1681–1738	204,800	3,530	7.0	1673–1729	5.4
1739–88	317,300	7,930	2.0	1739–74	2.6
1779–90	313,200	26,100	5.5	1776–1807	1.9
*1791	25,000	—	—	—	—
Total	864,300				

* Estimate.

Sources: Saint Domingue population data from Table 19. Jamaican rates of net natural decrease calculated from data of Le Page, "Jamaican Creole," pp. 74, 81. See text, Ch. 2, fn. 26, and pp. 75–77.

the Leeward Islands, but French Guiana followed curious spurts and pauses peculiar to itself. Louisiana also went its own way, and apparently stopped importing slaves after about 1778. Guadeloupe, Martinique, and French Guiana, on the other hand, continued to import slaves well into the nineteenth century. Deerr's solution—that of making a rough comparison of the combined slave populations of Guadeloupe and Martinique to that of Barbados in 1789—is therefore bound to be very rough indeed. It yielded an estimate of 720,000 slaves imported by the two French islands during the whole period of the slave trade. A similar rough estimate can be derived from the closer analogy to the Leeward Islands. If the Leewards imported an estimated 346,000 slaves up to 1807, Guadeloupe and Martinique together might well have taken twice that number—say, 692,000 up to 1807 and another 50,000 or so after the end of the Napoleonic Wars. A range of rough estimates therefore seems to lie between about 690,000 and 720,000.

TABLE 21

ESTIMATED SLAVE IMPORTS INTO MARTINIQUE AND GUADELOUPE

Colony and period	Slaves imported	Annual average	Growth rate of slave population (%)	Assumed rate of net natural decrease (%)	Precedent
Martinique					
To 1663	4,000	—	—	—	—
1664–1735	121,600	1,690	4.2	5.4	Jamaica (1673–1729)
1736–87	182,200	3,500	0.8	4.2	Barbados (1734–66)
1788–1831	48,900	1,110	0.0	1.3	Martinique (1832–37)
1852–61	9,100	910	—	—	—
Total	365,800				
Guadeloupe					
To 1699	10,000	—	—	—	—
1700–78	211,400	2,680	3.2	5.4	Jamaica (1673–1729)
1779–1818	36,500	910	0.0	1.1	Guadeloupe (1732–37)
1819–31	27,000	2,080	1.2	1.1	Guadeloupe (1732–37)
1852–61	5,900	590	—	—	—
Total	290,800				
Total both islands 656,600					

Source: Population data for the French Antilles from Table 19. Jamaican rate of natural decrease from Table 20. Barbadian rate of natural decrease calculated from data of Tables 13 and 14. See text, pp. 80–82.

Given the uncertainty of the basic data, a more careful calculation may be hardly more valid than these educated guesses. On the other hand, the same form of calculation used for estimating the slave imports into Saint Domingue can be used again for the French Lesser Antilles, with the result shown on Table 21. Sheer guesswork is still required for Martinique before 1663 and for Guadeloupe before 1699. Thereafter, the experience of Jamaica in its first phase of expansion is a precedent for assuming net natural decrease of 5.4 per cent until 1735 for Martinique and until 1778 for Guadeloupe.

After 1736, the slave population of Martinique grew much more slowly. Its growth rate of 0.8 per cent over the period 1736–87 was nearly the 0.9-per-cent rate of Barbados over 1734–66. Barbados' net natural decrease for that period can therefore serve as a precedent. Then after 1788 Martinique attained a slightly fluctuating but relatively constant slave population—a situation that lasted until the virtual end of slave imports in the 1830's.[31] Deaths among the slaves still exceeded births, and some slave imports were necessary to maintain the population level. Data are not available for calculating the rate of natural decrease for a population at an equivalent stage of maturity and with a similar growth rate of zero. But the population history of Martinique itself provides a clue. Slave imports ceased to be significant after 1831. During the next seven years, the slave population decreased consistently at an overall rate of 1.3 per cent.[32] Assuming that a trickle of illicit imports would be balanced by an equivalent number of manumissions, this percentage can be taken as a guide to the probable rate of slave imports during the previous period, 1788–1831.

Guadeloupe reached a similar level of stability in the period 1779–1818. In this case, the Guadeloupe rate of population de-

31. Slave population in the Lesser Antilles must have fluctuated considerably in the wartime conditions of 1792–1815. Slaves (and their masters) moved from island to island, and death rates may have been high. The French managed, however, to introduce some new slaves from Africa, imports of 3,558 being recorded for Martinique during year XIII (1804–5). (A. Moreau de Jonnès, *L'Esclavage*, pp. 11–12.)

32. Moreau de Jonnès calculated the natural rates of increase and decrease for the French sugar colonies of this period, using the birth and death records for the slave population. He found that Martinique appeared to have a population with a balanced birth and death rate of about 30 per 1000 per annum, but this rate is not sufficient to account for the marked drop of population in the period after 1832. For all three colonies in the French Caribbean, therefore, the rates of decrease calculated from the slave population figures for 1832 and 1837 are preferred to those calculated from birth and death figures.

cline after 1831 is a possible indication of the rate of net natural decrease, not only for 1779–1818 but also for 1819–31 when the slave population of the island began to grow again through immigration.

In one sense, the slave trade of the French Antilles ended in 1831, when France granted British anti-slave-trade patrols the right of search on the high seas. Small numbers may have been imported illicitly after that time, but they can be ignored for present purposes.[33] A form of legal slave trade, however, was reintroduced in the 1850's. Between 1852 and 1861, the French government adopted the theory that a slave might be purchased in Africa, "liberated" on shipboard and transported to the Antilles as a worker under contract.[34] Whatever the legal theory, this was certainly a continuation of the slave trade. Some 15,000 slaves were authorized under this plan between 1852 and 1861 and delivered to the Antilles.

Slave imports into French Guiana and Louisiana were comparatively minor, but they are more difficult to estimate with

33. Gaston Martin, *Histoire de l'esclavage dans les colonies françaises* (Paris, 1948), p. 256.

34. P. Chemin-Dupontès, *Les Petites Antilles* (Paris, 1909), pp. 201–2; P. Lasascade, *Esclavage et immigration: La question de la main-d'oeuvre aux Antilles* (Paris, 1907), p. 73. Only a fine line separates these imported "contract" workers from the equivalent British source of additional African-born population for the West Indies—the recruitment of contract workers from among the recaptives taken from slavers captured by the Royal Navy. The fact that these workers were theoretically free to choose whether or not to go to America, and the further fact that some of them were genuinely free recruits from the Kru coast of present-day Liberia, seems to make it inappropriate to count them as part of the slave trade. If they are to be counted, however, the numbers landed in various West Indian colonies between 1841 and 1867 are given in Roberts, *Population of Jamaica,* p. 110 as follows:

Jamaica	10,000	St. Vincent	1,040
British Guiana	13,970	St. Lucia	730
Trinidad	8,390	St. Kitts	460
Grenada	1,540		

The demographic consequence of these imports is uncertain, since it is not known how many took advantage of the promised repatriation at the end of their labor contract.

accuracy. Louisiana had a particularly checkered history. After a long period on the periphery of the Spanish empire, real economic development began only with the foundation of New Orleans by the French in 1718. The colony was again returned to Spain in 1763, but with Britain now in possession of the eastern bank of the Mississippi. In 1800, Louisiana was ceded to France, and France sold its claim to the United States in 1803.

With this variety of jurisdictions, few records are reported in the literature, and even the estimates of slave population may be quite wide of the facts. One report based on French records, for example, claims that 7,000 slaves were imported between 1718 and 1735. If the slave population reached only the reported total of 3,400 in 1735, this figure seems inordinately high, though not impossible. It can therefore be accepted for the period up to the end of 1734. If Louisiana had followed the pattern of other sub-tropical mainland colonies in North America, the slave population may actually have begun to increase naturally from some point in the late eighteenth century. Given Louisiana's nineteenth-century reputation for bad health conditions, however, it seems appropriate to assume that the rate of net natural decrease may have been about 2 per cent per year. At that rate, it would have required 21,300 slaves imported in 1735–84 to produce the slave population of 16,500 by 1785. Since slave imports from that date to annexation by the United States can be taken as negligible, the total slave trade to Louisiana up to 1803 can be estimated very uncertainly at about 28,300.[35]

French Guiana is simply an enigma. The slave population grew relatively slowly—at an annual rate of 2.3 per cent over the period 1695–1806. That colony also had a reputation for bad health conditions, and the long period 1695–1806 would include a probable high death rate near the beginning, following the pattern of the Caribbean colonies. A long-term estimated net natural decrease of 4.5 per cent per year might therefore be about right. Combined with the rate of growth and the popula-

35. Gray, *History of Agriculture,* 1:335, for estimated imports of 1718–35. The calculations here follow the formulae outlined in Ch. 2, fn. 26.

TABLE 22

REVISED SLAVE-IMPORT ESTIMATES FOR THE FRENCH CARIBBEAN

Colony	Deerr		Revised
Saint Domingue	820,000		864,300
Martinique	375,000		365,800
Guadeloupe	375,000		290,800
Minor territories	80,000		79,300
Louisiana to 1803		28,300	
French Guiana		51,000	
Total	1,650,000		1,600,200

Sources: Deerr, *History of Sugar*, 2:280–82; Tables 20 and 21 above. See also text, pp. 82–84.

tion numbers, an estimate comes to 37,000 slaves imported between 1695 and 1806, and this figure is accepted for lack of something better.

In the late war years, 1807–13, French Guianese slave imports appear to have been negligible, but they began again in the postwar period, as they did for the French Antilles. The slave population grew at an annual rate of 2.7 per cent from 1814 to 1831, but it then decreased at 2.3 per cent annually from 1831 to 1837, once the trade had stopped.[36] These two rates in conjunction suggest that some 14,100 slaves were required over 1814–30 to produce the reported population of 1831. The result is a very uncertain estimate of 51,000 slaves imported into French Guiana during the whole period of the slave trade, and the total imports into the French colonies can be put at roughly the levels shown in Table 22.

THE DUTCH WEST INDIES AND GUIANA

The Dutch carried a high proportion of the seventeenth-century slave trade, and they remained an important source of supply into the eighteenth. But many, if not most, of the slaves they

36. Moreau de Jonnès, *L'Esclavage*, p. 60.

carried were destined for other peoples' colonies. The Dutch islands in the West Indies, like Curaçao and Aruba, were mainly trading stations with insignificant agricultural production and insignificant numbers of retained slaves. Surinam, Demerara, Berbice, and Essequibo in Guiana, however, were true plantation colonies with a slave population of more than 100,000 by 1790.[37] On the basis of this population and a comparison with Barbados, Deerr allowed a total import of 500,000 slaves into Surinam and Berbice and 350,000 into Demerara and Essequibo —thus including the future British Guiana as part of the Dutch colonies for purposes of his tabulation—and he allowed a further 50,000 for the Dutch islands.[38]

Dutch scholarship has not yet produced carefully constructed estimates, but Dutch estimates tend to be much lower than Deerr's figures. Some give less than 100,000 for the entire slave trade to Surinam. The authoritative study of Rudolf van Lier put the total slave imports into Dutch Guiana at 300,000 to 350,000.[39] This, however, appears to be too low in terms of the length of the slave trade to these colonies and the slave population at the end of the eighteenth century. While a reliable estimate is not possible from the present literature, 500,000 is accepted here for the whole of Dutch America during the whole of the slave trade, including present-day Guyana.

The Danish West Indies

The Danish West Indies (now the American Virgin Islands) functioned more as trading posts than as true centers of the South Atlantic System. Their total slave population of around 20,000 at the end of the eighteenth century was not therefore the result of demographic processes comparable to those of the

37. Deerr, *History of Sugar,* 1:280.
38. Deerr, *History of Sugar,* 1:283.
39. See L. C. Vrijman, *Slavenhalers en Slavenhandel* (Amsterdam, 1937), pp. 38, 110; "Slavernij" in *West Indische Encyclopaedia* (Amsterdam, 1927), p. 639; R. van Lier, *Samenleving in een Grensgebeid: een sociaal-historische studie van de Matschappij in Suriname* (The Hague, 1949), pp. 125–26.

true "sugar islands." Deerr's estimate of 75,000 slaves imported in the course of the trade is likely to be high. Danish archival records published by Westergaard more than a half-century ago indicate a much lower rate. For the period 1687–1754, Westergaard shows retained imports of 16,889, or an annual average of 248 slaves.[40] The Danish slave trade was much larger than this, but most of it went to foreign colonies. It may not be unreasonable simply to extend Westergaard's annual average to the remaining years of the century, giving a further sum of 11,160 for 1755–99, and a total estimate for the whole period of the slave trade in the neighborhood of 28,000.

Total Estimates and Geographical Distribution

A total estimate of slaves imported into the Americas, based mainly on country-by-country import estimates, is shown in Table 23 in the same categories as Deerr's estimates. This table should be understood to indicate a range of possibility, not a set figure of 9,566,000 or even 10 million, to be repeated in the textbooks as Dunbar's estimates were. There are too many holes in the data, too many calculations subject to doubt, too much danger of double counting, and too much uncertainty about normal levels of natural decrease or increase among slave populations—especially those outside the heartland of the South Atlantic System.

While it is doubtful that the revised estimates of Table 23 are too low, it is easily possible that they will be too high—and some of the data supporting this possibility will appear in later chapters. Meanwhile, the total can stand as one kind of calculation among others—in this case an import-based estimate. The only competing similar estimate is that of Noel Deerr. His figure is 25 per cent higher than this one, but, if his mammoth miscalculation of the slave trade to North America is modified, his total would be 8,869,000, or 7 per cent lower. Within the limits of uncertainty imposed by the basic quality of the data, the two

40. W. Westergaard, *The Danish West Indies Under Company Rule (1671–1754)* (New York, 1917), pp. 320–26.

TABLE 23

DEERR'S ESTIMATES OF SLAVES IMPORTED DURING THE WHOLE PERIOD OF THE ATLANTIC SLAVE TRADE, WITH REVISIONS

Region	Deerr	Revision
Old-World traffic	200,000	175,000
Spanish America, asiento period	450,000	700,000
Spanish America, post-asiento period	550,000	852,000
Brazil	3,325,000	3,647,000
British Caribbean	1,900,000	1,665,000
British North America	1,500,000	275,000(to 1790)
United States, 1786–1808	420,000	70,000(1791–1807)
United States, 1809–61	1,000,000	54,000(1808–61)
French Caribbean and Guiana	1,650,000	1,600,000
Dutch Caribbean and Guiana	900,000	500,000
Danish West Indies	75,000	28,000
Total	11,970,000	9,566,000

Sources: Deerr, *History of Sugar*, 2:284; Tables 4, 5, 8, 9, 10, 18, 22. See also text, pp. 49, 72–75, 84–86.

estimates are therefore in substantial agreement with one another. While neither claims to be a final answer, it is extremely unlikely that the ultimate total will turn out to be less than 8,000,000 or more than 10,500,000.

A total number, however, has only a limited meaning for history. Whether the figure is 8 million, 10 million, or 15 million, this largest dimension of the Atlantic slave trade is simply too all-embracing for comparison. As a measure of human misery, 2 million slaves brought to the Americas is already such a terrifying thought that no multiplier could make it seem any worse. As a measure of the relative importance of recent inter-continental migrations, any figure in the range indicated is smaller than the nineteenth- and twentieth-century movement of Europeans overseas. And it is equally clear that more Africans than Europeans arrived in the Americas between, say, 1492 and 1770. The total might also have meaning for the demographic and social history

TABLE 24

A SPECULATIVE GEOGRAPHICAL DISTRIBUTION OF SLAVE IMPORTS DURING THE WHOLE PERIOD OF THE ATLANTIC SLAVE TRADE (000 OMITTED)

Region and country		No.		%
Grand total		*9,566*		*100.0**
Old World traffic		*175*		*1.8*
Europe		50		0.5
Madeira, Canaries, Cape Verde Is.		25		0.3
São Thomé		100		1.0
North America		*651*		*6.8*
Territory of the United States		427		4.5
British North America	399		4.2	
Louisiana	28		0.3	
Middle America		224		2.3
Mexico	200		2.1	
Central America and Belize	24		0.3	
Caribbean Islands		*4,040*		*42.2*
Greater Antilles		2,421		25.3
Haiti	864		9.0	
Dominican Republic	30		0.3	
Cuba	702		7.3	
Puerto Rico	77		0.8	
Jamaica	748		7.8	
Lesser Antilles		1,619		16.9
US Virgin Is.	28		0.3	
British Virgin Is.	7		0.1	
Leeward Is.	346		3.6	
Guadeloupe	291		3.0	
Martinique	366		3.8	
St. Vincent, St. Lucia, Tobago, & Dominica	70		0.7	
Grenada	67		0.7	
Trinidad	22		0.2	
Barbados	387		4.0	
Dutch Antilles	20		0.2	
Bahamas	10		0.1	
Bermuda	5		0.1	

TABLE 24 (*Continued*)

South America		*4,700*		*49.1*
The Guianas		531		5.6
Surinam & Guyana	480		5.0	
French Guiana	51		0.5	
Brazil		3,647		38.1
Bahia	1,200		12.5	
Other	2,447		25.6	
Spanish South America		522		5.5
Argentina, Uruguay, Paraguay, & Bolivia	100		1.0	
Chile	6		0.1	
Peru	95		1.0	
Colombia, Panama, & Ecuador	200		2.1	
Venezuela	121		1.3	

* Percentages have been rounded.
Sources: Tables 4, 11, 17, 18, 22. See also text, pp. 49, 72–75, 84–86.

of Africa, but the present knowledge of African historical demography is still too weak to make that meaning clear.

Other dimensions of the trade, below the level of the grand total, add far more to historical knowledge. When the data of Table 23 are rearranged according to approximate territorial, regional, and continental totals, a new pattern appears. (See Table 24.) Even if the range of accuracy were as large as plus or minus 50 per cent for any geographical total, the table suggests some revisions of accepted historical beliefs. Contrary to the parochial view of history that most North Americans pick up in school, the United States was only a marginal recipient of slaves from Africa. The real center of the trade was tropical America, with almost 90 per cent going to the Atlantic fringe from Brazil through the Guianas to the Caribbean coast and islands. The highest ratio of slave immigration to geographical area is found in the Lesser Antilles.

These data take on additional meaning if they are set against other estimates of the recent distribution of Afro-American populations. The figures assembled by Angel Rosenblat can be used here as representative of the broad pattern that emerged in the

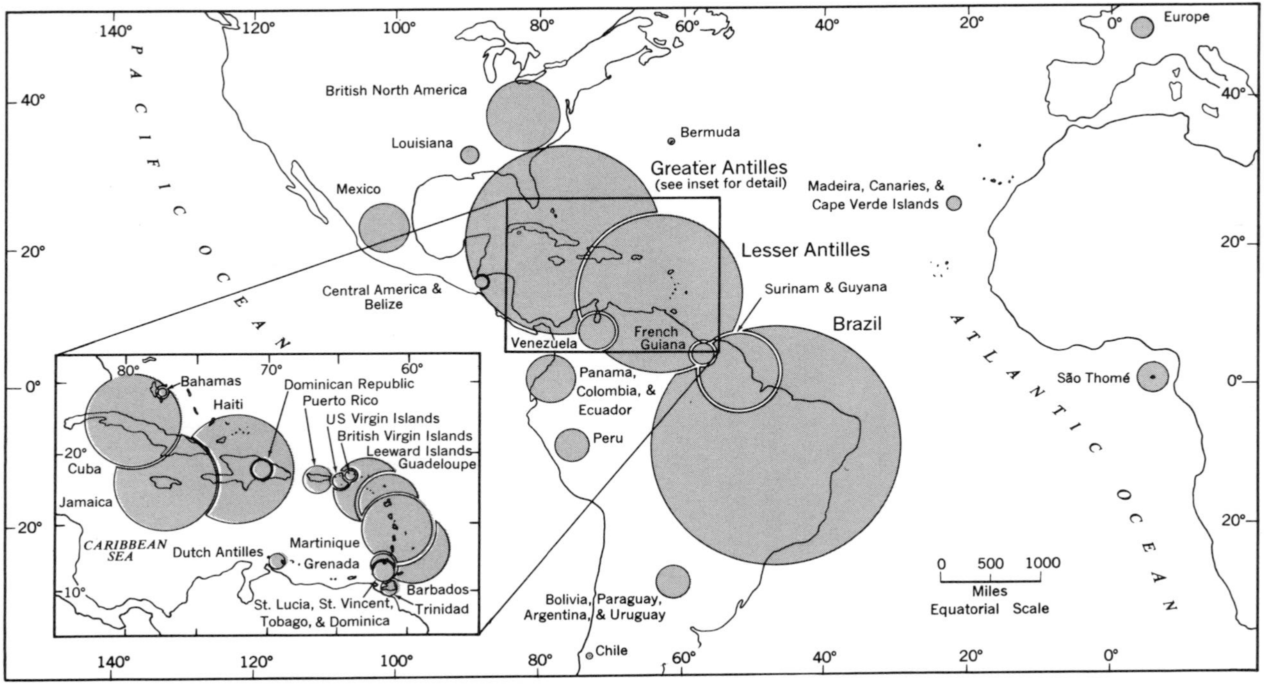

Fig. 5. Slave imports during the whole period of the Atlantic slave trade. Fig. by UW Cartographic Lab.

TABLE 25

RELATION OF SLAVE IMPORTS TO POPULATION OF AFRICAN DESCENT, C.1950 (000 OMITTED)

Region and country	Estimated slave imports		Estimated population partly or entirely of African descent	
	No.	%	No.	%
United States & Canada	*427*	*4.5*	*14,916*	*31.1*
Middle America	*224*	*2.4*	*342*	*0.7*
Mexico			120	0.3
Central America			222	0.5
Caribbean Islands	*4,040*	*43.0*	*9,594*	*20.0*
South America	*4,700*	*50.0*	*23,106*	*48.2*
Surinam & Guyana			286	0.6
French Guiana			23	†
Brazil			17,529	36.6
Argentina, Uruguay, Paraguay, & Bolivia			97	0.2
Chile			4	†
Peru			110	0.2
Colombia, Panama, & Ecuador			3,437	7.2
Venezuela			1,620	3.4
Total	9,391	100.0*	47,958	100.0*

* Percentages have been rounded.
† Less than 0.05%.
Sources: Angel Rosenblat, *La población indígena y el mestizaje en América*, 2 vols. (Buenos Aires, 1954), 1:21; consolidation of data in Table 24.

mid-twentieth century.[41] The population data for 1950, as shown in Table 25, represent all people of partial or full African descent, and they must be taken as extremely imprecise at best. Not only are some census data inadequate; the classification of "Negro" or "colored" is often at the whim of the census taker in

41. Zelinsky, "Historical Geography of the Negro Population of Latin America," has also traced Negro populations in part of the New World, and in a more authoritative way than Rosenblat. Zelinsky, however, presented a series of maps without publishing the numerical data on which they were based.

racially mixed societies. The contrasts are nevertheless too outstanding to escape notice. Though the United States had about one-third of the total Afro-American population in 1950, it imported less than 5 per cent of the slaves. At the other extreme, the Caribbean islands with more than 40 per cent of the slave imports had only 20 per cent of the Afro-American population. Brazil was nearly balanced between these extremes, with 38 per cent of the imports and 37 per cent of the Afro-American population of 1950.

Social historians and historical demographers have been slow to pay attention to comparative data of this kind. One aspect of the table that seems to cry out for a more adequate explanation is the long-standing and high growth rate among the Afro-Americans in the United States. Yet most of the United States historians simply note it in passing, if at all, as though it were the natural and expected course of events.

The Tannenbaum hypothesis, which is still widely followed, suggests that the Latin colonies enjoyed a milder form of slavery than those of the Dutch or English, partly on account of a Catholic humanitarianism and partly because of legal traditions that protected slaves from their masters.[42] This may have been true at some times and in some places, but one measure of well-being is the ability to survive and to multiply. Cuba, for example, received about 7 per cent of the whole slave trade to the Americas, yet the Negro and mulatto population of the island in 1953 was only about 1.5 million, or just over 3 per cent of the Afro-American population of the Americas. Other colonies with a Latin tradition were still more striking in this respect. At the end of the slave trade to Saint Domingue in 1791, the slave input was more than twice that of the United States, yet the surviving slave population was only 480,000—compared with a United States slave population of about 4.5 million at emancipation in 1861.

42. See F. Tannenbaum, *Slave and Citizen;* S. M. Elkins, *Slavery* (Chicago, 1959); H. S. Klein, *Slavery in the Americas: A Comparative Study of Virginia and Cuba* (Chicago, 1967).

One tempting explanation is the tropical climate, especially before the development of modern tropical medicine after the middle of the nineteenth century. This certainly played a role, but the experience of Colombia, Panama, and Ecuador suggests that disease is not the only explanation. That region of northwestern South America appears to have imported only 2 per cent of the total slave trade, yet it emerged in 1950 with 7 per cent of the Afro-American population. The quantitative evidence also suggests some significant social differences within Latin America. Rosenblat's estimates, for example, show 82 per cent of the Afro-Americans of Colombia, Ecuador, and Panama as mulatto, while the corresponding figure for Brazil is only 60 per cent, and only 10 per cent for Haiti. Here again the full explanation will have to wait for more careful and extensive comparative research.

In short, the principal value of these tables, and of this quantitative survey, is not mere quantitative accuracy—not simply the substitution of "right numbers" for wrong ones. For that matter, numbers are only projections with a wide range of possible inaccuracy. Their value is not in being correct, but in being correct enough to point out contradictions in present hypotheses and to raise new questions for comparative demography and social history.

CHAPTER 4

DISTRIBUTION THROUGH TIME: THE FIFTEENTH, SIXTEENTH, AND SEVENTEENTH CENTURIES

The number of slaves landed in the New World, and their distribution in space, is only a first step toward the numerical analysis of the slave trade. It may not even be a very important step. Grand totals are simply large numbers, whose real meaning often lies in the smaller numbers behind the global figure. The slave trade was a process, constantly changing and closely integrated with other processes in the Atlantic economy over more than four centuries. As with most economic processes, the changes are more important than the totals, and the slave trade was a pattern of changing sources of supply, changing destinations, and changing rates of flow. Sometime, when more basic research has been done, historians will be able to construct a reasonably accurate numerical picture of the trade as a variable stream of forced migrants, drawn from diverse and shifting tributaries, and flowing to an equally various and changing set of destinations. And they will be able to explain why change took place. That time is not yet, and it may even be too soon to try; but the historical literature already contains a large body of useful data. An outline of the present state of knowledge therefore seems to be called for, if only as a point of departure.

The Fifteenth and Sixteenth Centuries

The first century and a half of the Atlantic slave trade are necessarily obscure. Estimates can only be based on scattered guesses and incomplete records, and these have already been used in projecting the early imports into Spanish America and the slave-importing regions of the Old World. For the fifteenth-century slave trade, we have little more than a general impression that these slaves came dominantly from a region stretching south of the Senegal River to the vicinity of present-day Sierra Leone, with only a scattering exported from other parts of West or Central Africa. By the sixteenth century, however, Spanish American samples identifying slaves by ethnic origin begin to give a much clearer statistical picture of the regions actually affected by the trade.

Two samples have been published for the mid-sixteenth century. One from Peru was compiled by James Lockhart from the notarial registers of Lima and Arequipa between 1548 and 1560. Two hundred and fifty-six Afro-Peruvians are mentioned in these records, of whom 207 (or 80 per cent) were African-born: the rest were identified as originating in Spain, Portugal, or the Caribbean. (See Table 26.) Almost three-quarters of those from Africa came from the Senegambia and present-day Guinea-Bissau, a region on which the Portuguese concentrated early in the sixteenth century—in their terms, the "Guinea of Cape Verde," or the coastal regions conveniently reached from the Cape Verde Islands.[1]

A Mexican sample was compiled and published by Aguirre Beltrán from an inventory of the property of Hernando Cortés, drawn up in 1549. In this case, only 123 slaves were listed as born in Africa, and only 83 were identified by place of origin.

1. For sixteenth-century fashions in coastal nomenclature in Africa see W. Rodney, "Portuguese Attempts at Monopoly on the Upper Guinea Coast, 1580–1650," *Journal of African History*, 6:307 (1965); Vianna Filho, "O trabalho do engenho."

Table 26

Ethnic Origins of Afro-Peruvians, 1548–60

Sixteenth-century nomenclature	No.	%	Modern nomenclature and location
Senegambia and Guinea-Bissau	*154*	*74.4*	
Jelof	45	21.7	Wolof (Senegal)
Fula	1	0.5	Fulbe (hinterland of the Senegambia)
Berbesi	18	8.7	Serer (Senegal)
Mandinga	15	7.2	Malinke (probably Gambia)
Cazanga	4	1.9	Kassanga (Casamance)
Bañol	8	3.9	Banyun (Guinea-Bissau)
Biafara	40	19.3	Biafada (Guinea-Bissau)
Bran	23	11.1	Bram or Bola (Guinea-Bissau)
Other West Africa	*32*	*15.5*	
Zape	8	3.9	Landuma, Baga, Temne, and related peoples (coastal Sierra Leone)
Tierra Nova	20	9.7	Eastern Guinea coast generally (?)
São Thomé	3	1.4	Shipping point, which drew both from Dahomey-Southern Nigeria and from Congo-Angola region
Ambo	1	0.5	Northwest Bantu, vicinity of Mt. Cameroons
Central and southern Africa	*21*	*10.1*	
Manicongo	13	6.3	Bakongo (lower Congo River)
Enchicho	2	1.0	Tio or Teke (southern Congo-Brazzaville)
Angola	1	0.5	Probably Ambundu (hinterland of Luanda)
Mozambique	5	2.4	Shipping point, southeastern Africa generally
Total	207	100.0	

Source: Data from J. Lockhart, *Spanish Peru, 1532–1560* (Madison, 1968), p. 173.

TABLE 27

ETHNIC ORIGINS OF AFRO-MEXICANS, 1549

Sixteenth-century nomenclature	No.	%	Modern nomenclature and location
North Africa	*1*	*1.2*	
Zafi			Safi, Morocco (shipping point, nonspecific)
Senegambia and Guinea-Bissau	*73*	*88.0*	
Tucuxuy	1	1.2	Tukulor (Senegal Valley)
Gelofe	14	16.9	Wolof (Senegal)
Berbesi	6	7.2	Serer (Senegal)
Mandinga	9	10.8	Malinke (Gambia Valley)
Cazanga	1	1.2	Kassanga (Casamance and Guinea-Bissau)
Bran	23	27.7	Bram, Gola, or Burama (Guinea-Bissau)
Biafara	14	16.9	Biafada (Guinea-Bissau)
Bañol	5	6.0	Banyun (Guinea-Bissau)
Other West Africa	*5*	*6.0*	
Zape	4	4.8	Landuma, Baga, Temne, and related peoples (coastal Sierra Leone)
Terra Nova	1	1.2	Eastern Guinea coast generally (?)
Central and southern Africa	*4*	*4.8*	
Manicongo	2	2.4	Bakongo (lower Congo Valley)
Mozambique	2	2.4	Southeastern Africa generally
Total	83	100.0*	

* Percentages have been rounded.
Source: Data from Aguirre Beltrán, *Población negra*, pp. 244–45.

The numbers are too small to be statistically viable taken alone, but Table 27 shows a regional distribution remarkably similar to that of the Peruvian sample.[2] The Senegambia, for example, contributed 36 per cent to the Mexican sample and 38 per cent to

2. The original text is published in H. Cortés, *Documentos inéditos relativos a Hernán Cortés* (Mexico, D.F., 1935), pp. 242–78.

the Peruvian. The whole "Guinea of Cape Verde" provided 74 per cent for Peru and 88 per cent for Mexico. The remainder of both samples was drawn from scattered sources along the coast of West, Central, and even southeast Africa, with no group accounting for more than 6 per cent of either sample. These similarities argue that both samples must represent a better statistical picture of the Spanish-American slave imports of the previous decades than their numbers alone suggest.

As a result, it is possible to advance speculatively one further step and combine the two samples as though they were one. (See Table 28.) This combined sample may then represent the distribution of sources for the whole slave trade flowing to Spanish America, and also to Europe, Madeira, the Canaries, and the Cape Verde Islands; and this representation may well be valid for roughly the quarter-century, 1526–50. With this much information, one can also project a possible rate of flow from various regions of Africa. Loss in transit may have been high, perhaps as high as 25 per cent. The estimates of annual flow to Europe (300), the Atlantic Islands (200), and Spanish America (500) therefore suggest an annual export in these branches of the slave trade in the neighborhood of 1,300 slaves a year. The consequent drain of population for this part of the trade, by ethnic group and region, is represented on Table 28.

Although this projection may appear far-gone in the realm of speculation, one more step can be taken. Table 28 represents only the trade flowing to the Caribbean and points north. Brazil was not yet importing slaves, but São Thomé was a major importing territory, whose slaves were unlikely to have come from the distant coasts of the Senegambia. Annual exports from Angola to São Thomé in about 1530 were, indeed, reported at a level of four to five thousand a year.[3] While this figure is far too high to have been sustained for a full quarter-century, it supports the estimate that São Thomé was the largest single importer of slaves at this period. If an annual average of 750 is allowed São Thomé, if the loss in transit is estimated at a low

3. J. Vansina, *Kingdoms of the Savanna* (Madison, 1966), p. 53.

TABLE 28

PROJECTED CONTRIBUTION OF AFRICAN REGIONS AND ETHNIC GROUPS TO THE NORTHERN AND TRANSATLANTIC SLAVE TRADE, 1526–50

Region and ethnic group	Annual average export No.	%
Senegambia	*499*	*37.6*
Wolof	271	20.4
Fulbe	4	.3
Tukulor	4	.3
Serer	110	8.3
Malinke	110	8.3
Guinea-Bissau	*543*	*40.8*
Kassanga	23	1.7
Banyun	60	4.5
Biafada	249	18.7
Bram	211	15.9
Sierra Leone	*56*	*4.2*
Temne and related peoples	56	4.2
Cape Mount to Cameroon	*114*	*8.6*
"Tierra Nova"	97	7.3
São Thomé re-exports	13	1.0
Cameroon coast (Ambo)	4	.3
Congo-Angola	*82*	*6.2*
Bakongo	69	5.2
Tyo or Teke	9	.7
Ambundu	4	.3
Southeastern Africa	*32*	*2.4*
Total	1,330*	100.0*

* Percentages and totals have been rounded.
Sources: Tables 26, 27.

figure of, say, 5 per cent, and if the sources of these imports are speculatively divided between the Bights of Benin and Biafra (20 per cent) and the Congo-Angola area (80 per cent), the

TABLE 29

CONJECTURAL PROJECTION OF TOTAL SLAVE EXPORTS FROM AFRICA TO THE ATLANTIC SLAVE TRADE, 1526–50

Region	Annual average exports	
	No.	%
Senegambia	499	23.5
Guinea-Bissau	543	25.6
Sierra Leone	56	2.6
Cape Mount to Cameroon	272	12.8
Congo-Angola	714	33.7
Southeastern Africa	32	1.5
Total	2,120*	100.0*

* Percentages and totals have been rounded.
Source: Table 28. See also text, pp. 99–100.

whole distribution of the slave trade by origin in Africa would be similar to that shown in Table 29.

This sequence of steps from the relatively hard data of the Spanish notaries to the speculations of Table 29 is obviously one of decreasing accuracy, but even the last step is accurate enough to tell something about the origins of the sixteenth-century slave trade. One generalization sometimes found in the older literature held that the slave trade began in the region immediately south of the Sahara and then moved southeastward along the African coast in step with increasing European maritime prowess. While this may have been true of the fifteenth-century trade, it was no longer so in the sixteenth. The vast majority of slaves in this period were supplied from two areas—the Guinea of Cape Verde and the region just south of the Congo mouth. The choice of these areas had little to do with distance from Europe. The large proportion of Wolof is explained not by European but by Senegambian history. The middle decades of the sixteenth century were a time when the empire of Jolof, previously dominant throughout the region between the Senegal and the Gambia, broke into a series of separate kingdoms. This disintegration of a large state meant warfare, and warfare prolonged as Cayor tried to make itself dominant over the other successor states of the Jolof empire.[4] The result was war prisoners for sale in large numbers, so that Wolof were frequently found in sixteenth-century America, though they never again provided significant numbers for the slave trade.

The large flow from the Congo is again partly the result of African political history, but with more direct European participation. This quarter-century in the history of the kingdom of Kongo was the period when the early good relations with Portugal began to deteriorate, when the central authority of the kingdom declined, and when the Portuguese began their exploration and penetration of the kingdom of Ndongo. Beyond these events on the supply side of the slave trade, an important fact on the demand side was the creation of a plantation sector on the island of São Thomé which led to a new Portuguese policy and new Portuguese actions on the coast of Central Africa. The Portuguese might have gone elsewhere for their slaves, but the decades of peaceful relations and Christian influence in Kongo, stretching back to the late fifteenth century, gave them an opening too convenient to be passed over.[5]

Other aspects of the tables are harder to explain. It is clear that the source of the trade was still coastal. Every ethnic name in Tables 26 and 27 is found today within fifty miles of the coast or a navigable waterway. Given the fact that the Portuguese built their fort at Elmina on the coast of present-day Ghana as early as 1481, the relatively small number of slaves who might have been from the Gold Coast is impressive. Clearly the presence of Europeans on a section of the coast was not in itself a cause for large-scale export of slaves. The large numbers drawn

4. D. P. Gamble, *The Wolof of Senegambia* (London, 1957), p. 173.

5. For the history of Kongo and Angola in the sixteenth and seventeenth centuries see Vansina, *Kingdoms of the Savanna;* G. Balandier, *Daily Life in the Kingdom of the Kongo* (New York, 1968).

from present-day Guinea-Bissau therefore require an explanation that is not yet available.

Toward the end of the sixteenth century, estimates of slave flows from Africa can rest on a different kind of record. As the Spanish empire strengthened its bureaucratic controls, and particularly after the union of the Spanish and Portuguese crowns in 1580, Spanish shipping records became more systematic. These records have been intensively studied in the monumental work of Pierre and Hugette Chaunu, *Séville et l'Atlantique* (1955–60). Although the Chaunus were principally concerned with the flow of trade between Spain and the Americas, they also published tables drawn from the records of the Spanish-controlled slave trade from 1551 to 1640.

These records are principally the series of licenses issued for individual ships permitted to supply slaves to Spanish America. The ships themselves were usually foreign and normally Portuguese, and each permit specified the number of slaves to be carried to the Americas and the section of the African coast from which they were to be taken. From these records, the Chaunus drew up a table of the Spanish-controlled slave trade for each quinquennium. (See Table 30.)

The fact that the Spanish records identified African origin according to shipping points means that some aspects of the table require interpretation. Cape Verde, for example, meant neither the actual cape where Dakar now stands nor the Cape Verde Islands, but rather the "Guinea of Cape Verde" stretching roughly from the Cape Verde peninsula to the Sierra Leone River. This category therefore includes much the same people who were shipped from the Canary Islands. The Canaries drew their slaves from the nearby mainland of coastal Mauritania, but the desert peoples of Mauritania in turn drew their slaves from the much denser populations of sedentary people south of the Sahara—in short, from the hinterland of the Guinea of Cape Verde. The categories "Canaries" and "Cape Verde" therefore have to be understood as a consolidated total of slaves originat-

TABLE 30

…TION OF SLAVE SHIPS AUTHORIZED BY THE SPANISH GOVERNMENT, 1551–1640, ACCORDING TO REGION OF SUPPLY IN AFRICA

Period	Total	Canaries	Cape Verde	Guinea	São Thomé	Angola	Mixed	Un-known
1551–55	15	—	15	—	—	—	—	—
1556–60	15	—	15	—	—	—	—	—
1561–65	25	—	25	—	—	—	—	—
1566–70	9	—	9	—	—	—	—	—
1571–75	16	—	11	4	1	—	—	—
1576–80	2	—	1	—	—	—	—	1
1581–85	22	—	16	2	1	—	3	—
1586–90	59	6	7	25	3	1	15	2
1591–95	105	3	18	26	—	6	51	1
1596–1600	188	11	8	90	1	4	17	57
1601–5	97	20	2	22	—	4	1	48
1606–10	174	—	2	96	—	3	3	70
1611–15	9	—	1	2	—	2	—	4
1616–20	139	—	6	17	7	104	2	3
1621–25	125	—	8	14	5	82	16	—
1626–30	59	—	—	—	—	50	6	3
1631–35	80	—	1	2	2	64	8	3
1636–40	83	—	1	2	—	76	4	—
Total	1,222	40	146	302	20	396	126	192
%		3.3	11.9	24.7	1.6	32.4	10.3	15.7

Source: H. and P. Chaunu, *Séville et l'Atlantique,* Table 188, 6:402–3 with minor changes for apparent arithmetic error.

ing roughly in the present-day Gambia, Senegal, and Guinea-Bissau.

Similar considerations apply in interpreting the other coastal designations. "Guinea" has always been an unstable concept. Early in the sixteenth century it referred to the whole western coast of Africa from the Senegal to the Orange River. Here it can be taken to include the whole east-west coast from around Cape Mount or the Sierra Leone River to the Bight of Benin. The Bight of Biafra at this period is more likely to have come under the heading of "São Thomé," though the entrepôt at São Thomé drew slaves from the region of Angola as well. "Angola" itself changed in meaning through time. It began as a title, Ngola, borne by the ruler of Ndongo, and its first European meaning referred quite precisely to the immediate hinterland of Luanda. In later usage, the sense was extended, not only to the present-day colony of Angola, but frequently to the whole coast from Cape Lopez to Benguela. At this period, it was undoubtedly used in this broader sense.

The Chaunu data of Table 30 are presented as the number of ships authorized for each section of the coast, but this can be readily translated into the number of slaves. As the Chaunus point out, the size of ships in the slave trade was remarkably uniform at this period, averaging 118 toneladas (each tonelada being equal to approximately 2.8 cubic meters capacity). In addition, the ships were licensed on the basis of tonnage, so that the number of toneladas was equal to 80 or 90 per cent of the number of piezas de India authorized. If 85 per cent is taken as the norm, this means that the average ship of 118 toneladas would have carried 139 piezas. (See Table 31.)

When the Chaunu totals are recalculated in this way to give equivalents in piezas de India, they are remarkably close to the totals reported elsewhere in the literature for the period after 1595. Aguirre, for example, gives the figure of 132,594 piezas as the total allotment for all asientos of the period 1595–1640, while 133,996 is the equivalent figure derived from the Chaunu data for the period 1595–1640—a difference of only 1 per cent.[6] The Chaunu data should therefore be interpreted as a nearly-complete sample for the period after 1595, but only a small and somewhat biased sample for earlier years.

Piezas were not, of course, individuals, nor were the numbers authorized, and even loaded on the African coast, likely to have been delivered in the Americas. It was to the merchants' advantage to deliver fewer slaves than authorized,[7] and the loss in

6. Aguirre Beltrán, *Población negra,* p. 220.
7. Chaunu, *Séville et l'Atlantique,* 1:310–13.

Table 31

Distribution of Slave Exports from Africa Authorized by the Spanish Government, in Piezas de India, 1551–1640, According to Region of Supply in Africa

Years	Total*	Canaries	Cape Verde	Guinea	São Thomé	Angola	Unknown
1551–55	2,100	—	2,090	—	—	—	—
%	100.0	—	100.0	—	—	—	—
1556–60	2,100	—	2,090	—	—	—	—
%	100.0	—	100.0	—	—	—	—
1561–65	3,500	—	3,480	—	—	—	—
%	100.0	—	100.0	—	—	—	—
1566–70	1,300	—	1,250	—	—	—	—
%	100.0	—	100.0	—	—	—	—
1571–75	2,200	—	1,530	560	140	—	—
%	100.0	—	68.7	25.0	6.2	—	—
1576–80	300	—	140	—	—	—	140
%	100.0	—	50.0	—	—	—	50.0
1581–85	3,100	140	2,360	420	140	—	—
%	100.0	4.5	77.3	13.6	4.5	—	—
1586–90	8,200	1,810	1,230	4,130	420	330	280
%	100.0	22.1	15.0	50.3	5.1	4.1	3.4
1591–95	14,600	2,370	4,370	5,410	—	2,320	140
%	100.0	16.2	29.9	37.0	—	15.9	1.0

TABLE 31 (CONTINUED)

Years	Total*	Canaries	Cape Verde	Guinea	São Thomé	Angola	Unknown
1596–1600	26,100	2,200	2,900	19,660	200	1,200	—
%	100.0	8.4	11.1	75.2	0.8	4.6	—
1601–5	13,500	5,600	550	6,150	—	1,190	—
%	100.0	41.5	4.1	45.6	—	8.8	—
1606–10	24,200	90	550	22,500	90	960	—
%	100.0	0.4	2.3	93.0	0.4	4.0	—
1611–15	1,300	—	250	500	—	500	—
%	100.0	—	20.0	40.0	—	40.0	—
1616–20	19,300	70	970	2,430	970	14,460	420
%	100.0	0.4	5.0	12.6	5.0	74.8	2.2
1621–25	17,400	—	2,120	2,210	760	12,270	—
%	100.0	—	12.2	12.8	4.4	70.7	—
1626–30	8,200	—	440	70	—	7,690	—
%	100.0	—	5.4	0.9	—	93.7	—
1631–35	11,100	—	140	800	340	9,420	420
%	100.0	—	1.3	7.2	3.1	84.7	3.8
1636–40	11,500	—	210	560	—	10,770	—
%	100.0	—	1.8	4.8	—	93.3	—
Total	169,900	12,280	26,670	65,400	3,060	61,110	1,400
%	100.0	7.2	15.7	38.5	1.8	36.0	0.8

* Figures have been rounded to nearest ten; row totals, to nearest hundred.
Source: Data from Chaunu, *Séville et l'Atlantique*, 6:402–3.

transit may have run as high as 20 to 25 per cent. At the same time, unlicensed smugglers were also active in the slave trade. If these imponderables are assumed to counter one another, the numbers of piezas authorized are probably a reasonable indication of the numbers of slaves actually landed in the Americas, legally or illegally.

The real value of the Chaunu data, however, is their relative, not their absolute, quantities. In spite of large categories of "unknown" and "mixed voyage" in Table 30, a marked change through time is obvious. The shifting sources within Africa show still more clearly, if less accurately, in Table 31, where these two categories have been redistributed. The "mixed voyage" can be assigned to particular regions on the assumption that it loaded an equal number of slaves in each authorized region. In cases where the number of identified voyages is large enough, the "unknowns" can be redistributed according to the proportion of the known. This has been done in Table 31 in all cases where the unknowns exceeded 5 per cent.

The result is a highly variable pattern of trade, shifting from a heavy dependence on the Senegambia to an equally heavy dependence on Angola as the principal source of supply. Other estimates found in the literature tend to confirm both the general level of the trade and the shift in source. On the import side, the Cartagena customs house reported an import of 6,884 slaves over the period 1585–90.[8] Given the central importance of Cartagena in the Spanish commercial system, this figure is consonant with that of 8,200 authorized for the Spanish empire as a whole during 1586–90. One-year export estimates tend to be higher than the authorized levels. Walter Rodney, for example, reports three different estimates of slaves exported from the Guinea of Cape Verde for 1600, 1622, and 1644, all three in the region of 3,000 a year.[9] Given the annual averages for "Cape Verde" in each of the quinquennia represented in Table 31, 3,000 appears to be a reasonable round figure for the probable exports in the

8. Rodney, "Portuguese Monopoly," p. 309.
9. Rodney, "Portuguese Monopoly," p. 313.

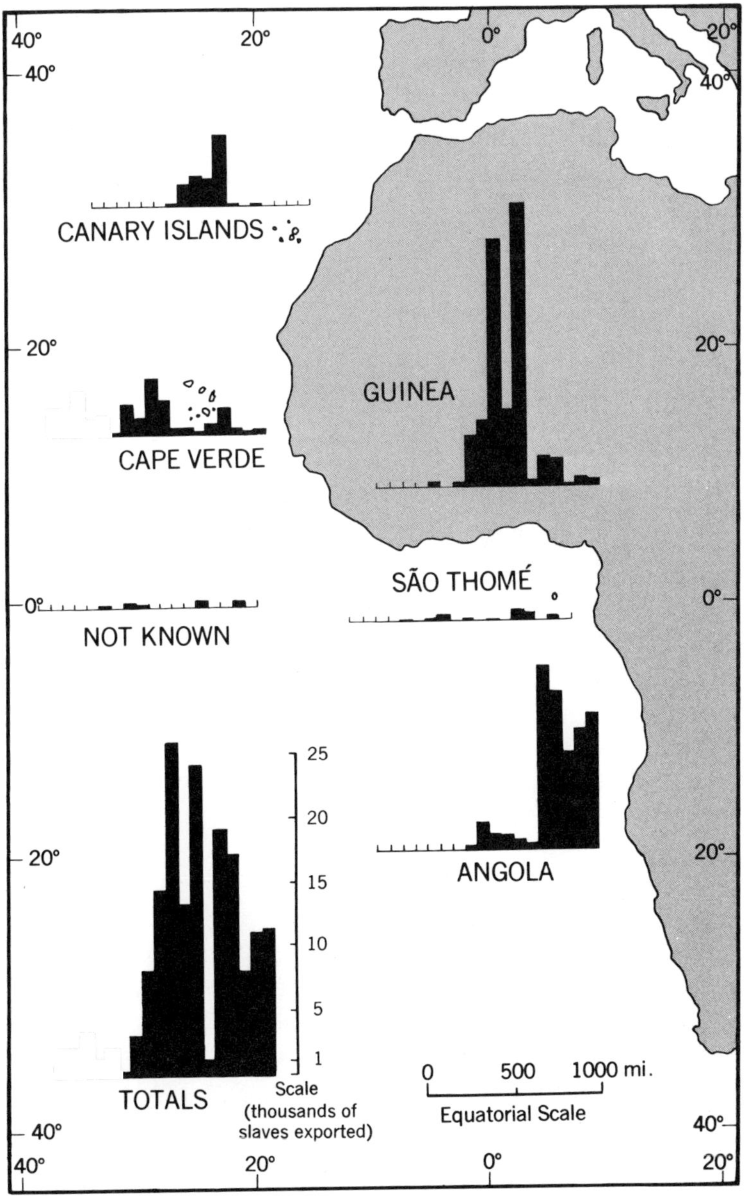

Fig. 6. African sources of the slave trade to Spanish America, 1551–1640. The bars represent quinquennial divisions between these dates. Fig. by UW Cartographic Lab. Data from Chaunu, *Séville et l'Atlantique,* 6:402–3. See Table 31.

best recent year shortly before 1600 and again before 1622. In short, these are not out of line with the Chaunu data—provided they are taken to represent a single year and not a long-term annual average.

The shift in source from Upper Guinea to south of the Congo is also confirmed by other information. A study of the slave population of the Audiencia of the Las Charcas (now Bolivia) shows Wolof as the dominant African ethnic element in the middle decades of the sixteenth century, followed by larger numbers from the Bight of Biafra in the second half of the century, and then by a sharp shift to Angola in about 1594. By 1600, Angola was the most important source of supply for this area.[10] A little later the same dominance was even more pronounced in Chile, where 132 out of 183 slaves sold in 1615 were listed as "Angolas." In this case the term was apparently used in a narrow sense, since Bakongo were listed separately, though they were only 2 per cent of the total.[11]

This evidence suggests that southern South America became dependent for slaves on Angolan sources even before the rest of Spanish America did. Official government authorizations, as shown by the Chaunu study, shifted sharply from Guinea to Angola only after 1616. Yet Las Charcas made the same change in the 1590's, and Chile must have done so in the years 1610–15. The difference in timing is nevertheless explicable. By the end of the sixteenth century, the sugar industry on São Thomé first stabilized and then declined in the face of Brazilian competition.[12] This meant a reduced demand for Angolan slaves in the Gulf of Guinea itself, while Brazil and southern South America were readily accessible across the South Atlantic. In addition, the Spanish had re-founded Buenos Aires in 1580, opening an overland route across the pampa to Bolivia and Chile. Given the

10. I. Wolff, "Negersklaverei und Negerhandel in Hochperu 1545–1640," in R. Konetzke and H. Kellenbenz, eds., *Jahrbuch für Geschichte von Staat, Wirtschaft, und Gesellschaft Lateinamerikas,* 1:157–86 (Cologne, 1964), p. 166.

11. R. Mellafe, *Esclavitud negra en Chile,* p. 200.

12. Mauro, *Portugal et l'Atlantique,* pp. 190–91.

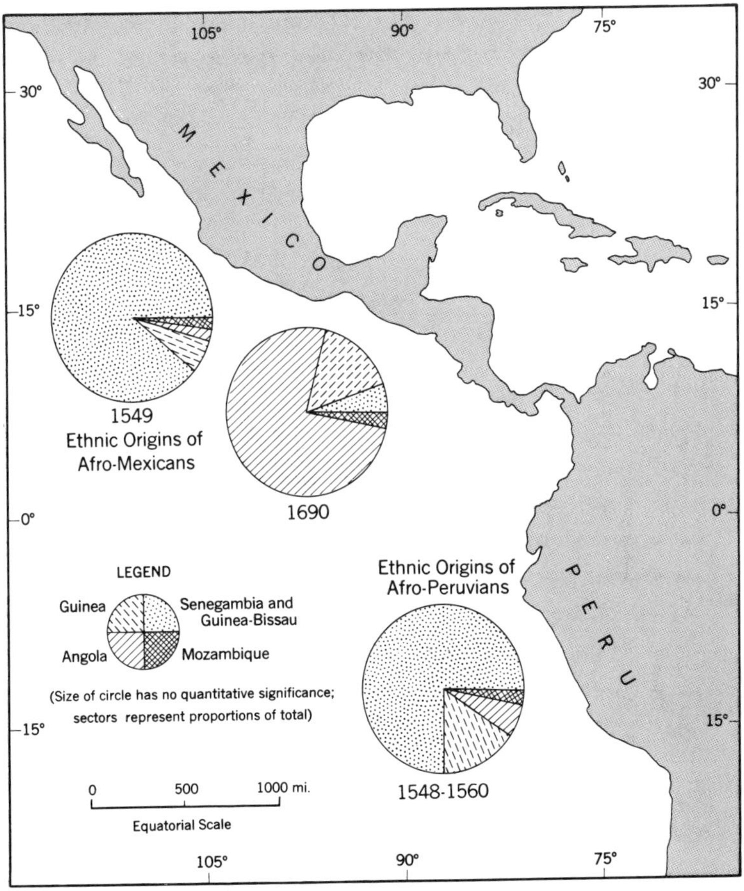

Fig. 7. African origins of Afro-Peruvian and Afro-Mexican populations of the sixteenth and seventeenth centuries. Fig. by UW Cartographic Lab. Data from Tables 26, 27, and 33.

union of the Hispanic crowns at this period, Buenos Aires and its hinterland may well have secured slaves by re-export from Brazil, rather than through a direct trade from Africa. If so, the pampa trade route would have escaped notice in the Chaunu tables. It flourished, in any case, only until 1622, when the Spanish government prohibited overland trade and insisted that all slaves for the Pacific coastal colonies come by way of Panama. Even if this provision were not completely enforced, it would have the effect of diverting "Angolas" into the legal route to Spanish America by way of the Caribbean.[13]

Other explanations for the early seventeenth-century shift to Angola can be found in African conditions. The first upward step of the Chaunu series for Angola, in 1616–20, can be associated with a new scale of Portuguese hostilities against Ndongo after 1608 and especially after 1614, when the Portuguese accepted the Jaga as allies. From then until well beyond 1640, the Portuguese were engaged in military operations in the hinterland of Luanda, providing new sources of slaves—both directly captured and secured through trade with African allies.[14]

A late seventeenth-century ethnic sample of Afro-Mexican slaves illustrates the longer-term influence of the shift to Angola. Out of 499 slaves belonging to the Colegio de San Pedro and San Pablo, 402 (80 per cent) were African-born. Among these, the relative positions of West and Central Africans was the reverse of the sixteenth-century mixture. West Africans had dropped to 21 per cent, from about 90 per cent of the earlier samples. Central Africa now contributed three-quarters of the total, and even the West African sources had shifted eastward to the Bights of Benin and Biafra: less than 2 per cent now came from Senegambia, and only 4 per cent from Guinea-Bissau.

Neither the size of the fifteenth- and sixteenth-century slave trade, nor its variation through time, can be measured in detail. On the other hand, the rather slight evidence that does exist, the spot estimates and short-term records, are actually measures of the rate-of-flow, from which the total import estimates of Tables 4 and 5 were derived. It is therefore possible, with no greater degree of inaccuracy, to rearrange these estimates by quarter-centuries in order to see the changing flows and changing destinations of the trade. (See Table 33.) The Chaunu data are some help for the Spanish-American trade at the very end of the sixteenth century. Recent reconsideration of the Portuguese posi-

13. Wolff, "Negersklaverei," p. 180.
14. Vansina, *Kingdoms of the Savanna*, pp. 124–42.

Table 32

Ethnic Origins of Afro-Mexicans at the End of the Seventeenth Century

Seventeenth-century nomenclature	No.	%	Modern nomenclature and location
West Africa	*84*	*20.9*	
Guinea (unspecified)	22	5.5	
Gelofe	3	0.7	Wolof (Senegal)
Caboverde	2	0.5	Lebu (?), possibly Upper Guinea generally
Berbesi	1	0.2	Serer (Senegal)
Bran	8	2.0	Bram (Guinea-Bissau)
Biafara	5	1.2	Biafada (Guinea-Bissau)
Bañol	2	0.5	Banyun (Guinea-Bissau)
Bioho	1	0.2	Bissago (Guinea-Bissau)
Xoxo	1	0.2	Susu (Guinea-Conakry)
Zape	2	0.5	Temne etc. (Sierra Leone)
Mina	1	0.2	Akan (Gold Coast)
Arara	6	1.5	Fon, Gun, and related peoples (coastal Dahomey)
Arda	9	2.2	Ardra (coastal Dahomey)
Carabalí	6	1.5	Kalabari, shipping point for Ijo or Ibo (Eastern Nigeria)
São Thomé	14	3.5	Shipping point, probably Bight of Benin peoples generally
Terra Nova	1	0.2	Eastern Guinea coast generally
Central Africa	*303*	*75.4*	
Balala	2	0.5	Lala (Cameroon, Gabon)
Lunga	1	0.2	From coastal region north of the Congo mouth, possibly Rungu
Anchico	2	0.5	Tio or Teke (Congo-Brazzaville)
Longo	1	0.2	Sorongo, Bakongo sub-group
Congo	24	6.0	Bakongo and others from the lower Congo River basin
Angola	271	67.4	Shipping point, hinterland of Luanda generally
Matamba	1	0.2	Upper Kwango
Banguela	1	0.2	Benguela, shipping point
Southeastern Africa	*15*	*3.7*	
Zozo	1	0.2	Xhosa (Cape Province, South Africa)
Cafre	7	1.7	Probably Nguni (Cape and Natal)
Mozambique	7	1.7	Southeastern Africa generally
Total	402	100.0	

Source: Data from Aguirre Beltrán, *Población negra*, pp. 244–45.

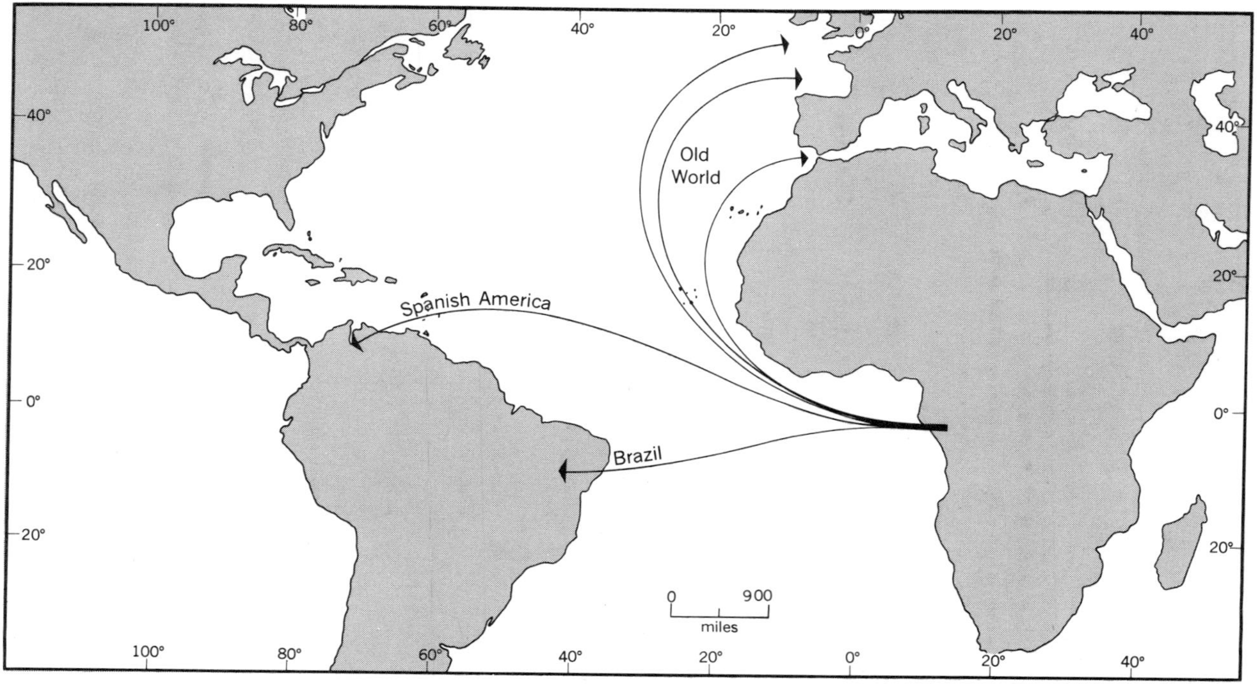

Fig. 8. Destinations of the Atlantic slave trade, 1451–1600. Fig. by UW Cartographic Lab. Data from Table 33.

tion in the Atlantic between 1570 and 1670 by Frédéric Mauro provides a reasonably reliable guide for Brazil.[15]

Contrary to the usual impression of the earlier literature, the Old-World slave trade was and remained dominant to the middle of the sixteenth century. The trade to Europe itself was preponderant to the end of the fifteenth century, though Madeira, the Canaries, and Cape Verde Islands became significant importers over the century 1476–1575. Slave imports into Madeira and the Canaries, however, had virtually ended by the end of the sixteenth century.[16] The Cape Verde Islands continued to import a few slaves into the seventeenth century, and, even later, populations moved back and forth between the islands and the adjacent mainland. For most purposes, though, the slave migration to these groups of islands was completed by 1600. So too was the direct slave trade from Africa to Europe: most African slaves who entered Europe after 1600 came as re-exports from the West Indies. They are therefore ignored here.

São Thomé is a continuous problem, little studied by historians but clearly of crucial importance to the slave trade of the sixteenth century. The distribution of its imports through time is therefore largely a matter of conjecture. Effective settlement began in 1493. A guess at 1,000 slaves a year for the 1490's is therefore possible for the last quarter of the fifteenth century. Thereafter, the only basis for estimation is a rough picture of sugar plantations rapidly expanding in the first half of the sixteenth century, then declining but still drawing a significant flow of slaves into the seventeenth century.

These estimates are too uncertain to support strong generalizations or penetrating questions. As a revisionist point, however, the relative importance of the Old-World trade is too striking to be an altogether false impression. It shows here as 55 per cent of the whole slave trade to 1600, and, if Deerr's higher estimate for

15. Mauro, *Portugal et l'Atlantique,* p. 180.

16. See Mauro, *Portugal et l'Atlantique,* pp. 178–79, 185–86, 190–91, for the fortunes of sugar planting on Madeira, the Azores, the Cape Verde Islands, and São Thomé.

TABLE 33

ROUGH ESTIMATES OF THE ATLANTIC SLAVE TRADE, 1451–1600, BY IMPORTS OF MAJOR IMPORTING REGIONS (000 OMITTED)

Region	1451–75	1476–1500	1501–25	1526–50	1551–75	1576–1600	Total
Europe	12.5	12.5	12.5	7.5	2.5	1.3	48.8
Atlantic Islands	2.5	5.0	5.0	5.0	5.0	2.5	25.0
São Thomé	—	1.0	25.0	18.8	18.8	12.5	76.1
Spanish America	—	—	—	12.5	25.0	37.5	75.0
Brazil	—	—	—	—	10.0	40.0	50.0
Total	15.0	18.5	42.5	43.8	61.3	93.8	274.9
Annual average	0.6	0.7	1.7	1.8	2.5	3.8	1.8
Mean annual rate of increase		0.8%	3.3%	0.1%	1.3%	1.7%	1.5%

Source: See text, pp. 112–15.

the Atlantic Islands were accepted, it would be higher still. Even in the last quarter of the century, when the South Atlantic System was firmly established in the New World, the Old-World destinations appear to account for 17 per cent of the total slave trade.

A second point that stands out, even though some of these estimates may be quite inaccurate, is the rapid rate of increase. The mean rate of increase is 1.5 per cent, with the greatest increase falling between the last quarter of the fifteenth century and the first quarter of the sixteenth. This particular jump may be exaggerated, but it seems clear that the slave trade began with a very high growth rate—not a mere trickle or a relatively constant rate of flow over this first century and a half.

THE SEVENTEENTH CENTURY

Although the first forty years of the seventeenth century are still within range of the Chaunu data, the outlines of the slave trade are no more certain than they were a century earlier. Up to 1640, what with the union of the Hispanic crowns and only minor incursions by the north Europeans, estimates may be a bit more accurate than they had been, or were to be during the rest of the century. From the 1640's onward, Dutch, English, French, Brandenburgers, Danes, Swedes, Genoese, and even Courlanders entered the picture. If they kept records, these are now scattered through the archives of three continents, and the situation is further complicated by the fact that the Dutch, Danes, and many smaller carriers either had no plantation colonies of their own or carried more slaves than their own colonies could absorb. They therefore supplied the French, English, and Spanish with illegal slaves whose arrival was not recorded at the customs houses. Some guesses can be made, informed by overall estimates based on slave-population data, but any conclusions must be tentative until the records of the Dutch West India Company are more fully exploited.

Perhaps the Spanish-American data are most accurate for this period. The Chaunu compilation and asiento data indicate an annual average import of 3,000 for the first quarter-century and 2,100 for the period 1626–40. This rate of import can be extended to 1650, but after that probable accuracy drops sharply. From 1640, the resumption of Portuguese independence broke the pattern of Portuguese asientos. Illegal Dutch imports replaced the legal asientos as the main source of supply until the mid-1660's and even later. Estimates for the second half of the century are therefore merely impressions based on the levels at which the Spanish tried to negotiate asiento contracts.[17]

Many of the same conditions applied to Portuguese America. The Dutch were even more active in Brazil than they were in the Caribbean. The common opinion of Brazilian historians, summed up by Goulart and confirmed by Mauro, puts Brazilian imports at 4,000 a year in the first half of the century, rising to 7,000 in the third quarter, and then dropping slightly.[18] Meanwhile, São Thomé also continued to import slaves. One asientista, holding

17. See Scelle, *La Traite négrière*, 1:473–503, 506, 566–67, 569; 2:26–27.
18. Mauro, *Portugal et l'Atlantique*, p. 180; Goulart, *Escravidão*, p. 116.

the contract for 1624–26, sent 42 per cent of his slaves to Brazil, 51 per cent to Spanish America, and 7 per cent to São Thomé.[19] São Thomé's share in this case was not far from that shown in Table 34 for the second quarter of the century.

The French and English colonies pose another kind of problem. With time-series of imports into Barbados and Jamaica, plus population data from a variety of Caribbean islands, it was possible in Chapter 3 to calculate possible rates of net natural decrease among the slave populations. These, in turn, served as the basis for estimating annual average slave imports over a period of years, and finally for estimating the total slave imports into each colony over the whole period of the slave trade. These total estimates, however, cannot easily be subdivided into the imports by quarter-centuries or any other short run of time. Short-term influences like war and peace, epidemic and famine, make it necessary to base these estimates on long periods, which would allow short-term factors to balance out. These longer time periods, however, yield generalized annual average rates of import which undoubtedly hide great annual variation, and even wide variation between average rates over shorter periods of five or ten years each.

If, therefore, the annual average rates of import calculated for each of the French and English colonies in Chapter 3 are used to redistribute the total estimated immigration into time periods (as in Table 34), the result for any individual time period is liable to be less accurate than the long-run total. But this source of distortion will be more serious in individual cells of Table 34 than in the quarter-century totals and the row-totals by region, where some of these errors may balance out.

In addition to the categories of Table 34, a small number of slaves were imported by other colonies such as Virginia, South Carolina, and a few of the smaller Caribbean colonies. Though several thousand people were involved in these movements, a category of "other" is not required. Until a colony became sufficiently developed to absorb a whole cargo direct from Africa, its

19. Mauro, *Portugal et l'Atlantique*, p. 175.

slave imports took the form of small lots carried by ships in the inter-colonial trade. Consequently, the slaves would already have been counted as imports into another colony.

The projections of Table 34 can be checked and illuminated by reference to partial data found elsewhere in the literature. This kind of cross-checking raises some problems in regard to the

TABLE 34

ROUGH ESTIMATES OF THE ATLANTIC SLAVE TRADE, 1601–1700, BY IMPORTS OF THE MAJOR IMPORTING REGIONS (000 OMITTED)

Region and country	1601–25	1626–50	1651–75	1676–1700	Total no.	Total %
Old World	*12.8*	*6.6*	*3.0*	*2.7*	*25.1*	*1.9*
São Thomé	12.5	6.3	2.7	2.4	23.9	
Europe	0.3	0.3	0.3	0.3	1.2	
Spanish America	*75.0*	*52.5*	*62.5*	*102.5*	*292.5*	*21.8*
Brazil	*100.0*	*100.0*	*185.0*	*175.0*	*560.0*	*41.8*
British Caribbean	—	*20.7*	*69.2*	*173.8*	*263.7*	*19.7*
Jamaica	—	—	8.0	77.1	85.1	
Barbados	—	18.7	51.1	64.7	134.5	
Leeward Is.	—	2.0	10.1	32.0	44.1	
French Caribbean	—	*2.5*	*28.8*	*124.5*	*155.8*	*11.6*
Martinique	—	1.5	22.8	42.2	66.5	
Guadeloupe	—	1.0	3.0	8.7	12.7	
Saint Domingue	—	—	3.0	71.6	74.6	
French Guiana	—	—	—	2.0	2.0	
Dutch Caribbean	—	—	*20.0*	*20.0*	*40.0*	*3.0*
Danish Caribbean	—	—	—	*4.0*	*4.0*	*0.3*
Total	187.8	182.3	368.5	602.5	1,341.1	100.0
Annual average	7.5	7.3	14.7	24.1	13.4	
Mean annual rate of increase	+2.8%	−0.1%	+2.8%	+2.0%	+1.9%*	

* Mean annual rate of increase between 1576–1600, and 1676–1700.
Sources: Tables 4, 5, 13, 15, 18, 20, 21, 22. See also text, pp. 116–19.

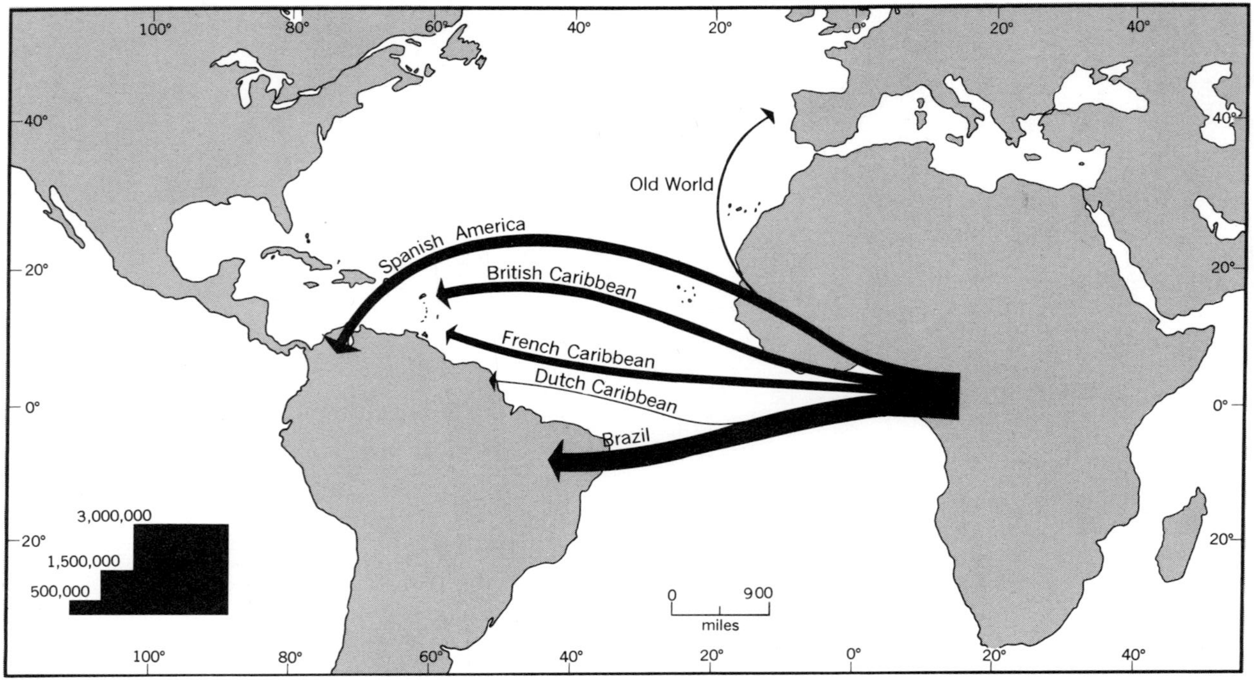

Fig. 9. Destinations of the Atlantic slave trade, 1601–1700. Fig. by UW Cartographic Lab. Data from Table 34.

French slave trade. The projections of Table 34 suggest a French colonial import in excess of about 4,980 slaves a year in the last quarter of the seventeenth century, but it is very doubtful on other evidence that French shipping of this period regularly carried as many as 2,000 a year. Two thousand a year was, indeed, the goal set in the stipulations of the French government for slave trade companies chartered in 1679 and 1696,[20] and none of the companies actually succeeded in meeting this goal as a regular practice. The carrying capacity of the whole French slave trade has been estimated at only 1,000 slaves a year in 1670–72.[21] La Rochelle, the leading slaving port of France at this period, sent out only 42 ships in the 23 years, 1671–93.[22] The Senegal Company appears to have carried an annual average of 1,520 slaves in 1682–84,[23] but this also seems to have been its most successful performance.

At these rates, at least three-quarters of the imports into French colonies were carried by non-French shipping—or else the projections are far too high. *Some* were undoubtedly carried by foreigners. Otherwise the slave populations of Martinique, Guadeloupe, and Saint Domingue together could not have reached the level of 44,000 reported in 1701.[24] But it is also possible that the projections are somewhat inflated by the double counting of slaves moving in the inter-colonial trade, and French shipping data suggest that the projections are more likely too high than too low.

The English slave trade of the late seventeenth century has been more carefully studied than the French. K. G. Davies' work

20. L. Peytraud, *L'Esclavage aux Antilles françaises avant 1789* (Paris, 1897), p. 137.

21. Gaston Martin, *L'Esclavage,* p. 21.

22. M. Delafosse, "La Rochelle et les îles au xviie siècle," *Revue d'histoire des colonies,* 36:241 (1949); Gaston Martin, *Nantes au xviiie siècle: L'Ere des négriers (1714–1774)* (Paris, 1931), p. 115.

23. E. Donnan, *Documents Illustrative of the History of the Slave Trade to America,* 4 vols. (Washington, 1930–35), 1:101.

24 Donnan, *Documents,* 1:97–101; Ly, *Compagnie du Sénégal,* pp. 155–56.

TABLE 35

THE SLAVE TRADE OF THE ROYAL AFRICAN COMPANY, BY ORIGIN AND DESTINATION, 1673–89

Region	No. slaves	%	Annual average
Coastal origin of slaves exported:			
Senegambia & Sierra Leone	10,700	12.0	
Windward Coast	24,400	27.3	
Gold Coast	18,600	20.9	
Ardra & Whydah	14,000	15.7	
Benin & the Calabars	6,000	6.7	
Angola	10,700	12.0	
Other & unknown	4,800	5.4	
Total	89,200	100.0	5,250
Imported into:			
Barbados	26,200	38.4	
Jamaica	22,900	33.6	
Nevis	6,900	10.1	
Other & unknown	12,200	17.9	
Total	68,200	100.0	4,010

Source: Calculation based on Davies, *Royal African Company*, pp. 225, 233, 361–63. Export percentages are those of 1680–85.

with the Royal African Company provides an invaluable body of numerical data. Even though the Company always traded in competition with illegal interlopers, it enjoyed a dominant position in the English sector of the trade between 1673 and 1689. For this period at least, its records provide a large sample of the origins, rates of flow, and destinations of the English slave trade. (See Table 35.)

Davies published annual figures for the value of the Company's exports to various regions of the African coast, and these form the basis for slave export estimates by region. They cannot be used directly, because the Company exported other goods from the African coast, but they can be adjusted to account for other African products. On Davies' own evidence, gold exports from the Gold Coast accounted for about 28 per cent of the value of exports from that region, and this has been allowed for in constructing Table 35.[25] In addition, the Senegambia and the region southward to Sierra Leone also exported a variety of other products, including wax, hides, and gold dust. In this case, an arbitrary 25 per cent allowance for non-slave exports was made in Table 35.

The number of slaves landed in the American colonies follows the Company's records, and the number exported from Africa can be calculated by reference to the usual level of loss in transit. That is, the Company's loss in transit over the years 1680–88 was 23.5 per cent of exports.[26] Extending this percentage to the whole period yields a total export of 89,200, which is then subdivided in Table 35 in proportion to the Company's adjusted "investment" in each region.

This pattern of African sources for the English trade contrasts sharply with the nearly contemporaneous sample of Mexican slaves in Table 32. The Gold and Windward Coasts accounted for 48 per cent of the English exports from Africa, but less than 1 per cent of the exports that went to Mexico. Even when Mexican slaves identified merely as coming from "Guinea" are credited to the Gold and Windward Coasts, the total is only 6 per cent of the sample. Bantu-speaking peoples from southern and Central Africa, on the other hand, make up 79 per cent of the Mexican sample and only 12 per cent of the English exports.

The pattern of English sources is also different from the pattern of West African exports to Spanish America in the sixteenth century, a phase of the slave trade that also had a West African emphasis. While the English drew more than 70 per cent of their slaves from the main east-west Guinea coast, from Cape Mount to Cameroons, the sixteenth-century Spanish trade drew only 9 per cent from these sources. (See Table 28.) Differences of this kind must have had a marked influence on Afro-American cultures in the New World. They underline once more the fact that

25. Davies, *Royal African Company*, p. 225.
26. Higham, *Leeward Islands*, p. 158.

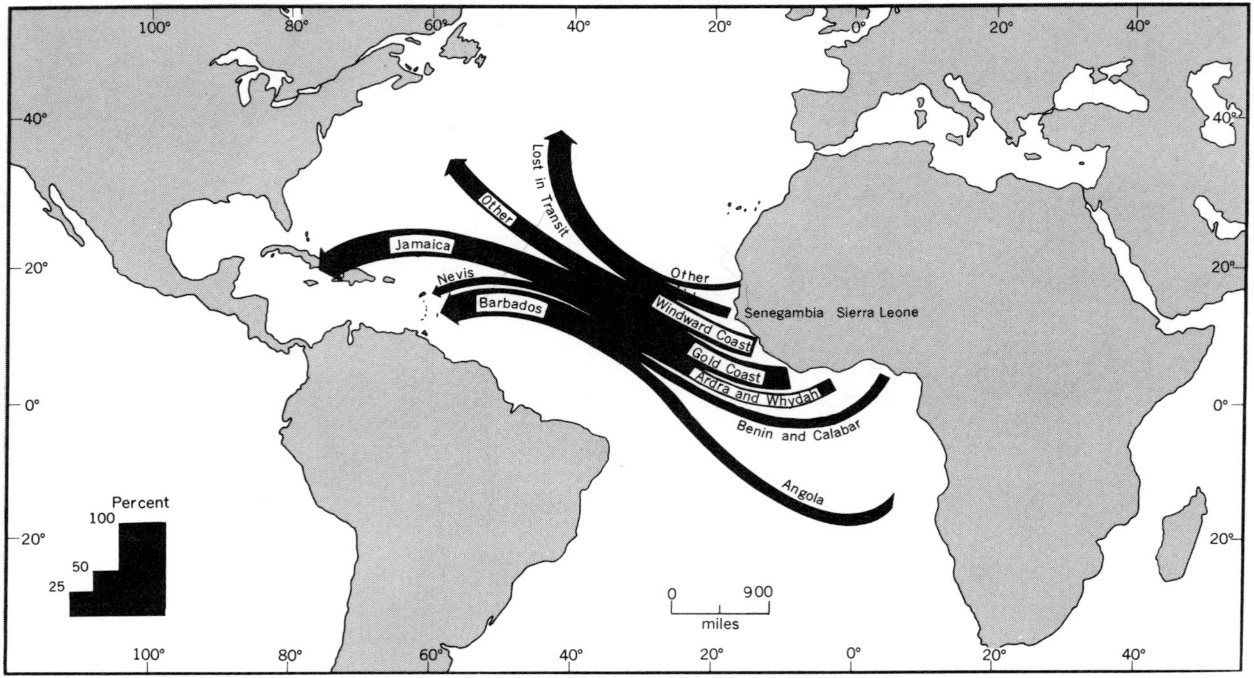

Fig. 10. The slave trade of the Royal African Company, 1673–89. Fig. by UW Cartographic Lab. Data from Table 35.

trading zones shifted in prominence with the passage of time, and that different slave-trading powers simultaneously patronized different parts of Africa.

For the English trade to English colonies, the Royal African Company's imports for 1673–89 were only 4,010 per year, while the projections based on import estimates in Table 34 suggest that the English colonies should have taken 6,950 a year in the final quarter of the seventeenth century. Part of this discrepancy is undoubtedly accountable to interlopers. The Gambia adventurers had a legal monopoly of the Senegambia trade until the end of 1677, but the Gambia was not a large supplier of slaves in any case. Other interlopers are known to have gone east of the Cape, into the zone of the East India Company which did little or nothing to keep them out. English colonies imported large numbers from southeast Africa and Madagascar, especially between 1675 and 1690, but the voyage to the Indian Ocean was long and expensive. The Company's own accounting of the interlopers operating in the years 1679–82 credited them with 29 per cent of the English slave trade of that period.[27] But interlopers would have to have had 42 per cent of the trade, if the English colonies actually did import the annual average of 6,950 assigned to them in Table 34. A possible discrepancy therefore remains. It is possible that the interlopers actually had a larger share of the trade, perhaps that Dutch smugglers were active, but the double-counting problem may also have inflated the estimates based on import data and slave populations. If so, the difference is not serious in terms of the accuracy to be expected, but it may be that the import estimates for the English colonies in Table 34 are 10 to 15 per cent too high.

Whether or not Table 34 is inflated in its estimates for French and English colonies, it is sufficiently accurate to show the major trends of the century's slave trade. The crucial event was the coming of the north Europeans, and especially the Dutch. They

27. Davies, *Royal African Company,* p. 225. This calculation disregards 4 interlopers that were captured and confiscated.

brought the "sugar revolution" to the Caribbean and began the shift that was to make the West Indian islands the heart of the eighteenth-century South Atlantic System. In time, this shift was to rebound to the interests of English and French planters, not Dutch shippers, but the straws in the wind should not obscure the fact that about 60 per cent of the slave trade in the seventeenth century still went to the Hispanic colonies, and about 40 per cent to Brazil alone.

Nor should the military and naval noise of the Dutch attack on Caribbean shipping, or the Dutch seizure of northeast Brazil in the second quarter of the century, obscure the meaning of these events for economic history. The traditional view sees the Dutch attack centered on the second quarter of the century, and it suggests that the slave trade should have sharply increased in that period. The projections of Table 34, on the other hand, show an actual decline. While it is possible, or even likely, that the slave trade continued to grow slightly at that period, it is hard to escape the conclusion that the initial Dutch impact was not simply additive. That is, the Dutch attempt to replace the Portuguese mastery over the trade of the South Atlantic was only partly successful. They were able to maintain the rate of slave imports into Brazil, to begin a new stream of slaves directed to the Lesser Antilles—but not, at the same time, to maintain the previous level of supply to Spanish America.

As a result, it was only after 1650 that the economic consequences began to be felt and the levels of the slave trade rose dramatically. Thus, in a rough way, the increased flow of slaves in the third quarter of the century can be attributed to the Dutch and some minor carriers, while the last quarter's increase probably owed more to the entry of the French and English. Even so, the rate of growth for the century as a whole was not remarkably different from that of the fifteenth and sixteenth centuries. The mean annual rate of increase in deliveries was 1.5 per cent in the earlier period (Table 33), and it rose only slightly, to 1.8 per cent in the seventeenth century.

CHAPTER 5

THE ENGLISH SLAVE TRADE OF THE EIGHTEENTH CENTURY

The eighteenth century saw the peak of the Atlantic slave trade, but increased size brought increased complexity. Historians have generally met the problem by restricting the scope of their studies—cutting back to the trade carried by one country, one port, or to the slaves received by a single colony overseas. The result is a large historical literature made up of many incommensurate studies covering scattered aspects of the whole. As a first step toward comparability of these data, the century can be arbitrarily divided into decennial units, and the English slave trade at least can be given decennial estimates by quantity, source, and destination for the whole period from 1691 to the legal end of the trade in 1808.

The political frontiers of the European colonies in the New World provide convenient standard units of destination, but the political units on the African side are less clearly defined in the literature. European traders and planters had a somewhat distorted and confused picture of African political geography, but they had a much clearer view of their commercial contacts on the African coast. It is therefore possible to deal with coastal regions of shipment, even where the actual origins in the interior are vague. According to the conventions of the time, several coastal regions of Africa were known by name, and these distinctions can be made still more precise in order to arrive at a standard series of conventional coastal regions in Africa.

The first of these is the conventional Senegambia, little changed from the sixteenth century and including the present-day Gambia and Senegal. A second region can be labelled Sierra Leone, but it would take in a good deal more than the present country. Instead, it would extend from the Casamance in the north to Cape Mount in the south, including the coastlines of Guinea-Conakry, Guinea-Bissau, and a very small part of Senegal and Liberia as well.

The third region would be the line of open breakers along the east-west coast from Cape Mount to Assini—mainly the present-day Ivory Coast and Liberia. The eighteenth-century English called it the "Windward Coast" (from a Gold Coast point of reference), though this should not be confused with the nineteenth-century "Windward Coast," a term sometimes used for the area on either side of Sierra Leone. A fourth region, the Gold Coast, presents no serious problem. In English usage at least, it has remained stable over several centuries as the coastal stretch from Assini on the west to the Volta in the east, roughly coterminous with the present-day Republic of Ghana. Here the Europeans built the greatest concentration of fortifications anywhere on the African coast—drawn by the gold trade to the interior and the existence of a series of rocky points with moderately safe landing beaches on the lee side, or by an occasional lagoon or river mouth where lighters could load and unload in security.

Farther east, coastal terminology is less stable over time, with terms like "the oil rivers" or "the slave coast" used at some periods but not in all. A fifth division, however, can be seen in the geographic Bight of Benin, taken here to include everything from the Volta to the Benin River. The core of this region in the eighteenth century was the somewhat narrower "slave coast" of present-day Togo and Dahomey. In the same way, the Bight of Biafra can be taken as a sixth region, centered on the Niger

TABLE 36

THE ENGLISH SLAVE TRADE, 1680–1800, BY AFRICAN REGION OF ORIGIN, EXPRESSED IN PERCENTAGES OF VARYING SAMPLES

<table>
<tr><th>Period</th><th>Senegambia</th><th>Sierra Leone</th><th>Windward Coast</th><th>Gold Coast</th><th>Bight of Benin</th><th>Bight of Biafra</th><th>Central Africa</th><th>Other</th></tr>
<tr><td>1. 1680–85</td><td colspan="2">12.0</td><td>27.3</td><td>20.9</td><td>15.7</td><td>6.7</td><td>12.0</td><td>5.4</td></tr>
<tr><td>2. 1688</td><td colspan="2">12.0</td><td>38.0</td><td>18.4</td><td>12.3</td><td>5.2</td><td>11.3</td><td>2.8</td></tr>
<tr><td>3. 1713</td><td>14.6</td><td>4.2</td><td>10.4</td><td>31.2</td><td>39.6</td><td>—</td><td>—</td><td>—</td></tr>
<tr><td>4. 1724</td><td>6.4</td><td>10.6</td><td>5.3</td><td>38.3</td><td>21.3</td><td>3.2</td><td>14.9</td><td>—</td></tr>
<tr><td>5. 1752</td><td>7.0</td><td colspan="3">32.0</td><td>5.2</td><td>40.4</td><td>12.7</td><td>2.6</td></tr>
<tr><td>6. 1771</td><td>7.0</td><td colspan="2">25.4</td><td>16.0</td><td colspan="2">49.5</td><td>2.1</td><td>—</td></tr>
<tr><td>7. 1771</td><td>6.7</td><td>2.0</td><td>31.0</td><td>13.1</td><td>3.0</td><td>44.2</td><td>—</td><td>—</td></tr>
<tr><td>8. 1788</td><td>0.9</td><td>4.7</td><td>5.4</td><td>13.5</td><td>16.8</td><td>29.0</td><td>29.7</td><td>—</td></tr>
<tr><td>9. 1798</td><td colspan="3">6.2</td><td>6.8</td><td>3.0</td><td>38.2</td><td>45.8</td><td>—</td></tr>
<tr><td>10. 1799</td><td>0.3</td><td colspan="2">9.8</td><td>9.7</td><td>1.0</td><td>44.8</td><td>34.4</td><td>—</td></tr>
</table>

Sources: Data from Davies, *Royal African Company*, pp. 225, 233, 363; Le Page, "Jamaican Creole," pp. 61–65; Donnan, *Documents*, 2:308–9, 454–56, 598; Edwards, *British West Indies*, 2:56. See also text, pp. 130–32.

Delta and the mouths of the Cross and Duala rivers to the east. Its bounds were the Benin River on the west and Cape Lopez to the south, in present-day Gabon. Then, from Cape Lopez south to the Orange River a number of different trading regions existed in fact, but the data are not sufficient to distinguish among them. The term Central Africa will therefore be used here as a seventh unit, though the term "Angola" in its broadest sense had the same meaning. Finally, the eighth region is the coast of southeastern Africa, from the Cape of Good Hope to Cape Delgado and including the island of Madagascar. In fact, few slaves were ever sold from the coast south of the present-day country of Mozambique, and the term Mozambique was sometimes used for this whole region.

Since the ethnic make-up of a particular New-World colony depended partly on ethnic market-preferences in that colony, the most effective guide to the changing source of the English slave trade as a whole is a series of samples that indicate the distribution of shipping. Suitable data were assembled recently by R. B. Le Page and reused more extensively by Orlando Patterson for assessing the ethnic make-up of the Jamaican slave populations.[1] Table 36 represents a slightly modified resetting of these data, consisting of ten samples from different dates over the period 1680–1799.

Rows 1, 2, and 4 are based on the distribution of "investment" by the Royal African Company for the years or periods indicated. The first two are derived from K. G. Davies' data in the same manner as the distribution of exports shown in Table 35.[2] That is, 28 per cent of the Company's exports to the Gold Coast are assumed to have been returned in gold, not slaves. Twenty-five per cent of the "investment" in the Senegambia is also taken as payment for other commodities. Row 4 is a similar recalculation of data on the Royal African Company's investment, first

1. Le Page, "Jamaican Creole," pp. 61–65; Patterson, *Sociology of Slavery*, pp. 113–44.

2. Davies, *Royal African Company*, pp. 225, 233, 363.

published by Elizabeth Donnan and later used by Le Page.[3] Row 3, on the other hand, is a different kind of sample. It is based on a contract between the Royal African Company and the South Sea Company, which called for the delivery of 4,800 slaves and stipulated the areas from which they were to be drawn. It can therefore be taken as a contemporaneous estimate of the relative importance of these areas for the slave trade.[4]

Rows 5, 6, 7, 9, and 10 are based on still another kind of sample. Each represents the capacity of ships sailing from English ports for Africa, along with their declared destinations. Again, the measure is not performance, but expectation. Some of these surely failed to find cargoes where they expected and therefore moved to another area. Others may have sailed for the Americas partially loaded. In addition, rows 5, 7, 9, and 10 include sailings from the port of Liverpool only, while row 6 is a calculation based on all slavers sailing from England.[5] Rows 9 and 10 are a little different from the others in this group. By this time, the capacity of a slaver was defined by law and determined by tonnage: these columns actually represent the declared outbound tonnage from Liverpool for various African destinations.

Row 8, on the other hand, is nothing more than the knowledgeable estimate of Robert Norris, a prominent slave trader. Though he gave these data as the distribution of the whole of the European slave trade, his knowledge is more likely to be

3. Le Page, "Jamaican Creole," p. 61.

4. Donnan, *Documents,* 2:308–9.

5. Data in row 5 from *Williamson's Liverpool Memorandum Book* (Liverpool, 1743), compiled by G. Williams, *History of the Liverpool Privateers and Letters of Marque with an Account of the Liverpool Slave Trade* (London, 1897), pp. 675–77 and calculated by Le Page, "Jamaican Creole," p. 62.

Row 6 from B. Edwards, *British West Indies,* 2:56.

Row 7 calculated from Donnan, *Documents,* 2:454–56 by Le Page, "Jamaican Creole," p. 63.

Row 8 from Donnan, *Documents,* 2:598.

Rows 9 and 10 from Williams, *Liverpool,* pp. 681–84, calculated by Le Page, "Jamaican Creole," p. 64.

accurate for the English part of the trade; his estimates can therefore be interpreted in this sense.

None of these ten samples is likely to be accurate within a few percentage points, but, as statistical samples, they are far larger than modern statistics demands. (Smaller and more accurate samples would, in fact, be more useful.) They can, nevertheless, be taken as a reasonable guide to the sources of the English slave trade, and the discrepancies between rows 6 and 7, both of which represent some kind of estimate for 1771 (one from all English ports and the other from Liverpool alone), are a guide to the degree of accuracy to be expected elsewhere on Table 36.

The time-series of slaves exported from Africa by English shipping is harder to establish than the proportionate distribution by source, but three different methods are available. One method begins with import estimates from the Americas, translated into export figures by reference to an expected loss in transit. A second is based on shipping data, either for all British shipping sailing for Africa, or for a particular port, incorporating in the calculation an estimate of that port's share of the total British slave trade. A third possibility is to work from the value of British exports to Africa and the ordinary price of slaves on the African coast at a particular time.

Of these, the third is perhaps the most difficult and uncertain. It was attempted recently for the period 1701–73 by Kenneth W. Stetson.[6] He began with time-series of the annual exports from Britain to Africa in the eleven principal articles in this trade. These quantities, given in the raw data at the fictitious "official values," were adjusted to actual values according to an unweighted commodity price index. Stetson then divided his total value of exports to Africa by the average price of slaves in each year to determine the approximate number of slaves that could have been purchased at that year's "investment" in African trade.

6. K. W. Stetson, "A Quantitative Approach to Britain's American Slave trade, 1700–1773," unpublished Master's thesis, University of Wisconsin, 1967.

He produced a table of decennial totals arrived at by two alternate means of calculation—one assuming that all exports to Africa would be returned in the form of slaves, the other attempting to account for the non-slave returns (Table 37).

TABLE 37

STETSON'S PROJECTED SLAVE EXPORTS FROM AFRICA BY WAY OF THE BRITISH SLAVE TRADE, 1701–73

Period	No. exported assuming total exports to Africa returned in slaves	No. exported allowing for value of non-slave exports from Africa
1701–10	110,500*	90,400
1711–20	81,300	61,000
1721–30	170,100	134,700
1731–40	150,200	107,100
1741–50	91,200	77,600
1751–60	145,800	121,800
1761–70	323,000	293,200
1771–73	128,300	114,200
Total	1,200,600	1,000,000

* Figures have been rounded.
Source: Stetson, "Britain's American Slave Trade," p. 37.

The second form of estimation, based on shipping, is not possible before 1750 for lack of data. After 1750, however, the number of ships sailing for Africa is reported for the years 1750–76. The total is 588 ships from Bristol and 1,868 ships from Liverpool. London shipping to Africa is listed only for 1750–53, but the annual average of 10 ships for the period 1750–53 can be projected at this same level until 1776.[7] The total for all three ports for 1750–76 can therefore be put at 2,726 ships. At the average capacity of 248 slaves per ship (the loading rate for the

7. Pitman, *British West Indies,* p. 67.

whole of the British slave trade in 1771), these ships would have had a capacity of 676,000 slaves, or an annual average capacity of 25,040.[8]

From 1776 through 1787, published returns indicate the number and tonnage of British ships clearing for the African coast.[9] These data can be converted to an estimate of slaves loaded at the rate of 2 slaves per ton, considered to be normal at the time.[10] In fact, some ships were chronically overloaded, while others were unable to find a full cargo. The translation is therefore only approximate.

For the period 1788 through 1793, I have not been able to find full returns for the whole of the British slave trade, but returns for the port of Liverpool alone cover both the annual number

8. Another set of returns for Liverpool alone (Williams, *Liverpool,* p. 678) gives a different total of 1,892 ships sailing for Africa in 1751–76, but this list includes some non-slave ships which were presumably left off the total given by Pitman.

9. PP, 1789, *Accounts and Papers,* xxiv (633), pp. 60 ff.

10. The estimate of 2 slaves per ton is confirmed somewhat by a later series of returns from Liverpool, which show both sailings expressed in the number of ships and the number of tons each year from 1783 through 1793. This series is paralleled by a second series of returns showing the number of Liverpool ships landing slaves in the British West Indies over the same time period, giving again the number of ships and the number of slaves landed. These data indicate that the average ship sailing from Liverpool for Africa was of 170 tons burden, that 878 Liverpool ships landed 303,737 slaves in the British West Indies (an average of 346 per ship and 2.03 per ton), and that 95.3 per cent of the Liverpool sailings to Africa were in the slave trade—the remainder returning directly to England from Africa with cargoes of ivory, timber, and so on. (Williams, *Liverpool,* pp. 678, 685.) A more precise calculation might be made by adjusting the average of 2.03 slaves landed per ton in accordance with the experience of the Nantes slave trade of this period, where losses in transit amounted to 5.01 per cent during the peace following the War of the American Revolution (D. Rinchon, *Le Trafic négrier, d'après les livres de commerce du capitaine gantois Pierre-Ignace-Liévin van Alstein.* Vol. 1 [Paris, 1938], pp. 282–301). On this basis, slaves loaded would have been 2.13 per ton, but the imprecision of the other data hardly justifies such a fine calculation. The two lists of returns, which form the basis of the calculation, are themselves in minor disagreement, and the peacetime years represented in the sample were a period when ships were probably loaded more nearly to capacity than was possible during the war years, 1776–83.

and tonnage of ships sailing for Africa and the number of slaves actually landed by Liverpool slavers in British colonies. Of these two forms of shipping record, the number landed is taken to be the more accurate, even though it has to be translated into a probable number purchased by reference to a coefficient of loss in transit. The losses in transit are systematically recorded for the French slave trade of this period, and they have been used in constructing the estimates found in Table 38.[11] The Liverpool trade, however, was only a part of the whole. In 1776–87 the share of the trade held by each English port is known, and Liverpool held 69.4 per cent of the trade for the last three recorded years (1785–87). Similar returns are again available in 1795–97, when Liverpool controlled 83.1 per cent of the English slave trade.[12] For lack of more precise knowledge, it seems acceptable to assume that Liverpool's share of the trade rose in equal annual steps from 1788 through 1793. No ships at all sailed to Africa from Liverpool in 1794, and it is assumed that the same was true of other ports at this critical juncture in the Napoleonic wars.

For the period 1795–1804, total British tonnage sailing for Africa is again recorded, and the legal capacity of a slaver was now set at 1.6 slaves per ton. Assuming the law was obeyed, or that disobedience was balanced by failure to fill out a cargo, these tonnages can be converted to an estimated number of slaves loaded.[13] For the last years of the English slave trade, only Liverpool records are available, but they are recorded with tonnages from 1805 until the last legal date at which a slaver could sail from a British port, 30 April 1807. It seems fair to

11. Williams, *Liverpool,* p. 685. See Gaston Martin, *L'Ere des négriers;* Rinchon, *Le Trafic négrier.* The coefficients of lost/sold used here were based on Gaston Martin, *L'Ere des négriers,* p. 115, for the 1750's and 1760's, and on Rinchon, *Le Trafic négrier,* pp. 248–305, for the 1770's and later. See below, p. 279, and Table 79.

12. Williams, *Liverpool,* p. 680.

13. This law was obviously hard to enforce, but many ships arrived in the West Indies with fewer slaves than full capacity. See W. Young, *The West India Common-Place Book . . .* (London, 1807), pp. 7–8.

assume that Liverpool in these years sustained the share of the British slave trade it held in 1802–4, amounting to 89.8 per cent of the total.[14] Estimates based on these shipping data are therefore possible from 1751 to 1807, and they are shown as decennial totals on Table 38.

TABLE 38

ESTIMATED SLAVE EXPORTS FROM AFRICA CARRIED BY THE ENGLISH SLAVE TRADE, 1751–1807, BASED ON SHIPPING DATA

Years	No. exported
1751–60	250,400*
1761–70	250,400
1771–80	196,000
1781–90	325,500
1791–1800	325,500
1801–7	266,000
Total	1,613,800
Annual average	28,310

*Figures have been rounded.

Sources: Pitman, *British West Indies,* p. 67; PP, 1789, *Accounts and Papers,* xxiv (633), pp. 60 ff; Williams, *Liverpool,* pp. 678, 680, 685. See text, pp. 133–36.

The final method for estimating British-carried exports from Africa is to begin with imports into the American colonies. K. W. Stetson made one estimate of this kind. He began with the North American colonies, taking the partial data in the U.S. Census Bureau's *Historical Statistics of the United States* as the basis for decennial estimates. His total of 255,100 slaves imported into the southern mainland colonies for the period 1701–75 is acceptable enough, being close to the calculations of other authorities.

For the West Indies, Stetson began with the same recorded imports into Jamaica and Barbados used by Deerr (and in the calculations in Chapter 3). Instead of comparing these to slave-

14. Williams, *Liverpool,* pp. 678, 680.

Table 39

Stetson's Projection of Slave Imports into British America, 1701–75

Years	Jamaica		Barbados		Southern mainland North America		Other British colonies		Total	
	No.	%	No.	%	No.	%	No.	%	No.	%
1701–10	22,400*	22.9*	37,600	38.4	9,000	9.2	28,800	29.4	97,900	100.0
1711–20	25,200	21.9	42,400	36.8	10,800	9.4	36,900	32.0	115,300	100.0
1721–30	38,000	32.8	21,100	18.2	9,900	8.5	46,800	40.4	115,900	100.0
1731–40	42,200	24.9	27,700	16.3	40,500	23.9	59,100	34.9	169,400	100.0
1741–50	54,200	26.0	31,700	15.2	58,500	28.0	64,200	30.8	208,500	100.0
1751–60	63,800	32.6	30,500	15.6	41,900	21.4	59,700	30.5	195,800	100.0
1761–70	62,300	26.7	33,300	14.3	69,500	29.8	68,000	29.2	233,100	100.0
1771–75	39,500	35.5	16,100	14.5	15,000	13.5	40,800	36.6	111,400	100.0
Total	347,600	27.9	240,400	19.3	255,100	20.5	404,300	32.4	1,247,400	100.0

* Figures and percentages have been rounded.

Source: Stetson, "Britain's American Slave Trade," pp. 13–15, 41, 48.

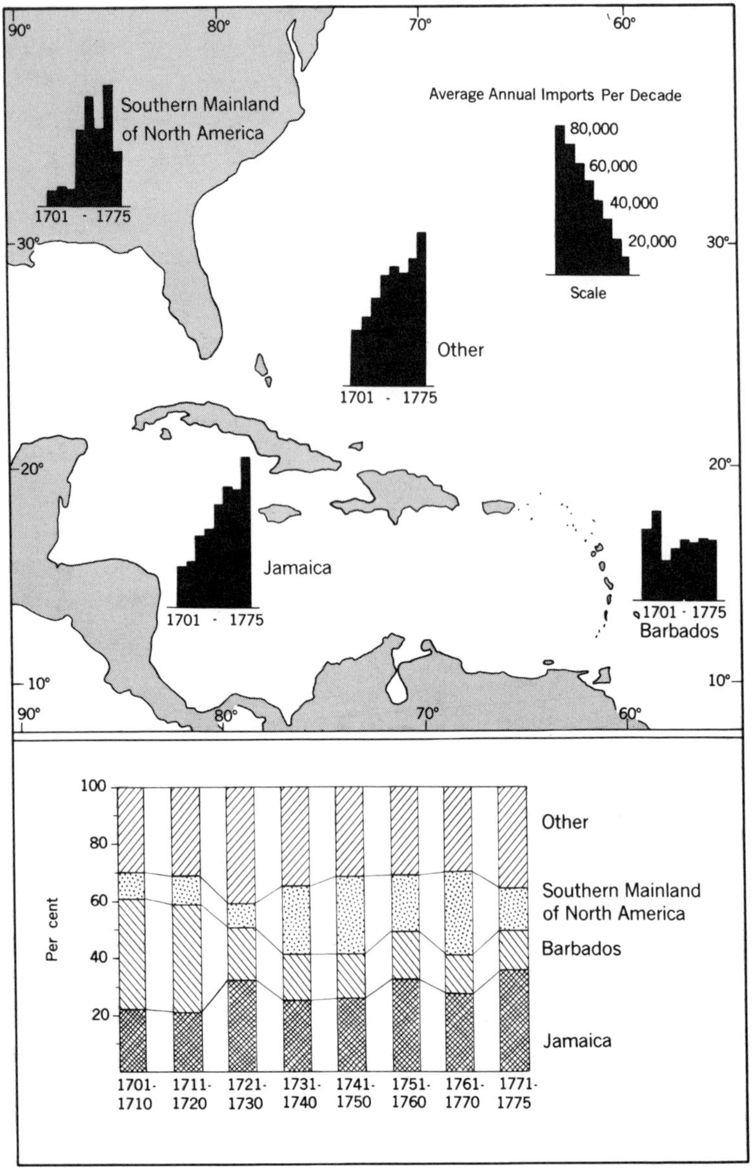

Fig. 11. Destinations of the British slave trade, 1701–75. Fig. by UW Cartographic Lab. Data from Table 39.

population figures, however, he assumed that the number of slaves imported would vary with sugar production. Thus, he found the relationship between slaves imported into Barbados and Jamaica and the sugar production of those two islands for each year. He then estimated the slave imports into the rest of the British Caribbean by reference to the sugar production there. The result is shown in Table 39.[15]

A second series of export estimates based on the slave imports of the American colonies can be constructed from the calculations in Chapter 3. Where the imports were not actually recorded, they can be projected by reference to long-term population increase. As with Table 34, however, this procedure may distort the distribution through time. Twenty-year periods or longer have therefore been adopted for Table 40, and the distribution of imports into North America is based on Stetson's data shown in Table 39.

The data of Tables 39 and 40 are still set in the form of imports into the British American colonies. The final step, translating these figures into British exports from Africa to the British colonies, is shown in cols. 3 and 4 of Table 41. Here the loss at sea is accounted for by analogy to the experience of the French slave trade in the eighteenth century. Gaston Martin's study of the Nantes slave trade indicates that the number of slaves purchased in Africa was 22.2 per cent higher than the number landed during the period 1715–41.[16] This figure is accepted as a general coefficient of loss in transit for the whole period 1701–60. In the second half of the century, however, losses decreased. Acceptable coefficients can, however, be derived from Gaston Martin's work until 1770, and from Rinchon's similar work on the slave trade of Nantes thereafter. They are .179 for the 1750's, .168

15. Stetson calculated from two alternate sets of estimates of Jamaican slave imports. The figure used here is the mean of the two, which is different from the Le Page data used elsewhere in this study, but not significantly so.

16. Gaston Martin, *L'Ere des négriers*, p. 115.

Table 40

Estimated Slave Imports into British American Territories, 1701–1810, Based on Slave Population Data (000 Omitted)

Territory	1701–20	1721–40	1741–60	1761–80	1781–1810	Total	%
North America	19.8	50.4	100.4	85.8	91.6	348.0	19.9
Jamaica	53.5	90.1	120.2	149.6	248.9	662.4	37.9
Barbados	67.8	55.3	57.3	49.3	22.7	252.5	14.4
Leeward Is.	30.0	44.5	67.9	67.9	91.6	301.9	17.3
St. Vincent, St. Lucia, Tobago, & Dominica	—	—	—	33.5	36.6	70.1	4.0
Trinidad	2.5	2.5	2.5	2.5	12.4	22.4	1.3
Grenada	3.8	3.8	14.5	27.5	17.3	67.0	3.8
Other	2.5	2.5	5.0	5.0	10.0	25.0	1.4
Total	179.9	249.1	367.8	421.1	531.1	1,749.2	100.0
Annual average	9.0	12.5	18.4	21.1	17.7	15.9	
Mean annual rate of increase over previous period	1.1%	1.6%	2.0%	0.7%	−0.7%	0.8%	

Sources: Tables 13, 15, 17, and 39. See text, pp. 57, 139.

for the 1760's, .115 for the 1770's, and .053 for the 1780's.[17] For the wartime decades that followed, a somewhat higher coefficient of .180 (equivalent to about a 15 per cent loss at sea) is chosen arbitrarily. The longer time-periods of Table 40 are subdivided by simple division, so that no great accuracy should be expected from decennial totals in col. 4 of Table 41.

Table 41 sums up the results of estimating British-carried slave exports from Africa by the three separate methods, each of which is based on an entirely independent body of data. In spite of the marked difference between individual decennial figures that should be comparable, the general similarity in the range of the totals over several decades is excellent evidence of the general magnitude of the British slave trade at this time.

In fact, the similarity is greater than a superficial comparison of totals will indicate. Only cols. 1 and 2 would be expected to give identical results if they had been perfectly calculated from perfect data. Cols. 3 and 4 do not claim to represent the whole of the British slave trade, only slaves exported in British ships to British colonies. Nor are they expected to be in agreement with each other. Col. 3 should be higher than col. 4: Stetson counted gross imports, while col. 4 excludes known re-exports. This difference is considerable. As Table 6 shows, Jamaican re-exports came to more than 200,000 between 1701 and 1807, or more than 1,900 a year. This amounts to 11.8 per cent of the British trade to the British colonies only, as shown in Table 40. And, since Stetson used the ratio of Jamaican slave imports to sugar production as a gauge for imports into other colonies as well, his estimates in col. 3 should be higher than those of col. 4 by at least that percentage. In fact, they are 12.0 per cent higher, which means that the two projections based on American imports (cols. 3 and 4) are nearly in agreement. The agreement between these two sets of estimates, however, may not be evi-

17. Rinchon, *Le Trafic négrier,* pp. 282–301. The coefficient for the 1770's is based on data for 1773–77, that for the 1780's on data for 1788–92. See Table 79 below.

TABLE 41

A COMPARISON OF DIFFERENTLY BASED ESTIMATES OF BRITISH SLAVE EXPORTS FROM AFRICA 1700–1807 (000 OMITTED)

Years	(1) Export potential	(2) Shipping data	(3) Import estimates based on production	(4) Import estimates based on demography	(5) Preferred series
1701–10	110.5		119.6	109.9	119.6
1711–20	81.3		140.9	109.9	140.9
1721–30	170.1		141.6	152.2	141.6
1731–40	150.2		207.0	152.2	207.0
1741–50	91.2		254.8	224.7	254.8
Subtotal 1701–50	*603.4*		*863.9*	*748.9*	*863.9*
1751–60	145.8	250.4	230.8	216.8	230.8
1761–70	323.0	250.4	272.3	245.9	273.3
Subtotal 1751–70	*468.9*	*500.8*	*503.1*	*462.7*	*503.1*
1771–80		196.0		234.8	196.0
1781–90		325.5		186.4	325.5
1791–1800		325.5		208.9	325.5
1801–7		266.0		208.9	266.0
Subtotal 1751–1810		*1,613.8*		*1,301.7*	*1,616.1*
Total 1701–1810				2,050.6	2,480.0

Sources: Col. 1: Stetson's estimates based on the purchasing power of British exports *to* Africa. From Table 37, col. 1.
Col. 2: Estimates based on declared destinations of ships sailing from England. From Table 38.
Col. 3: Stetson's estimates based on recorded imports, plus projections for the West Indian colonies based on sugar production and projections for the North American colonies based on population. From Table 39.
Col. 4: Recorded imports plus projections based on population data. From Table 40. This column represents *only* British exports to British colonies.
Col. 5: A summation of col. 3 to 1770 and col. 2 from 1771 onward.

dence that both are accurate. Both are, in fact, subject to the danger of double-counting as a result of the movement of slaves from one colony to another.

With the better data of the eighteenth century, compared to

the seventeenth, it is possible to see the dimensions of the double-counting problem a little more clearly, especially in regard to North America. In the northern mainland colonies, most slaves were imported in small numbers incidental to the West India trade. New York and New Jersey, for example, imported 4,551 slaves over the whole period 1715–67, but only 930 of these were African-born.[18] The rest were West Indians, and even the African-born may have lived for a time in the Caribbean colonies. Again, the New England colonies as a group imported only 6 African-born slaves over the four years 1769–72.[19] With this evidence, the safest course is simply to disregard the slave imports of the northern colonies.

The southern mainland colonies did, however, import slaves directly from Africa, especially after the economy of each had achieved the critical mass necessary to give it a market capable of absorbing a whole cargo of one or two hundred slaves at a time. Elizabeth Donnan's published data for the southern colonies illustrate this point. In her long but possibly incomplete list of slave ships entering Virginia between 1710 and 1769, most came from either the West Indies or nearby colonies, but with cargoes of a few individuals to a few dozen. A much smaller number of ships from Africa brought about 86 per cent of the 53,500 slaves recorded on the list. Furthermore, the proportion directly from Africa increased with the passage of time. In the earliest recorded period, 1710–18, only 56 per cent of the slaves were direct exports from Africa, the remainder being re-exports from other colonies. And the same pattern reappears in the development of Georgia. Partial lists for the period 1755–65 show no imports at all from Africa—only from other colonies—and, when the direct slave trade to Georgia began after 1766, the proportion of slaves arriving directly from Africa was low at first.[20]

18. Herskovits, *Negro Past,* p. 45.

19. Bureau of the Census, *Historical Statistics of the United States,* p. 769.

20. Donnan, *Documents,* 4:175–234, 612–25. The tabulation is partly that of Herskovits, *Negro Past,* pp. 46–47.

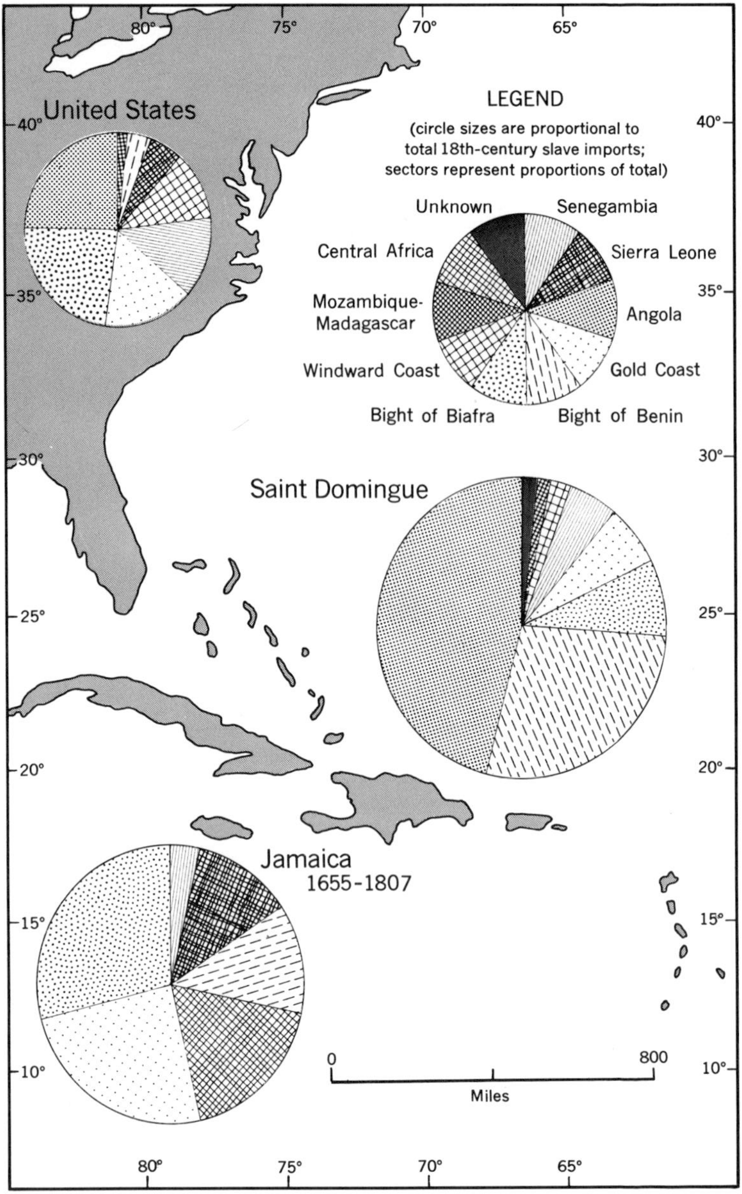

Fig. 12. Origins of slaves in Jamaica, Saint Domingue, and the United States in the eighteenth century. Fig. by UW Cartographic Lab. Data from Tables 45, 46, and 60.

South Carolina, however, was a direct importer from Africa at an early date, and its eighteenth-century development was the closest mainland approximation to the West Indian plantation pattern. Donnan's list of slaves imported is compiled from newspaper advertisements for "new Negroes," including some re-exported from the West Indies immediately after their arrival from Africa. It therefore ignores whatever inter-colonial trade in creole or "seasoned" slaves may actually have existed. Even so, some 3 to 4 per cent of the 65,000 slaves recorded for 1733–85 are listed with only an American point of origin.[21]

If the Virginia and North Carolina samples are taken together, assuming that the pattern of Virginian exports was roughly true for the Chesapeake Bay region as a whole, at least 4 per cent of the slaves entering by way of South Carolina and about 14 per cent of those entering the Chesapeake were actually re-exports, mainly from the West Indies. If these percentages were true of the whole period 1701–75, *at least* 20,000 slaves entering the southern mainland colonies have been counted twice in Stetson's calculations. The error amounts to less than 2 per cent of Stetson's total estimate, a negligible amount within the expected limits of accuracy—but what of the possibility that the inter-colonial trade was still more extensive? Error from this source could be far more substantial.

Comparison between the import-derived estimates and those of cols. 1 and 2 is mildly encouraging. The shipping estimates have a high level of expected accuracy. Although their total for 1751–1810 is 24.0 per cent greater than col. 4 over the same period, col. 4 represents exports to British colonies only. Jamaican re-exports alone came to 112,000 over these years (Table 6), representing an 8.6 per cent increase over col. 4.[22] If additional flows from the British slave trade to foreign colonies were equal

21. Donnan, *Documents,* 4:235–587. Tabulation from Herskovits, *Negro Past,* p. 48.

22. That is, when the decennial figures of Table 6 are multiplied by the same coefficients for loss at sea as those used in translating the import figures of Table 40 to the export figures of Table 41, col. 4.

to the Jamaican re-exports, estimated total British slave exports based on the data of col. 4 could come to 1,525,700—a figure directly comparable to the total of 1,613,800 in col. 2. With this adjustment, col. 2 exceeds col. 4 by 5.8 per cent, well within the expected limits of the data.

The low total for col. 1 is more disturbing. While the calculation may be faulty, it is also possible that all three of the other sets of estimates are a little too high. Col. 2, for example, would be too high if a considerable number of ships were unable to load to capacity in Africa. The estimates in cols. 3 and 4 are both susceptible to the danger of double counting.

These considerations suggest that Stetson's import estimates (Table 41, col. 3) are unacceptably high as estimates of the British slave trade to British colonies only—both on the score of double-counting and on that of neglecting re-exports. They may, however, be an accurate reflection of British slave exports to all destinations. By neglecting Jamaican re-exports and then using Jamaican data to calculate the number of slaves imported into the other British colonies, they contain the unconscious assumption that the gross imports for the whole of the British Caribbean will be in proportion to the gross imports of Jamaica and Barbados. This may be as fair as any other method of incorporating an allowance for re-exports. Stetson's time-series has an additional advantage over the series based on demographic data: it is based on annual calculations, which should have a greater degree of short-run accuracy.

Stetson's figures can therefore be adopted as the preferred series of estimates of British slave exports to all destinations from 1701 to 1770. From 1771 to 1810, the series based on shipping data appears to be the most accurate. The combination (Table 41, col. 5) gives a general time-series from 1700 to 1810, which is used for Table 43 below and its derivatives.

One other way of calculating the size of the British slave trade in the eighteenth century has not been mentioned up to this point. This method is to take a one-year estimate of the total British-carried slave trade and treat it as an annual average valid for adjacent years as well. A similar device was used for guessing at the slave trade of the fifteenth and early sixteenth centuries, but with considerable doubt as to the reliability of the process. Now, with the data of Table 41, it is possible to check the reliability of contemporaneous one-year estimates against the area of agreement found in three independent bodies of data.

A search of the literature produced eight separate one-year estimates scattered through the eighteenth century. One report for 1720 mentions a total of 146 ships in the British slave trade, capable of carrying 36,050 slaves.[23] A second gives 87 ships from London in 1725 with a capacity of 26,400 slaves, plus 63 ships from Bristol with a capacity of 16,950. The total can be taken as nearly the total British slave trade, since Liverpool had not yet entered it—or 150 ships with a capacity of 43,390 slaves.[24] In 1749, Bristol and Liverpool together sent out 117 ships with a capacity of 39,840, while London sent out eight additional ships. At the same rate per ship, the London capacity was 2,720 slaves, giving a British total for the year of 42,560.[25] Other reports, more often repeated in the literature, give an export capacity for the British slave trade of 53,100 slaves in 1768 and 47,100 slaves in 1771.[26] Robert Norris's famous estimate given to the Board of Trade in 1787 put the total British slave trade of that period at 38,000,[27] and James Bandinel gathered two additional estimates for his semi-official study of the slave trade—41,000 on the eve of the American Revolution, and 55,000 in 1798.[28]

In Table 42, these one-year estimates are compared to the preferred time-series from Table 41—that is, to the data in col. 5

23. Williams, "Golden Age of the Slave System," pp. 65–67.

24. Pitman, *British West Indies,* pp. 67–68; C. M. MacInnes, *England and Slavery* (Bristol, 1934), pp. 34–36.

25. Pitman, *British West Indies,* p. 67.

26. Pitman, *British West Indies,* p. 70; Edwards, *British West Indies,* 2:56.

27. Great Britain, Privy Council, *Report of the Lords of the Committee of Council for Trade and Foreign Plantations . . .* (London, 1789), Part II. (Hereafter *Board of Trade Report.*)

28. Bandinel, *Trade in Slaves,* pp. 63, 105.

of Table 41—and the comparison takes two forms. To arrive at a total estimate for 1701–1807, each of the one-year estimates can be taken as an annual average, representative of the period both before and after it, to the midpoint between its date and that of the next estimate in the series (Table 42, col. 3). On this basis, the general total for 1701–1807 would be 4,662,900 slaves exported from Africa by way of the British slave trade, or 88 per cent more than the preferred series from Table 41.

The second form of comparison is to set the one-year estimate against the annual average indicated by the preferred time-series. In this case, every single one of the one-year estimates is higher than the equivalent annual average, often with a high ratio of difference (Table 42, col. 5).

TABLE 42

A COMPARISON OF ONE-YEAR ESTIMATES OF BRITISH SLAVE EXPORTS FROM AFRICA WITH THE LEVEL OF CALCULATED DECENNIAL ANNUAL AVERAGES (000 OMITTED)

Year	(1) Estimated export	(2) Applied to the years	(3) Period estimate	(4) Calculated decennial annual av.*	(5) Ratio of one-year estimate to calculated time-series
1720	36.1	1701–22	794.2	14.1	2.56
1725	43.4	1723–36	607.6	14.2	3.06
1749	42.6	1737–58	937.2	25.5	1.67
1768	53.1	1759–69	584.1	27.2	1.95
1771	47.2	1770–73	188.8	19.6	2.41
1775	41.0	1774–80	287.0	19.6	2.09
1787	38.0	1781–93	494.0	32.6	1.17
1798	55.0	1794–1807	770.0	32.6	1.69
Total			4,662.9		

* From Table 41.

Sources: Table 41; Williams, "Golden Age of the Slave System," pp. 65–67; Pitman, *British West Indies*, pp. 67–70; MacInnes, *England and Slavery*, pp. 34–36; Edwards, *British West Indies*, 2:56; *Board of Trade Report*, Part II. See text, pp. 146–48.

How to explain such a marked difference? The annual averages of Table 41 agreed so closely, in spite of independent data and different forms of calculation, that it hardly seems possible they were all wrong. The explanation is probably psychological. The authority making an estimate, or the author quoting one, will tend to look for a "normal" year—one, for example, without warfare to interfere with the usual flow of trade. Thus, seven of the eight years represented in Table 42 were peacetime years, though peace was hardly a typical condition for eighteenth-century England. The single exception was 1798, a wartime year but also a boom year for the slave trade, being the second highest year in the whole history of the Liverpool trade. The choice of years therefore distorts the picture and guarantees an overestimate, but this is not to say that the men who originated these figures were trying to make the trade appear larger than it actually was. They knew that the trade varied greatly from year to year. (Indeed, in the time-series of Liverpool tonnages sailing for Africa, which are a complete time-series from 1751 to 1807, the highest figure for any decade is invariably at least twice the lowest.)[29] A merchant or government official at the time was hardly likely to think in terms of long-term annual averages, but rather in terms of maximum capacity in a good year. If the one-year estimates are understood in this sense, they are in close agreement with the projections of Table 41. They only become inaccurate if they are misinterpreted as long-term averages—but they are nevertheless responsible for many of the high estimates of the total slave trade found in the historical literature.

Having a reasonably accurate quantitative picture of the British slave exports from Africa, and having the set of ten distribution estimates shown in Table 36, it is now possible to put them together as a set of decennial projections of the number of slaves carried from each of the conventional coastal regions by the English traders over the course of the eighteenth century. The result is shown in Table 43.

29. Williams, *Liverpool,* p. 678.

Table 43

Possible Volume Exported by the English Slave Trade, by Coastal Region of Origin in Africa, 1690–1807

Coastal region	(1) 1690–1700	(2) 1701–10	(3) 1711–20	(4) 1721–30	(5) 1731–40	(6) 1741–50	(7) 1751–60	(8) 1761–70	(9) 1771–80	(10) 1781–90	(11) 1791–1800	(12) 1801–7	(13) Total
Senegambia	9,200	17,500	20,600	9,100	13,900	17,300	16,200	19,100	13,700	2,900	1,000	800	141,300
%	9.3	14.6	14.6	6.4	6.7	6.8	7.0	7.0	7.0	0.9	0.3	0.3	5.5
Sierra Leone	2,700	5,000	5,900	15,000	14,900	15,500	9,000	4,100	2,900	15,300	11,700	9,600	111,600
%	2.7	4.2	4.2	10.6	7.2	6.1	3.9	1.5	1.5	4.7	3.6	3.6	4.3
Windward Coast	37,800	12,400	14,700	7,500	18,400	25,500	28,600	65,100	46,800	17,600	13,700	11,200	299,300
%	38.0	10.4	10.4	5.3	8.9	10.0	12.4	23.9	23.9	5.4	4.2	4.2	11.6
Gold Coast	18,300	37,300	44,000	54,200	56,100	59,400	36,500	43,600	31,400	43,900	27,000	22,100	473,800
%	18.4	31.2	31.2	38.3	27.1	23.3	15.8	16.0	16.0	13.5	8.3	8.3	18.4
Bight of Benin	12,200	47,400	55,800	30,200	27,300	26,800	12,000	8,400	6,100	54,700	6,500	5,300	292,700
%	12.3	39.6	39.6	21.3	13.2	10.5	5.2	3.1	3.1	16.8	2.0	2.0	11.3
Bight of Biafra	5,200	—	—	4,500	45,100	71,300	93,200	126,300	90,900	94,400	135,100	110,400	776,400
%	5.2	—	—	3.2	21.8	28.0	40.4	46.4	46.4	29.0	41.5	41.5	30.1
Angola and Mozambique	11,200	—	—	21,100	28,600	34,400	29,300	5,700	4,100	96,700	130,500	106,700	468,300
%	11.3	—	—	14.9	13.8	13.5	12.7	2.1	2.1	29.7	40.1	40.1	18.2
Other and unknown	2,800	—	—	—	2,700	4,600	6,000	—	—	—	—	—	16,100
%	2.8	—	—	—	1.3	1.8	2.6	—	—	—	—	—	0.6
Total	99,400	119,600	140,900	141,600	207,000	254,800	230,800	272,300	196,000	325,500	325,500	266,000	2,579,400
													100.0
Annual average	900	12,000	14,100	14,200	20,700	25,500	23,100	27,200	19,600	32,600	32,600	38,000	21,900

Sources: Tables 36, 41; Davies, *Royal African Company*, p. 143. See text, pp. 127–46.

In fact, the table is extended for one decade back into the seventeenth century. The records of the Royal African Company are available through K. G. Davies' work, and they indicate both the Company's landings of slaves in the New World and the distribution of its "investment" in Africa. The Company can therefore be credited with 16,300 slaves landed in the eleven-year period, 1690–1700. The problem at this period comes from growing trade of the "interlopers," whose activities were illegal until the end of June 1698. After that, much the same group of merchants continued in the legal slave trade as "separate traders." The first years of legal competition were covered, fortunately for historians, by a government enquiry, which showed 75,000 slaves imported into the American colonies by the separate traders (July 1698–1707), as against 18,000 for the Company.[30] This gives the separate traders an annual average of 7,890, which may be applied to the period from 1 July 1698 to the end of 1700. The illegal period before 1698 is harder to deal with, but it is clear that the interlopers had been steadily gaining on the Company. Since an estimate of their trade for 1673–89 has already been made, and the interlopers' trade for this period came to an annual average of 1,620 slaves landed, one rough solution is simply to take the mean of the interlopers' annual average performance for 1673–89 and the separate traders' performance for 1698–1707. This figure, 4,760 a year, might then be a reasonable guess for the non-company trade of 1690 through June 1698. On this basis, the total British slave imports into the New World for the eleven years 1690–1700 would be about 76,500. Adjusted to an export rate by reference to the Company's mean loss in transit of 23 per cent, the total export for the period would be about 99,400.

The short run of official returns for the period 1698–1701 incidentally provides a further check on Stetson's import estimate. If the annual averages reported for the separate traders and the Company together from mid-1698 to 1707 were also

30. Davies, *Royal African Company*, p. 143.

valid for 1701–10, the number of slaves landed by British ships would have been 97,890—compared to Stetson's estimate of 97,935 (rounded to 97,900 in Table 39).

The distribution of the total for 1690–1700 (and of the decennial estimates that follow it) according to conventional regions of the African coast is not as straightforward as one might hope. The sources of the British slave trade in Africa (Table 36) are not always completely known, nor as precise as one might like in distinguishing the seven conventional trading zones. As a result, the projections of Table 43 include interpolations, which are legitimate if their limitations are understood, but will nevertheless have the effect of smoothing out some of the actual discontinuities in the time-series of exports from a particular section of the coast. For example, the distribution for the 1690's follows the Royal African Company's distribution of investment in 1688 (from Table 36), but the Company's combined investment for Sierra Leone and Senegambia is divided between these two regions following the proportions that appear to have been in effect in 1713.

Further interpolations follow this pattern. The distribution pattern for 1713 has been used for 1701–10, for lack of an appropriate sample within that decade. In 1721–30, the sample for 1724 is available (from row 4, Table 36), but a sample for the 1730's is again missing. A rough approximation can be found by taking the mean of the distributions for 1724 and 1752, but the 1752 sample lumps together Sierra Leone, the Windward Coast, and the Gold Coast. This aggregate must then be distributed somewhat conjecturally by taking the mean of the samples for 1724 and 1771 (rows 4 and 7, Table 36). The 1740's present the same problem, which is solved in the same manner; only this time the sample for 1752 is weighted 2-to-1 against that for 1724. For the 1750's, the 1752 sample is used, but with the undivided aggregate subdivided in proportion to the mean of the samples for 1724 and 1771 (row 7). Both the 1760's and the 1770's can be based on the sample of 1771, but Table 36 shows two different samples for that year. The first of these (row 6) is probably more accurate, but its consolidated totals are here redistributed according to the proportions of the second. The probable distribution for the 1780's follows readily enough from the sample of 1788, but consolidated totals again appear at the end of the nineties. In this case, it was assumed that Senegambia's share in 1798 remained unchanged at 0.3 per cent. The consolidated totals for the Windward Coast and Sierra Leone in the data for 1798 and 1799 were then redistributed in proportion to the data for 1788. The sources for the 1790's and for 1801–7 were projected as the mean of the samples for 1798 and 1799.

The result in Table 43 is therefore a somewhat speculative outline, whose calculations down to the last hundred slaves and the tenths of one per cent should not obscure its unreliability. If all has gone well, any figure in the table should be accurate within about 20 per cent of actuality. Where the data have been weak, as some certainly have been, not even that much can be expected.

Until the archives have been more fully exploited, it will be difficult to check long-range projections of this kind against other forms of data. The one-year estimates scattered through the literature are themselves suspect, but one time-series of annual export figures from the Gold Coast is available for 1758–68.[31] It shows the typical pattern of great variation from one year to the next, and an annual average of 3,700 slaves exported by British shipping. This figure can be compared to the annual average of 4,010 shown in the table for the two decades 1751–70. The projected average is 8.4 per cent higher than the recorded average for 1758–68, a very satisfactory result as far as it goes, though by no means conclusive.

The broad pattern of the English slave trade is nevertheless clear enough. The secular trend was steadily upward to the peak

31. Committee of the Company of Merchants Trading to Africa to Arthur Heywood, 20 June 1771, Public Record Office, London, T. 70/39, f. 3. The list is presented as an annotation to a letter from Richard Brew, a merchant at Cape Coast, and it carried the title, "A list of the slaves annually shipt off from the Gold Coast of Africa to the British Settlements in America," with no further identification of the source.

of the 1780's and 1790's. The very high annual rate of export from 1801 to 1807 is, of course, accountable to the planters' expectation that the trade would soon be cut off by Parliamentary action. It therefore constituted a short-term peak, of the kind that had occurred before in the years immediately following the peace of 1763 and the peace of 1783. The sustained peak of the English slave trade had already passed.

The use of these formal decennial totals tends to obscure the annual variation, but a decade is not long enough to smooth out the variations caused by war and peace in Europe. France and England were, after all, at war in 1689–97, 1702–13, 1739–48, 1755–63, 1779–83, 1793–1802, and 1803–15. In each period of warfare where control of the sea lanes was contested, the slave trade declined, but the unfilled demand of the American colonies was supplied in the peacetime years that followed. This explains the high level of the trade in the 1760's and 1780's, following the temporary drop of the 1750's and 1770's.

On the African side, supply was far more irregular. No one region supplied as much as a third of the British slave exports. No region supplied a steady or systematic response to the European demand. Only the Bight of Biafra showed a pattern of sustained long-run supply, but the Biafran source only began to be significant in the 1730's. Meanwhile, the Gold Coast and the Bight of Benin, which had supplied more than half the British exports of 1701–30, had become minor sources for the trade of the 1790's.

Table 43 has one further interesting implication. The proportions in col. 13 represent the approximate ethnic balance of the British slave trade as a whole. Since the great majority of slaves imported into British colonies were imported between 1690 and 1807, this column is also a guide to the probable mixture of African peoples in any of them.

But this guide is only approximate. Each colony received a somewhat different ethnic input. One cause of variation was the changing make-up of the British slave trade. A colony that imported heavily in the early part of the eighteenth century would receive a correspondingly high proportion of Akan peoples from the southern Gold Coast, and of Fon and Gun from southern Dahomey. Another, which may have received its largest number of slaves in the 1790's and later, would have drawn more heavily on the Ibo and their neighbors, and on Bantu-speaking peoples from the hinterland of Angola.

Market preferences also played a role. Slave buyers distinguished between African cultures following a set of stereotyped "national characters" highlighting traits that seemed important to slave owners—industry, proneness to rebellion, faithfulness, honesty, or physical suitability for field work. Such stereotypes differed through time and from one colony to another, but they could have a marked influence on the price offered in particular American markets. Since they were also known to merchants and supercargoes in the slave trade, they influenced the way in which slaves of a particular African origin would be distributed in the New World. The extent of this influence differed with time and place. Some markets showed less ethnic prejudice than others. Large markets like Jamaica, which took a large proportion of all British slave imports, could not depart drastically from the ethnic mixture offered by the British slave trade and still

TABLE 44

SLAVES IMPORTED INTO BRITISH GUIANA, 1803–7, BY ORIGIN

Region of origin	Slaves imported (%)	British exports from Africa, 1801–7 (%)
Windward Coast	31.7	4.2
Gold Coast	37.8	8.3
Bight of Benin	—	2.0
Bight of Biafra	8.6	41.5
Central Africa	11.1	40.1
Other or unknown	10.8	3.9
Total	100.0	100.0

Sources: Table 43, col. 12; Herskovits, *The Myth of the Negro Past*, p. 49.

meet the demand for workers. Smaller colonies had greater leeway. A place like British Guiana could import a very different mixture from that carried by the British trade as a whole, and the contrast at the end of the slave trade is illustrated in Table 44.

Other local samples of imports show similar variations, even between nearby colonies like Virginia and South Carolina, and the pattern of ethnic input to both was different from that of the Caribbean colonies. The most useful large samples are those collected and published by Elizabeth Donnan, and these serve as the basis for cols. 1 and 2 of Table 45.[32] Of the two, the South Carolina sample is far more accurate. The Virginia sample was based on naval officers' reports to London, but nearly half of the ships from Africa were listed simply as "from Africa." Many others were listed as from "Guinea," and these listings have been redistributed according to the proportion of more specific listings by coastal region from Sierra Leone, the Windward Coast, and the Gold Coast. The term "Guinea" undoubtedly included some from the Bight of Benin as well, but no specific listings appear from that region.

The comparative laxness of the Virginian listings is not mere chance. Donnan came to the conclusion that the Virginians, in contrast to their South Carolinian neighbors, were simply not so interested in ethnic origins.[33] The South Carolina planters, on the other hand, had strong ethnic prejudices which were reflected in the Charleston slave market. They preferred above all to have slaves from the Senegambia, which meant principally Bambara and Malinké from the interior at this period, and they generally

32. Donnan, *Documents*, 4, passim. The tabulations of Herskovits, *Negro Past*, pp. 46–47 have been used as the basis for the Virginia sample, with the "Guinea" category redistributed to conventional coastal regions adopted for this study. For the South Carolina sample, the tabulation of W. S. Pollitzer, "The Negroes of Charleston (S.C.); A Study of Hemoglobin Types, Serology, and Morphology," *American Journal of Physical Anthropology*, 16:244 (1958), has been used with adjustment to the conventional coastal regions.

33. Donnan, *Documents*, 4:234*n*.

TABLE 45

SLAVES IMPORTED INTO THE NORTH AMERICAN MAINLAND, BY ORIGIN

Coastal region of origin	Per cent of slaves of identifiable origin imported by			(4) Speculative estimate, all imported into North America (%)
	(1) Virginia, 1710–69	(2) South Carolina, 1733–1807	(3) British slave trade, 1690–1807	
Senegambia	14.9	19.5	5.5	13.3
Sierra Leone	5.3	6.8	4.3	5.5
Windward Coast	6.3	16.3	11.6	11.4
Gold Coast	16.0	13.3	18.4	15.9
Bight of Benin	—	1.6	11.3	4.3
Bight of Biafra	37.7	2.1	30.1	23.3
Angola	15.7	39.6	18.2	24.5
Mozambique-Madagascar	4.1	0.7	*	1.6
Unknown	—	—	0.6	0.2
Total	100.0	100.0	100.0	100.0

* Included in Angola figure.
Sources: Table 43, col. 13; Donnan, *Documents*, 4, *passim*. See text, p. 156.

had a prejudice against short people. As second choice, they would take slaves from the Gold Coast, but they had a marked dislike for those from the Bight of Biafra.[34] The South Carolina sample therefore deviates markedly from the ethnic make-up of the whole English slave trade of 1690–1807 (from col. 13, Table 43), while the Virginian sample resembles the distribution of the whole. To judge from the sample, however, Virginia also showed some preference for Senegambia and its hinterland, and the aversion to Ibo and others from the Bight of Biafra is missing. The slightly high percentage for the Bight of Biafra may, indeed, be a reflection of South Carolinian prejudice, in the sense that

34. E. Donnan, "The Slave Trade into South Carolina before the Revolution," *American Historical Review*, 33:816–17 (1927–28).

Biafran slaves unacceptable in Charleston may well have been sold in the nearest convenient market.

With the help of the Virginia and South Carolina samples, it is possible to project a highly speculative picture of the general ethnic make-up of slave imports into the North American mainland. The South Carolina slave market supplied many of the slaves for North Carolina and Georgia, and small samples of Georgian slave imports from Africa after 1766 show a heavy but non-quantifiable bias toward Senegambia and Sierra Leone—thus approximating the South Carolinian pattern.[35] Most other slaves for the southern mainland plantations were imported through the ports of Chesapeake Bay. According to Stetson's estimates for 1701–75, about 54 per cent came by way of Chesapeake Bay and 46 per cent by way of South Carolina.[36] To allow for those who came as re-exports from the West Indies, the sources of the British slave trade as a whole should also be taken into account. The estimated ethnic input from Africa to the United States (col. 4, Table 45) is therefore based on a combination of the South Carolina pattern, the Virginia pattern, and the whole British slave trade, each being weighted at one-third.

Of the British colonies, Jamaica presents the best possibility of constructing a relatively reliable and complete cross-tabulation of changing ethnic origins through time. (See Table 46.) The time-series of slave imports is relatively reliable in this case, and a number of samples of Jamaican imports by ethnic origin have been collected by R. B. Le Page and Orlando Patterson.[37] These can be set against Le Page's time-series of Jamaican imports to show the proportional derivation of newly imported Afro-Jamaicans at various periods of time.[38] In the second half of the seventeenth century, for example, a sample of 11,313 African-born slaves sold in Kingston between 1685 and 1692 provides a

35. Donnan, *Documents,* 4:620–25.

36. Stetson, "Britain's American Slave Trade," p. 48.

37. Le Page, "Jamaican Creole," pp. 61–65; Patterson, *Sociology of Slavery,* pp. 113–44. My conclusions, however, are not quite those of either author.

38. Le Page, "Jamaican Creole," p. 74.

useful base line.[39] Many of the slaves imported at this period came from the eastern Caribbean, and some of these may have been creoles, but those who were African-born would be represented in the sample. Its principal deficiency is the fact that the conventional Sierra Leone, Gold Coast, and Windward Coast are combined in a single category called "Guinea," but this total can be subdivided in proportion to the distribution of the whole British slave trade at that period (following col. 1, Table 43); and the result serves as a rough guide to Jamaican imports through 1701.

No local samples from Jamaica are available for the first half of the eighteenth century. The construction of Table 46 must therefore fall back on the possibly weak assumption that Jamaica followed the ethnic distribution in the whole English slave trade of the time.[40] After 1750, however, local data are again available. The distribution for 1751–75 is based on a sample of 16,254 slaves sold by the Kingston firm of Hibberts and Jackson between 1764 and 1774.[41] The distribution for 1776–91 is based, in turn, on a sample of 27,205 slaves sold by three different Jamaican firms between 1779 and 1788,[42] while the final column for 1792–1807 takes its percentages from a sample of 17,321 slaves sold by two firms between 1793 and 1799.[43] In these last two columns, the neat quarter-century divisions are abandoned in favor of a periodization adjusted to the chronological mid-points between two adjacent samples.

The ethnic distribution of Jamaican slave imports, as projected here, makes an interesting comparison to the patterns of the English slave trade as a whole. As expected, the deviation from the pattern of the broader trade in the second half of the eighteenth century was small. One departure of the Jamaican

39. Patterson, *Sociology of Slavery,* pp. 134–35. Patterson gives the total as 11,281, apparently copying an error of addition in his source.

40. That is, col. 2 of Table 46 follows the mean of cols. 3 and 4 of Table 43, while col. 3 of Table 46 follows col. 5 of Table 43.

41. *Board of Trade Report* (1789), part III.

42. *Board of Trade Report* (1789), part III.

43. Le Page, "Jamaican Creole," p. 84.

Table 46

Slaves Imported into Jamaica, 1655–1807: A Speculative Approximation by Coastal Region of Origin

Origin	(1) 1655–1701	(2) 1702–25	(3) 1726–50	(4) 1751–75	(5) 1776–91	(6) 1792–1807	(7) Total
Senegambia	4,200	6,700	8,600	1,000	2,600	4,600	27,700
%	4.8	10.5	6.7	0.6	2.1	2.7	3.7
Sierra Leone	800	4,700	9,200				
%	0.9	7.4	7.2	28,500	—	10,300	81,400
Windward Coast	11,400	5,100	11,400	16.5	—	6.0	10.9
%	12.9	7.9	8.9				
Gold Coast	5,500	22,300	34,700	67,300	47,100	13,900	190,800
%	6.3	34.8	27.1	39.0	38.3	8.1	25.5
Bight of Benin	24,300	19,500	16,900	23,800	18,300	—	102,800
%	27.6	30.5	13.2	13.8	14.9	—	13.8
Bight of Biafra	6,800	1,000	27,900	43,300	49,500	83,500	212,000
%	7.7	1.6	21.8	25.1	40.2	48.6	28.4
Central Africa	34,800	4,800	17,700	8,800	5,500	59,500	131,100
%	39.5	7.5	13.8	5.1	4.5	34.6	17.5
Unknown and other	200	—	1,700	—	—	—	1,900
%	0.2	—	1.3	—	—	—	0.3
Total	88,000	64,000	128,000	172,500	123,100	171,900	747,500
Annual average	1,900	2,700	5,100	6,900	7,700	10,700	4,900

Sources: Table 43; Le Page, "Jamaican Creole," pp. 61–65, 74, 84; Patterson, *Sociology of Slavery*, pp. 134–35, 137–39; Edwards, *British West Indies*, 2:60–80; *Board of Trade Report*, part III.

slave buyers appears, indeed, to be a reflex of market preferences elsewhere. If North Americans would pay inflated prices for slaves of Senegambian origin, all the more reason for a Jamaican planter to put his money elsewhere. But the Jamaicans also had preferences of their own. If Bryan Edwards fairly represented the Jamaican planting class, they took a very favorable view of Akan peoples and had a low opinion of Ibo and others from the Niger Delta and the Cross River hinterland.[44] This attitude in turn had its reciprocal in the eastern Caribbean, where Akan were avoided as "prone to revolt."[45]

The way in which such a preference might affect the flow of slaves is illustrated by a comparison of projected exports and imports. From 1751 to 1790, British exports from the Gold Coast available in the Americas came to about 138,300 slaves, and Jamaica apparently bought about 111,500 of this total. In short, while Jamaica only took about a quarter of the total British slaves delivered in the New World, it bought about 80 per cent of those from the Gold Coast.[46] But this pattern did not continue after 1791. After that date, the Jamaican share of Gold Coast slaves fell slightly below the general average of the English trade as a whole (comparing Table 43, cols. 11 and 12, with Table 46, col. 6). This change might be explained by the Akan reputation for rebelliousness, which could be a powerful influence on buyers whose fear of slave revolt was raised to the point of panic by the great revolt in Saint Domingue in 1791.

The possibility of such shifts in preference raises a new question, unanswerable on present evidence: if market preferences could influence the ethnic distribution of slaves to New-World

44. Edwards, *British West Indies,* 2:60–80.

45. Patterson, *Sociology of Slavery,* pp. 137–39.

46. That is, the projected Gold Coast exports (cols. 7–10 of Table 43) reduced in each decade by the relevant loss in transit of the French slave trade at this time (see note 19, above and Table 79, below), compared to the Jamaican imports of Gold Coast slaves projected in Table 46, col. 4, plus 15/16 of the Gold Coast total in col. 5. The Jamaican share of the whole English-carried slave trade is indicated by similar adjustments in the quantities shown in the "total" row for the same dates (Tables 43 and 46).

destinations, could they also affect the economic demand for slaves from particular parts of Africa? The sharp drop in British slave exports from the Gold Coast in the 1790's could have been caused by changed supply conditions, but it also might have owed something to the general fear of employing Akan peoples on the American plantations. Only a much more profound study of the records of individual firms, and of African responses to European demand at particular times and places, can answer questions of this kind. The example, however, points up both the usefulness of quantitative evidence in raising new questions, and its inability to answer many of them.

CHAPTER 6

THE FRENCH SLAVE TRADE OF THE EIGHTEENTH CENTURY

The best studies of the French trade are focused on the trade of a particular port town, and especially on Nantes—the French equivalent of Liverpool as the principal slave trading port in the eighteenth century. They therefore correspond to the now-old but invaluable work of Gomer Williams on the port of Liverpool. But they are based on a different kind of evidence. English shipping data are derived from the captain's declaration on clearing for a foreign destination. The best of the French evidence is the captain's *déclaration de retour,* which should exist in the archives of each French port active in the slave trade. In fact, these series are incomplete, but they exist most fully for Nantes between 1715 and 1774, and they can be supplemented by other records to give a reasonably complete picture of the Nantes slave trade to the eve of the French Revolution. Since the French trade in slaves was inconsequential until after the Peace of Utrecht in 1713, and again dropped to nothing between 1792 and the end of the century, the time-series for Nantes shipping covers all important portions of the eighteenth century. The déclarations de retour are also a firmer kind of evidence than English shipping data, since they record performance rather than intent.

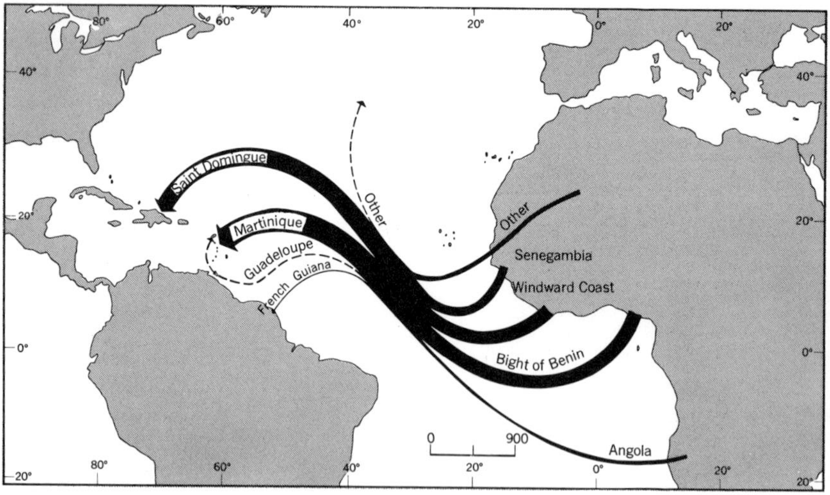

Fig. 13. The slave trade of Nantes, 1715–45: above, 1715–20; facing upper, 1729–33; facing lower, 1738–45. Fig. by UW Cartographic Lab. Data from Table 47.

These records for the port of Nantes have been exploited by two historians, Gaston Martin and Father Dieudonné Rinchon, with differing aims and results.[1] Gaston Martin's study was explicitly focused on the slave trade of Nantes between 1715 and 1775. He used the déclarations de retour to show the movement of the trade according to quantities carried, losses in transit, origins in Africa, and destinations in America. The statistical result, tabulated according to the conventional coastal regions established in Chapter 5, is shown in Table 47.

Rinchon's study was a more general discussion of the eighteenth-century slave trade, and he published an appendix listing all ships known to have sailed from Nantes between 1748 and

1. Gaston Martin, *L'Ere des négriers;* D. Rinchon, *Le Trafic négrier.* See also Rinchon, *La Traité et l'esclavage des congolais par les européens* (Brussels, 1929); *Les Armaments négriers au xviiie siècle* (Brussels, 1956); *Pierre-Ignace-Liévin van Alstein, Capitaine négrier* (Dakar, 1964).

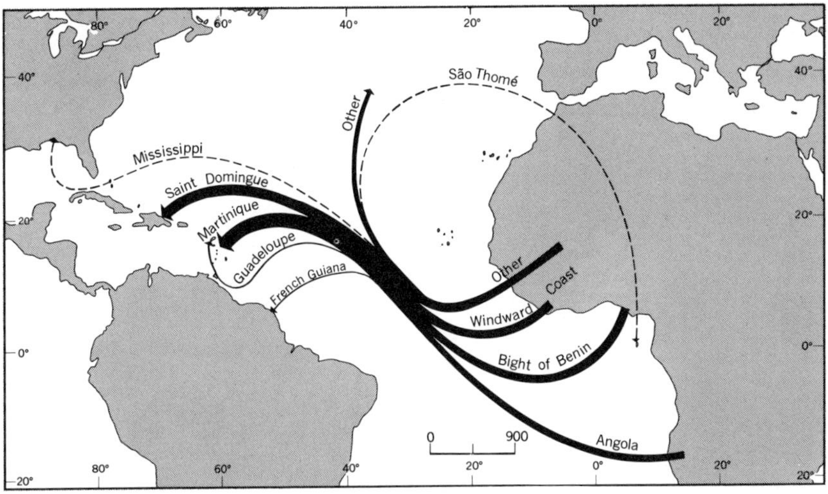

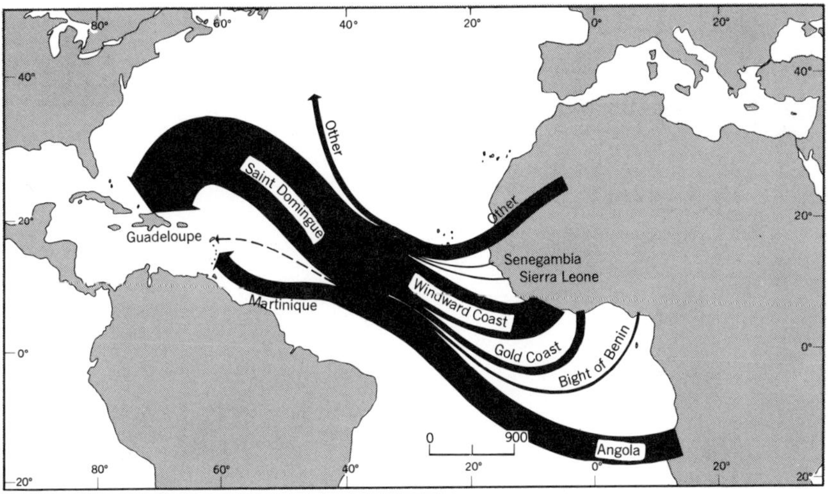

1792. This list was drawn from the déclarations de retour, supplemented by other records when the déclarations were missing. In all, it contains records of 910 ships, with substantially full data including origin, destination, and number of slaves carried for

TABLE 47

GASTON MARTIN'S DATA CONCERNING THE SLAVE TRADE OF NANTES, 1715–75, BY ORIGIN IN AFRICA AND DESTINATION IN THE NEW WORLD

Region	% of ships by time period*						
	1715–20	1721–28	1729–33	1734–37	1738–45	1749–55	1764–74
Region of embarkation							
Senegambia	20.6	15.5	—	—	2.8	4.6	6.0
Sierra Leone	—	—	—	—	3.4	—	1.4
Windward Coast	31.7	46.5	25.8	32.0	46.3	—	—
Gold Coast	—	—	—	8.0	8.9	—	12.9
Bight of Benin	33.3	21.1	24.2	28.0	4.8	—	17.1
Angola	6.3	12.7	19.4	20.0	30.0	25.2	31.3
Unknown and other	7.9	4.2	30.6	12.0	3.8	70.2	31.3
Total	100.0	100.0	100.0	100.0	100.0	100.0	100.0
No. slaves bought	*24,200*	*19,100*	*16,400*	*8,700*	*55,000*	*50,300*	*69,300*
No. ships	*63*	*71*	*62*	*25*	*180*	*151*	*217*
Destination							
Saint Domingue	41.3	42.3	33.9	40.0	72.7	74.2	80.2
Martinique	52.4	46.4	48.4	60.0	19.4	23.8	3.7
Guadeloupe	1.6	2.8	3.2	—	0.6	—	4.6
French Guiana	3.2	2.8	3.2	—	—	—	2.3
Mississippi	—	—	1.6	—	—	—	—
São Thomé	—	—	1.6	—	—	—	—
Puerto Rico	—	—	—	—	—	—	2.3
Cuba	—	—	—	—	—	—	0.5
Lost and other	1.6	5.6	8.0	—	7.2	2.0	6.4
Total	100.0	100.0	100.0	100.0	100.0	100.0	100.0
No. slaves sold	*19,000*	*15,400*	*14,300*	*7,200*	*45,300*	*42,500*	*60,100*

* The years 1746–48 and 1756–63 are omitted on account of wartime conditions and negligible traffic.

about 450 of them. Unlike Gaston Martin's study, Rinchon's data were neither tabulated nor discussed in detail, but they have been coded for electronic computation; and, in the process, some missing data have been supplied by statistical inference. Where the number of slaves carried was missing from the list, the tonnage was often supplied. With this list, the number of slaves carried per ton of capacity was not the same with all sizes of vessel. The ships were therefore divided into six different tonnage categories, and the average number of slaves carried by each category was used as an estimate for the slaves carried by a particular ship. In this way supplementary estimates could be constructed in order to complete the import data for 909 of the 910 ships listed. The number of slaves exported from Africa could then be calculated by reference to the mean loss in transit experienced by the 450 ships whose loss in transit is recorded.[2] The tabulated result of these calculations applied to Rinchon's data appears in Table 48, arranged according to Rinchon's own set of four conventional trade regions in Africa.

Rinchon's data are not commensurate with those produced by Gaston Martin's study, even though both used the déclarations de retour at Nantes. Rinchon assigned a ship to a particular year according to its date of departure from Nantes, while Gaston Martin used the date of return. Since most voyages began in one

2. The overall rate of loss in transit on the fully recorded voyages was 14.3 per cent, but certain are inexplicably listed as having sold more slaves in the American colonies than they bought in Africa. If these cases are set aside, the rate of loss is 15.2 per cent. This latter percentage of loss is the one used in constructing the tables below. Part of the data on Rinchon's list has been coded and punched on IBM cards, which are available on loan from the Data and Computation Library, University of Wisconsin, Madison, Wis. The coded data include, for each ship, date of departure from Nantes, tonnage, size of crew, site of trade in Africa, number of slaves purchased, site of trade in the Americas, number of slaves sold, date of return to France, number of crew members deceased during the voyage, estimated number of slaves sold (when missing from the original list) projected according to tonnage figures. References to Rinchon's data are to the list, *Le Trafic négrier*, pp. 247–305, unless otherwise noted.

TABLE 48

RINCHON'S DATA CONCERNING THE SLAVE TRADE OF NANTES, 1748–92, BY REGIONAL ORIGIN IN AFRICA

Years	Slaves purchased											
	Senegal		Guinea		Angola		Mozambique		Unknown		Total	
	No.	%	No.	%	No.	%	No.	%	No.	%	No.	%
1748–51	700	2.5	15,600	55.2	11,000	38.7	—	—	1,000	3.6	28,400	100.0
1752–55	2,300	8.0	15,300	52.1	10,600	36.3	—	—	1,000	3.6	29,300	100.0
1763–67	600	1.4	23,200	56.5	17,300	42.1	—	—	—	—	41,100	100.0
1768–72	1,500	4.5	18,200	55.4	13,100	40.1	—	—	—	—	32,800	100.0
1773–77	200	0.8	18,300	61.9	10,700	36.3	—	—	300	1.0	29,500	100.0
1778–82	2,000	54.5	1,700	45.5	—	—	—	—	—	—	3,700	100.0
1783–87	6,000	9.9	23,800	39.4	27,300	45.2	3,000	5.0	400	0.6	60,500	100.0
1788–92	1,300	2.0	24,600	37.1	37,400	56.5	800	1.2	2,200	3.3	66,300	100.0
Total	14,600	5.0	140,700	48.3	127,600	43.8	3,800	1.3	4,900	1.7	291,600	100.0

Source: Data from Rinchon, *Le Trafic négrier*, pp. 247–305.

calendar year and ended in another, the difference is considerable. In addition, Gaston Martin limited himself to the déclarations de retour, while Rinchon supplemented these records with other data. This means that Gaston Martin's study is based on a large sample, not a complete listing even of the Nantes slave trade. Rinchon's list is as nearly complete as records permit and Jean Meyer has recently gone over the archival data for the period 1783–92 in a way that reinforces Rinchon's data for that period. Meyer's total estimate of slaves landed in the Americas by ships from Nantes came to 115,500, as against 109,018 for Rinchon's list with supplementary estimates based on tonnage.[3]

In order to make the results of the Rinchon and Gaston Martin data comparable to the decennial tables already constructed for the English slave trade, two separate operations are necessary. One is to use appropriate portions of the two surveys as the basis for a decennial sample of the sources in Africa from which the Nantes shippers exported slaves, assuming in this case that the Nantes trade is a fair sample of the French slave trade as a whole. The second is to discover as nearly as possible the number of slaves exported by the French in each decade. Both operations can be attempted simultaneously on a decade-by-decade basis, but the process necessarily involves a certain amount of statistical projection, and even a little sheer guesswork. The results, as shown in Table 49, will therefore inevitably be less accurate, though more complete, than the data presented by either Rinchon or Gaston Martin.

Data are insufficient for the French slave trade before 1711, but Gaston Martin's study serves as a guide to 1711–20. The Nantes shipping returning to port in 1715–20 provides a sample of the coastal trading areas frequented by the French during the whole decade, and the "unknown" category can be redistributed in proportion to the known sources of slaves in Africa.

The size of the French slave trade in this decade is somewhat

3. J. Meyer, "Le Commerce négrier nantais (1774–1792)," *Annales, Economies, Sociétés, Civilisations,* 15:120–29 (1960).

TABLE 49

FRENCH SLAVE EXPORTS FROM AFRICA, 1711–1800: DECENNIAL ESTIMATES BY COASTAL ORIGIN IN AFRICA, BASED ON SHIPPING DATA

Coastal region	(1) 1711–20	(2) 1721–30	(3) 1731–40	(4) 1741–50	(5) 1751–60	(6) 1761–70	(7) 1771–80	(8) 1781–90	(9) 1791–1800	(10) Total
Senegambia	10,300	13,400	12,300	7,700	6,300	2,300	4,000	17,400	3,400	77,100
%	22.4	15.5	10.8	8.4	8.7	2.0	4.0	6.4	5.7	8.1
Sierra Leone	—	—	—	2,900	2,100	3,800	—	—	—	8,800
%	—	—	—	3.2	2.9	3.3	—	—	—	0.9
Windward Coast	15,900	40,100	36,800	39,800	28,200	—	—	—	—	160,800
%	34.5	46.5	32.2	43.6	38.9	—	—	—	—	16.8
Gold Coast	—	—	9,100	7,600	5,400	30,200	19,300	66,200	8,900	146,700
%	—	—	8.0	8.3	7.4	26.2	19.5	24.4	15.0	15.4
Bight of Benin	16,700	18,200	32,100	4,100	2,900	31,500	36,000	30,100	4,100	175,700
%	36.2	21.1	28.1	4.5	4.0	27.3	36.4	11.1	6.8	18.4
Bight of Biafra	—	—	—	—	—	—	—	14,900	2,000	16,900
%	—	—	—	—	—	—	—	5.5	3.4	1.8
Angola	3,200	10,900	23,000	25,800	25,300	47,500	38,800	129,000	38,800	342,300
%	6.9	12.7	20.1	28.3	34.9	41.2	39.3	47.5	65.1	35.8
Mozambique	—	—	900	—	—	—	—	8,700	1,100	10,700
%	—	—	0.8	—	—	—	—	3.2	1.8	1.1
Unknown & other	—	3,600	—	3,300	2,300	—	800	5,200	1,300	16,500
%	—	4.2	—	3.6	3.2	—	0.8	1.9	2.2	1.7
Total	46,100	86,200	114,200	91,200	72,500	115,400	98,800	271,500	59,600	955,500
%	100.0	100.0	100.0	100.0	100.0	100.0	100.0	100.0	100.0	100.0

Sources: Tables 47 and 48; Gaston Martin, *L'Ere des négriers*, p. 117, and graph; Weber, *Compagnie des Indes*, p. 483; Dardel, *Rouen et Havre*, p. 403; Delcourt, *La France au Sénégal*, p. 398; Malvezin, *Bordeaux*, 3:208–9; Rinchon, *Le Trafic négrier*, pp. 25–27. See text, pp. 169–79.

uncertain. The first years, to the peace of Utrecht in April 1713, were the final years of a long and unsuccessful war. In spite of the French diplomatic success in securing the asiento privilege from the Spanish Crown, the slave trade of these years must have been insignificant. After the peace, the old privileged companies, the Compagnie de Guinée and the Compagnie du Sénégal, were in a failing condition, though both continued to carry slaves. Then, for the period 1716–20, the slave trade was freed from company regulation, though it was restricted to the ports of Nantes, Rouen, La Rochelle, and Bordeaux. Desmarets, the Contrôleur-Général, estimated in 1713 that the French ports could send out 12 to 15 ships a year, if they were allowed to do so freely, without the encumbrance of a chartered company. Gaston Martin, seeing that more than 10 ships a year returned to Nantes in 1715–20, claimed that this estimate was low (and Nantes was the principal port for the Compagnie de Guinée). A guess seems called for, and 15 ships a year for 1713–20 would perhaps include a small allowance for wartime traffic as well. Since the Nantes captains bought an average of 384 slaves per ship, the export from Africa carried by the whole French slave trade can be estimated at 46,100 for 1711–20.[4]

With the decade 1721–30, a new problem arises. In September 1721, the Compagnie des Indes absorbed the older privileged companies. At first, it merely licensed private traders, but from the beginning of 1723 through the first four months of 1725 it undertook its monopoly over the French slave trade on its own account. Since the Company used other ports, no slavers returned to Nantes in either 1725 or 1726, but the Company's records show 15,928 slaves delivered to the West Indies during their 2⅓ years of direct participation in the trade.[5] Assuming that their rate of loss in transit was the same as that of the Nantes traders in the bracketing periods 1720–24 and 1727–31, this

4. Gaston Martin, *L'Ere des négriers,* pp. 115, 117.

5. H. Weber, *La Compagnie française des Indes (1604–1875)* (Paris, 1904), p. 483.

implies an export from Africa of 19,500 slaves, or 8,400 a year.[6] For lack of other evidence, this annual average can serve as a general estimate for the full eight years 1721–23.

Another source is available for the last two years of the decade. In the mid-eighteenth century, an official named Dernis prepared an annual list of slaves imported into the French colonies by French shipping, distinguishing the number of slaves carried by ships from each French port over the sixteen-year period, 1725/26 through 1740/41. His annual series, however, included only the private traders; the Company's trade was shown only as a sixteen-year total.[7] Gaston Martin was suspicious of these figures, which were based on returns filed by the Chambres de Commerce at each port, on grounds that these returns were not always accurate.[8] On the other hand, Gaston Martin's own total for deliveries to the New World by Nantes shippers, which made no claim to be exhaustive, came to 47,100, while Dernis's equivalent figure for the sixteen-year period was 55,900; they are, at least, in the same range.

If Dernis is accepted as a basis for estimating the French slave trade of 1729 and 1730, his import figures can be translated into

6. Gaston Martin, *L'Ere des négriers,* p. 115, has a table giving annual numbers of ships trading for slaves, numbers of slaves exported, and numbers of slaves dying in transit. But the number dying en route does not represent the total number of slaves lost from shipwreck, capture at sea by the enemy in wartime, and the like. This number can be found, however, by using the data on slaves sold in America represented in a graph tip-in at the back of Gaston Martin's work. For the whole of 1715–75, 14.5 per cent of the slaves exported died on the voyage, but the total losses were 16.2 per cent. Here and below where Gaston Martin's data are used, the total losses, rather than deaths from disease, will be taken into account.

7. The table is contained in a mss. volume, "Histoire abrégée des compagnies de commerce qui ont été établies en France depuis l'an 1626," Archives d'Outre-Mer, Série F^2, no. 18, p. 415. It has been reprinted many times, beginning with Peytraud, *L'Esclavage,* p. 138, more recently in Rinchon, *L'Esclavage des congolais,* p. 93, and P. Dardel, *Navires et marchandises dans les ports de Rouen et du Havre au xviiie siècle* (Paris, 1963), p. 403.

8. Gaston Martin, *L'Ere des négriers,* p. 168.

export estimates by reference to loss in transit suffered by Gaston Martin's sample from Nantes. The resulting figure for these two years is 19,200, giving a general estimate of 86,200 for the decade 1721–30. With the Nantes sample at about 40 per cent of the whole French trade, the sample is used as a guide to the probable distribution of the whole to various trading zones on the African coast.[9]

The estimates for the 1730's can be found by the same method, again using Dernis's data adjusted from import to export figures by reference to Gaston Martin's sample from Nantes.[10] On this basis, the total French exports for the decade come to 114,200 slaves, but the literature presents a problem in assigning this total to the conventional regions of export. The Nantes sample appears to be made up entirely of non-Company trade; it will therefore contain a bias against those areas where the Company of the Indies tried to exercise its monopoly on its own account, as

9. Since Dernis did not work with calendar years, his import figure for 1729–30 was calculated to be twice the annual average of the three years, 1728/29 through 1730/31 for the non-Company trade, plus twice the annual average of the Company's deliveries over the whole sixteen-year period (1725/26–1740/41)–a total of 16,900. This was then adjusted to an export estimate by reference to the coefficient of slaves lost/slaves sold (.135) in these two years, as indicated by Gaston Martin's Nantes sample, yielding an export total of 19,200.

An alternative way of making the estimate would be to use Gaston Martin's export figure for the Nantes traders of 1729–30 as a base, finding the total French slave trade for these years by reference to the Nantes share (37.7 per cent) indicated for these years by Dernis. The result is an export estimate of 16,800 for the two years, but the earlier form of calculation is preferred.

10. That is, Dernis gives the non-Company trade as 63,000 slaves imported into the Americas during the decade, 1731/32–1740/41. In addition, the annual average of his consolidated figure for the Company trade of 1725/26–1740/41 suggests a Company import figure of 27,300 for the decade 1731–40. The total import would therefore be 90,300, translated into an export estimate by reference to the coefficient of slaves lost/slaves landed (.265) derived from Gaston Martin's sample of the Nantes trade of 1731–40. The result is a total export estimate of 114,200 for the French slave trade of that decade.

it did east of the Cape of Good Hope and in the Senegambia. For these areas, some independent evidence has been published. Delcourt tabulated the Company's Senegambian exports for 1732–41, and the annual average for these years provides a guide to 1731 as well, giving a total of 9,700 for the decade. The Company also exported at least 750 slaves from Madagascar to the American colonies.[11] But the Nantes sample shows no traffic at all with either Senegambia or southeast Africa.

One solution, adopted here with more than the usual uncertainty, is to apply the proportional distribution indicated by the Nantes sample for 1734–37, but to apply this only to the quantities indicated by Dernis for the non-Company trade of the decade. The larger picture of French exports can then be filled out by adding the recorded amounts for the Company's exports from Senegambia and Madagascar. The result will be the proportional distribution by region shown in Table 49, col. 3, but this method will also yield a decennial export estimate of only 90,100—as opposed to 114,200 where Dernis's figures for the Company's trade are used. The higher figure will be accepted, though only with a warning of possible error and with a distribution along the coast following the proportions of the lower one.

After 1741, the Dernis data are no longer available, and wartime conditions in the latter part of the decade made the French slave trade unstable. Indeed, it virtually disappeared after 1745. The Nantes trade, however, gives a clue to the size of the non-Company trade. Gaston Martin recorded 42,800 slaves exported from Africa by Nantes shippers over the period 1741–50. This figure is almost certainly lower than the actual trade of Nantes. This defect can, however, be taken into account. In moving from Gaston Martin's partial total to a general total for the French slave trade, it can be assumed that his data were incomplete to approximately the same degree over the whole period from 1735 to 1755. Since the proportion of Gaston Mar-

11. A. Delcourt, *La France et les établissements français au Sénégal entre 1713 et 1763* (Dakar, 1952), p. 398; Weber, *Compagnie des Indes,* p. 483.

tin's total to the figure for the whole French slave trade is calculable for both the late 1730's and the early 1750's, interpolation can provide a possible proportion for the 1740's as well. Gaston Martin's sample of imports for 1736–40 comes to 42.6 per cent of the Dernis figure for non-Company imports over the equivalent period, 1736/37–1740/41. For 1750–55, Malvezin has published a total figure for the French slave imports, and Gaston Martin's import figure for the same period is 56.9 per cent of that total.[12] The mean of the bracketing percentages is 49.8. If Gaston Martin's sample of the slaves *exported* during 1741–50 were that percentage of the total, the total would have been in the vicinity of 85,900. But this figure is still not complete, since it leaves out the Company's trade, which carried on into the 1740's, though often with chartered ships which may have turned up in the Nantes sample. Nevertheless, it seems appropriate to add something for the Company's trade, at least until 1745. The Company's exports from 1 October 1738 to 30 September 1744 are recorded at 6,300 slaves—an annual average of 1,050, which can be used to estimate the Company's exports for 1741–45 at 5,300.[13]

The result is a total estimate for the French slave trade of 1741–50 at about 91,200, which can be distributed to the conventional coastal trading zones according to Gaston Martin's sample for 1738–45—with the exception of the Company's exports, which are assigned entirely to Senegambia.

With the decade 1751–60, the differing basis of calculation in the two surveys of the Nantes slave trade poses a difficult problem. Following Gaston Martin's figures based on the *return* of a ship to Nantes, the postwar boom in the French slave trade of 1749 and 1750 is assigned to the decade 1751–60, but Rinchon's list according to the date of departure assigns the same set of voyages to the 1740's. One solution is to ignore both Nantes surveys in favor of Malvezin's calculation that the French slave

12. T. Malvezin, *Histoire du commerce de Bordeaux,* 4 vols. (Bordeaux, 1890–93), 3:208.

13. Gaston Martin, *L'Ere des négriers,* p. 341.

trade delivered 12,200 slaves a year to the West Indies in the period 1750–55.[14] Since the war began again in 1755, and French slavers stayed in port until after the peace in 1763, five years at this rate should account for the French slave trade of 1751–55—total deliveries of 61,000 being equivalent to total exports of 72,500 at the rate of loss reported by Gaston Martin for the period (lost/sold, 1751–55, .188).

With the 1750's, the Nantes shipping data cease to be a reliable guide to origins of slaves transported by the French slave trade. Gaston Martin was forced to assign 70 per cent to the category "other and unknown." While Rinchon's unknown category came to only 3.2 per cent of his total, his treatment of "Guinea" as a single category covers over the really significant detail. Rather than discard the shipping data out of hand, however, the origins of the French slave trade for the 1750's through the 1790's are projected in Table 49 as far as possible from data of this kind—but only to be subjected later on to critical examination in the light of other data.

Some estimate for the period 1751–60, for example, can be made by using Rinchon's categories as far as possible, but redistributing his large category of "Guinea" following the distribu-

14. Malvezin, *Bordeaux,* 3:208. An alternate calculation can be made using Rinchon's data for the Nantes slave trade as soon as it becomes available in 1748. The difference between Rinchon's mode of listing by sailing date and Gaston Martin's list according to date of return can be adjusted by assuming that ships returning in 1742–48 sailed in 1741–47. This Rinchon-based calculation would show total French exports for 1741–50 as 99,300—as opposed to 91,200 following Gaston Martin and then Malvezin.

For 1751–60, on the other hand, the estimate based on Rinchon shows a total French export from Africa as 59,400—as opposed to 72,500 following Malvezin. In short, the method followed in the text differs from the alternate based on Rinchon in that it shifts about 10 per cent of the total French exports for 1741–60 from the 1740's into the 1750's. The total for the two decades together is roughly equal, no matter which data are used—being 158,600 following Rinchon from 1748 onward, as against 163,700 following Gaston Martin and then Malvezin (Table 49, cols. 4 and 5).

tion of French shipping within that region according to Gaston Martin's prewar figures for 1738–45. This projection would be correct, of course, only if the French slave traders returned to their prewar sources of supply.

After the Seven Years War and the complete interruption of the French slave trade, Rinchon's data are far more complete than that of Gaston Martin—listing, for example, 195 ships for the 1760's compared with only 141 in Gaston Martin's survey. Since Rinchon's more thorough listing appears to be complete or nearly complete for the Nantes trade, the Nantes trade can be used to estimate the whole French slave trade. Malvezin reports that Nantes carried 51 per cent of the whole during the three-year period, 1762–64,[15] and this percentage can be accepted as generally true of the 1760's. Since Rinchon's import total for 1761–70 was 50,380, the import total for the whole French slave trade could be put at 98,800, which in turn can be translated into an export estimate by reference to the coefficient of lost/sold based on Gaston Martin (.168)—hence a total estimate of French exports from Africa at 115,400 slaves in that decade. Again, this total can be only roughly assigned to coastal areas on the basis of shipping data, with some confidence in the major division into Guinea, Angola, Mozambique, and Senegambia following Rinchon's data—but somewhat less in the redistribution of the Guinea total into its subdivisions following Gaston Martin's indications for 1764–70.[16]

For the 1770's, the total French slave trade can be estimated in much the same way. Only this time it is necessary to assess the Nantes share of the trade according to the mean of Malvezin's figure for 1762–64 and a one-year (and hence doubtful) figure for 1785.[17] The result at 43 per cent suggests a decline in the fortunes of the Nantes traders. The whole French trade, for that matter, also declined from the levels of the 1760's—presumably

15. Malvezin, *Bordeaux,* 3:209.
16. Gaston Martin, *L'Ere des négriers,* p. 287.
17. Rinchon, *Le Trafic négrier,* pp. 25–27.

because the backlog of demand created by the Seven Years War had been filled in the 1760's, and the new War of the American Revolution interfered with trade in the last years of the decade. Rinchon's import figure for Nantes over the period 1771–80 is 38,100, yielding an estimate for the imports of the whole French slave trade at 88,600 following Rinchon's sample of loss at sea for 1773–77 (lost/sold, .115); this implies an export figure of 98,800. Distribution according to coastal regions again follows Rinchon for the major categories, with Guinea subdivided according to Gaston Martin's analysis for 1771–75.

The period 1781–90 was clearly the all-time peak of the French slave trade, but the data for a firm estimate are not strong. The one-year sample of 1785 assigned 35 per cent of the whole French trade to Nantes,[18] but the Nantes total was much higher than it had been—some 90,240 slaves landed in the Americas during the decade. These figures, combined with Rinchon's sample of losses in transit at 5 per cent in 1788–92, suggest total French exports in the vicinity of 271,500 slaves. As for the distribution of trading zones in Africa, the Rinchon breakdown is still useful for the major coastal regions, but the subdivision of the Guinea trade must rest on a single sample for 1785; and this one lists only the Bight of Biafra and the Gold Coast. It can nevertheless serve as a weak basis for a guess that the French trade with Sierra Leone and the Windward Coast had become negligible; the balance of the "Guinea" total can be assigned to the Bight of Benin, where the French were traditionally important.

In the final decade of the century, 1791–1800, French slavers sailed from Nantes only in 1791 and 1792, and Rinchon's data are less complete than they are for earlier decades. They do, however, include tonnage figures, which suggest some 19,820 slaves sold in the Americas by Nantes shipping in these years. If the Nantes share of the total French trade remained unchanged at 35 per

18. Rinchon, *Le Trafic négrier*, pp. 25–27.

cent, and if the loss at sea was at 5 per cent as reported by Rinchon for 1788–92, the total French exports can be estimated at 59,600. The distribution of that trade in Africa is highly uncertain, if shipping data alone are used, but Rinchon's data indicate that "Guinea" provided 25.5 per cent of the total, and this can then be subdivided in the same proportions used in dealing with the trade of the 1780's.

In spite of the weakness in the distribution data from the 1750's onward, other evidence suggests that the total estimates of French exports from Africa may not be far wrong. Meyer's study confirms Rinchon's data for the 1780's. An unsigned document in the colonial records of the Archives Nationales in Paris gives the annual French imports of slaves into the French colonies for the three years 1774–76—the annual average being 16,000.[19] This can be checked against Rinchon's export figures for 1773–77 (from Table 48). Assuming that Nantes controlled about 35 per cent of the French slave trade, and that the losses at sea were approximately 10 per cent (following Rinchon's data for the same period, Table 79 below) the annual average imports of the French slave trade of 1773–77 would have been 15,200. There is, in addition, a British estimate of 1787, putting the French slave trade at 20,000 a year.[20] This is certainly far too low; official French figures for the four years 1785–88 published by Peytraud indicate an annual average import of 31,800.[21] This is in line with the Rinchon data on Nantes exports from Africa for 1783–87 (from Table 48). Taking the Nantes trade at 35 per cent of the total, these data

19. "Mémoire sur la traite des noirs au côtes d'Affrique et sur les moyens de l'encourager," 1778, unsigned, Archives Nationales, colonies, C^6, 17. Another unsigned memoir from the same series has been published by J. Machat, *Documents sur les établissements français et l'Afrique occidentale au xviiie siècle* (Paris, 1906), pp. 132–33. This document mentions an ordinary French export before the War of the American Revolution as about 15,000 slaves a year.

20. *Board of Trade Report,* quoted in D. Macpherson, *Annals of Commerce,* 4 vols. (London, 1805), 4:152.

21. Peytraud, *L'Esclavage,* pp. 139–40.

Table 50

Rinchon's Data Concerning the Slave Trade of Nantes, 1748–92, by Destination in the Americas

	Slaves sold								
Destination	1748–51	1752–55	1763–67	1768–72	1773–77	1778–82	1783–87	1788–92	Total
Saint Domingue	13,900	20,200	28,400	22,900	24,600	800	39,300	31,100	181,000
%	60.1	80.4	83.2	88.9	92.6	24.5	75.8	54.3	73.4
Martinique	6,700	2,600	1,700	200	—	—	50	—	11,300
%	29.2	10.4	5.1	0.7	—	—	0.1	—	4.6
Guadeloupe	200	100	1,400	200	500	200	—	400	2,900
%	0.9	0.5	4.1	0.8	1.8	4.9	—	0.7	1.2
French Guiana	—	100	1,100	300	400	400	—	—	2,300
%	—	0.4	3.3	1.4	1.4	11.6	—	—	0.9
Puerto Rico and Cuba	—	—	1,300	1,600	—	—	—	400	3,300
%	—	—	3.9	6.1	—	—	—	0.7	1.3
Trinidad	—	—	—	—	—	—	—	400	400
%	—	—	—	—	—	—	—	0.7	0.2
Surinam	—	—	—	—	—	—	—	200	200
%	—	—	—	—	—	—	—	0.3	0.1
Unknown	2,300	2,100	200	600	1,100	1,900	12,500	24,800	45,400
%	9.9	8.3	0.5	2.2	4.2	59.0	24.2	43.3	18.4
Total	23,100	25,200	34,100	25,800	26,500	3,100	51,800	57,200	246,800
%	100.0	100.0	100.0	100.0	100.0	100.0	100.0	100.0	100.0

Source: Data from Rinchon, *Le Trafic négrier*, pp. 247–305.

indicate a general French annual export of 34,600, or 31,100 slaves imported, allowing for a 10-per-cent loss in transit.

The distribution of the French slave trade in the Americas is reasonably clear from Gaston Martin's study of the Nantes trade (Table 47). From the 1780's onward, however, the Nantes data are less specific about destination than about origin in Africa. Rinchon's data therefore contain a very large "unknown" category after 1778. A tabulation is shown below in Table 50, though it tells little more than the fact that most of the French slave trade of this period was directed toward Saint Domingue. Rinchon apparently let a misprint slip through in publishing his list. It shows no deliveries at all to Guadeloupe, but some to Grenada in almost every time period, even though Grenada had been transferred to England. Table 50 is corrected on the assumption that Guadeloupe is intended in place of Grenada.

In spite of deficient data toward the end of the eighteenth century, the broad pattern of French deliveries to the Americas is clear. Guadeloupe and Martinique received a declining proportion of a growing total as the decades passed. In this respect, they were like Barbados or the Leeward Islands in the English sphere, having limited land for sugar cultivation and an improving rate of net natural decrease with the passage of time. Saint Domingue, on the other hand, was like Jamaica, receiving higher proportions of an increasing trade as the century wore on—but receiving a much higher proportion of the whole French trade than Jamaica did of the English trade.

Saint Domingue was also like Jamaica in the ethnic make-up of its slave imports compared to the ethnic proportions in the French slave trade as a whole. (See Table 51.) Importing more than three-quarters of the whole French supply, Saint Domingue had little choice but to take a nearly random sample of the slaves exported from Africa by French shipping. The only marked deviation shown in the Rinchon data is a low proportion from Senegambia, but, following the pattern of the English trade, this is probably accountable to high prices offered elsewhere for people shipped from Senegambia—not to an avoidance of Senegambians by the Saint Domingue planters. Martinique, on the other hand, showed a marked bias against the Bantu-speaking peoples from Central Africa and a preference for West Africans —a striking contrast to nearby Guadeloupe, which appears (in a rather small sample) to have bought what the trade had to offer. French Guiana (again on a small sample) appears to have had a very strong pro-Senegambian bias, some preference for West Africans, and an avoidance of Central Africans.

TABLE 51

REGIONAL ORIGIN OF SLAVES IMPORTED INTO THE FRENCH CARIBBEAN COLONIES, 1748–92, BASED ON RINCHON'S SAMPLE OF THE NANTES SLAVE TRADE

Importer	% of total imports derived from					Total slaves imported
	Senegambia	Guinea	Angola	Mozambique	Unknown	
Total Nantes slave trade	5.0	47.8	44.2	1.3	1.7	246,800
Saint Domingue	3.7	48.9	45.8	0.8	0.8	181,000
Martinique	8.4	65.5	26.2	—	—	11,300
French Guiana	15.9	58.3	25.8	—	—	2,300
Guadeloupe	2.4	54.0	43.6	—	—	2,900

Source: Data from Rinchon, *Le Trafic négrier*, pp. 247–305.

These apparent market biases were, in turn, reflected in the way exports from particular parts of Africa were distributed. Table 52 is another arrangement of the Rinchon data, showing the proportional distribution in the New World of slaves exported from each of the three major shipping areas in Africa, where both origin and destination were recorded. The greater part from all three went to Saint Domingue, as might be expected from its dominant place in the economy of the French

TABLE 52

DISTRIBUTION IN THE AMERICAS OF SLAVES EXPORTED BY THE NANTES SLAVE TRADE, 1748–92

	(1)	% of col. 1 to			
Exporting region	% of known destination	Saint Domingue	Martinique	Guadeloupe	French Guiana
Africa generally	80.1	91.6	5.7	1.5	1.2
Senegambia	65.6	83.1	11.6	0.9	4.5
Guinea	83.9	89.6	7.5	1.6	1.4
Angola	80.4	94.5	3.4	1.4	0.7

Source: Data from Rinchon, *Le Trafic négrier*, pp. 247–305.

Caribbean. But slaves from Senegambia and its hinterland went disproportionately to Martinique and French Guiana. Those from Guinea went disproportionately to Martinique, while those from Central Africa went disproportionately to Saint Domingue.

Another kind of evidence shows the ethnic origins of people in the Francophone Caribbean in far more detail. Under the slave regime, planters, lawyers, or notaries had reason to produce lists of slaves—for parish records, property records of individual estates, lists of runaways or slaves for sale. These lists often identified the African-born slaves by nationality of origin. Beginning in 1961, Professor G. Debien and a group of collaborators began publishing lists of this kind in a series of articles, which finally came to a total of 73 separate lists.[22] While only a few slaves on each list might have a precise or recognizable African national origin, the totals of several lists are often large enough to be considered as sample data. (See Tables 53–58.)

Tabulation, however, presents problems of interpretation. Terminology has changed in some cases since the eighteenth cen-

22. G. Debien and others, "Les Origines des esclaves des Antilles," *Bulletin de l'IFAN*, 23:363–87 (1961); 25:1–41, 215–66 (1963); 26:166–211, 601–75 (1964); 27:319–71, 755–99 (1965); 29:536–58 (1967).

tury. The lawyers or planters who made up these lists recognized cultural variants; but they rarely knew much about Africa itself, and the typology they used was neither that of the contemporaneous Africans nor that of present-day ethnographers. For Senegambia, at least four of the eighteenth-century designations are still in use, but their meanings have changed. The term "Senegal" itself, now a river and a republic, then meant first of all the town of Saint Louis and secondly the river. A slave identified as Senegalese might therefore be either (a) an individual shipped from Saint Louis, whatever his nationality, (b) a Wolof of Cayor or Walo in the immediate vicinity of the town, or, (c) a Pular-speaker from Futa Toro in the middle valley of the Senegal.[23] In the same sense, the eighteenth-century "Bambara" was a catch-all term for slaves brought from the far interior and sold to Saint-Louisian slave dealers at one of the trading posts in Gadiaga, near the head of navigation on the Senegal River. Some of these slaves may well have been Bambara in the present-day sense of language and culture, but the eighteenth-century term was more geographical than cultural.

Two tendencies were at work. One was the European habit of identifying nationalities customarily shipped from a particular African port by the name of the port, as in the case of "Senegalese." The second was to pick one ethnic or linguistic term to identify a much larger group, as in the case of "Bambara." These tendencies make for confusion and overlapping terminology. "Poulard" is clearly the present-day Pular language, but Pular-speakers might also be classified as Senegalese, or, if they came from Futa Jallon they might turn up on a West Indian list as "Timbo" or "Timbu" from the name of the capital of the largest state in that region. These overlapping variants make it difficult to equate ethnic identifications with particular coastal regions of the slave trade. "Mandingue" (or Mandingo in English) was originally a term attached to the Malinke-speaking people of the

23. Debien and others, "Origines des esclaves," 26:181 (1964).

Gambia valley, but it later spread to all speakers of Mande languages. An individual identified as Mandingue might therefore have originated anywhere from the Gambia eastward to the present-day northern Ghana and western Upper Volta, and he might have been shipped from any part of the coast between the Senegal and the Gold Coast.

In spite of these difficulties, it is possible to make at least a rough identification of most national names appearing on the eighteenth-century lists from the French Antilles. In Sierra Leone and vicinity, "Théminy" and "Guimonée" are variants of Temne, but the term probably meant almost anyone from coastal Sierra Leone. "Soso," in the same way, probably meant a wider group than the Susu of present-day Sierra Leone and Guinea-Conakry. "Timbo" could mean people from Futa Jallon, but it may also have been used for those who passed through this important commercial center on their way to the coast.

Even greater uncertainty applies along the Windward Coast. The "Canga" and "Misérables" were people shipped from the vicinity of Cape Mesurado, near present-day Monrovia.[24] Cap Lahou was another shipping point that became an ethnic term. The "Aquia" are conjecturally the Akwa, or Mbato. Only two other recognizable names appear to come from the hinterland of the Windward Coast, the Kissi of upper Guinea-Conakry and the Bobo of Upper Volta. Of these the Kissi might also have been shipped by way of Sierra Leone, and people called Bobo might have been shipped from Gold Coast ports. Even today the term Bobo is subject to a good deal of confusion, and in the eighteenth century it probably had an even wider meaning than it does now.[25]

For the Gold Coast, "Mine," the name most commonly found, is another shipping point, the ancient fort at Elmina, but the

24. Moreau de Saint-Méry, *Description de la partie française de l'isle Saint-Domingue,* 3 vols. (Paris, 1958; first published 1797), 1:49.

25. See G. Moal, "Note sur les populations 'Bobo'," *Bulletin de l'IFAN,* série B, 29:418–30(1957).

name had long since been extended to mean any of the Akan peoples. In Portuguese usage of the eighteenth century it was used still more broadly to mean almost anyone from West Africa, but more narrowly those from the Slave Coast on the Bight of Benin. "Coromanti" and its variants were similar and derived from the Dutch fort at Kormantin, less than twenty miles east of Elmina. In English usage it, rather than Mina, was used for Akan peoples generally, but what distinction could have been in the mind of a West Indian lawyer more than five thousand miles away when he wrote "Mine" rather than "Coromanti" against a man's name?

In any event, either "Mine" or "Coromanti" was more restricted than "Côte d'Or." The eighteenth-century French sometimes used it in the narrow sense of the English "Gold Coast," but they also had a tendency to extend the region westward, as far as Cap Lahou in the present-day Ivory Coast.[26] In the hinterland, "Bandia" is modern Bandja, but it apparently meant all Guang-speaking peoples. "Denira" is conjecturally "Denkyera," and "Domba" can be taken as Dagomba.[27]

The same terminological imprecision reigned along the Bight of Benin. Ardra or Arada is a form of Allada, the African kingdom in present-day southern Dahomey, but it probably should be interpreted as "people sold by Allada," not "people from Allada." And, by the late eighteenth century, the term had already extended to mean almost anyone shipped from the Bight of Benin ports. In much the same way, "Nago" originally referred to a sub-group of the northern Yoruba, but it gradually

26. Moreau de Saint-Méry, *La Partie française de Saint-Domingue*, 1:49–50. This westward extension of the term, "Gold Coast," in French usage is a curious contrast to the Portuguese terminology, which moved the equivalent term, "costa da mina," from the Gold Coast to the Bight of Benin, thus an eastward shift.

27. Another possibility is a place named as "Damba" in a treaty between Portugal and Matamba in 1683 and presumably located to the north and east of the kingdom of Kongo. See D. Birmingham, *Trade and Conflict in Angola* (Oxford, 1966), p. 131.

stretched to include any Yoruba-speaking people—and perhaps any sent to the coast by Oyo. It is possible that "Ado" and "Attanquois" both refer to people from Otta, which would mean southwestern Yoruba. "Faeda" is a French variant of the place-name also known as Fida, Juda, Whydah, and now Ouidah, a major slaving port. Judging from the small numbers so classified, however, it may actually have meant people from that part of the coast, not merely those shipped through Ouidah. The same degree of uncertainty is present with "Adia" (Adja), "Fon" and "Fonseda" (Fon), and Popo. These are all peoples found in the coastal region of Dahomey and Togo, or its immediate hinterland, but the terms may have been used in the eighteenth century in a somewhat broader sense.

Further inland, only a few ethnic names occur on the lists, suggesting that a single name may have been applied in the fashion of "Bambara" to whole groupings or regions. "Quiamba" and "Thiamba" (Chamba) are the only listed representatives of the broader Gurma cluster, which also includes such people as the Basair, Gurma, Konkomba, and Moba. It is unlikely that the eighteenth-century term was used even in a relatively narrow sense of designating the whole Gurma cluster. For the English on the Gold Coast, Chamba simply meant any slaves brought down from the region north of Ashanti, or anyone speaking one of the Gur languages.[28] The Tem cluster in G. P. Murdock's classification is represented sometimes by "Nambo" (Namba) and sometimes by "Cotocoli" (Kotokoli), but the two terms never occur on the same list. Apparently they were alternates for

28. For this identification see S. W. Koelle, *Polyglotta Africana,* ed. Hair and Dalby (Sierra Leone, 1963), p. 7; G. C. A. Oldendorp, *Geschichte der Mission der Evangelischen Brüder auf den Caraibischen Inseln S. Thomas, S. Croix, und S. Jan,* 2 vols. (Barby, 1777), p. 271; and G. P. Murdock, *Africa: Its Peoples and Their Culture History* (New York, 1959), p. 80. See also Capt. John Adams, *Remarks on the Country Extending from Cape Palmas to the River Congo* (London, 1823), pp. 43–45; and for the history of the Bight of Benin and its hinterland, R. Cornevin, *Histoire du Togo* (Paris, 1959), and *Histoire du Dahomey* (Paris, 1962).

a broader but indefinite category. The same pattern extends to the Bargu cluster, represented by the terms "Barba" (Bariba) and "Samba" (Somba), but again the two are never found on a single list. Further east, in present-day Nigeria, the Nupe are listed as "Tacoua," "Tapa," or other similar variants derived from the Yoruba or Fon names for Nupe.[29] This, however, is the northernmost name from Nigeria found on any of the lists before the 1790's, when Gbari and Hausa appear for the first time.

Along the Bight of Biafra, where the English long dominated the slave trade, nomenclature follows the English fashion, though this was no more precise than the French. The "Moco" or Moko were a diverse range of peoples and cultures shipped from slave ports on the lower Cross River. "Calabari" could mean people shipped from Kalabari (or New Calabar), in which case they would be Ibo or Ijo, or it could refer to Old Calabar, in which case it might be Efik, Ibibio, or even carry much the same meaning as Moko. The "Bibi" of the French records is equivalent to the English Ibibio,[30] but even today the term refers to a group of related and similar cultures rather than a single people. Other terms may be quite narrow in their origins: the "Ara" that occur on one list may possibly be the "Aro," an Ibo subgroup.

Once south of Cape Lopez, listed "nationalities" are still more loosely used. "Congo," which really meant Bakongo in the early sixteenth century, had now become generalized to any Bantu-speaking people from western Central Africa. Nor is the "Mondongue" of the lists equivalent to present-day Mondonga. At best, it meant the man in question came from the interior, roughly to the north and east of the Congo mouth, just as "Angola" referred equally vaguely to the region south and east of the Congo. Thus the term "Congo" encompassed both of the other two general terms from the area. Only one entry in the Debien samples suggests a more narrowly defined ethnic group

29. D. Forde, "The Nupe," in D. Forde, ed., *Peoples of the Niger-Benue Confluence* (London, 1955), p. 17.

30. Oldendorp, *Mission der Evangelischen Brüder,* 1:285.

TABLE 53

ETHNIC ORIGINS OF SLAVES ON THE SUGAR ESTATE OF REMIRE, FRENCH GUIANA, 1690

Region and ethnic group	No.	%
Senegambia	*12*	*18.5*
"Cap-Vert" (Cape Verde Islands)	3	4.6
"Bambara"	5	7.7
Fulbe	3	4.6
Wolof	1	1.5
Gold Coast	*3*	*4.6*
"Cormanti"	3	4.6
Bight of Benin	*33*	*50.8*
"Foin" (Fon)	12	18.5
"Arada"	7	10.8
"Juda" (Ouidah)	7	10.8
Popo	6	9.2
"Ayo" (Oyo Yoruba)	1	1.5
Bight of Biafra	*6*	*9.2*
Calbary (Kalabari)	6	9.2
Central Africa	*11*	*16.9*
Congo	11	16.9
Total	65	100.0

Source: Data from Debien and others, "Origines des esclaves," sample no. 32.

from Central Africa: this is a single "Mousondi," clearly identifiable as a Sonde from the Kwango if the term was used in its African sense.

The peoples of southeastern Africa are lumped together as "Mozambique," possibly including those from Madagascar as well. The only recognizable exceptions are one "Baravie," who could have been from any part of the broad Maravi culture stretching from present-day Malawi down to the lower Zambezi,[31] and one "Maqua," who was probably a genuine enough

31. Murdock, *Africa,* p. 294.

Makwa from the immediate hinterland of Mozambique City.

In spite of problems of interpretation, the most common European error was to use a narrow ethnic or linguistic name, or a coastal shipping point, to stand for a larger and more diverse assortment of peoples. It is therefore possible to arrange the Debien samples with fair accuracy according to the conventional coastal regions. The result is a statistical picture of the sources of the French slave trade, which can be checked against similar data derived from shipping figures.

Since the Debien lists represent many different parts of the French Antilles, the total sample from any single time and place is not always large. A few of the small samples are nevertheless interesting as historical evidence, though weak as statistical samples. Table 53, for example, shows the origins of African-born slaves on a single plantation of French Guiana in 1690. The

TABLE 54

REGIONAL ORIGIN OF SLAVES IMPORTED INTO FRENCH GUIANA, COMPARED WITH THE REGIONAL ORIGIN OF THE WHOLE FRENCH SLAVE TRADE

	% of imports derived from		
Import sample	Senegambia	Guinea	Central Africa
Total Nantes slave trade, 1748–92*	5.0	47.8	44.2
French Guiana, 1748–92*	15.9	58.3	25.8
Remire plantation, French Guiana, 1690†	18.5	64.6	16.9

* From Table 51.
† From Table 53.

sample tells very little by itself, but when it is compared to the origins of the later slave population of French Guiana, and to the origins of the whole French slave trade of the period 1748–92, an interesting pattern emerges. (See Table 54.) The Guaynese deviation from the pattern of the French slave trade in 1748–92 is in the direction of the distribution patterns of Remire plantation almost a century earlier, and this deviation applies to percentages of slaves derived from each of the three major exporting regions. This pattern suggests a hypothesis—that French Guiana (and perhaps other colonies) developed market preferences based on experience with the first slaves to arrive, that planters sought to buy more people from the ethnic groups they were accustomed to.

The statistical viability of the Debien lists is strongest for Saint Domingue toward the end of the eighteenth century. Lists from Saint Domingue can therefore be grouped together by decades, from the 1760's through the 1790's, to produce four separate tables that may be representative of the ethnic distribution of the African-born population of that colony.[32] (See Tables 55–58.) Slaves identified as coming from "Africa" or "Guinée" are left out of account, and the rest are grouped according to the conventional coastal regions.

This body of data can serve not only as a possible ethnic sample for Saint Domingue; it should also be representative of the French slave trade as a whole. Saint Domingue took too large a percentage of that trade to exert strong ethnic preferences. These samples therefore provide a check on the ethnic distribution indicated by shipping data, which are notably weak

32. These tabulations, being arranged according to conventional decades and conventional coastal areas, are slightly different from those of Professor Debien and his colleagues. Since their tabulations follow more closely the chronology and sources of the data themselves, they are to be preferred for the analysis of West Indian history. The need to find commensurates for purposes of the present study occasionally produces a slight distortion. In this case, Debien and his colleagues compiled a very large sample of maroons or escaped slaves in Saint Domingue during 1790–91. They find this sample, no. 73, to be atypical of the whole slave population in significant ways. It is therefore set aside for present purposes. If, however, it were to be included, the result would be to increase the percentages from Mozambique and Central Africa shown in Tables 57 and 58. While the sample is set aside, it nevertheless suggests that these tables underestimate the contribution of Bantu-speaking Africa, which became especially important in the late 1780's. See Debien and others, "Origines des esclaves," esp. 27:784–99, 29:536–58.

Table 55

Ethnic Origins of African-Born Slaves, Saint Domingue, 1760–70

Region and ethnic group	No.	%
Senegambia	*23*	*12.2*
"Senegal"	4	2.1
"Bambara"	19	10.1
Sierra Leone	*5*	*2.7*
"Timbou" (Futa Jallon)	5	2.7
Windward Coast	*2*	*1.1*
"Maminy" (Mamini Kru)	1	0.5
Bobo	1	0.5
Gold Coast	*17*	*9.0*
"Mine" (Akan)	16	8.5
"Coromanti" (Akan)	1	0.5
Bight of Benin	*52*	*27.7*
"Arada" (Coastal Dahomey-Togo)	29	15.4
"Foëda" (Ouidah)	1	0.5
"Adia" (Adja)	1	0.5
"Thiamba" (Chamba or Gurma)	6	3.2
"Cotocoli" (Kotokoli or Tem)	1	0.5
"Barba" (Bariba or Bargu)	1	0.5
"Nago" (Oyo Yoruba)	11	5.9
"Ado" (Otta or southwest Yoruba)	1	0.5
"Tacoua" (Nupe)	1	0.5
Bight of Biafra	*28*	*14.9*
Ibo	23	12.2
"Moco" (Northwest Bantu)	1	0.5
"Bibi" (Ibibio)	4	2.1
Central Africa	*60*	*31.9*
"Congo"	56	29.8
"Mondongue"	4	2.1
Mozambique	*1*	*0.5*
"Baravie" (Maravi)	1	0.5
Total	188	100.0

Unidentified, one each classified as: Saga, Tagar, Apapa, Baourou, Tobouca

Source: Data from Debien and others, "Origines des esclaves," samples no. 1, 6, 7, 20, 21–29.

Table 56

Ethnic Origins of African-Born Slaves, Saint Domingue, 1771–80

Region and ethnic group	No.	%
Senegambia	*10*	*5.7*
"Senegal"	4	2.3
"Bambara"	6	3.4
Windward Coast	*4*	*2.3*
"Canga" (hinterland of Mesurado)	1	0.6
"Aquia" (Akwa or Mbato)	1	0.6
Bobo	2	1.1
Gold Coast	*11*	*6.3*
"Mine" (Akan)	11	6.3
Bight of Benin	*73*	*42.0*
"Arada" (Coastal Dahomey-Togo)	17	9.8
"Foëda" (Ouidah)	2	1.1
"Adia" (Adja)	6	3.4
"Fon" (Fon)	1	0.6
"Thiamba" (Chamba or Gurma)	14	8.0
"Cotocoli" (Kotokoli or Tem)	4	2.3
"Barba" (Bariba or Bargu)	3	1.7
"Nago" (Oyo Yoruba)	25	14.4
"Attanquois" (Otta or southwestern Yoruba)	1	0.6
Bight of Biafra	*12*	*6.9*
Ibo	11	6.3
"Calabari"	1	0.6
Central Africa	*64*	*36.8*
"Mondongue"	1	0.6
"Congo"	63	36.2
Total	174	100.0

Unidentified, one each classified as: Magi, Robo, Calfat, Menanda, Guiala, Fonseda, Niiac, Isaïa

Source: Data from Debien and others, "Origines des esclaves," samples no. 1, 2, 6, 7, 20, 21–29.

Table 57

Ethnic Origins of African-Born Slaves, Saint Domingue, 1781–90

Region and ethnic group	No.	%
Senegambia	*63*	*11.1*
"Senegal"	18	3.2
"Bambara"	35	6.2
"Poulard" (Fulbe)	1	0.2
"Mandingue" (Malinke)	9	1.6
Sierra Leone	*2*	*0.4*
"Timbo" (Futa Jallon)	1	0.2
"Soso" (Susu)	1	0.2
Windward Coast	*18*	*3.2*
"Misérables" (Cape Mesurado)	11	1.9
"Canga" (hinterland of Mesurado)	1	0.2
"Aquia" (Akwa or Mbato)	1	0.2
Cap Lahou	3	0.5
Bobo	2	0.4
Gold Coast	*41*	*7.2*
"Côte d'Or"	15	2.6
"Mine" (Akan)	12	2.1
"Cormanti" (Akan)	8	1.4
"Bandia" (Bandja or Guang)	1	0.2
"Damba" (Dagomba)	4	0.7
"Denira" (Denkyera)	1	0.2
Bight of Benin	*196*	*34.5*
"Arada" (Coastal Dahomey-Togo)	107	18.8
"Foëda" (Ouidah)	5	0.9
"Adia" (Adja)	10	1.8
"Thiamba" and "Quiamba" (Chamba)	15	2.6
"Cotocoli" (Kotokoli or Tem)	11	1.9
"Barba" (Bariba or Bargu)	3	0.5
"Nago" (Oyo Yoruba)	41	7.2
"Tapa" and "Tacoua" (Nupe)	4	0.7
Bight of Biafra	*65*	*11.4*
Ibo	58	10.2
"Moco" (Northwest Bantu)	3	0.5
"Calabari"	1	0.2
"Bibi" (Ibibio)	2	0.4
"Ara" (Aro)	1	0.2

TABLE 57 (*Continued*)

Region and ethnic group	No.	%
Central Africa	*183*	*32.2*
"Mondongue"	2	0.4
"Angola"	1	0.2
"Congo"	180	31.7
Total	568	100.0

Unidentified, one each classified as: Alemcoua, Bengassi (possibly Benga, Northwest Bantu), Mombo, Coida.

Source: Data from Debien and others, "Origines des esclaves," samples no. 1, 4, 8, 48–58.

for the second half of the eighteenth century. A comparison of results is illustrated by Table 59. The projections according to shipping data are derived from Table 49, following the barely-plausible assumption that the slaves present in Saint Domingue at any time would represent some who had landed in the current decade, some who had arrived the previous decade, and still others who had come during a decade earlier still. For lack of demographic information, the three decades are weighted evenly. Thus, the percentage indicated on the basis of shipping data in any one decade is derived from the mean of the number of slaves shown in Table 49 as the export from that region of Africa over the past three decades, but in this instance the "unknown" category is removed from the calculation in order to make the percentages comparable to those from Debien's samples.

At first glance, Table 59 indicates a wild lack of correlation between the two types of data, but a closer examination of the good and bad correlations leads to some interesting conclusions. It should be kept in mind that the large categories—Senegambia, Guinea, Congo-Angola, and Mozambique—are based on Rinchon's list of Nantes shipping, which came to about a third of the whole French slave trade in this period. Subdivisions within the

Table 58

Ethnic Origins of African-Born Slaves, Saint Domingue, 1791–1800

Region and ethnic group	No.	%
Senegambia	*59*	*10.4*
"Senegal"	13	2.3
"Bambara"	28	4.9
"Poulard" (Fulbe)	4	0.7
"Mandingue" (Malinke)	14	2.5
Sierra Leone	*11*	*1.9*
"Théminy" (Temne)	1	0.2
"Soso" (Susu)	10	1.8
Windward Coast	*19*	*3.3*
"Canga" (hinterland of Mesurado)	7	1.2
Kissi	1	0.2
Cap Lahou	9	1.6
Bobo	2	0.4
Gold Coast	*50*	*8.8*
"Côte d'Or"	26	4.6
"Mine" (Akan)	10	1.8
"Cromanti" (Akan)	8	1.4
"Bandia" (Bandja or Guang)	6	1.1
Bight of Benin	*175*	*30.7*
"Arada" (Coastal Dahomey-Togo)	63	11.1
"Foëda" (Ouidah)	2	0.4
"Adia" (Adja)	12	2.1
"Thiamba" and "Quiamba" (Chamba)	17	3.0
"Cotocoli" (Kotokoli or Tem)	7	1.2
"Barba" (Bariba or Bargu)	3	0.5
"Nago" (Oyo Yoruba)	53	9.3
"Tapa" and "Taqoua" (Nupe)	7	1.2
"Samba" (Somba)	1	0.2
"Gambary" (Gbari)	2	0.4
Hausa	8	1.4
Bight of Biafra	*51*	*8.9*
Ibo	44	7.7
"Bibi" (Ibibio)	7	1.2

TABLE 58 (*Continued*)

Region and ethnic group	No.	%
Central Africa	*197*	*34.6*
"Mondongue"	19	3.3
"Congo"	176	30.9
"Mousondi" (Sonde)	2	0.4
Mozambique	*8*	*1.4*
"Mozambique"	7	1.2
"Maqua" (Makwa)	1	0.2
Total	570	100.0

Unidentified, one each classified as: Alemcoua, Téméré, Natcamba, Thémésse, Bagné, Mioc, Bagui; two classified as Dambau (possibly Dagomba).

Source: Data from Debien and others, "Origines des esclaves," samples no. 1, 3, 9–10, 16–17, 28, 30–31, 33, 48–58, 70, 71.

Guinea total, however, were based on much more sketchy outlines and samples. Good correlations for the major areas would therefore support the general validity of Debien's samples, while bad correlations within the broad category of Guinea would not deny it.

This is, in fact, the apparent result. The large categories with a viable statistical base in both Debien's samples and the sample of Nantes shipping show a moderately good correlation. For the two types of data used to derive the figures for Guinea as a whole, each of the totals over the four decades is within 4.2 per cent of their mean, and the figures are even closer in the 1760's and 1770's.[33] For Congo-Angola, each total over the four decades

33. For Guinea, a decade-by-decade comparison of the two methods gives figures that are within 2.3 per cent of their mean for the 1760's; within 1.1 per cent for the 1770's; within 8.0 per cent for the 1780's; and within 11.1 per cent for the 1790's—an average of 5.6 per cent deviation from the mean.

TABLE 59

A COMPARISON OF ALTERNATE MEANS OF ESTIMATING THE ORIGINS OF AFRICAN-BORN SLAVE POPULATIONS OF SAINT DOMINGUE, 1760–1800

Coastal region & source of data	Distribution (%)			
	(1) 1760–70	(2) 1771–80	(3) 1781–90	(4) 1791–1800
Senegambia				
Shipping data	6.0	4.4	4.9	5.9
Debien	12.2	5.7	11.1	10.4
Sierra Leone				
Shipping data	3.2	2.1	0.8	—
Debien	2.7	—	0.4	1.9
Windward Coast				
Shipping data	24.9	9.9	—	—
Debien	1.1	2.3	3.2	3.3
Gold Coast				
Shipping data	15.8	19.4	24.1	22.3
Debien	9.0	6.3	7.2	8.8
Bight of Benin				
Shipping data	14.1	24.8	20.3	16.6
Debien	27.7	42.0	34.5	30.7
Bight of Biafra				
Shipping data	—	—	3.1	4.0
Debien	14.9	6.9	11.4	8.9
Congo-Angola				
Shipping data	36.1	39.3	44.9	48.9
Debien	31.9	36.8	32.2	34.6
Guinea*				
Shipping data	58.0	56.2	48.3	42.9
Debien	55.4	57.5	56.7	53.6
Mozambique				
Shipping data	—	—	1.8	2.3
Debien	0.5	—	—	1.4

* The total of all coastal regions from Sierra Leone through the Bight of Biafra.

Sources: Tables 49, 55–57. See text, pp. 191–95.

is within 11.1 per cent of their mean.[34] For the numerically weaker regions like Mozambique and Senegambia, however, the sample size is too small for any such correlation to appear. The only one of the smaller regions for which the four-decade totals show a correlation falling within the range of 20 per cent is Sierra Leone, where the deviation is about 10 per cent.

Even with this lack of correlation, the data assembled in Table 59 tell something about the relative value of shipping data as against the demographic samples, especially in regard to the Guinea coast. The consolidated total for Guinea in the shipping data was first taken from Rinchon's list and then subdivided. The subdivisions therefore do not reflect on the accuracy of the total. The Guinea total based on Debien's Saint Domingue sample, on the other hand, is the sum of the subdivisions. Here, the relatively good correlation between the Guinea total and Rinchon's Nantes sample indicates the greater probable accuracy of the subtotals as well.

The first conclusion is therefore to reject the pattern of origins projected for the Guinea coast from shipping data alone (Table 49, cols. 5–9). As a second step, it is necessary to reconstruct the projections for this part of the coast following Debien's samples. The result is shown in Table 60. This can be done in a very rough way by again assuming that one-third of a population sample arrived in the decade of the sample, one-third in the previous decade, and one-third a decade still earlier. Thus, the percentage of slaves exported from Sierra Leone in the 1760's should approximate the mean percentage of Sierra Leoneans shown in the Debien samples of the 1760's (Table 55), the 1770's (Table 56), and the 1780's (Table 57). But these calculations have been used in Table 60 only to subdivide the consolidated Guinea total derived from the sample of Nantes shipping. In

34. For Congo-Angola, a decade-by-decade comparison of the two methods gives figures that are within 6.2 per cent of their mean for the 1760's; within 3.3 per cent for the 1770's; within 16.5 per cent for the 1780's; and within 17.1 per cent for the 1790's—an average of 10.8 per cent deviation from the mean.

TABLE 60

FRENCH SLAVE EXPORTS FROM AFRICA, 1751–1800: DECENNIAL ESTIMATES BASED ON SHIPPING DATA COMBINED WITH POPULATION SAMPLES FROM SAINT DOMINGUE

	Slaves purchased					
	(1)	(2)	(3)	(4)	(5)	(6)
Coastal region	1751–60	1761–70	1771–80	1781–90	1791–1800	Total
Senegambia	6,300*	2,300	4,000	17,400	3,400	33,400
%	8.7	2.0	4.0	6.4	5.7	5.4
Sierra Leone	900	1,200	800	2,400	500	5,800
%	1.3	1.0	0.8	0.9	0.9	0.9
Windward Coast	1,200	2,500	2,900	6,800	1,000	14,400
%	1.6	2.2	2.9	2.5	1.6	2.3
Gold Coast	5,300	8,800	7,300	16,000	2,400	39,800
%	7.3	7.6	7.4	5.9	4.1	6.4
Bight of Benin	23,600	40,000	35,300	65,700	8,600	173,200
%	32.6	34.7	35.7	24.2	14.4	28.0
Bight of Biafra	7,500	13,000	9,100	20,400	2,500	52,500
%	10.4	11.3	9.2	7.5	4.2	8.5
Angola	25,300	47,500	38,800	129,000	38,800	279,400
%	34.9	41.2	39.3	47.5	65.1	45.2
Mozambique	—	—	—	8,700	1,100	9,800
%	—	—	—	3.2	1.8	1.6
Unknown & other	2,300	—	800	5,200	1,300	9,600
%	3.2	—	0.8	1.9	2.2	1.6
Total	72,500	115,400	98,800	271,500	59,600	617,800
%	100.0	100.0	100.0	100.0	100.0	100.0

* Figures and totals have been rounded.
Sources: Tables 55–58.

other respects, Table 60 follows the shipping data of Table 49. It should also be noted that this subdividing process has unequal validity depending on the decade. The Debien sample is too small to be useful for the 1750's. Therefore, the estimates for 1751–60 have to depend on population samples for the 1760's and

1770's only. Toward the end of the century, the samples are larger and presumably more accurate, but the population data run out after 1800. Therefore the subdivisions for 1781–90 are based only on the data for the 1780's and 1790's, while those for 1791–1800 are based on the population sample for that decade alone.

The tables derived from Debien's lists also tell something about the actual origins of people shipped from a particular coastal area, in spite of the uncertainty of eighteenth-century nomenclature. The fact that "Bambara" dominate the Senegambian samples, for example, confirms the qualitative impression of travellers and slave dealers, that most slaves sold off that coast were brought down from the hinterland beyond the heads of navigation on the Senegal and Gambia rivers. This pattern is in sharp contrast to the sixteenth-century samples of Senegambian slaves in the Americas, which were mainly made up of Wolof, Serer, or peoples from the banks of the two rivers.

The data are also occasionally useful for their negative evidence. The absence of any ethnic name from northern Nigeria before the 1790's, for example, suggests that the slave trade along the Bight of Biafra had not yet begun to draw on the hinterland of the Ibo country, as it was to do in the nineteenth century.

Only the Bight of Benin, however, provides enough regional data to show a statistical pattern of changing sources of slaves within the region. For purposes of Table 61, the "nationalities" recognized in the West Indies can be divided into a coastal zone about 150 kms wide, a northern hinterland, a northeast hinterland, and a far northeast, beyond the "middle belt" of present-day northern Nigeria. The numbers are too small to tell very much about any particular decade, but the totals for all four decades shake some of the generalizations found in the literature. In some accounts, for example, the Yoruba are mentioned as entering the slave trade only in the nineteenth century, whereas the Yoruba make up at least a fifth of the sample for every decade from the 1760's onward. Another view holds that most slaves were drawn from the "middle-belt," from small and

Table 61

Ethnic Origins of Saint Domingue Slaves from the Bight of Benin, 1760–1800

Region and ethnic group	(1) 1760–70 No.	%	(2) 1771–80 No.	%	(3) 1781–90 No.	%	(4) 1791–1800 No.	%	(5) Total No.	%
Coastal region	*32*	*61.5*	*27*	*37.0*	*122*	*62.2*	*77*	*44.0*	*258*	*52.0*
"Arada"	29		17		107		63		216	43.5
Ouidah	1		2		5		2		10	2.0
Adja	1		6		10		12		29	5.8
Fon	—		1		—		—		1	0.2
Otta	1		1		—		—		2	0.4
Northeast hinterland (Oyo Yoruba only)	*11*	*21.2*	*25*	*34.2*	*41*	*20.9*	*53*	*30.3*	*130*	*26.2*
North hinterland	*9*	*17.3*	*21*	*28.8*	*33*	*16.8*	*35*	*20.0*	*98*	*19.8*
"Kotokoli"	1		4		11		7		23	4.6
Bariba	1		3		3		3		10	2.0
Nupe	1		—		4		7		12	2.4
Somba	—		—		—		1		1	0.2
"Chamba"	6		14		15		17		52	10.5
Far northeast	—		—		—		*10*	*5.7*	*10*	*2.0*
Gbari	—		—		—		2		2	0.4
Hausa	—		—		—		8		8	1.6
Total	52		73		196		175		496	

Sources: Tables 55–58, samples consolidated.

segmentary societies unable to defend themselves against the forces of the better-organized states nearer to the coast. More than half of this sample, however, is coastal. The only evidence of a progressive movement inland is, indeed, the appearance of the far northeast in the last decade of the century.

CHAPTER 7

MAIN CURRENTS OF THE EIGHTEENTH-CENTURY SLAVE TRADE

While the French and English slave trade of the eighteenth century is susceptible to detailed projections indicating coastal regions of export, the same detail is not yet possible in dealing with other national branches of the trade. The French and English trade together nevertheless constitutes something like a 50-per-cent sample of the whole, over the period 1701–1810. The slave trade to Brazil, though known in less detail, can be added to produce a somewhat larger if more generalized sample of the whole Atlantic slave trade in its most important century.

The Portuguese Slave Trade of the Eighteenth Century

Unlike the historians of the French and English slave trade, the Portuguese and Brazilian authorities have been concerned with the total number of slaves imported into Brazil. After their publications of estimate and counter-estimate over the past thirty years, one can accept the consensus reported by Mauricio Goulart in his *Escravidão africana no Brasil* as a crucial point of departure.[1]

Though Goulart's import estimates appear to be less secure than the calculations based on French or English shipping data, they should be at least as accurate as the import estimates for the

1. The key passages for the eighteenth-century estimates are found on pp. 203–9, 209–17, and 265–66.

French and British West Indies. Many of the problems are the same. Provincial records give time-series for parts of the trade; but these records are incomplete and they may have been incompletely explored. In addition, slaves were re-exported from one Brazilian province to another, both overland and by sea. The West Indian problem of possible double counting from this source therefore reappears. Other re-exports moved southward toward the Spanish sphere around the Rio de la Plata, where 12,500 of the legal entries from 1742 to 1806 are recorded as having come from Brazil.[2] Re-export to the northwest, into the Guianas or the Caribbean, is also possible, and it may have taken place in significant numbers.

In other respects, the records of the Brazilian and Portuguese slave trade are different from those of the French and English. No single port dominated the trade in the manner of Liverpool or Nantes. At all periods, both Portuguese and Brazilian shipping were engaged, so that long runs of shipping data from a single port are not a helpful indicator of the size of the whole trade. On the other hand, the Portuguese posts in Africa preserved long series of export figures. Those from Luanda after 1734 and Benguela after 1759 were found in the Lisbon archives and published by Edmundo Correia Lopes.[3] More recently, David Birmingham published additional lists from the same source, which carry the annual export series for Luanda back to 1710 with only a few years missing.[4]

Goulart used the Correia Lopes figures, which are less complete than Birmingham's and differ from them in minor ways, but the differences are relatively trifling. Goulart's figure for Luanda exports over 1711–40, for example, are filled out with estimates, but they come to 229,500 slaves exported, while Birmingham's more complete figures (plus interpolation where required) add up to 215,700 for the same period. Other differences in later years or in Benguela exports are still more minor. The

2. Studer, *Trata de negros,* p. 325.
3. Goulart, *Escravidão,* pp. 203–9.
4. Birmingham, *Trade and Conflict in Angola,* pp. 137, 141, 154.

TABLE 62

GOULART'S ESTIMATED SLAVE IMPORTS INTO BRAZIL, 1701–1810, BY REGIONAL ORIGIN

Decade	From Costa da Mina	From Angola	Total
1701–10	83,700	70,000	153,700
1711–20	83,700	55,300	139,000
1721–30	79,200	67,100	146,300
1731–40	56,800	109,300	166,100
1741–50	55,000	130,100	185,100
1751–60	45,900	123,500	169,400
1761–70	38,700	125,900	164,600
1771–80	29,800	131,500	161,300
1781–90	24,200	153,900	178,100
1791–1800	53,600	168,000	221,600
1801–10	54,900	151,300	206,200
Total	605,500 (32.0%)	1,285,900 (68.0%)	1,891,400

Sources: Birmingham, *Trade and Conflict in Angola,* pp. 137, 141, 154; Goulart, *Escravidão,* pp. 203–9. See text, pp. 206–7.

Angola column in Table 62 is based on Correia Lopes, supplemented by Birmingham's data for the missing years.[5]

As presented in Table 62, these data are shown as imports into Brazil, rather than exports from Africa. This practice follows from Goulart's assumption that the number of ships sailing legally and paying taxes would be less than the total trade. He assumed, furthermore, that other ships arriving from Mozambique or the coast of present-day Guinea-Bissau would make the total still higher. As a result, he inferred that unrecorded exports might be about equal to the expected 10-per-cent loss in transit, therefore the recorded Angolan export figures would constitute a Brazilian import estimate—an estimate that would include all Brazilian imports other than those from the Costa da Mina, equivalent to the conventional regions from the Windward Coast westward to the Bight of Biafra.

5. That is, Luanda: Birmingham (with interpolations), 1711–30, Correia Lopes (with interpolations), 1731–1800; Benguela: Birmingham, 1755–58, Correia Lopes, 1759–1800.

This assumption seems reasonable. The Mozambique trade may have been important, but the old "Guinea of Cape Verde" was no longer a key source of slaves for Brazil. Barreto estimated the normal eighteenth-century exports from Guinea-Bissau at about 1,500 slaves a year, but the recorded exports from Bissau over the seven years 1788–94 show an annual average of only 700, almost entirely directed toward Maranhão.[6] Even at the higher figure, this would fit easily within Goulart's assumption.

The most important West African source of slaves for Brazil was the Bight of Benin. When the Dutch captured Elmina castle in the 1630's, they first tried to cut the Portuguese out of the Guinea slave trade altogether. This proved to be impossible in practice, and the Portuguese were allowed to return—but only on payment of a 10-per-cent duty on all trade goods brought to the coast, payable at Elmina. But payment did not open up the trade of the Gold Coast itself, it merely bought Dutch permission to trade at four ports on the Bight of Benin—Grand Popo, Ouidah, Jaquin, and Apa. As a result the Portuguese took to calling this area the Costa da Mina, and in time the term spread in Portuguese usage to include more loosely any part of the broad region from Cape Mount to Cape Lopez,[7] as Portuguese trade spread somewhat as well. In 1721 the Portuguese built their own fort at Ouidah, and they less often paid blackmail to the Dutch; but their greatest trading interest remained in the Bight of Benin.

The best available data for measuring the level of Portuguese trade on the Costa da Mina are the recorded imports into Bahia. That province had a special interest in the Mina trade, with a marked market preference for "Minas" or West Africans over "Angolas" or Bantu-speaking peoples, and Bahia had the added advantage of producing a type of tobacco that was highly prized

6. Barreto, *História da Guiné,* p. 287; G. Faro, "O movimento comercial do porto de Bissau de 1788 a 1794," *Boletim cultural da Guiné Portuguesa,* 14:231–58 (1959).

7. L. Vianna Filho, "O trabalho do engenho," p. 16.

in West Africa—not merely in preference to other American tobacco, but also in preference to other Brazilian tobacco, even that from neighboring regions.[8] Bahian archives contain records of slaves imported from the Costa da Mina for 62 years of the eighteenth century, and Goulart's estimate of Brazilian slave imports from West Africa is based on these records plus estimates for the first decades of the century and some interpolation. The problem, however, is to move from the relatively secure estimates for Bahia to a total for all Brazil. Goulart guessed that an additional 90,000 slaves from the Costa da Mina would have been imported into other parts of Brazil over the century 1701–1800.[9] The estimated imports from the Costa da Mina, as shown in Table 62, are constructed by taking the Goulart figures for Bahia, plus the additional 90,000 slaves distributed in proportion to the Bahia totals for each decade.

Although these figures for imports from the Costa da Mina are shown in Table 62 as Goulart stated them, there is some reason to believe that they are probably too high. The guesswork in setting the non-Bahia imports from the Costa da Mina at 90,000 has no archival base, and 90,000 is an 18-per-cent increase over the Bahia figures. In addition, Goulart's estimates for the first decades of the century may be too high. There is no doubt but that the gold rush in Minas Gerais greatly increased the demand for slaves in Brazil in the 1690's and the decades that followed,

8. In 1807, for example, slaves from the Costa da Mina sold in Bahia at about 100$000 each, as against 80$000 for newly imported slaves from Angola (Goulart, *Escravidão*, p. 265). For the Bahia tobacco trade see P. Verger, "Rôle joué per le tabac de Bahia dans la traite des esclaves au Golfe du Bénin," *Cahiers d'études africaines*, 4:349–69 (1964). Verger's important work, *Flux et reflux de la traite des nègres*, was available too late in 1968 to be used fully to form the conclusions of this chapter. Verger's statistical data and calculations of the numbers of slaves imported from the Bight of Benin to Bahia—based on the number and capacity of ships sailing from Bahia with tobacco—confirm the conclusions already reached by Goulart on other evidence. See Verger, "Mouvement de navires," p. 31; *Flux et reflux*, Appendix II, pp. 651–69.

9. Goulart, *Escravidão*, pp. 209–17.

and this rebounded on the slave trade of Bahia. Between 1681 and 1700, 76 ships a decade sailed to Africa from Bahia. In the decade 1701–10 the number had increased to 217 ships.[10] But, if Goulart's estimated imports into Bahia are accurate, each ship would have had to carry 550 slaves. Ships of that size existed, but English and French slavers of the eighteenth century tended to carry only about 250 to 300 slaves each, and a sample of 21 ships carrying slaves into Bahia in 1728–29 averaged only 425 slaves each.[11]

The decennial estimates of slaves imported into Brazil as shown in Table 63 therefore include an arbitrary reduction of about 10 per cent in Goulart's estimate of the flow from the Costa da Mina to Brazil for the period 1701–1800, a reduction made by taking Goulart's import figure as an export figure and thus disregarding a loss in transit of about 10 per cent. The Goulart figure for Brazilian imports from the Costa da Mina in 1801–10, however, is based on actual import records for at least a part of the decade and for all major Brazilian ports. That decade, and the whole of the Angola import estimate, are therefore translated into an export estimate by adding a 10-per-cent allowance for probable loss in transit. The result in Table 63 is a set of export estimates in which the modified data of Table 62 are combined with the French and English estimates in Tables 43 and 49 to give a general picture of decennial exports by the three major trading nations and from the two principal trading regions in Africa.[12]

The Minor Trading Nations in the Eighteenth-Century Slave Trade

Table 63 should represent a very broad picture of the eighteenth-century slave trade, but the "big three" were not alone. Aside from *really* minor carriers like Brandenburg, the Dutch and

10. Verger, "Le Tabac de Bahia," p. 358.
11. Verger, *Flux et reflux,* p. 661.
12. Table 63 is slightly distorted by the form of Goulart's estimates, which include exports of Guinea-Bissau with those of Angola, rather than grouping them with the Costa da Mina.

Table 63

Projected Exports of the Portuguese, English, and French Slave Trade, 1701–1810 (000 Omitted)

Region and carrier	1701–10	1711–20	1721–30	1731–40	1741–50	1751–60	1761–70	1771–80	1781–90	1791–1800	1801–10	Total	%
West Africa													
Total exports	*230.3*	*267.6*	*271.4*	*322.8*	*332.9*	*286.2*	*373.1*	*281.0*	*381.7*	*267.0*	*219.8*	*3,233.8*	*58.9*
Portuguese	83.7	83.7	79.2	56.8	55.0	45.9	38.7	29.8	24.2	53.6	60.4	611.0	
English	119.6	141.0	120.5	175.7	215.8	195.5	266.6	191.8	228.8	195.0	159.4	2,009.7	
French	27.0*	42.9	71.7	90.3	62.1	44.8	67.8	59.4	128.7	18.4	—	613.1	
Central and Southeast Africa													
Total exports	*80.0*	*64.0*	*105.8*	*172.7*	*203.3*	*190.5*	*191.7*	*187.6*	*403.7*	*355.2*	*273.1*	*2,227.6*	*40.6*
Portuguese	77.0	60.8	73.8	120.2	143.1	135.9	138.5	144.7	169.3	184.8	166.4	1,414.5	
English	—	—	21.1	28.6	34.4	29.3	5.7	4.1	96.7	130.5	106.7	457.1	
French	3.0*	3.2	10.9	23.9	25.8	25.3	47.5	38.8	137.7	39.9	—	356.0	
Other and unknown origin													
Total exports	—	—	*3.6*	*2.7*	*7.9*	*8.3*	—	*0.8*	*5.2*	*1.3*	—	*29.8*	*0.5*
General total	310.3	331.6	380.8	498.2	544.1	485.0	564.8	469.4	790.6	623.5	492.9	5,491.2	100.0

* Estimate.

Sources: Tables 43, 49, 60, and 62 with modifications.

Table 64

Some Estimates of the Slave Trade of Principal Carriers in 000's Exported from Africa

Carrier	(1) 1768 No.	(1) 1768 %	(2) 1780 No.	(2) 1780 %	(3) 1788 No.	(3) 1788 %	(4) 1788 No.	(4) 1788 %	(5) 1798 No.	(5) 1798 %	(6) Mean %	(7) Estimated or projected total exports*	(8) Estimated or projected annual average	(9) Mean % of "big-three" subtotal	(10) % of "big-three" export estimates, 1761–1810
England	53.1	51.0	32.8	46.9	38.0	51.3	36.0	48.5	55.0	57.9	51.1	1,385.3	27.7	58.0	47.1
France	23.5	22.6	15.0	21.4	20.0	27.0	18.0	24.2	—	—	19.0	546.4	10.9	21.6	18.5
Portugal	8.7	8.4	18.0	25.7	10.0	13.5	12.0	16.2	25.0	26.3	18.0	1,010.4	20.2	20.4	34.4
Subtotal	*85.3*		*65.8*		*68.0*		*66.0*		*80.0*		*88.1*			100.0	100.0
Dutch	11.3	10.9	3.0	4.3	4.0	5.4	4.0	5.4	—	—	5.2	173.6†	3.5†		
Danes	1.2	1.2	1.2	1.7	2.0	2.7	2.0	2.7	—	—	1.7	56.8†	1.1†		
US	6.3	6.1	—	—	—	—	2.2	3.0	15.0	15.8	5.0	166.9†	3.3†		
Total	104.1	100.0	70.0	100.0	74.0	100.0	74.2	100.0	95.0	100.0	100.0	3,338.3			

* Based on estimated exports of 1761–1810 for England, France, and Portugal (Table 63).

† Projected figures.

Sources: Col. 1 quoted from Ad. Mss. 18960, f. 37, by Pitman, *West Indies*, p. 70; col. 2 quoted from undated "Mémoire sur la côte d'Afrique," from Archives Nationales, K 907, nos. 38 and 38bis, by J. Machat, *Documents sur les établissements français et l'Afrique occidentale au xviiie siècle* (Paris, 1906), pp. 132–33 (internal evidence indicates a date between 1779 and 1783); col. 3, estimate of Robert Norris, quoted from *Board of Trade Report*, by Pitman, *West Indies*, p. 71; col. 4, from W. Young, *West India Common-Place Book* (London, 1807), p. 5; col. 5, from J. Bandinel, *Some Account of the Trade in Slaves from Africa* (London, 1842), p. 105; col. 6, from cols. 1–5; col. 7, from Tables 43, 49, and 63; col. 8, from cols. 6 and 7; col. 9, from cols. 1–5; col. 10, from Tables 43, 49, and 63; see also text, pp. 213–17.

Danes were active throughout the century. North American shipping, considered part of the British slave trade to 1783, became increasingly important after the American Revolution, and Spain entered the direct slave trade to some degree in the second half of the eighteenth century. The historical literature is notably weak in its treatment of these minor national branches of the trade. None of them can be traced quantitatively over a period of years or decades without the help of archival research which is yet to be done. Historians sometimes make statements about the relative importance of the minor carriers, but these statements appear to rest solely on contemporaneous estimates, laying out the distribution of the trade by national carriers. Estimates of this kind are notoriously weak as an indication of long-run performance. They are weaker still, because the estimating authority was usually connected with the slave trade of a particular European country: his knowledge of the amount of business done by foreigners might well be faulty. But these estimates are at least worthy of critical examination.

Five estimates are widely quoted, all of them lying between the years 1768 and 1798, and these are summarized in cols. 1 through 5 of Table 64.[13] In each case, the percentage of the total trade allowed to each carrier is the crucial figure. (The absolute number of slaves exported in a particular year may or may not be true for that year, but it cannot be taken as an annual average for a trade as variable as this one.) The share of the trade assigned to the "big three"—England, France, and Portugal—is remarkably consistent in all five estimates. Even though France dropped from the trade after 1792, leaving its share to be picked

13. Two additional sets of estimates available in the French archives have been set aside because they duplicate or nearly duplicate the published estimates shown in Table 64. One unsigned document, for example, gives estimates claimed to be for 1778, but they are nearly identical with the English estimates for 1768 in Table 64, col. 1 (Archives Nationales, colonies, C^6 17, "Mémoire sur la traite des noirs," July 1782). A second document gives estimates for about 1778 nearly identical with those in Table 64, col. 2 (A.N., colonies C^6 17, unsigned, untitled, undated, in folder for 1778, but datable by internal evidence to 1782 or later).

up by England and Portugal, the lowest percentage assigned to the big three (in 1768) and the highest (in 1780) vary from the mean of 88.1 per cent by only 7.1 per cent. The minor traders therefore appear to have carried only about 12 per cent of the total slave trade, at least for the period 1761–1810.

Given this measure of agreement in the five samples, they can be used experimentally to make still more explicit projections of the possible share in the slave trade held by the Netherlands, Denmark, and the United States. The samples are chronologically concentrated on the 1780's, but the presence of an earlier and later sample helps to make them more broadly representative of the whole period 1761–1810. The mean of the five samples, as shown in col. 6, can therefore be taken as a consensus of contemporaneous estimates. The three major carriers are assigned 88.1 per cent of the whole trade, and their exports from Africa over the period 1761–1810 can be taken from Tables 43, 49, and 63. If, as shown in col. 7, the number of slaves exported by the big three is known, the number carried by the three minor trading nations can be projected in proportion to the mean percentages in col. 6. The result is the fifty-year annual average export of slaves from Africa in col. 8.

These projections are merely experimental and should not be taken too seriously. Cols. 9 and 10, showing the percentage shares of the big three alone, first according to the five samples and then according to the long-run estimates from earlier tables, are a measure of the degree of accuracy to be expected. On the other hand, the annual averages indicated for the Dutch trade are reasonably consistent with other estimates found in the literature. One authority put the Dutch trade at 8,000 to 10,000 a year before the war of 1779–83—and at about 4,000 a year during the peace that followed.[14] Another gives a short-run calculation of 6,300 a year for 1767–68, though the annual average may have

14. *Board of Trade Report,* Part IV.

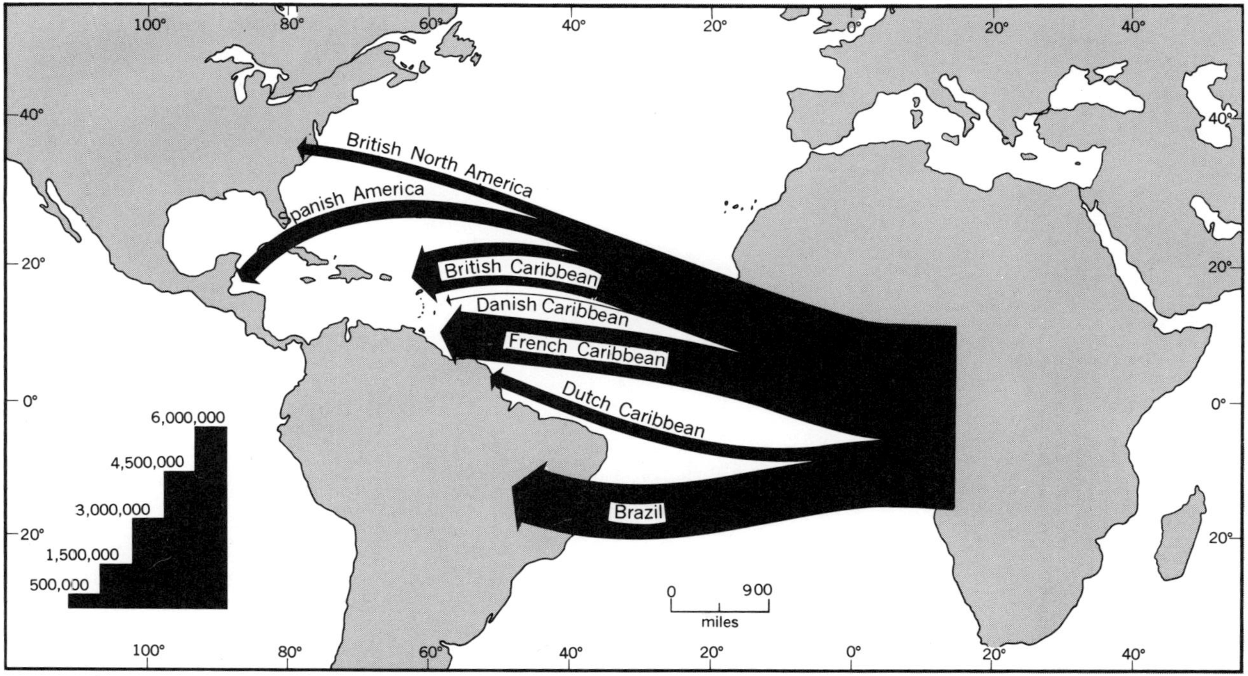

Fig. 14. Destinations of the Atlantic slave trade, 1701–1810. Fig. by UW Cartographic Lab. Data from Table 65.

Table 65

Estimated Slave Imports into American Territories, 1701–1810 (000 Omitted)

Region and country	1701–20	1721–40	1741–60	1761–80	1781–1810	Total No.	Total %
British North America and US	*19.8*	*50.4*	*100.4*	*85.8*	*91.6*	*348.0*	*5.8*
Spanish America	*90.4*	*90.4*	*90.4*	*121.9*	*185.5*	*578.6*	*9.6*
British Caribbean	*160.1*	*198.7*	*267.4*	*335.3*	*439.5*	*1,401.3*	*23.2*
Jamaica	53.5	90.1	120.2	149.6	248.9	662.4	
Barbados	67.8	55.3	57.3	49.3	22.7	252.5	
Leeward Islands	30.0	44.5	67.9	67.9	91.6	301.9	
Dominica, St. Lucia, St. Vincent, and Tobago	—	—	—	33.5	36.6	70.1	
Trinidad	2.5	2.5	2.5	2.5	12.4	22.4	
Grenada	3.8	3.8	14.5	27.5	17.3	67.0	
Other BWI	2.5	2.5	5.0	5.0	10.0	25.0	
French Caribbean	*166.1*	*191.1*	*297.8*	*335.8*	*357.6*	*1,348.4*	*22.3*
Saint Domingue	70.6	79.4	158.7	195.0	286.0	789.7	
Martinique	33.8	42.9	70.1	70.1	41.5	258.3	
Guadeloupe	53.5	53.5	53.5	52.2	24.4	237.1	
Louisiana	1.2	8.3	8.5	8.5	1.7	28.3	
French Guiana	7.0	7.0	7.0	10.0	4.0	35.0	
Dutch Caribbean	*120.0*	*80.0*	*80.0*	*100.0*	*80.0*	*460.0*	*7.6*
Danish Caribbean	*6.0*	*3.3*	*6.7*	*5.0*	*3.0*	*24.0*	*0.4*
Brazil	*292.7*	*312.4*	*354.5*	*325.9*	*605.9*	*1,891.4*	*31.3*
Total	855.1	926.3	1,197.2	1,309.7	1,763.1	6,051.7	100.0
Annual average	42.8	46.3	59.9	65.5	58.8	55.0	
Mean annual rate of increase (%)	2.5	0.4	1.3	0.4	−0.4	0.8	

Sources: Tables 5, 8, 9, 10, 20, 21, 22, 39, 40, 62.

been as high as 20,000 a year in the first decades of the eighteenth century.[15]

Experimental as they are, the totals shown in col. 7 are one kind of estimate of the whole slave trade over a half-century. Since the English and French totals are both mainly derived from shipping data, they can be taken as projected exports based on shipping data; and they can be checked in part against other estimates based on import data from the Americas. Import estimates for the whole eighteenth century, following the calculations in Chapters 2 and 3, are summarized in Table 65.

With two sets of estimates, derived from differing bodies of data, it is at least possible to see whether they are consistent. Since the Portuguese import estimates for the eighteenth century are actually based on export figures from Africa, they have to be left out of account. For the rest, the exports according to shipping data, less loss in transit, should approximately balance the imports of all the Americas except Brazil. For the whole of 1761–1810, non-Portuguese slave traders appear to have exported 2,328,000 slaves (Table 64, col. 7) translated into potential imports by allowing a loss in transit of 15 per cent. As a result, some 1,979,000 slaves were available to satisfy the imports of the non-Brazilian New World, estimated at 2,141,000 slaves over the same period (following the summary in Table 65). In short, shipping-based estimates fall short of import-based estimates by about 8 per cent. Given the limited quality of the data, particularly of the samples in Table 64, this result is satisfactory in showing a general area of agreement. It *may* suggest either that the carrying capacity of the minor carriers is somewhat underestimated by the samples, or that the double-counting problem has led to an overestimate of imports into some American colonies. The data are too weak to show which possibility is more probable.

The carrying capacity of the minor trading nations—and inci-

15. R. van Lier, *Maatschappij in Suriname,* p. 125; Vrijman, *Slavenhalers,* p. 38; article "Slavenhandel," in *West Indische Encyclopaedie,* p. 635.

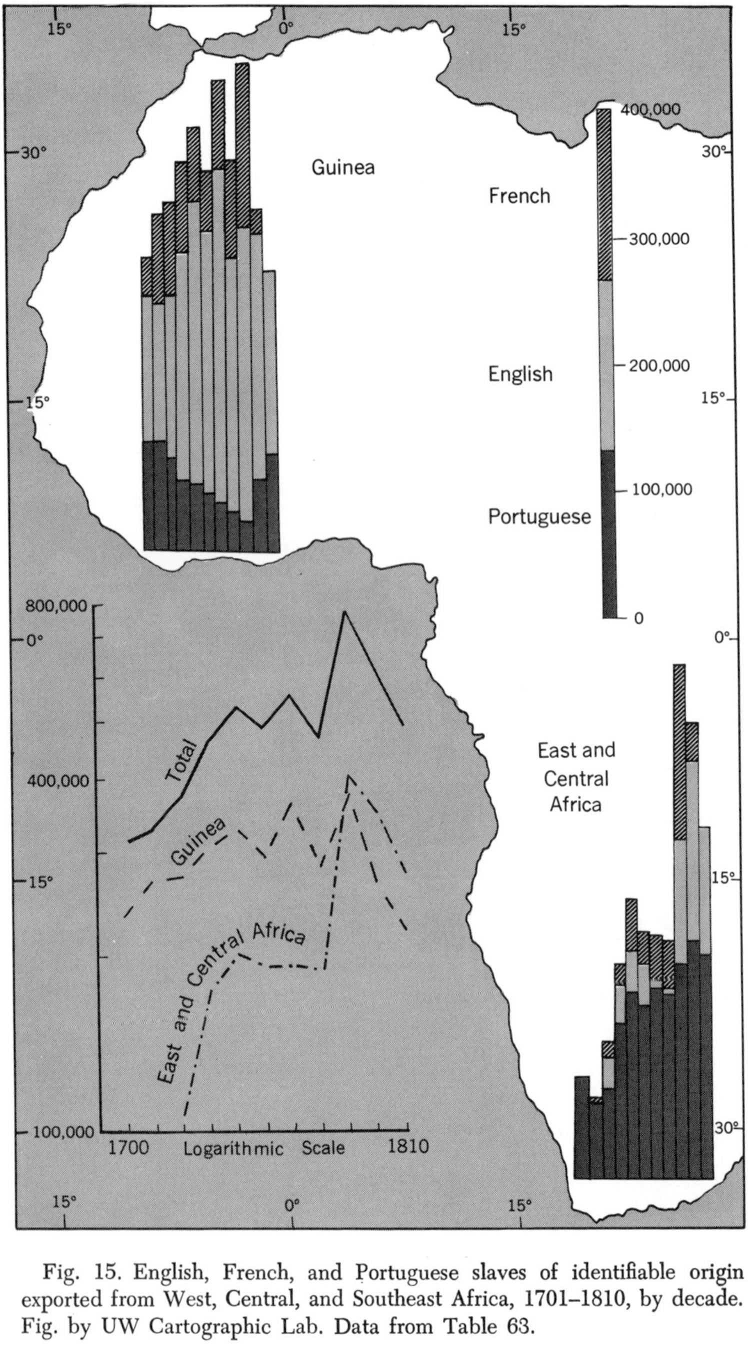

Fig. 15. English, French, and Portuguese slaves of identifiable origin exported from West, Central, and Southeast Africa, 1701–1810, by decade. Fig. by UW Cartographic Lab. Data from Table 63.

dentally the possible inconsistency of shipping data and import data—can also be examined for the whole period 1701–1810 by comparing the export data for France and England (Table 63) with the import summary for the Americas as a whole (Table 65). Again, the slave trade to Brazil has to be left out, since Portuguese exports and Brazilian imports are derived from the same body of data. The British slave exports, however, are mainly derived from shipping data. Allowing for a 15-per-cent loss in transit, British slave traders should have had about 2,108,000 slaves for sale in the Americas over the whole 110-year period. Since the imports of the British colonies—plus an estimated half of the slaves imported into the United States after 1781—are shown at 1,704,000 slaves, the British should have had a surplus of 404,000 slaves available for sale to foreign colonies. This figure is consistent with the estimated re-export of 206,000 slaves from Jamaica during the period 1701–1810 (Table 6), but it raises more severe problems when taken in conjunction with the estimated imports of other colonies.

The French slave trade, for example, is generally considered to have supplied less than the full imports of the French colonies. The data of Tables 49 and 63 indicate that this was indeed the case in 1701–1810. At a 15-per-cent loss in transit, the French exports from Africa allow only 838,000 slaves for purchase in the Americas, only 62 per cent of the estimated imports into French colonies. The deficit of 511,000 would therefore have to come from the British surplus, combined with other supplies from the Dutch, Danes, or North Americans.

Meanwhile, Spanish America imported an estimated 579,000 over 1701–1810, while the Dutch and Danish colonies themselves imported 484,000, and that portion of the North American imports not included with the British imports is another 46,000. If these imports are added to the French deficit, they come to a total of 1,619,000 slaves—with no visible means of supply other than the British surplus and the minor trading nations. This level of imports would require 1,215,000 slaves delivered to the Americas by minor traders during the whole period 1701–1810—29 per cent of the non-Portuguese imports, or 20 per cent of the whole slave imports including Brazil.

Here is indeed a discrepancy. None of the contemporaneous estimates for the second half of the eighteenth century credits the minor slave trading nations with so important a share of the slave trade. (The estimates of Table 64 assign them only 11.9 per cent of the trade during 1761–1810.) Several explanations are possible. One is that the minor traders, and especially the Dutch, carried a much larger share of the trade in the early eighteenth century, before the date of any of the estimates quoted in Table 64. Another possibility is a large re-export trade from Brazil northeastward to the Caribbean, or even of direct Portuguese trade from Angola to the West Indies. (If this were the case, the Brazilian import estimates are inflated.) Still another is the likely possibility that the authorities responsible for the sample estimates in Table 64 systematically underestimated the number of slaves carried by the minor trading nations. Four of the authorities were, after all, English, and one French. They clearly mistook the size of the Portuguese slave trade of 1761–1810, assigning it only 18 per cent of the total slaves exported from Africa, while Brazilian historians tend to agree on a figure at least twice as large.

It is also possible either that the export data of Table 63 are too low, or the import data of Table 65 are too high. The danger of double counting implicit in the flow of re-exports from one colony to another has already been mentioned. This possibility seems more likely than an underestimate of exports from Africa, but a clear solution is not possible on present evidence. In any event, the discrepancy is well within the margin for error to be allowed in interpreting estimates of the kind given here.

African Sources of the Eighteenth-Century Slave Trade

Table 63 can also serve as a broad perspective on the African sources of the French, English, and Portuguese slave trade. The main trends of the exports from West Africa, Central and East

TABLE 66

PROJECTED EXPORTS OF THAT PORTION OF THE FRENCH AND ENGLISH SLAVE TRADE HAVING IDENTIFIABLE REGION OF COASTAL ORIGIN IN AFRICA, 1711–1810

Region	1711–20	1721–30	1731–40	1741–50	1751–60	1761–70	1771–80	1781–90	1791–1800	1801–10	Total
Senegambia	30,900*	22,500	26,200	25,000	22,500	21,400	17,700	20,300	4,400	800	191,700
%	16.5	10.0	8.2	7.4	7.6	5.5	6.0	3.4	1.1	0.3	5.8
Sierra Leone	5,900	15,000	14,900	18,400	9,900	5,300	3,700	17,700	12,200	9,600	112,600
%	3.2	6.7	4.7	5.4	3.4	1.4	1.3	3.0	3.2	3.6	3.4
Windward Coast	30,600	47,600	55,200	65,300	29,800	67,600	49,700	24,400	14,700	11,200	396,100
%	16.4	21.2	17.3	19.3	10.1	17.4	16.9	4.1	3.8	4.2	12.1
Gold Coast	44,000	54,200	65,200	67,000	41,800	52,400	38,700	59,900	29,400	22,100	474,700
%	23.5	24.2	20.5	19.8	14.2	13.5	13.2	10.1	7.7	8.3	14.4
Bight of Benin	72,500	48,400	59,400	30,900	35,600	48,400	41,400	120,400	15,100	5,300	477,400
%	38.8	21.6	18.6	9.1	12.1	12.5	14.1	20.3	3.9	2.0	14.5
Bight of Biafra	—	4,500	45,100	71,300	100,700	139,300	100,000	114,800	137,600	110,400	823,700
%	—	2.0	14.2	21.1	34.1	35.9	34.0	19.4	35.9	41.5	25.1
Central and southeast Africa	3,200	32,000	52,500	60,200	54,600	53,200	42,900	234,400	170,400	106,700	810,100
%	1.7	14.3	16.5	17.8	18.5	13.7	14.6	39.6	44.4	40.1	24.7
Total	187,000	224,200	318,500	338,100	295,000	387,700	294,000	591,800	383,800	266,000	3,286,100
%	100.0	100.0	100.0	100.0	100.0	100.0	100.0	100.0	100.0	100.0	100.0

* Figures and totals have been rounded.
Sources: Tables 43, 49 (through the 1740's), and 60 (1751–1810) leaving aside category of "other" or "unknown."

Africa, and the two together are illustrated by the semi-logarithmic presentation in Fig. 15. While roughly 59 per cent of the Atlantic slave trade came from West Africa over the whole period 1701–1810, as against 41 per cent from the Bantu-speaking portion of the continent, the growth of trade proceeded quite differently in the two major regions. During the early part of the century, West African exports increased at an annual average of 0.9 per cent between the decade of the 1700's and that of the 1740's. The Central and East African exports meanwhile supplied most of the total growth, increasing at 3.9 per cent per annum between the 1710's and the 1740's. In the mid-century, exports from both regions reached a plateau of relative stability, West African exports alternating from decade to decade in response to the pattern of Anglo-French warfare at sea—showing increasingly higher peaks and lower troughs, but little long-term growth. The last burst of the eighteenth-century slave trade came almost entirely from Central and southeastern Africa, which more than doubled its exports between the 1770's and 1780's. Thereafter, exports from this region too began to fall through the 1790's and the decade of the 1810's. The warfare of the Napoleonic period undoubtedly had a strong influence on the pattern of declining exports from both Central and West Africa in these decades, but this time there was to be no postwar boom meeting a backlog of American demand. The real beginning of the downward spiral of African slave exports therefore came with the 1790's—not, as often pictured, after the passage of the British act abolishing the slave trade in 1808.

A more intimate, if less general picture of the slave exports from the conventional coastal zones is possible through a combined table of Anglo-French exports over the century from 1711–1810 (Table 66). The Portuguese and the minor carriers may have used other sources of supply, but the French and English together carried more than half the trade of the century, and their total exports from a particular region establish a link between the numerical patterns of their trade and the main lines of African political history.[16] Fig. 16 shows the rise and fall of exports from each of the six coastal zones.

It is clear from these data that no coastal region exported slaves at a consistently high rate. Nor is the export curve of any region closely tied to the export curve from Africa as a whole. The consolidated slave exports from West Africa, as illustrated in Fig. 15, apparently responded to the demand of the European slave dealers and ultimately to the rhythm of war and peace between European powers on the Atlantic, but no coastal zone responded in quite that pattern. The high point for the Senegambia, for example, was in the 1710's, possibly even earlier. Sierra Leone reached one peak of export in the 1740's, followed by a second in the 1780's—a pattern in common with that of the Gold Coast. Exports from the Windward Coast also reached two decennial maxima, this time in the 1740's and 1760's. The Bight of Benin, on the other hand, shows a beginning pattern nearly

16. While it is possible that the pattern of trade in the hands of non-English and non-French merchants was drastically different from the Anglo-French trade, there is no evidence that it was. The trade of any one of the minor traders did, indeed, tend to be concentrated in a few regions, to take advantage of commercial contacts or the presence of trading forts. The Portuguese, for example, traded heavily with the Bight of Benin, while the Danes concentrated on the Gold Coast. The little evidence available, however, suggests that some minor traders were found almost everywhere along the coast. One set of estimates showing the distribution of this trade in about 1778 is found in the Archives Nationales, but its authority is uncertain. (A. N., colonies, C^6 17, folder for 1778, unsigned, undated, untitled.) This document assigns the Portuguese, Dutch, and Danish exports as follows (in annual numbers of slaves exported):

Coastal origin	*Portuguese*	*Dutch*	*Danes*
Casamance to Bissagos Islands	1,000		
Gold Coast		1,500	1,000
Bight of Benin	4,000		200
Bight of Biafra	2,000		
Gabon to Congo		1,500	
Congo to Cape Negro (Angola proper)	12,000		
Total	19,000	3,000	1,200

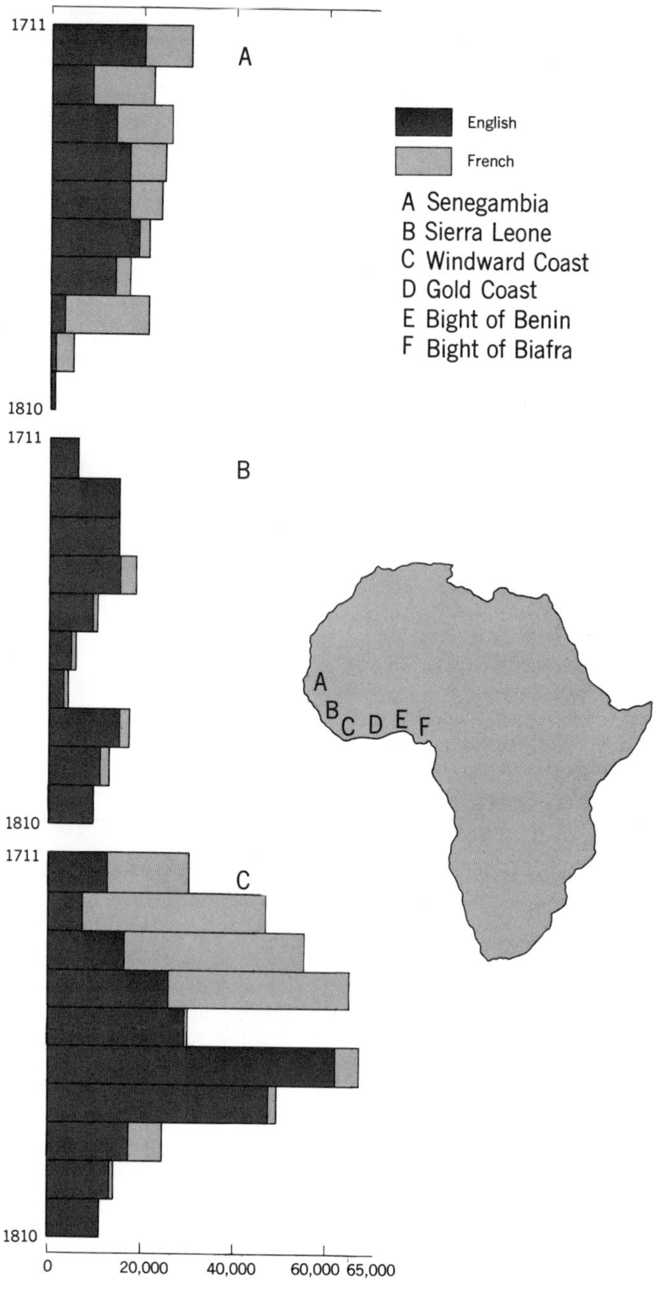

Fig. 16. Anglo-French slave exports from West Africa, 1711–

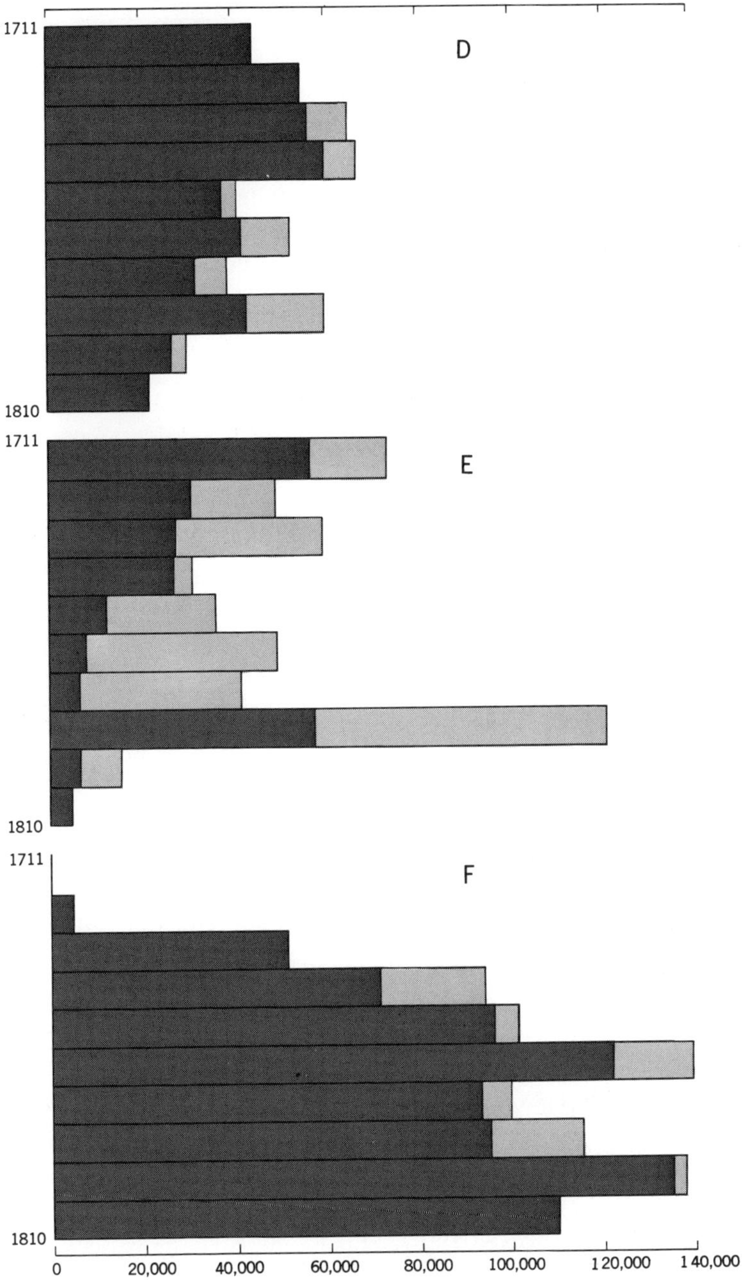

1800, by decade. Fig. by UW Cartographic Lab. Data from Table 66.

reciprocal to that of the Gold Coast. While the Gold Coast exports were rising steadily from the 1710's to the 1740's, those from the Bight of Benin were falling, though they rose suddenly in the 1780's to more than twice the low point of the 1770's. By contrast, the Bight of Biafra was a negligible supplier until the 1730's, but its export then grew very rapidly to levels that were more consistently maintained than those of any coastal zone other than Senegambia.

In short, the exports of an individual region responded far more to local supply conditions than they did to the demand of European traders. The Senegambian peak in the 1710's, for example, appears to be associated with the establishment of a French post in Gadiaga on the upper Senegal at the end of the eighteenth century, and possibly with political disturbances in the region of Segu with the rise of power of Marmari Kouloubali (1712–55).[17] Otherwise the exports of the Senegambia were remarkably even, though the Anglo-French division of the total varied greatly through time.

Other variations can be explained, at least speculatively, by periods of warfare that produced large numbers of prisoners for sale. The sharp peak of Sierra Leone exports in the 1720's through the 1740's may well reflect the disorders accompanying the Fulbe jihad in Futa Jallon. Other variations are hard to explain. The second Sierra Leone peak in the 1780's is something of a mystery. So too are the sharp variations in the supply of slaves from the Windward Coast. Cape Mount to Assini is certainly the region of coastal Africa whose eighteenth-century history is least well known. The pattern of trade there, however, suggests that the supply of slaves was not drawn from the distant hinterland, but from scattered sources close to the coast. A French survey of the late 1770's listed all of the known slave-supply ports of Africa with the expected annual export capacity of each. For the Windward Coast, it named no less than 35 separate ports, none of them credited with a supply of more than 500 slaves a year. By contrast, ports with a developed network of

17. L. Tauxier, *Histoire des Bambara* (Paris, 1942), pp. 69 ff.

trade routes to the interior—such as the Gambia, Ouidah, or the major ports along the Bight of Biafra or the coast of Angola—were rated at an export capacity of 1,000 to 6,000 a year. But each of these ports served a much wider area: in constrast to the 35 ports of the Windward Coast, only 27 were listed for all of Africa east of the Volta River.[18]

On the Gold Coast, the rise of exports through the 1740's correlates well enough with the rise and consolidation of Ashanti, though the variations from the 1750's onward are hard to associate with particular periods of warfare in Ashanti and beyond.

The Bight of Benin also conforms to the pattern of known political change. The early peak of the 1710's was based mainly on the exports from Ouidah at its height before the Dahomean conquest of the late 1720's. On other evidence, Colin Newbury judged the zenith of the Ouidah trade to have been reached by about 1716.[19] Some slaves were later sent down from Dahomey through Ouidah, but the trade on this coast tended to shift eastward to Porto Novo (Ajashe), Badagry, Apa, and even Lagos at the very end of the eighteenth century. The second Bight-of-Benin peak of the 1780's is associated with these newer currents, especially with slaves from Oyo during the reign of Alafin Abiodun (c. 1770–89). He greatly enlarged the Oyo slave trade, and he established Oyo control over both Porto Novo and a corridor leading south from metropolitan Oyo to the port.[20] The Bight of Benin is one area where the Anglo-French pattern of exports need not be taken in isolation. The Portuguese estimates for exports from West Africa (Table 63) were so nearly derived from the Bight of Benin exclusively that they may be added to the Anglo-French totals to obtain a more inclusive

18. Archives Nationales, colonies, C^6 18, "Etat des esclaves de la côte d'Afrique," unsigned, undated, but presumed to be 1783.

19. C. W. Newbury, *The Western Slave Coast and Its Rulers* (Oxford, 1961), p. 22.

20. I. A. Akinjogbin, "The Oyo Empire in the Eighteenth Century—A Reassessment," *Journal of the Historical Society of Nigeria,* 3:457–59 (1966); Peter Morton-Williams, "The Oyo Yoruba and the Atlantic Trade 1670–1830," *Journal of the Historical Society of Nigeria,* 3:25–45(1964); P. Verger, "Le Tabac de Bahia," pp. 364–68.

picture of the exports from that region.[21]

The Bight of Biafra seems to be an exception to the prevailing West African pattern of slave supply dependent on political events. Here political change followed the appearance of European demand. The Oil Rivers and the estuary of the Cross River had been small-scale sources of slaves during the seventeenth century, though both the Dutch and the Portuguese had occasionally traded there.[22] The rise of exports from the 1730's onward is associated with political reorganization. The trading states of Kalabari and Bonny, which developed stronger monarchies under the Amakiri and Pepple dynasties, began to spread controlled trade networks into the interior. The Efik trading communities of the lower Cross River were meanwhile passing through a similar structural change,[23] and all appear to have acted in response to the rising European demand for slaves, reflected in increasing prices through the eighteenth century. Throughout the region, political reforms led to more efficient institutions for gathering slaves and transporting them to the coast, including devices like the manipulation of the Arochuku oracle among the Ibo to produce slaves for export without depending on large-scale warfare.[24] The sustained high level of exports from the Bight of Biafra may possibly be explained by the success of these innovations.

A similar response may also explain the immense increase in slave exports from Central Africa in the 1780's. Whether moved

21. The numerical totals of the combined Anglo-French-Portuguese exports from the Bight of Benin (from Tables 63 and 66) are as follows:

1711–20	156,200	1761–70	87,100
1721–30	127,600	1771–80	71,200
1731–40	116,200	1781–90	144,600
1741–50	85,900	1791–1800	68,700
1751–60	81,500	1801–1810	65,700

22. A. F. C. Ryder, "Dutch Trade on the Nigerian Coast."

23. G. I. Jones, *The Trading States of the Oil Rivers* (London, 1963), esp. pp. 43–48; D. Forde, ed., *Efik Traders of Old Calabar* (London, 1956).

24. See K. O. Dike, *Trade and Politics in the Niger Delta 1830–1885* (Oxford, 1956), pp. 37–41.

by higher prices or other, more local reasons, African merchants serving both the Angolan ports and the slave ports north of the Congo mouth began to lengthen their reach into the interior. By the 1780's the routes from the Congo mouth reached inland and north to the lower Ubangi, while in the south the Ovimbundu traders began in the 1770's to supply Benguela from the farther interior. A central route leading due east from Luanda through Kassange, the capital of Imbangala, had long since carried some European trade goods as far as the east coast, and it appears to have acquired a set of important feeder routes during the 1780's and 1790's. Changes in demand, and perhaps restricted supplies elsewhere in Africa, also had something to do with the great Angolan slave rush of the 1780's and 1790's. The English and French slavers had a backlog of demand based on the prosperity of the plantation regime in Jamaica and Saint Domingue, and on the wartime interruption of trade until 1783. Their purchases on the Central African coast account for almost the entire increase in the exports of that period, while Portuguese-carried exports rose only slightly. Unfortunately, the data are not precise enough to show which of the three principal routes into the interior was most responsible for the increased supply of slaves.[25]

Mozambique also became a significant source of slaves for the Atlantic trade in the 1780's, after an earlier phase of importance in the seventeenth century. This time, the principal impetus came from the French in the Mascarene Islands, who were developing a plantation complex like that of the West Indies. Exports from Mozambique City began to increase in the 1770's reaching a peak at around 9,000 a year in about 1790, and French slave traders of the Indian Ocean seem to have met local demand well enough to divert about 5 to 10 per cent of this trade to the Atlantic. Other exports from Mozambique and the east coast were carried by the Portuguese, especially to southern South America, where about 40 per cent of the slaves imported

25. J. Vansina, "Long Distance Trade Routes in Central Africa," *Journal of African History,* 3:375–90(1962).

in the region of the Rio de la Plata between 1742 and 1806 were from southeastern Africa.[26]

But new supplies from Mozambique also depended on an African response to demand. In this case, the innovators were not coastal traders but the Yao of the interior, who turned from their customary ivory trade to supply slaves as well, drawing on the area bordered by the Zambezi in the south, Lake Nyasa to the west, and the Rovuma River to the north.[27]

26. Studer, *Trata de negros,* p. 325.
27. M. Zimmermann, "The French Slave Trade at Moçambique, 1770–1794," unpublished M.A. thesis, University of Wisconsin, 1967.

CHAPTER 8

THE SLAVE TRADE OF THE NINETEENTH CENTURY

The dimensions of the nineteenth-century slave trade have always been a matter of controversy—political controversy at the time and historical controversy since. This outcome is hardly unexpected. As the trade was made illegal, those who practiced it tried to keep their dealings to themselves. At the same time, the anti-slavery forces tried to provide as much publicity as possible for the trade that continued. The result was a great deal of writing about a subject on which no one could possibly be very well informed.

Legal abolition, however, was a gradual process, shutting off the sources of information a little at a time. It began with Danish abolition in 1805,[1] continued with the British and North American acts taking effect in 1808. Still later, after the Peace of Vienna, a series of piecemeal abolition acts were passed by all of the European maritime powers—though often passed unwillingly under diplomatic pressure from Great Britain. Formal legal abolition rarely meant an actual end of the trade. Neither Spain, Portugal, France, the United States, nor Brazil (after independence in 1822) immediately took effective measures to enforce its own legislation. By treaty with Britain, the Portuguese slave

1. Georg Nørregard, *Danish Settlements in West Africa, 1658–1850* (Boston, 1966), p. 184.

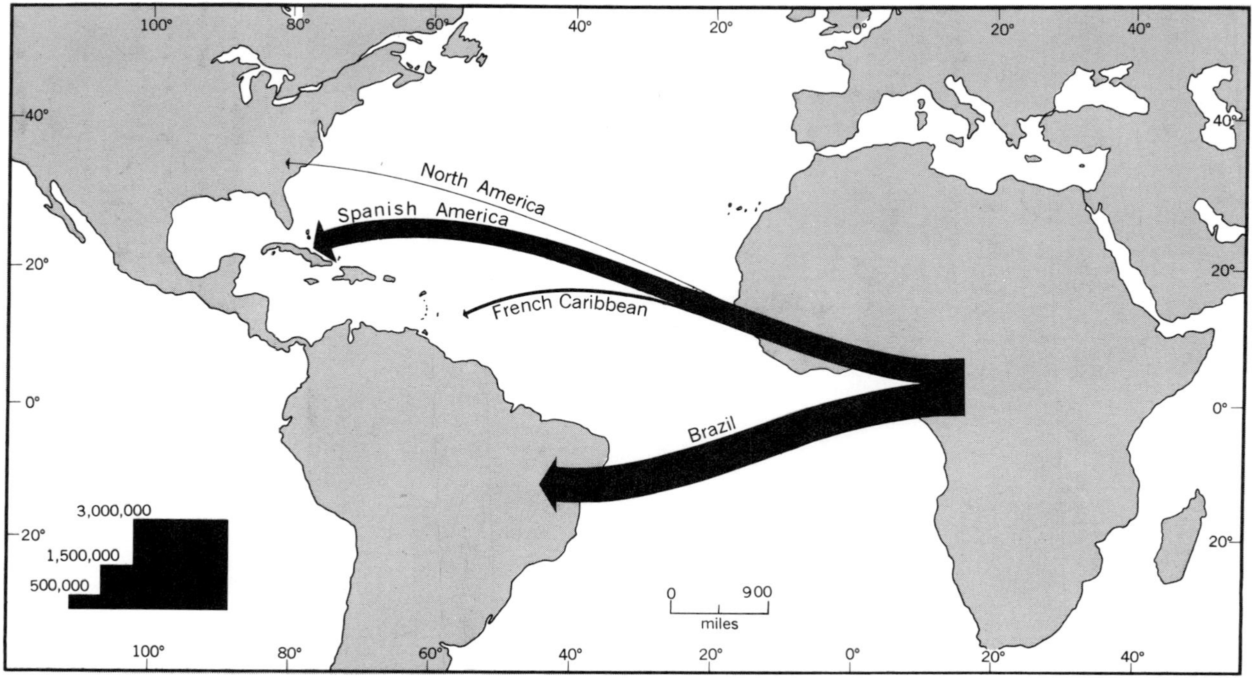

Fig. 17. Destinations of the Atlantic slave trade, 1811–70. Fig. by UW Cartographic Lab. Data from Table 67.

traders were safe from British cruisers south of the equator until 1839, and Brazilian slavers enjoyed the same privileged sanctuary until 1845. The end of general legality for the trade, however, marks the end of regular and official shipping data from the slave-trading nations. If such exist, they remain buried in the archives.

The principal source of information about the nineteenth-century slave trade is therefore the anti-slavery group, which, especially in Great Britain, used publicity as a major weapon. Having persuaded the country to suppress the foreign slave trade as a matter of national policy, private opponents of the slave trade won the help of public institutions. From 1815 into the 1870's, the Foreign Office and the navy took up the fight against the slave trade, putting their much larger resources into the tasks of investigation, negotiation, and suppression. In the process, they left behind enormous quantities of archival material which has not yet been fully mined for quantitative data.

Meanwhile, a great deal of information about the trade was published for Parliament, including estimates and samples that are among the best and the worst available from that period. The Foreign Office with its overseas representation had the means to find out a great deal. But it also acquired a commitment to the policies it initiated. Like the anti-slavery propagandists themselves, the Foreign Office sometimes found it useful to make the slave trade appear as evil as possible, by making it appear as large as possible.

This tendency appears especially in a famous set of estimates presented to Parliament in 1848. Over the years 1810–39, they show an annual average exceeding 100,000 slaves exported from Africa, an annual average of 135,800 for 1835–39, and an average loss in transit to the New World of 25 per cent.[2] These estimates could have been honest guesswork, but the total is impossible measured against American slave populations, agricultural production, or any other index. It was not even consistent with other

2. PP, 1847–48, xxii (623), p. 8.

Table 67

Estimated Slave Imports of American Territories, 1811–70 (000 Omitted)

Territory	1811–20	1821–30	1831–40	1841–50	1851–60	1861–70	Total	
							No.	%
United States	*10.0*	*10.0*	*10.0*	*10.0*	*10.0*	*1.0*	*51.0*	*2.7*
Spanish Caribbean	*86.3*	*124.6*	*140.2*	*58.2*	*130.5*	*66.2*	*606.0*	*31.9*
Cuba	79.9	112.5	126.1	47.6	123.3	61.5	550.0	
Puerto Rico	6.4	12.1	14.1	10.6	7.2	4.7	55.1	
French Caribbean	*31.4*	*46.0*	*3.6*	—	*15.0*	—	*96.0*	*5.1*
Martinique	15.2	15.2	1.5	—	9.1	—	41.0	
Guadeloupe	12.2	20.8	2.1	—	5.9	—	41.0	
French Guiana	4.0	10.0	—	—	—	—	14.0	
Brazil	*266.8*	*325.0*	*212.0*	*338.3*	*3.3*	—	*1,145.4*	*60.3*
Total	394.5	505.6	365.8	406.5	158.8	67.2	1,898.4	100.0
Annual average	39.5	50.6	36.6	40.7	15.9	6.7	31.6	
Mean annual rate of increase (%)	−2.0	2.5	−3.2	1.1	−9.4	−8.6	−3.1	

Sources: Tables 9, 10, 21; Goulart, *Escravidão,* p. 270. See text, pp. 235–36.

returns furnished to Parliament, presumably from the same source. In 1845, for example, the Foreign Office furnished a "Return of the Number of Slave Vessels arrived in the Transatlantic States since 1814," including a remarkably full sample of more than 2,000 slave ships known to the Foreign Office over the years 1817–43.[3] Unless the Foreign Office had found some new information between 1845 and 1848, its own records showed an annual average of 31,400 slaves over 1835–39—not 135,800. Some allowance would have to be made for slavers that slipped into port without notice, but Portuguese and Brazilian trade south of the equator was still open, and the Brazilian trade was legal until 1830. As for the mortality at sea, the rate of loss recorded on 826 ships in the period 1817–43 was 9.1 per cent, according to the published list of 1845—not 25 per cent, as estimated in 1848.

Unfortunately, more historians of the slave trade seem to have believed the Foreign Office estimates of 1848 than took the trouble to tabulate its excellent body of raw data published in 1845. The 1848 estimates have thus become one cause of the chronic exaggeration of the trade still found in the historical literature, while the neglected Foreign Office listing of 1845 is the largest and most complete sample of the slave trade at any period in its entire history. It is, however, a large sample, not the complete record.

Imports into the Americas

For the larger dimensions of the nineteenth-century slave trade, import estimates remain the most complete guide. The estimates and calculations already made for particular countries are summarized in Table 67.

The largest single importer was certainly Brazil, and Goulart's summary of the findings of Brazilian historians continues to be acceptable. It is supported for the period 1840–51 by the estimates of the Foreign Office and by Brazilian government fig-

3. PP, 1845, xlix (73), pp. 593–633.

ures.[4] Brazilian imports for the 1820's and 1830's are more uncertain, and Goulart did not divide his total estimate for 1810–38 into annual subtotals. The table nevertheless can be taken as the approximate movement of the trade from one decade to the next, and the Foreign Office listing of 1845 appears to be approximately an 85-per-cent sample of Brazilian imports for the 1820's and a 60-per-cent sample for the 1830's. If the British representatives in Brazil were efficient in the period before 1830 of openly illegal slave imports, their information may actually have been nearly complete. In that event, the imports shown on Table 67 for the 1820's may be inflated by as much as 20 per cent.

The various import estimates for Cuba have already been discussed critically in Chapter 2, as have those for the French West Indies and the United States in Chapter 3. Table 67 merely summarizes the preferred estimates to cover the major aspects of the trade. Other minor currents are less known—some slave trade flowed into Texas while it was still part of Mexico and during its period of independence before joining the United States. Other occasional reports mention small shipments of slaves to various parts of continental South America. Although these minor flows have been omitted from Table 67, the Foreign Office sample for 1817–43 hints at some of the possibilities without being exhaustive. (See Table 68.)

The pattern of Table 68 tells something about the biases to be expected in the Foreign Office sample. The British representatives were clearly trying to accumulate data as complete as possible on Brazil and Cuba, the countries universally recognized at the time as the major importers. The rest were only occasionally reported, almost as a matter of chance when a ship here or a ship there came into the orbit of British information-gathering agencies. Even then, some of the destinations may be deceptive. The imports into the Bahamas, and perhaps into British Honduras, were probably en route to the United States. Those into Uruguay could be either for local use or re-export.

4. Goulart, *Escravidão*, p. 270. For other estimates see Gomes, "Tráfico africano no Brasil," p. 51; Taunay, *Tráfico africano*, pp. 291–93.

Table 68

Slaves Imported into the Americas by Ships Known to the British Foreign Office, 1817–43

Importing country	1817–20		1821–30		1831–40		1841–43		Total	
	No.	%	No.	%	No.	%	No.	%	No.	%
Brazil	44,100	96.3	277,200	81.2	147,500	75.4	48,500	69.2	517,300	79.2
Cuba	1,000	2.3	22,700	6.7	42,600	21.8	20,500	29.2	86,800	13.3
Bahamas	—	—	600	0.2	1,800	0.9	—	—	2,400	0.4
Danish WI	200	0.4	—	—	—	—	—	—	200	*
Puerto Rico	—	—	—	—	300	0.2	—	—	300	*
United States	—	—	100	*	—	—	—	—	100	*
Guadeloupe	—	—	300	0.1	—	—	—	—	300	*
Martinique	—	—	1,400	0.4	—	—	—	—	1,400	0.2
Uruguay	—	—	—	—	1,400	0.7	—	—	1,400	0.2
British Honduras	—	—	—	—	200	0.1	—	—	200	*
Surinam	500	1.1	600	0.2	—	—	—	—	1,100	0.2
Destination unknown	—	—	38,300	11.2	1,800	0.9	1,100	1.6	41,200	6.3
Total	45,800†	100.0†	341,300†	100.0†	195,600†	100.0†	70,100†	100.0†	652,800†	100.0†

* Less than 0.05%.
† Totals and percentages have been rounded.
Source: Data from PP, 1845, xlix (73), pp. 593–633.

Most of the minor importers are only represented by a single ship, though nine were known to have unloaded in the Bahamas, five each in Martinique and Uruguay, and three in Surinam. Still, these minor currents are small compared to a total of 1,703 ships on which data were extensive enough for inclusion in the table.

From a comparison of this tabulation of the Foreign Office sample with the other import estimates represented in Table 67, it appears that the British sources of information were far better for Brazil than for Cuba—as would be expected from the fact that Brazilian slavers had less reason to disguise their activities. For the two complete decades, the 1820's and 1830's together, the Foreign Office sample includes about 80 per cent of the Brazil imports, but only 27 per cent of the Cuban imports—as assessed in Table 67. For the whole transatlantic slave trade of these two decades, the sample is about 60 per cent of the whole.

The subsample for Brazil is not merely the largest; it is also the best supplied with full information. A total of 1,308 ships unloading 517,300 slaves over the 27-year period are documented fully enough in the Foreign Office sample to be separately tabulated according to the importing state in Brazil and the exporting coastal region in Africa. (See Table 69.) This tabulation certainly contains a bias owing to the illegality of the trade. Some of the bias is unpredictable, but some is clear. The imports from West Africa are certainly understated. The slave trade north of the equator was forbidden by Anglo-Portuguese and Anglo-Brazilian treaties, and the British navy patrolled the West African coast. On the face of it, one might not expect any slave trade at all with West Africa, especially when the trade south of the line was legal and open until 1830. Every state in Brazil could be reached by sea without going north of the equator, and British cruisers rarely patrolled south of the equator until the mid-1840's. Bahian tobacco, however, still enjoyed its special preference among African consumers in the Bight of Benin, and other traditional trade contacts were too important to be sacrificed. In the case of Bahia, shipping not only continued to go to

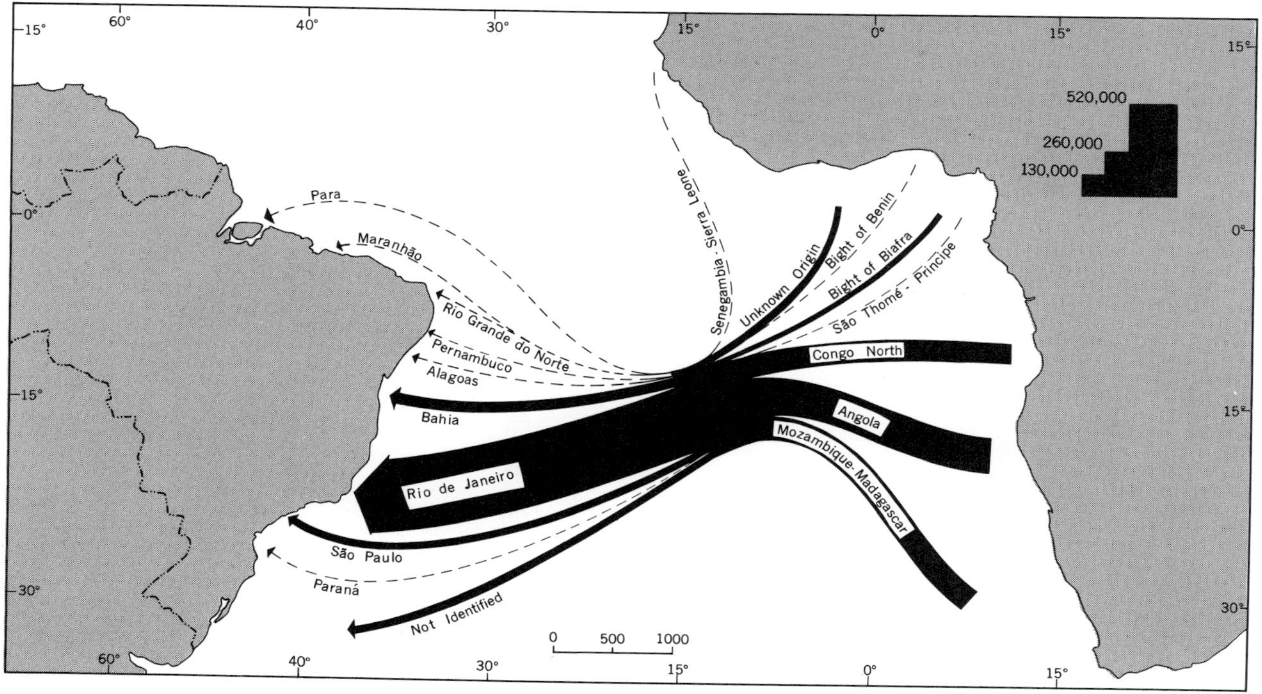

Fig. 18. The Brazilian slave trade, 1817–43. Fig. by UW Cartographic Lab. Data from Table 69.

Table 69

Brazilian Slave Trade Known to the British Foreign Office, 1817–43: The Imports of Brazilian States, by Origin in Africa

State	Senegambia and Sierra Leone	Bight of Benin	Bight of Biafra	Congo North	Angola	Mozambique and Madagascar	São Thomé and Principe	Unknown origin	Total	% of total Brazil imports
Pará	100*	—	—	—	500	600	—	—	1,300	0.2
%	9.5	—	—	—	43.2	47.4	—	—	100.0	
Maranhão	500	—	—	500	2,300	100	—	200	3,700	0.7
%	13.1	—	—	14.9	63.6	3.7	—	4.7	100.0	
Rio Grande do Norte	—	—	—	—	4,400	1,000	—	500	5,900	1.1
%	—	—	—	—	74.4	16.9	—	8.7	100.0	
Pernambuco	—	—	300	—	3,200	800	—	2,300	6,600	1.3
%	—	—	4.8	—	48.5	12.0	—	34.7	100.0	
Alagoas	—	—	—	—	900	700	—	—	1,600	0.3
%	—	—	—	—	58.5	41.6	—	—	100.0	
Bahia	—	1,200	12,600	26,200	4,100	2,300	600	8,000	55,100	10.7
%	—	2.1	22.9	47.6	7.5	4.3	1.1	14.5	100.0	
Rio de Janeiro	200	600	1,000	95,900	172,600	92,400	900	14,000	377,700	73.0
%	0.1	0.2	0.3	25.4	45.7	24.5	0.2	3.7	100.0	
São Paulo	—	2,000	—	5,700	11,000	13,200	11,100	2,100	35,100	6.8
%	—	5.7	—	16.3	31.4	37.7	3.0	6.1	100.0	
Paraná	—	—	—	—	2,200	1,500	—	600	4,300	0.8
%	—	—	—	—	51.5	34.1	—	14.4	100.0	
Not identified	—	1,100	—	2,500	16,200	3,700	100	2,600	26,200	5.1
%	—	4.3	—	9.4	62.0	14.0	0.4	10.0	100.0	
Total	800	4,900	13,900	130,800	217,500	116,300	2,700	30,300	517,300	100.0
%	0.2	1.0	2.7	25.3	42.1	22.5	0.5	5.9	100.0	

* Figures and totals have been rounded.
Source: Data from PP, 1845, xlix (73) pp. 593–633.

the Bight of Benin; British cruisers actually succeeded in capturing some 169 Bahian ships over the years 1815–50, most of them in West African waters.[5]

Table 69 uses African coastal zones slightly different from those of earlier tables. The conventional Senegambia and Sierra Leone supplied so few slaves that they are most conveniently combined in a single zone stretching from the Senegal to Cape Mount. The Gold and Windward Coasts drop out altogether, but the "Angola" of earlier tables can now be divided into two—"Congo North" taking in coastal points from Cape Lopez southward to and including the mouth of the Congo River, and "Angola," now taken as Angola proper, the region from Ambriz southward to Benguela. In addition, São Thomé and Principe, the two Portuguese islands in the Gulf of Guinea, have been tabulated separately, though both were merely entrepôts that drew their supplies from the nearby coast.

As the table shows, imports into Brazil were highly concentrated. The east-west coast took a bare 1 per cent of the identified imports. Southern Brazil took less than 1 per cent. But 80 per cent were drawn to the developing sugar and coffee estates of Rio de Janeiro and São Paulo, while Bahia and the northeast, the older home of the sugar industry, took only about 13 per cent.

The African origins of these slaves retained some aspects of the eighteenth-century pattern and lost others. Angola in the narrow sense now supplied a smaller proportion of Brazilian imports than the estimated 68 per cent that held for the period 1701–1810, but the shift was only a few miles up the coast to the region of Congo North. Since this region seems to have been the "Angola" of the French and English slavers in the eighteenth century, its export capacity was now available to serve Brazil. The bias of the table, however, must be taken into account here. Bahian captains bound for the Bight of Benin usually registered for a voyage to Malembo, Cabinda, or São Thomé, thus securing papers that would account for their legitimate presence near the

5. Verger, "Mouvement de navires," pp. 13–15.

Bight. Therefore, almost all the traffic shown in the table as originating in Congo North with destination Bahia came in reality from the Bight of Benin. Ships from Rio de Janeiro, on the other hand, lacked the old connection of the tobacco trade. Their trade with Congo North probably represents a genuine shift in source of supply.

Even with these biases taken into account, West Africa appears to have supplied a smaller proportion of Brazilian slave imports than it did in the eighteenth century. If all the ships of unknown origin, plus those recorded as sailing to Bahia from Congo North, are assigned to West Africa, that region still supplied less than 15 per cent of Brazilian imports.

Instead, Brazil began to draw more slaves than ever before from southeast Africa. There too, the fragmentary data now available suggest that Brazilian importers took over supplies that formerly had other outlets, rather than developing new sources within Africa itself. In this case, the supply they tapped was apparently the Yao trade route from the interior to Mozambique City, which had formerly gone on by sea to the Mascarene Islands. The city of Mozambique had reached an export capacity of about 9,000 slaves a year by 1790, only a small part of which flowed into the Atlantic slave trade. With an annual average of 4,300 slaves imported into Brazil from Mozambique each year, according to the sample for 1817–43, the actual imports from that area may well have been in the vicinity of 6,000 a year. This in turn implies an export from Mozambique of about 7,300, when allowance is made for loss in transit.

The retention of old patterns is especially clear in comparing the origin of the imports into northern and northeastern Brazil. Pará and Maranhão had traditionally drawn their slaves from Guinea-Bissau, and they appear on Table 69 importing three-fourths of the small supply of slaves listed from that region. Bahia, on the other hand, had always shopped for slaves on the Costa da Mina, and it continued to do so as much as possible.

Still another curiosity of the Brazilian slave trade is the great variation in the size of the cargo. It was not only variable according to the African region of export, but increased in a regular manner from the north and west, where the mean number of slaves landed per vessel was smallest, to the south and east, where it was largest. (See Table 70.) The preference for larger ships in the long voyage to the Indian Ocean is clear, but the regular progression along the West African coast is not so obvious.

TABLE 70

MEAN NUMBER OF SLAVES PER SHIP IMPORTED INTO BRAZIL, 1817–43, BY COASTAL REGION OF EXPORT

Senegambia	119
Sierra Leone	145
São Thomé-Principe	269
Bight of Benin	290
Bight of Biafra	310
Congo North	359
Angola	400
Mozambique	493
All points of origin	395

Source: Data from PP, 1845, xlix (73), pp. 593–633.

The Foreign Office sample is much less complete for the Cuban slave imports of 1817–43, and the port of embarkation in Africa is unknown in the case of more than 70 per cent of the ships listed. While 254 ships, importing a total of 86,800 slaves appear in the Cuban subsample for these years, the region of embarkation in Africa is given for only 71 ships carrying 25,700 slaves. The sample is therefore small, only about 10 to 15 per cent of the Cuban slave imports of the period, and its biases are too unpredictable to give it statistical viability for anything but the broadest indications.

It is possible, however, to make a better-educated guess at the origins of nineteenth-century slave imports into Cuba by combining the Foreign Office sample with data from other sources. Slaves captured by the British Navy in the course of the anti-slave-trade blockade of the West African coast were usually landed in Sierra Leone. In 1848, the Freetown census included information on the ethnic origins of the population that resulted.[6] This census did not include the whole colony, but it nevertheless constitutes a sample of some 13,273 representatives of the recaptives as a group. (See Table 71.) It has two known sources of bias. First, recaptives from nearby areas were often able to return home. Sierra Leone as a coastal region is therefore under-represented. Second, the British cruisers patrolled south of the equator only in the 1840's, and even then many of the recaptives from the south were not taken to Sierra Leone for adjudication. The region south of Cape Lopez is therefore badly under-represented. The table also poses some problems in assigning particular ethnic groups to coastal regions of export. Some of the Malinke, for example, could possibly have been shipped from the Senegambia, though British control of Bathurst at the mouth of the Gambia River reduced this possibility after 1817. The large block of Hausa is somewhat more of a problem, since some of them were certainly shipped from Bight-of-Benin ports. With these exceptions, however, Table 71 should be reasonably representative of slave exports from West Africa during the period covered by the Foreign Office sample.

Table 72, below, represents the Cuban import data from the Foreign Office sample, modified according to the indication of the Freetown census. Although great accuracy in detail is not expected from the Foreign Office sample, it should be reasonably accurate in major division between West Africa on one hand and East and Central Africa on the other. In Table 72, col. 1 therefore represents the Cuban subsample of the Foreign Office data for 1817–43. Col. 2 shows the percentage distribution by coastal region, with ships from São Thomé and Principe or listed with unknown origin omitted. Col. 3 shows an alternate projection with the West African total divided according to the proportions of the Freetown census (Table 71) rather than those of the Cuban import sample. Of the alternative projections, col. 3 is

6. PP, 1849, xxxiv [C. 1126], pp. 304–5.

Table 71

Ethnic Origin of Recaptives in Sierra Leone, 1848

Region and ethnic group	No.	%
Senegambia	*16*	*0.1*
Wolof		
Sierra Leone	*905*	*6.8*
Malinke	188	
Temne	5	
Fulbe	14	
Susu	51	
Mende, etc. (Koso)	609	
Sherbro	38	
Windward Coast	*60*	*0.5*
Basa, etc.		
Gold Coast	*168*	*1.3*
Akan, etc. (Kromantees)		
Bight of Benin	*8,459*	*63.7*
Fon, Gun, etc. (Popos)	1,075	
Yoruba	7,114	
Nupe	163	
Benin	107	
Bight of Biafra	*2,677*	*20.2*
Ibo	1,231	
Efik, Ibibio, etc. (Calabahs)	319	
Northwest Bantu (Moko)	470	
Hausa	657	
Angola-Mozambique	*439*	*3.3*
West coast generally (Congo)	421	
East coast generally (Mozambique)	18	
Other	*549*	*4.1*
Total	13,273	100.0

Source: Data from PP, 1849, xxxiv [C.1126], pp. 304–5.

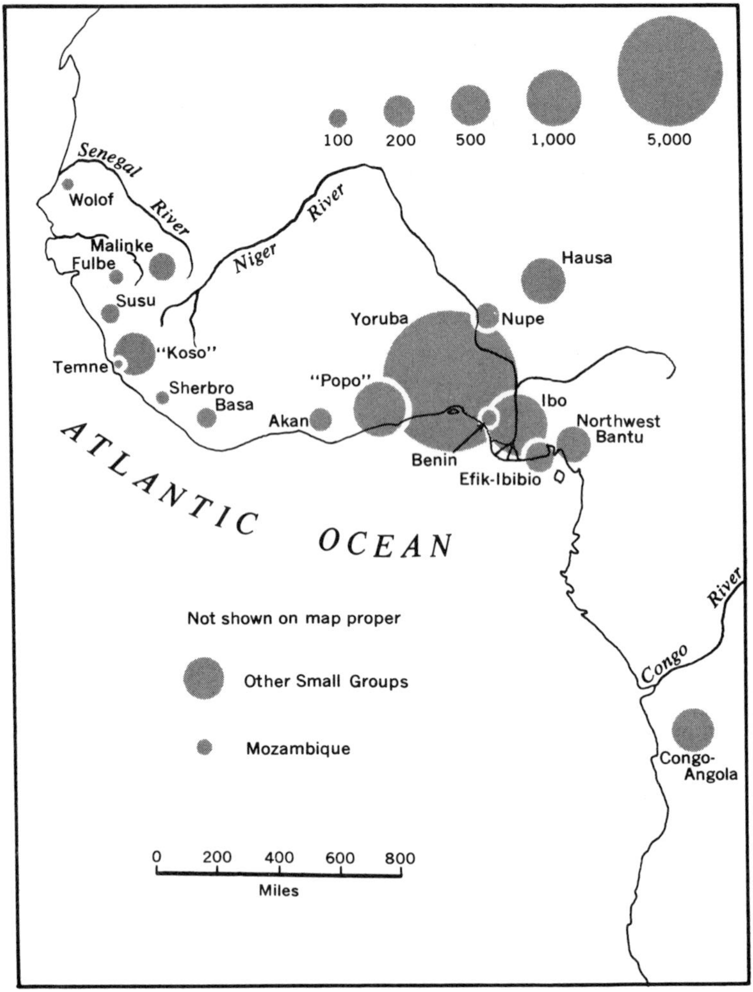

Fig. 19. Ethnic origins of recaptives in Sierra Leone, 1848. Names in quotation marks are census categories with no modern equivalent. Fig. by UW Cartographic Lab.

probably more accurate than col. 2, though col. 2 is certainly correct in showing a higher proportion from Sierra Leone.

The carriers of the nineteenth-century slave trade remain an unexplored aspect of the trade, though the records of the British

TABLE 72

ESTIMATED AFRICAN ORIGINS OF CUBAN SLAVE IMPORTS, 1817–43

Coastal region	Foreign Office sample: Crude %	Foreign Office sample: % with São Thomé-Principe and unknown categories omitted	Alternate projection using Freetown census of 1848 for distribution of origins within West Africa
Senegambia	—	—	0.1
Sierra Leone	2.5	10.6	3.3
Windward Coast	0.1	0.4	0.2
Gold Coast	1.1	4.6	0.6
Bight of Benin	3.9	16.1	31.1
Bight of Biafra	3.3	13.6	9.9
Congo North	3.1	13.0	13.0
Angola	2.7	11.3	11.3
Mozambique	7.1	29.5	29.5
Madagascar	0.2	1.0	1.0
São Thomé-Principe	5.7		
Origin unknown	70.3		
Total	100.0	100.0	100.0

Sources: Data from PP, 1845, xlix (73), pp. 593–633, and Table 71.

anti-slave-trade squadron, the Courts of Mixed Commission with judicial power over captured slavers, and private business records on four continents may someday open it more fully. The Foreign Office sample of 1845 mentions the names of 802 individual captains and 847 ships which could someday be correlated with other forms of evidence.

It also identifies the national flag of 621 ships delivering slaves to New-World destinations. The nineteenth-century slavers, like twentieth-century tankers, used flags of convenience, and they shifted from time to time according to the state of international treaties permitting search or seizure on the high seas. The flag of registration is not necessarily evidence as to the nationality of the owners, the captain, or the crew. It is, however, a visible dimension of the trade worth tentative examination. Table 73

TABLE 73

NATIONAL REGISTRATION OF SHIPS IMPORTING SLAVES INTO THE AMERICAS, 1817–43

Registration	% of total sample of slaves delivered to								Mean number delivered per ship
	Spanish Caribbean	Brazil	Bahamas & British Honduras	French & Danish WI	Uruguay	Surinam	Unknown	Total	
Portugal	14.2	50.0	0.8	0.1	0.1	—	0.9	66.1	404
Brazil	—	11.4	—	—	0.1	—	4.1	15.6	341
Spain	13.1	0.4	0.1	—	—	—	0.2	13.8	316
France	1.4	0.1	—	0.6	—	0.1	—	2.1	275
US	*	0.4	0.1	—	—	—	—	0.6	257
Uruguay	0.2	0.2	—	—	0.4	—	—	0.8	379
Netherlands	0.1	—	—	—	—	0.2	—	0.3	372
Denmark	0.2	0.3	—	—	—	—	—	0.5	367
Other†	0.2	0.1	—	—	—	—	—	0.2	—
Total	29.3	62.9	1.0	0.7	0.6	0.3	5.1	100.0	373

* Less than 0.05%.
† This category consists of one ship each of Argentine, Swedish, and Russian registry.
Source: Data from PP, 1845, xlix (73), pp. 593–633.

shows proportional deliveries by ships of various national registrations, following the Foreign Office sample for 1817–43.

Some aspects of Table 73 are as expected from the usual qualitative picture in the historical literature. The omnipresence of the Portuguese flag follows easily enough from the safety it enjoyed south of the line. But Brazilian ships had the same privilege, and they appear to have served only neighboring parts of South America. In the same way, the presence of the Uruguayan flag in the trade to Cuba is a little surprising, as is the fact that Uruguayan-flag ships apparently supplied more slaves to the New World than Uruguay itself imported.

The Nineteenth-Century Revival of the Old-World Traffic

The nineteenth-century movement of slaves from one part of Africa to another, or from the African mainland to the offshore islands, has been omitted from the general totals of Table 67. These enforced migrations were far more closely connected to the increased European activity in Africa during the pre-colonial century than they were to the great inter-continental migration from Africa. Some nevertheless formed a part of the Atlantic slave trade as well, in the technical sense of having been first enslaved and then transported by sea.

For varying periods, the United States, British, and French navies maintained squadrons off the West African coast and in American waters to intercept illegal slaves. The recaptives could rarely be returned to their homes. They were therefore dropped at some convenient coastal point, most often in Africa and most often of all in Sierra Leone, which served as the principal landing point for the United States navy as well as the British.[7] Others were carried to Liberia by the Americans. Still others were re-exported to the Americas as indented laborers or recruits into the British army, and some were "liberated" in Cuba or Brazil under conditions that were not very different from plantation slavery, whatever the legal status.

7. Duignan and Clendenen, *African Slave Trade*, pp. 54–55.

The various national anti-slave-trade squadrons actually caused sizable diversion of the slave trade. The British share was by far the largest, amounting to 149,800 recaptives landed alive between 1810 and 1864.[8] In addition, the United States navy captured at least 103 slavers between 1837 and 1862.[9] If these carried the same average number of slaves as those captured by the British, the number of recaptives landed alive would have been 8,100. The French captured at least a few hundred and may have taken more. The total for all three must have been in the neighborhood of 160,000, representing a diversion equal to about 8 per cent of the estimated imports into the Americas over the years 1811–70.

The anti-slavery movement also indirectly encouraged the invention of various legal disguises to achieve the fact of slavery without the name. The French in Senegal, for example, allowed slaves to be introduced into the colony, on condition that they be "freed" immediately and placed under an *engagement à temps* or indenture for a period of fourteen years. Indeed, the Senegalese government bought slaves for its own use and "liberated" them on the same terms, and it bought still others as forced recruits into the local military forces.[10] Some of these men served in other French dependencies as distant as Madagascar and French Guiana.[11] Even though they may not have been slaves under French law, they were certainly part of the African internal slave trade before they arrived in the colony, and those sent overseas in labor battalions could easily be considered as a part of the Atlantic slave trade.

8. C. Lloyd, *The Navy and the Slave Trade* (London, 1949), pp. 275–76.

9. Howard, *American Slavers*, pp. 213–23 contains a list of 107 ships libeled in United States district courts or made naval prizes. I have excluded four ships captured by British naval vessels and turned over to American authorities for prosecution. The list does not include all vessels arrested by naval patrols.

10. F. Zucarelli, "Le Régime des engagés à temps au Sénégal (1817–1848)," *Cahiers d'études africaines*, 2:420–61 (1962).

11. C. Faure, "La Garnison européene du Sénégal (1779–1858)," *Revue d'histoire des colonies*, 8:5–108 (1920).

In the second half of the nineteenth century, a similar quasi-slave-trade led from Angola to São Thomé and Principe. In this case the captives were legally "liberated" on the mainland before being transported to the island plantations as forced "contract workers." In theory they served only for a period of years, otherwise they were slaves in everything but law. Official Portuguese statistics count an annual average of 2,240 of these *serviçaes* shipped from Angola to the two islands between 1876 and 1900.[12]

African Sources in the Nineteenth Century

Even though the new illegality of the slave trade closed off some sources of information, the new European interest in Africa opened others. The effort to investigate African ethnology through the interrogation of slaves in the Americas goes back to Oldendorp's studies in the Danish West Indies, published in 1777.[13] More serious research on African peoples and cultures followed, much of it conducted in Africa itself. For the study of the slave trade, the most valuable single investigation was the work of S. W. Koelle in Sierra Leone of the 1840's. His own concern was linguistic, and his method was to interrogate the recaptives landed by the navy. In the process of building up more than 160 comparative vocabularies of African languages, he also recorded a great deal of other information about his informants—their homeland, their enslavement, and their subsequent personal histories as a part of the slave trade.[14] Among other questions, he asked each informant how many other people speaking his own language were present in Sierra Leone. If the numbers were small, the informant would often know the answer, and the larger groups are numerically represented in the Freetown census of 1848. The combination is therefore a very good picture of the ethnic origins of the recaptives—not, unfortunately, quite precise enough to be tabulated as a whole, but

12. J. Duffy, *A Question of Slavery* (Oxford, 1967), esp. p. 98.
13. Oldendorp, *Mission der Evangelischen Brüder.*
14. Koelle, *Polyglotta Africana.*

useful nevertheless. At the very least, Koelle's list of informants, based on his search for at least one speaker of as many languages as possible, shows the range of penetration of the nineteenth-century slave trade in West Africa. (See Appendix, and Figs. 20–24.) It shows, for example, a much deeper penetration than is indicated for the late eighteenth century by the Saint Domingue samples (Tables 55–58), and this suggests that the last burst of the Atlantic slave trade may have reached for new sources deeper in the interior than ever before.[15]

But Koelle's samples and the Freetown census suffer alike from under-representation of Central and Southeast Africa. This weakness can be corrected to a degree by reference to the Foreign Office sample of 1845, which is strong precisely where the Sierra Leone samples are weak. The fact that British cruisers did not capture slavers in the Angola trade also opened that trade to easier investigation by British representatives in Brazil. Table 74 shows the regional zone of origin for slaves landed in the Americas by a total of 1,711 ships. This sample of ships known to the Foreign Office can be taken to be more accurate for the two full decades, 1821–30 and 1831–40, than it is for either 1817–20 or 1841–43. In this last period, the Portuguese slavers south of the equator were subject to capture by the British, which probably accounts for the large percentage of slaves listed as having an unknown origin. Nor is the percentage allotted to West Africa (only 4.6 per cent of the total sample) likely to be accurate. That part of the African coast was patrolled and out-of-bounds to Portuguese, Spanish, and Brazilian ships. For the same reason, the distribution of origins within West Africa is probably less accurate than that shown in the Sierra Leone samples.

15. See P. D. Curtin and J. Vansina, "Sources of the Nineteenth Century Atlantic Slave Trade," *Journal of African History,* 5:185–208 (1964); P. E. H. Hair, "The Enslavement of Koelle's Informants," *Journal of African History,* 6:193–203 (1965). Both are based on data from Koelle, *Polyglotta Africana.*

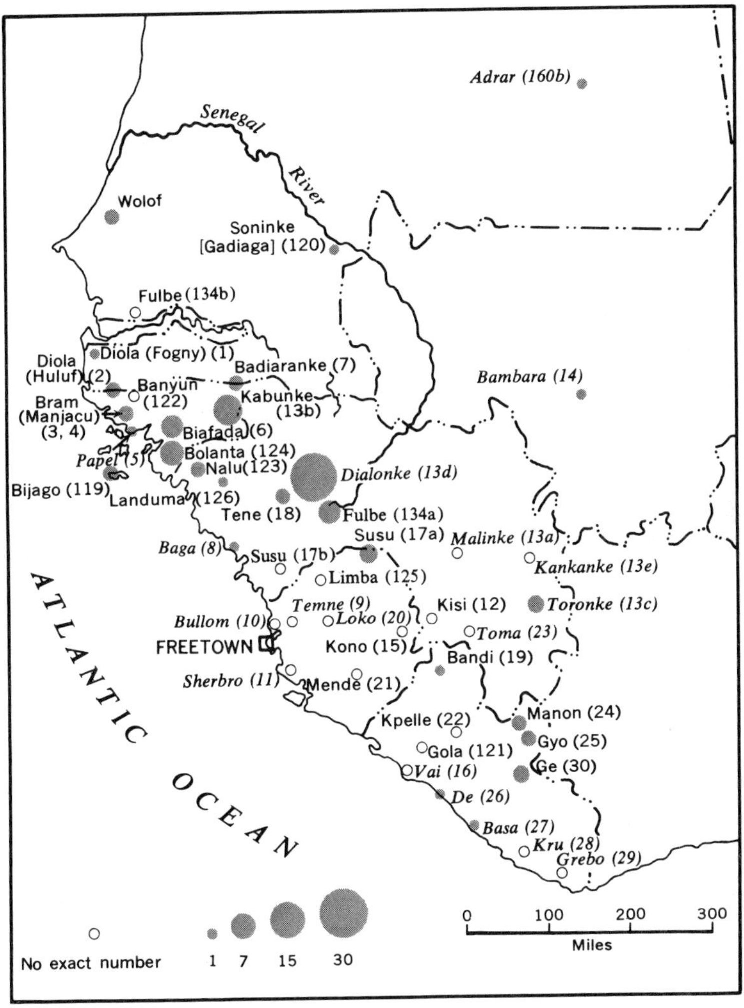

Fig. 20. Koelle's sample of recaptives in Sierra Leone, c. 1850: Senegambia, Sierra Leone, and their hinterland. (Numbers in parentheses refer to numbers in Appendix.) Fig. by UW Cartographic Lab.

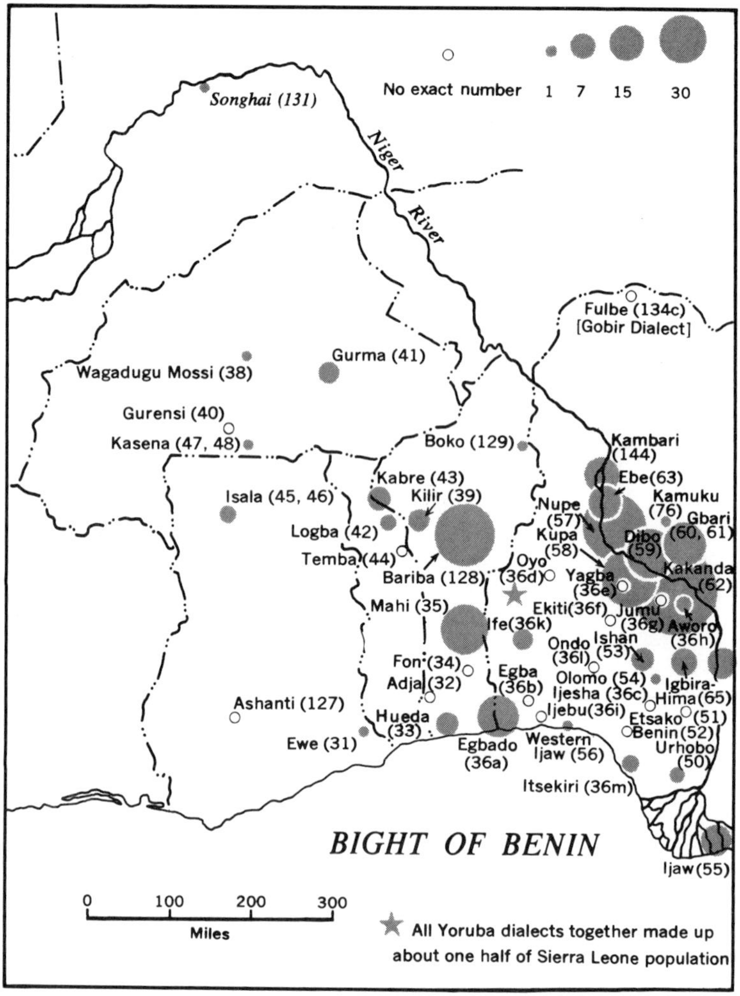

Fig. 21. Koelle's sample of recaptives in Sierra Leone, c. 1850: The hinterland of the Gold Coast and the Bight of Benin. (Numbers in parentheses refer to numbers in Appendix.) Fig. by UW Cartographic Lab.

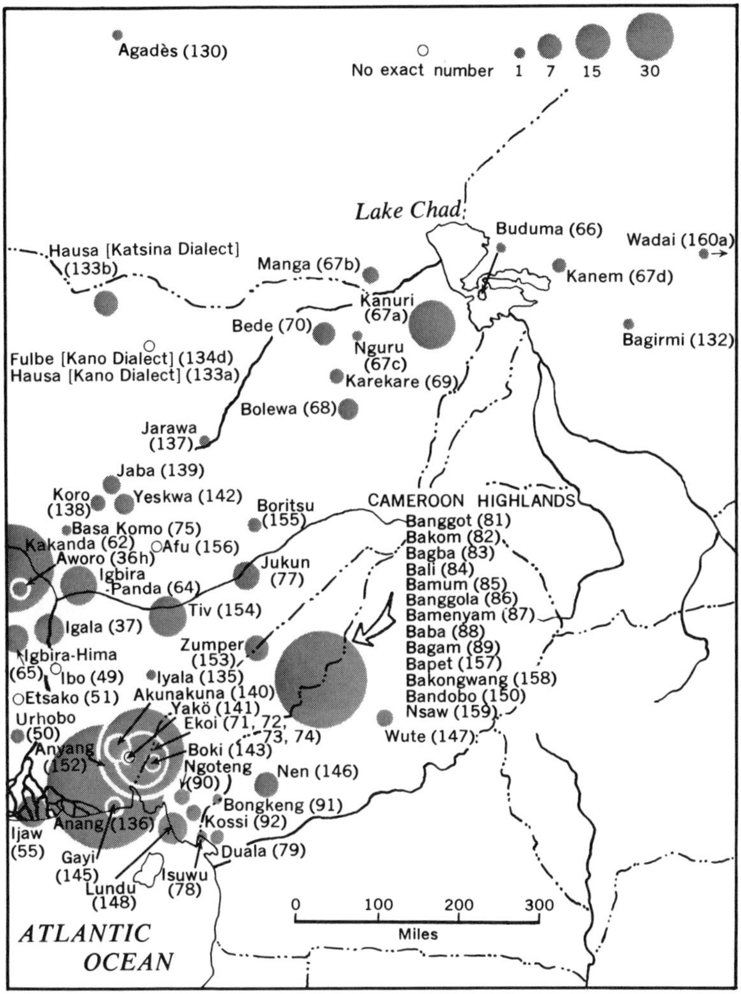

Fig. 22. Koelle's sample of recaptives in Sierra Leone, c. 1850: The Bight of Biafra and its hinterland. (Numbers in parentheses refer to numbers in Appendix.) Fig. by UW Cartographic Lab.

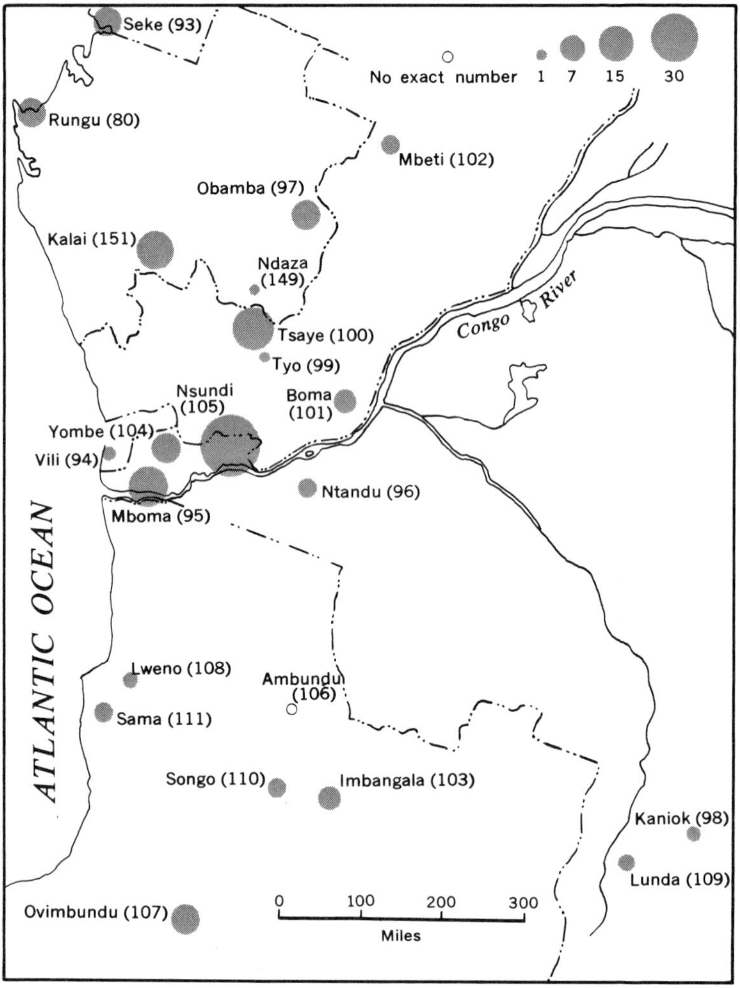

Fig. 23. Koelle's sample of recaptives in Sierra Leone, c. 1850: Central Africa. (Numbers in parentheses refer to numbers in Appendix.) Fig. by UW Cartographic Lab.

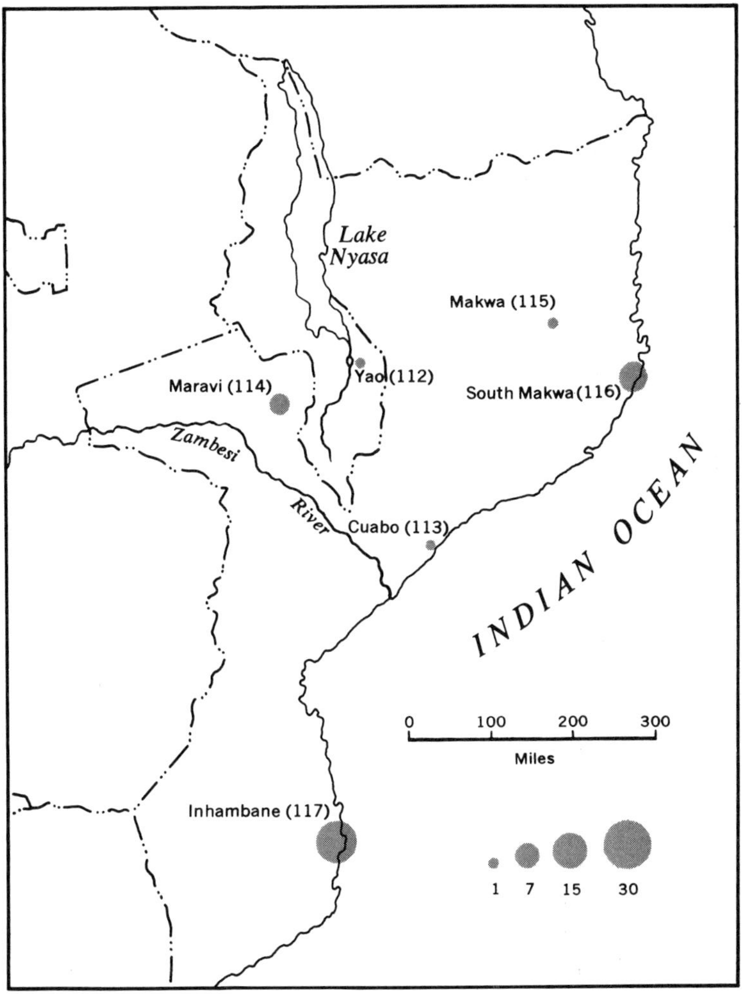

Fig. 24. Koelle's sample of recaptives in Sierra Leone, c. 1850: Southeastern Africa. (Numbers in parentheses refer to numbers in Appendix.) Fig. by UW Cartographic Lab.

TABLE 74

REGIONAL DISTRIBUTION IN PERCENTAGE OF SLAVES EXPORTED FROM AFRICA BY SHIPS KNOWN TO THE BRITISH FOREIGN OFFICE, 1817–43

Exporting region	1817–20	1821–30	1831–40	1841–43	Total
Senegambia	—	*	—	0.2	*
Sierra Leone	—	0.4	0.5	1.8	0.6
Windward Coast	—	*	—	—	*
Gold Coast	—	—	0.5	—	0.2
Bight of Benin	—	0.4	1.8	4.7	1.3
Bight of Biafra	—	4.4	0.9	—	2.6
Congo North	55.9	27.5	11.9	6.5	22.6
Angola	26.6	37.6	38.7	28.7	36.2
Mozambique	13.5	21.2	24.4	6.8	20.1
São Thomé-Principe	—	0.1	3.6	0.3	1.2
Origin unknown	4.0	8.3	17.7	51.0	15.4
Total	100.0	100.0	100.0	100.0	100.0

* Less than 0.05%.

Source: Data from PP, 1845, xlix (73), pp. 593–633. Based on the Foreign Office sample of slaves imported into the Americas.

Thus, Table 71 can be taken to be the best available sample for the larger ethnic groups in West Africa, while Table 74 is the best sample we have for Central and southeastern Africa. Even so, the two agree in pointing up a number of changes in the distribution of the West African slave trade—changes which had greatly altered the course of the trade since the eighteenth century. The Windward Coast had now practically ceased to be an export zone—so much so that Koelle was unable to locate a single recaptive speaking any language from eastern Liberia or the present-day Ivory Coast. The two larger samples also agree with Koelle's data in showing that the Gold Coast had dropped to insignificance as an exporter of slaves.

The West African slave trade now flourished in only two regions—the Bights taken together, and Sierra Leone. Even in the conventional region of Sierra Leone, the trade now avoided

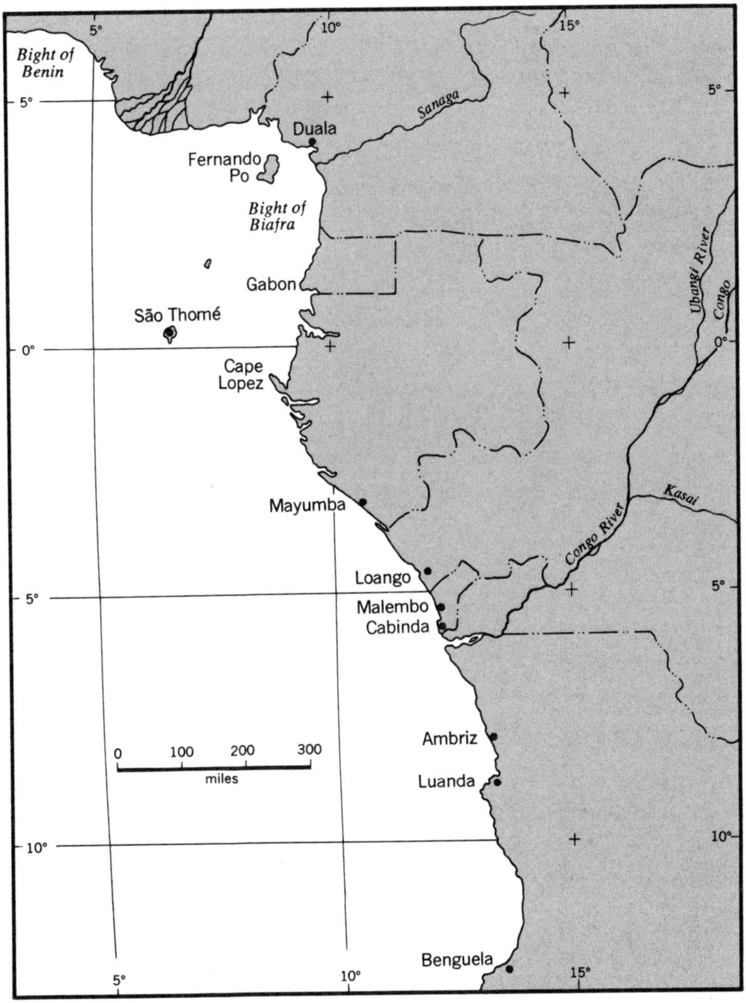

Fig. 25. Central Africa. Map by UW Cartographic Lab.

the Sierra Leone River and ports near it. It came instead from the region between Sherbro Island and Cape Mount, straddling the present-day border between Liberia and the Republic of Sierra Leone, or else from the river mouths to the north, in present-day Guinea-Conakry and Guinea-Bissau.

The Bights of Benin and Biafra, however, were more important than the conventional Sierra Leone, and this again is supported by both of the large samples. They disagree only as to the detail, and especially as to which of the Bights held a larger share of the trade. In this disagreement, the Freetown sample is certainly the more adequate, but the disagreement may not be outright contradiction. The large share given to the Bight of Biafra in the Foreign Office sample depends on a very large export listed for the 1830's only. This short-term figure could be accurate, and still leave the Freetown sample broadly representative for the early nineteenth century as a whole.

The shift to the Bights can be easily connected with political events on shore, including the break-up of Oyo, the Yoruba Wars that followed, and the chronic disorder all around the fringes of the Caliphate of Sokoto to the north. These events account not only for the large number of Yoruba in the Freetown sample, but also for the great increase since the eighteenth century in the proportion of Hausa found in the slave trade. Other peoples, such as the large numbers from the Cameroon highlands shown in Koelle's sample, were also caught on the fringes of Sokoto Fulbe expansion. Certain coastal peoples like the Ibo, who had once been such an important source of the eighteenth-century slave trade, now contributed less—only 9 per cent of the Freetown sample.

The nineteenth-century political history of Central Africa is less well known than that of Nigeria, but the Foreign Office sample constitutes a body of data that will someday be better explained by political changes within Africa. With a sample consisting of more than 100,000 slaves landed in the Americas by 1,018 ships over 1817–43—from Gabon in the north to Benguela in the south—it is possible to construct a tabulation with a reasonable degree of statistical validity. (See Table 75.)

Even without the support of detailed political history, Table 75 shows a variety of general patterns. One of these is the concentration of the trade on a few ports. Although this whole coastline stretches more than 1,000 miles, about three-quarters of

TABLE 75

THE SUPPLY OF SLAVES FROM CENTRAL AFRICAN PORTS AND REGIONS, BY SHIPS KNOWN TO THE BRITISH FOREIGN OFFICE, 1817–43

Exporting place	1817–20	1821–25	1826–30	1831–35	1836–40	1841–43	Total
Gabon	—	—	—	100	—	500	600
%	—	—	—	3.2	—	1.8	0.2
Cape Lopez	—	—	100	—	300	—	500
%	—	—	0.1	—	0.3	—	0.1
Mayumba	—	—	—	100	—	—	100
%	—	—	—	2.7	—	—	*
Loango	—	—	—	1,100	—	—	1,100
%	—	—	—	23.6	—	—	0.3
Malembo	—	14,900	11,900	—	—	—	26,800
%	—	14.6	9.8	—	—	—	7.0
Cabinda	25,200	23,400	36,400	—	14,200	3,300	102,500
%	66.7	22.9	30.0	—	15.0	13.4	26.6
Congo River	400	900	6,700	500	7,000	800	116,400
%	1.1	0.9	5.6	10.2	7.4	3.4	4.3
Angola, unspecified	6,700	36,800	33,100	1,600	58,600	7,300	144,100
%	17.6	36.0	27.3	36.2	61.8	29.4	37.4
Ambriz	—	9,600	15,400	300	2,800	2,400	30,600
%	—	9.4	12.7	7.1	3.0	9.7	7.9
Luanda	600	500	1,000	—	1,800	500	4,400
%	1.6	0.5	0.8	—	2.0	2.0	1.2
Benguela	4,900	15,900	16,700	800	9,900	10,100	58,400
%	13.0	15.6	13.8	17.0	10.5	40.4	15.1
Total	37,800†	102,000†	121,400†	4,500†	94,800†	25,000†	385,500†
%	100.0	100.0	100.0	100.0	100.0	100.0	100.0

* Less than 0.05%.
† Totals have been rounded.
Source: Data from PP, 1845, xlix (73), pp. 593–633. Based on the Foreign Office sample of slaves imported into the Americas.

the slaves exported came from the region between Cabinda in the north and Luanda in the south, a distance of only about 300 miles.

Again, the trade of this region appears to vary greatly through time, with rapid shifts from one port to another. This is partly accountable to the fact that several ports might serve the same trade route from the interior. The long trade route from the northeast, for example, could end with almost equal ease (political factors aside) at Loango, Malembo, Cabinda, or the mouth of the Congo River. If these four are taken together part of the great variation through time disappears, though it is also clear that this group of ports supplied a progressively smaller proportion of all Central African exports.

Other ports served other trade routes. The tabulated quantities shown for Angola, Luanda, and Ambriz can be taken to represent in a rough way the output of the central route from the interior, by way of Kassange, and it seems that this outlet attained its maximum role in the period 1836–40. The southern or Ovimbundu route, on the other hand, found its principal outlet in Benguela, and here a different pattern of supply appears—rising slave exports in each successive period to 1836–40, then a drop with the general drop for all regions in 1831–34 followed by a second period of increasing supply in the decade that followed. It would be convenient if we knew enough to associate these changing export quantities with the politico-economic patterns of inland trade. Unfortunately, this kind of association is not yet possible. The trade routes went far inland, but slaves also came from the coastal region itself. Koelle's sample, for example, turns up two individuals from Katanga, but 20 Mboma from the region of the Congo mouth. Traffic from ports serving the various inland routes is therefore suggestive of the possible trade along these routes, but nothing more.

The Foreign Office sample of 1845 also tells something about the nationality of the slavers serving various coastal zones. With the usual reservations about the actual nationality of a ship flying a given flag, it identifies the flag of registration in more

TABLE 76

NATIONAL REGISTRATION OF SHIPS EXPORTING SLAVES FROM AFRICA, 1817–43

Registration	% of total sample of slaves exported from								
	Sierra Leone, Windward Coast, Gold Coast	Bight of Benin	Bight of Biafra	Congo North	Angola	Mozambique, Madagascar	São Thomé, Principe	Origin unknown	Total
Portugal	0.7	0.3	—	3.7	26.9	16.2	2.5	15.3	65.6
Brazil	0.2	0.2	0.1	4.6	5.3	0.9	0.2	4.2	15.6
Spain	0.8	1.5	1.1	0.9	0.3	0.3	0.6	8.8	14.3
France	—	—	0.4	0.1	—	—	—	1.7	2.1
Uruguay	—	—	—	—	0.6	—	—	0.2	0.3
Netherlands	—	—	0.1	—	—	—	—	0.2	0.3
Argentina	—	—	—	0.1	—	—	—	—	0.1
Denmark	—	—	—	—	0.2	—	—	0.3	0.5
Other*	—	—	—	—	—	—	—	0.7	0.7
Total	1.7	2.0	1.6	9.3	33.3	17.5	3.2	31.4	100.0

* This category consists of one ship each of United States, Swedish, and Russian registry.

Source: Data from PP, 1845, xlix (73), pp. 593–633.

than 600 cases. This sample seems adequate as an indicator of Portuguese routes and markets, since 273 Portuguese ships are represented. (This number will, of course, include Brazilian ships as well for the period before 1822, but the distortion from this source should not be serious.) Brazilian and Spanish shipping are less well represented—82 ships for Brazil and 41 for Spain. For the other carriers, however, the sample is too small to be valid. (See Table 76.)

It is hardly surprising to find Spanish shipping concentrated in West Africa, with more than half of the identified voyages originating north of Cape Lopez. In spite of anti-slavery patrols, this region was most convenient to the Cuban market, and a longstanding commercial system in Africa itself assured a good supply, to say nothing of the Yoruba wars as a supply factor. Portuguese and Brazilian ships tended to stay south of the equator, even if all voyages of unknown origin are attributed to West Africa, but the Portuguese and Brazilians served somewhat different regions. The Portuguese enjoyed a near-monopoly over the new trade from southeast Africa, as might be expected from their traditional connections in Mozambique and the Indian Ocean. Portugal also was dominant in the Angola market, while Brazilian ships carried more slaves than the Portuguese did from Congo North and West Africa. This pattern also reflects a traditional commercial tie going back to the eighteenth century when ships from Brazil, rather than metropolitan Portugal, were dominant in the trade to the Costa da Mina.

CHAPTER 9

MAJOR TRENDS

It is now possible to look at the long-term movement of the Atlantic slave trade over a period of more than four centuries. Table 77 sums up the pattern of imports for each century, while Fig. 26 shows the same data drawn as a graph to semi-logarithmic scale. Together, these data make it abundantly clear that the eighteenth century was a kind of plateau in the history of the trade—the period when the trade reached its height, but also a period of slackening growth and beginning decline. The period 1741–1810 marks the summit of the plateau, when the long-term annual average rates of delivery hung just above 60,000 a year. The edge of the plateau was reached, however, just after the Peace of Utrecht in 1713, when the annual deliveries began regularly to exceed 40,000 a year, and the permanent drop below 40,000 a year did not come again until after the 1840's. Thus about 60 per cent of all slaves delivered to the New World were transported during the century 1721–1820. Eighty per cent of the total were landed during the century and a half, 1701–1850.

The higher rates of growth, however, came at earlier phases of the trade. The highest of all may have been an apparent growth at the rate of 3.3 per cent per year between the last quarter of the fifteenth century and the first quarter of the sixteenth, but the data for this early period are too uncertain for confidence in this figure. In the smoothed-out long-term annual averages of the graph, the growth of the trade was remarkably constant at a

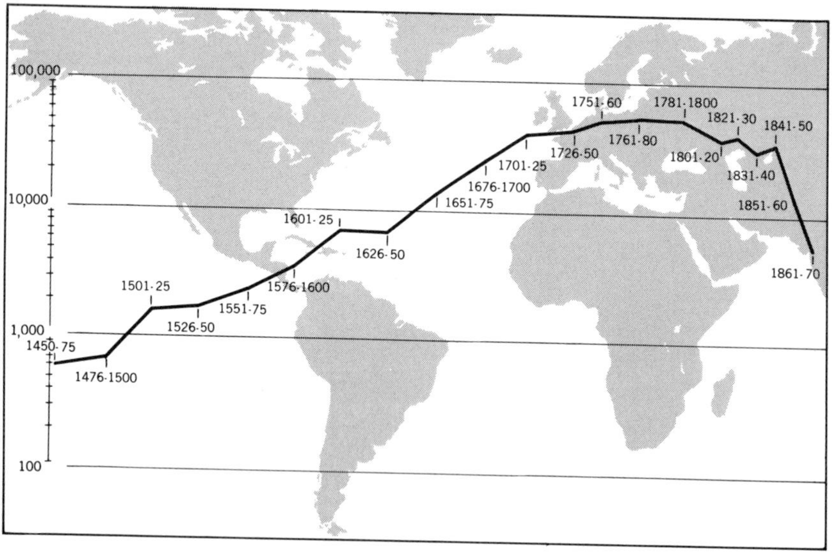

Fig. 26. Major trends of the Atlantic slave trade, in annual average number of slaves imported. Fig. by UW Cartographic Lab. Data from Tables 33, 34, 65, 67.

remarkably uniform rate over more than two centuries. Two periods of stability or possible decline occur, one between the first and second quarters of the sixteenth century and again between 1601–25 and 1626–50. Aside from these periods, the growth rate was an overall 2.2 per cent per year in the last half of the sixteenth century and the first quarter of the seventeenth, and at about the same rate during the equivalent period a century later. But during the first four decades of the eighteenth century, the growth rate was 0.7 per cent.

These trends are not surprising. They run parallel to the growth of the South Atlantic System traced in the literature on qualitative evidence. The nineteenth-century portion of the curve is less predictable from the present literature, but hardly surprising. The slave trade began to decline in the 1790's—not after 1808 with the legal abolition of the British trade—and this trend shows more clearly and precisely in the combined Anglo-

French-Portuguese shipping data (Table 63 and Fig. 15) than it does in the longer-term data of Fig. 26. One of the common older views of the slave trade holds that a last burst of imports took place between about 1802 and 1807, as planters sought to fill out their slave gangs before the trade became illegal. This pattern may be true of imports into the Anglo-Saxon territories, but not for the slave trade as a whole. Instead, the general trend shows a drop to the 1810's, then a rise in the 1820's. At first glance, the removal of British shipping from the trade in 1808 made no difference at all in the totals transported.

But this interpretation is probably mistaken. In the eighteenth century, warfare was the really important influence on the short-run rise and fall of the slave trade. There is no reason to expect this pattern to have changed at the end of the century. The drop of the 1790's seems to be accountable to the Napoleonic Wars, and it continued into the decade of the 1800's. After the wars, and especially after such a long period of warfare, an enormous backlog of demand would be expected, and the trade might well have shot up to meet that demand—had it not been for British abolition and the early work of the anti-slave-trade patrols at sea. The trade recovered somewhat in the 1820's, but the recovery was drastically dampened by the anti-slavery movement and by the shifts to new carriers (like Spain) and new sources (like Mozambique). In short, the quantitative impact of British abolition on the trade as a whole is obscured by other influences, but not completely missing.

The present projections also suggest a solution to some of the nineteenth-century controversies that still influence historical literature. Fig. 26 shows a high and sustained level of annual average import from the 1810's through the 1840's—not a sharp drop as a result of abolition, nor yet a boom carrying the slave trade to new heights in the 1830's. Although an annual average export in excess of 135,000 a year is still mentioned by some authorities, it is clearly based on the Foreign Office estimate of 1848, apparently made without sufficient evidence and with a clear political interest in trying to show Parliament that the

TABLE 77

ESTIMATED SLAVE IMPORTS INTO THE AMERICAS, BY IMPORTING REGION, 1451–1870 (000 OMITTED)

Region & country	1451–1600	1601–1700	1701–1810	1811–70	Total
British North America	—	—	*348.0*	*51.0*	*399.0*
Spanish America	*75.0*	*292.5*	*578.6*	*606.0*	*1,552.1*
British Caribbean	—	*263.7*	*1,401.3*	—	*1,665.0*
Jamaica	—	85.1	662.4	—	747.5
Barbados	—	134.5	252.5	—	387.0
Leeward Is.	—	44.1	301.9	—	346.0
St. Vincent, St. Lucia, Tobago, & Dominica	—	—	70.1	—	70.1
Trinidad	—	—	22.4	—	22.4
Grenada	—	—	67.0	—	67.0
Other BWI	—	—	25.0	—	25.0
French Caribbean	—	*155.8*	*1,348.4*	*96.0*	*1,600.2*
Saint Domingue	—	74.6	789.7	—	864.3
Martinique	—	66.5	258.3	41.0	365.8
Guadeloupe	—	12.7	237.1	41.0	290.8
Louisiana	—	—	28.3	—	28.3
French Guiana	—	2.0	35.0	14.0	51.0
Dutch Caribbean	—	*40.0*	*460.0*	—	*500.0*
Danish Caribbean	—	*4.0*	*24.0*	—	*28.0*
Brazil	*50.0*	*560.0*	*1,891.4*	*1,145.4*	*3,646.8*
Old World	*149.9*	*25.1*	—	—	*175.0*
Europe	48.8	1.2	—	—	50.0
São Thomé	76.1	23.9	—	—	100.0
Atlantic Is.	25.0	—	—	—	25.0
Total	274.9	1,341.1	6,051.7	1,898.4	9,566.1
Annual average	1.8	13.4	55.0	31.6	22.8
Mean annual rate of increase*	—	1.7%	1.8%	−0.1%	

* These figures represent the mean annual rates of increase from 1451–75 to 1601–25, from 1601–25 to 1701–20, and from 1701–20 to 1811–20.

Sources: Tables 33, 34, 65, and 67.

anti-slavery blockade had been effective. If the estimates here are correct, it *was* effective in diverting about 8 per cent of the trade, perhaps in keeping the trade from going even higher; but the trade nevertheless continued, at a level about a third less than its eighteenth-century peak. It was sustained first by the postwar boom of the 1820's, then by the sugar boom in Cuba and the coffee boom in Brazil. Really significant decline came only with the 1850's, when Brazil, the largest single importer, dropped from the trade. Steep as the final decline of the 1850's and 1860's appears to have been, the rate of import in the 1860's, the last important decade of the trade, nevertheless exceeded the rate for any period before the seventeenth century.

It would be premature to generalize about the impact of the slave trade on African societies over these four centuries. On the other hand, historians have already begun to do so. The range of opinion runs the gamut from the view that the slave trade was responsible for virtually every unfavorable development in Africa over these centuries, to the opposite position that even the slave trade was better than no trade, that it was therefore a positive benefit to the African societies that participated. Since the results of this survey could be brought into the argument on either side, it is appropriate to enter a few caveats.

One conclusion that might be drawn is that, in reducing the estimated total export of slaves from about twenty million to about ten million, the harm done to African societies is also reduced by half. This is obvious nonsense. The demographic consequences of moving any number of people from any society can have meaning only in relation to the size of the society, the time-period concerned, the age and sex composition of the emigrants and of the society from which they depart. Until we know at least the size of the African population that supplied the slaves, the demographic implications of the ten-million estimate are just as indeterminate as those of the twenty-million estimate. As for the social or political consequences of the slave trade to African societies, these would not necessarily vary directly with the number exported.

For that matter, the slave trade—even in its demographic consequences—was merely one aspect of the tightening web of intercommunication which followed the maritime revolution in the Atlantic basin. The new intensity of contact between Africa and Europe began to be felt by the 1480's, with the Americas entering shortly after 1500. The slave trade constituted a movement of people along these new lines of communication, but two other demographically important migrations took place along these same lines—the migration of diseases and the migration of food crops.

It is well known that the Old-World diseases virtually wiped out the American Indian populations of the tropical lowlands and caused a very sharp drop among other New-World populations. Given our present lack of knowledge about the epidemiological history of Africa, it is impossible to say what European (or even American) diseases were new to the tropical African disease environment—and hence what demographic consequences they may have had. For southern Africa, it seems clear that newly imported strains of smallpox and perhaps some other diseases effectively destroyed the integrity of the San or "Hottentot" community at the Cape. What similar events may have taken place in tropical Africa during the sixteenth and seventeenth centuries is not yet known.

As for the migration of food crops, at least two New-World crops were introduced into Africa by the sixteenth century: manioc and maize spread very widely and came to be two of the most important sources of food on that continent. If other factors affecting population size had remained constant, the predictable result would have been population growth wherever these crops replaced less efficient cultigens. Since this process took place over very large areas, it seems possible and even probable that population growth resulting from new food crops exceeded population losses through the slave trade. Whatever population loss may have followed the introduction of new diseases would have been temporary, while more efficient food crops tend to make possible a permanently higher level of population. It is even possible that, for sub-Saharan Africa as a whole, the net demographic effect of the three Atlantic migrations was population growth, not decline. Only further research in demographic and epidemiological history can give a firm answer.

But even if a firm answer were available, it would not solve the problem of assessing the impact of the slave trade on African societies. For statistics, "sub-Saharan Africa as a whole" is a useful entity, but not for this historical problem. People did not live in "sub-Saharan Africa as a whole." They lived in a series of particular African societies. The incidence of the slave trade was extremely variable, seriously affecting some regions while leaving others completely untouched. Useful analysis will therefore have to begin with particular societies, looking far beyond the narrowly demographic trends and seeing each society in its broader context. Only a systematic comparative study of the variety of different African responses to the European demand for slaves can expose the relevant evidence. The kind of quantitative evidence about the slave trade presented here is not completely irrelevant, but neither is it crucial.

One of the key questions to be answered, for example, is the possible role of the slave trade in social and political change. One model frequently found in the historical literature depicts the transformation of a previously peaceful peasant community into a militarized slave-catching society, where slave-raiding becomes an economic activity consciously pursued for the sake of the European imports that could be bought with slaves, and slaves alone. If the European demand for slaves did indeed force this kind of adaptation on African societies, the slave trade can be shown to have had disastrous consequences for the hunters as well as for the hunted. Alongside the destruction and death caused by the raids themselves, human resources and creative effort among the hunters must have been diverted from the pursuit of innovation and progress in other fields.

But another possibility, or model, is conceivable. African societies, like those of other people in other places, settled disputes by military means. Warfare produces prisoners-of-war, who can be killed, enslaved, or exchanged—but they may be a by-product of war, not its original cause. The African adaptation to the demand for slaves might be to change military tactics and strategy to maximize the number of prisoners, without actually increasing the incidence or destructiveness of warfare. In that case, the slave trade might have done little serious damage to the well-being of the African society.

Between these two extreme models, many mixed cases are obviously possible, and several of them appear to have existed historically. The crucial question is one of degree—which model was most common, or which tendency was dominant? The question asks for measurement, but the number of slaves exported (or even the ratio of slave exports to population) is no evidence of the way they were acquired. It tells even less about what might have happened if they had not been exported at all.

At best, the export data of the slave trade can be suggestive. If the dominant African pattern at the height of the slave trade was that of the militarized, slave-catching society, systematically preying on its neighbors, the export projections should show a relatively large and continuous supply of slaves from these hunter societies; and the slaves themselves should have been mainly from the less organized neighbors. This pattern does not emerge clearly from the slave-export data of eighteenth-century Africa. Some ports, notably the city-states of the Bight of Biafra, did produce a continuous supply that may imply slave-catching as an economic enterprise. Elsewhere, the rapid shift in sources of supply from one region to another suggests that by-product enslavement was the dominant feature, or that, if systematic slave-hunting were tried, it could not be maintained.

These weaknesses of quantitative evidence are important to keep in mind, if only because of a popular tendency to regard numbers as more "scientific" and reliable than other kinds of data. A great deal more could nevertheless be profitably done with the quantitative study of the slave trade. More and better samples of slave origins and better data on the numbers carried by the trade at particular times should make it possible to project the annual flow of slaves from particular societies, to take only one example. Even if the dimensions of the slave trade outlined here were as accurate as limited sources will ever allow—and they are not—still other dimensions of far greater significance for African and Atlantic history remain to be explored.

CHAPTER 10

A POSTSCRIPT ON MORTALITY

The cost of the slave trade in human life was many times the number of slaves landed in the Americas. For every slave landed alive, other people died in warfare, along the bush paths leading to the coast, awaiting shipment, or in the crowded and unsanitary conditions of the middle passage. Once in the New World, still others died on entering a new disease environment. Most of these losses are not measurable. More careful investigation of the slave trade within Africa should produce illuminating samples of the slaves' experience, but these could only be typical for a particular period and a particular place.

Mortality rates at sea, however, are measurable, and historians of the trade usually have produced an estimated rate of loss in transit. Among the recent English-language textbooks on African history, Robert Rotberg sets the loss of life during the maritime leg of the journey into slavery at 25 to 33 per cent. J. D. Hargreaves says it was about one-sixth (or half of the rate given by Rotberg) and J. D. Fage says it was "at least" one-sixth.[1] Donald L. Wiedner is still more precise: "Many of the trading records have been lost or destroyed, but enough has survived to permit at least an estimate of the percentage of slaves who died during the rigorous ocean voyage: about 12 per cent in French ships, contrasted with 17 per cent in Dutch and British ships;

1. Rotberg, *Political History,* p. 149; Hargreaves, *West Africa,* p. 36; Fage, *West Africa,* p. 82.

Portuguese losses in the early centuries ran about 15 per cent, but when the nineteenth-century abolitionists pressure forced the slave traders to take chances, the casualty rate rose to 25 to 30 per cent."[2]

Textbooks customarily cite no sources, and it is not clear where this information came from; but one source of the high estimate for the nineteenth-century slave trade is the Foreign Office report of 1848, which set the rate of loss at about 25 per cent.[3] Another source often cited in the literature for the eighteenth century is Rinchon's calculation from his compilation of Nantes shipping—that over the period 1748–82 the number of slaves sold in the Americas was 13 per cent lower than the number purchased in Africa. This figure, for example, was used recently by Basil Davidson as a general indicator of the rate of loss.[4] Thus the recent literature on the slave trade tends to put the mortality rate at sea somewhere between 13 per cent and 33 per cent.

This wide range is easily explicable: mortality rates varied greatly according to the route, the length of the voyage, the original disease environment of the slaves themselves, the care they received, and the chance occurrence of epidemics. Westergaard's archival survey of the Danish slave trade, for example, showed that individual voyages between 1698 and 1733 had mortality rates as low as 10 per cent and as high as 55 per cent.[5]

But some general tendencies are also discernible. One of these is a decreasing rate of loss over the eighteenth and nineteenth

2. Wiedner, *History of Africa,* p. 67.

3. PP, 1847–48, xxii (623), p. 8.

4. Davidson, *Black Mother,* p. 87. Davidson's figure of 13 per cent loss between 1748 and 1782 is based on Rinchon's own totals for these years alone. They disagree slightly with the gross loss of 14.33 per cent, found on recomputing the mortality rate from Rinchon's list of ships sailing from Nantes between 1748 and 1792 or with the figure of 15.2 per cent obtained if ships listed as selling more slaves than they had purchased are disregarded. These results may differ from Rinchon's own calculation because they include loss from capture and shipwreck as well as loss from disease. (See Rinchon, *Le Trafic négrier,* pp. 248–305, esp. p. 305.)

5. Westergaard, *Danish West Indies,* p. 144.

TABLE 78

LOSS OF SLAVES IN TRANSIT SUSTAINED BY THE SLAVE TRADERS OF NANTES, 1715–75

Period	Mortality from disease (%)	Mortality from all causes (%)
1715–19	12.2	19.1
1720–24*	19.1	22.4
1727–31	13.5	13.5
1732–36	18.4	18.4
1737–41	19.4	19.6
1742–45	11.1	16.8
1746–50	10.8	11.5
1751–55	15.8	15.8
1756–63	5.9	7.9
1764–68	13.2	13.2
1769–73	14.2	14.8
1774–75	5.3	8.6
Mean, 1715–75	14.5	16.2

* No shipping returned to Nantes in 1725–26.
Source: Martin, *L'Ere des négriers,* pp. 15 ff. and graph.

centuries. Goulart, who assembled a number of samples which he did not publish, concluded that the rate of mortality in transit to Brazil was in the region of 15 to 20 per cent in the sixteenth and seventeenth centuries, dropping to about 10 per cent by the early nineteenth century, and he supported this final estimate by citing a sample of some 12,000 slaves received in the first decade of the nineteenth century, with a loss at sea of 11.3 per cent.[6] Other samples show a similar trend in the English trade as well. The Royal African Company's records of total purchases and total deliveries over the period 1680–88 indicate a mean loss in transit of 23.4 per cent, with a maximum annual rate of 29 per cent in 1682 and a minimum rate of 14.3 per cent in 1687.[7] A

6. Goulart, *Escravidão,* p. 278.
7. Higham, *Leeward Islands,* p. 158.

century later, T. F. Buxton assembled data for a sample of 15,754 slaves exported in 1791 with a loss in transit of 8.75 per cent, and a second sample of 1792 showed a loss of 17 per cent among 31,554 slaves.[8] Though the annual variation continued to be great, the range was apparently lower.

Data for the French slave trade based on still larger samples surveyed over longer periods of time are available in the Nantes studies of Gaston Martin and Rinchon. Together they cover the entire period from 1715 to 1792, and they introduce new variables. Gaston Martin, for example, discriminated between loss from disease and total loss in transit—including other dangers like shipwreck, piracy, and enemy action. (See Table 78.) In this sample, the mortality rates were still variable, but they were markedly lower from 1742 to 1775 than they had been from 1715 to 1741.

Rinchon's data on the Nantes slave trade from 1748 to 1792 show the total loss only, measured in the difference between the number of slaves purchased and the number sold. These data were available for a total of 472 ships, but, for seven of these, the number sold in the Americas was listed as greater than the number purchased in Africa. While children may have been born at sea, the possibility of births exceeding deaths during the voyage seems so remote that these observations should be set aside. The result, in Table 79, is a sample of 465 ships.

Since Rinchon's compilation distinguished the four major trading zones in Africa, Table 79 makes it possible to examine loss in transit over different routes. The Mozambique sample is too small to be valid, though a high mortality would be expected on the long voyage from the Indian Ocean. Differing death rates over other routes are also explicable. A ship from Senegambia could move directly into the northeast trade winds for a relatively short and predictable passage to the Caribbean. The Guinea coast, however, had prevailing westerly winds and a strong current flowing toward the east. The usual voyage, and

8. Buxton, *African Slave Trade,* p. 124.

TABLE 79

LOSS OF SLAVES IN TRANSIT BY SHIPS FROM NANTES, 1748–92, BY COASTAL REGION OF EMBARKATION*

Time period	Senegal	Guinea	Angola	Mozambique	Total
1748–51	2.5 (2)	20.7 (53)	18.1 (25)	—	19.4 (80)
1752–55†	2.4 (6)	14.4 (53)	17.1 (27)	—	14.4 (86)
1763–67	22.9 (5)	19.1 (82)	13.2 (47)	—	17.2 (134)
1768–72	10.0 (4)	18.7 (46)	10.1 (28)	—	15.2 (78)
1773–77†	14.0 (1)	12.4 (41)	7.4 (28)	—	10.3 (71)
1788–92	—	7.1 (5)	1.9 (9)	22.3 (1)	5.0 (15)
Total	10.4 (18)	17.2 (281)	12.5 (164)	22.3 (1)	15.2 (465)

* In per cent of slaves purchased. Numbers in parentheses indicate number of ships in each sample. One ship with unknown point of embarkation is included in the total. One ship with no recorded loss in 1778–82 is included in the Guinea total.

† No sailings took place in 1756–62 and 1778–83 because of wartime. No data were provided for 1784–87.

Source: Data from Rinchon, *Le Trafic négrier*, pp. 248–302.

the route still recommended for sailing ships bound from the Guinea coast to the North Atlantic, took the ship south to the equator to pick up the southeast trades. Then in mid-ocean, it turned northward across the equatorial calms to catch the northeast trades for the Caribbean. Thus, a ship bound for the northern hemisphere had to cross the doldrums twice with slaves on board, each time taking a chance on prolonged calms which could mean shortages of food and water and a greater danger of disease in the crowded slave quarters. The voyage from Europe to Angola and return by the Caribbean was much the same, but in this case the first crossing of the equatorial calms took place with only the crew aboard. The voyage with full cargo should therefore have been shorter, and the mortality at sea less—as Rinchon's data indicate.

The British Foreign Office sample of 1845 provides some similar data on variations in loss at sea according to point of origin, and it tends to confirm the generalization that the loss at sea dropped with the passage of time. Out of a total sample of 826 ships with data on loss in transit known to the Foreign Office in the period 1817–43, the overall loss was at the rate of 9.1 per cent. This sample is most adequate for the slave trade to Brazil, represented by 692 ships of known origin. It is not statistically adequate for any other importing country, though the mortality rates by point of origin, shown in column 2 of Table 80, include the rate of loss on a total of 812 ships whose point of origin was known. Of these 32 landed their slaves in Cuba, and 88 had no identified destination.

TABLE 80

LOSS OF SLAVES IN TRANSIT AMONG SHIPS KNOWN TO THE BRITISH FOREIGN OFFICE, 1817–43*

Origin	Destination Brazil	Total sample
Sierra Leone	1.5	5.6
Bight of Benin	7.9	4.4
Bight of Biafra	3.7	4.9
Congo North	5.3	5.4
Angola	7.6	7.4
Mozambique	17.7	17.6
Mean	9.1	9.1

* In per cent of slaves lost.

Source: Data from PP, 1845, xlix (73), pp. 593–633.

The totals shown at the bottom of the two columns include all slave ships whose mortality data was known to the Foreign Office: they are therefore based on somewhat larger samples than are represented in the columns themselves. Since the mortality rates for the total slave trade appear to be nearly identical with those for the illegal but openly practiced trade to Brazil, they contradict the usual view that mortality rates rose steeply as the slave trade became illegal. A smaller sample based on 17 slavers captured by the United States navy between 1844

TABLE 81

LOSS OF SLAVES IN TRANSIT RELATED TO LENGTH OF VOYAGE, 1817–43*

Length of voyage in days	Destination Brazil	All destinations
10–19	—	7.9 (1)
20–29	5.1 (31)†	4.8 (47)
30–39	6.0 (60)	5.9 (83)
40–49	8.3 (19)	8.5 (25)
50–60	13.7 (18)	13.1 (21)
61 or more	25.9 (20)	22.0 (29)
All voyages in sample	9.7 (148)	9.0 (206)

* In per cent of slaves lost during voyage.

† Numbers in parentheses indicate number of ships in sample.

Source: Data from PP, 1845, xlix (73), pp. 593–633.

and 1864 suggests a somewhat higher rate, but not notably higher than the rates common in the eighteenth century. The ships in this group purchased a total of 10,744 slaves in Africa and lost 17.5 per cent in transit.[9]

The sample of voyages from Sierra Leone and the Bight of Benin to Brazil is too small to be meaningful—only three ships. Otherwise, the table shows a marked correlation between mortality rates at sea and length of voyage. It does not, however, show the higher rate for voyages from Guinea that turned up in Rinchon's data for the eighteenth-century French trade. A voyage from either of the Bights to Brazil might be a shorter distance than one from Angola, but its duration under sail should have been longer. Nevertheless, the mortality rates from ports north of the Congo and from Angola are higher than those from the Guinea coast. Only a speculative explanation is possi-

9. Quoted from L. C. Howard, "The United States Government and the African Slave Trade, 1837–1862," unpublished Ph.D. thesis, University of California, Los Angeles, by Duignan and Clendenen, *African Slave Trade,* p. 61.

ble. If, as appears likely, the slaves shipped from Angola and Congo North in the nineteenth century were drawn from the distant interior in any large proportion, a long journey within Africa might well contribute to a higher mortality rate at sea.

In other respects, mortality rates at sea appear to be closely related to the duration of the voyage. Full data are available for a sample of 206 ships appearing on the Foreign Office list of 1845. Time at sea is plotted against mortality rates in Table 81, and the correlation coefficient (Pearson's product-moment correlation) between mortality rate and duration of voyage is 0.47 for this sample.

The historical literature rarely mentions the mortality rate for the crews of slave ships, though it was known in the eighteenth century and earlier that Europeans entering the disease environment of West Africa as adults died at spectacular rates. The shores of the Gulf of Guinea were famous as the "white man's grave," and a frequently-quoted sailor's song warned:

> Beware and take care
>   Of the Bight of Benin:
> For one that comes out,
>   There are forty go in.

Other versions give other figures in the last line, but some ships actually did lose their crews at rates approaching this one. *Marie Gabrielle* of Nantes lost 31 out of 39 on one voyage in 1769.[10] Europeans newly arrived at trading posts on the Gulf of Guinea usually sustained a death rate of about 50 per cent in the first year of residence. Fortunately for the sailors, their stay was shorter and their death rates lower, but the slave trade was dangerous nevertheless. Rinchon's study of the Nantes trade of 1748–92 included data on the crew mortality of 598 ships, and the results are summarized in Table 82.

A comparison of Table 82 with the slave mortality on many of these same ships (Table 79) shows some interesting differences. The death rate per voyage among the crew was uniformly higher

10. Martin, *L'Ere des négriers,* p. 43.

TABLE 82

CREW MORTALITY PER VOYAGE AMONG SLAVERS FROM NANTES, 1748–92, BY COASTAL REGION OF EMBARKATION*

Period	Senegal	Guinea	Angola	Mozambique	Mean
1748–51	10.8 (2)	20.6 (50)	18.5 (24)	—	19.7 (76)
1752–55†	4.8 (6)	15.9 (49)	14.2 (20)	—	14.5 (75)
1763–67	33.9 (3)	20.9 (61)	22.5 (41)	—	21.9 (105)
1768–72	10.8 (4)	17.2 (48)	18.6 (28)	—	17.3 (80)
1773–77	12.5 (1)	13.2 (40)	7.8 (26)	—	11.1 (68)
1778–82	5.4 (2)	33.4 (2)	—	—	19.4 (4)
1783–87	20.6 (14)	17.2 (53)	16.4 (54)	14.1 (3)	17.2 (124)
1788–92	—	12.1 (31)	14.1 (33)	—	13.3 (66)
Mean	15.9 (32)	17.3 (334)	16.5 (226)	14.1 (3)	16.9 (598)

* In per cent of deaths from all causes. Three ships having unknown points of embarkation are included in the total. Numbers in parentheses indicate number of ships in sample.

† No sailings took place in 1756–62 because of wartime.

Source: Data from Rinchon, *Le Trafic négrier*, pp. 248–302.

than the death rate among slaves in transit at the same period. The data are so consistent and regular in this respect that this can be taken as a normal circumstance of the eighteenth-century slave trade. Even more unexpectedly, the death rate of slaves in transit fell progressively through the period, but that of the crew remained nearly at the same level. Apparently, the slave traders discovered ways to improve health conditions for slaves in transit, but they were less successful in meeting the dangers of malaria and yellow fever, the principal killers of strangers to the West African coast. Marked improvement in treating these diseases came only in the 1840's, while the dysentery and lung diseases that were the principal causes of death among the slave-passengers could be reduced by better sanitation and less crowded conditions.[11] But the contrasting causes of death among

11. See P. D. Curtin, "'The White Man's Grave': Image and Reality, 1780–1850," *Journal of British Studies*, 1:94–110 (November, 1961); "Epidemiology and the Slave Trade."

the two groups should not be overemphasized. In Rinchon's data, the two death rates moved together through time.

Crew death rates, moreover, did not show a marked response to the region of trade. Indeed, the lowest rates were found on the voyage to Mozambique, where the slave death rate was highest, though here again the Mozambique sample is too small to be decisive. On the western coasts of Africa, the lowest slave death rate, on the voyage from Senegal, was almost 7 percentage points below the highest, while the equivalent difference among crew death rates was only 1.4 per cent. Apparently, neither the length of the voyage nor the region of trade was crucial to crew mortality, which probably responded far more to other factors such as chance epidemics or the length of time spent on the African coast. Even the Guinea coast, which enjoyed the worst reputation, was only slightly more dangerous than the other three regions.

The historical literature on the slave trade contains no comparable sample of crew mortality in any other national branch of the trade—not, at least, for such a long run of time. But smaller samples of the English trade toward the end of the eighteenth century indicate that mortality there was at least as high as it was among the French. Thomas Clarkson assembled some samples in the 1780's, for the Privy Council's investigation of the Africa trade. One was based on the muster rolls of all 88 ships sailing for tropical Africa from Liverpool in 1786 and returning before September 1787. The total crew strength was 3,170 men, of whom only 45 per cent returned with the ship on which they sailed. Some 20 per cent died or were lost at sea, and 35 per cent deserted or were discharged in Africa or the Americas. He took a second sample from Bristol shipping, this time beginning in 1784 and taking each ship in order until he had a total of 24 vessels, with an initial crew strength of 910 men. Of these, 50 per cent returned with the ship, 24 per cent died or were lost at sea, and 26 per cent deserted or were discharged overseas.

In order to make this Bristol sample comparable with crew mortality on other maritime trade routes, Clarkson took further samples of Bristol ships sailing for other destinations, each sample consisting of the first 24 ships leaving Bristol from 1784 onward. He then adjusted the results so as to produce comparable figures in terms of mortality per 910 men per annum. Adjusting these once more to give the more common measurements in deaths per thousand per annum yields the results shown in Table 83.

TABLE 83

THOMAS CLARKSON'S SAMPLES OF CREW MORTALITY IN THE ENGLISH SLAVE TRADE, 1784–88

Crew	Bristol sample 1784–85* (%)	Liverpool sample 1786–87† (%)
Returned with ship	50.0	45.0
Dead or lost	23.7	20.3
Deserted or discharged overseas	26.3	34.7

* 910 men † 3,170 men

MORTALITY PER THOUSAND PER ANNUM IN SELECTED TRADES, BRISTOL SHIPPING, 1784 FF.

Slave trade	219
East India trade	41
West India trade	23
St. Petersburg trade	11
Newfoundland trade	11
Greenland trade	10

Source: Data from Thomas Clarkson to Lords of Trade and Plantations, 27 July 1788, *Board of Trade Report*, Part II.

The indications of these data are in line with other statistical studies of the British army serving overseas in the early nineteenth century. West Africa was by far the most dangerous overseas region for European troops, as well as for European sailors, while other tropical environments were notably less dangerous. Temperate environments outside Europe, on the other hand, showed death rates equivalent to that of British soldiers serving in Britain itself.[12]

These data about crew mortality in the slave trade raise some interesting questions about the slave trade as a whole. It has often been assumed that the slave trade was a profitable enterprise. While this was almost certainly the case for the merchants involved, and for their West Indian and Brazilian customers, it may be that the social cost of the trade—the cost to European society as a whole—was far greater than its benefits, again to European society as a whole. European historians have been quick to point out that African slave dealers sold their fellow Africans for private profit, contrary to the true interests of African societies. It is at least worth asking whether this might not have been true of European merchants as well. If the African disease environment claimed the life of half the European merchants, factors, officials, and soldiers sent out to man the slave trading posts, the social cost was already high. If, in addition, the slave trade cost the life of one sailor out of five, each voyage; and if the West Indian disease environment killed about 130 per thousand per annum among newly arrived soldiers and planters (as British military surveys of the nineteenth century indicate), then the cost to European society was indeed considerable. Unfortunately, the question of social profitability is not susceptible to ordinary cost accounting, and the problem posed here may be unanswerable. It is nevertheless significant that the South Atlantic System was a cruel and wasteful operation—most damaging for the slaves themselves, but deadly even for those who were free and voluntary participants.

12. Curtin, "Epidemiology and the Slave Trade," esp. p. 203.

REFERENCE MATTER

APPENDIX

KOELLE'S LINGUISTIC INVENTORY

The table below is a summary of the information contained in the introduction to Koelle's *Polyglotta Africana.* In most cases, Koelle furnished the name of the informant or informants, data about the lapse of time since each had left his home country, some hint as to the location of that country, the number of speakers of that language present in Sierra Leone in the later 1840's, and occasionally other information about the circumstances by which these individuals became commodities of the slave trade. The summary below adds a more common modern name for each group or language, its location in modern political geography, and the approximate date at which each informant was originally captured. The major categories follow Koelle's linguistic classification, but the individual languages and dialects have been renumbered as a key to Figs. 21–25.

An earlier version of this list was published in an appendix to Curtin and Vansina, "Sources of the Nineteenth Century Atlantic Slave Trade," *Journal of African History,* 5:185–208 (1964). Since that article went to press, the *Polyglotta Africana* has appeared in a new printing, and uncertain cases have been more precisely identified by David Dalby, "Provisional Identification of Languages in the *Polyglotta Africana,*" *Sierra Leone Language Review,* 1:83–90 (1964). Still other corrections were made by E. M. Chilver and others, "Sources of the Nineteenth-Century Slave Trade: Two Comments," *Journal of African History,* 6:117–20 (1965), and I am grateful to Mr. Joseph J. Lauer for a personal communication on the languages of Casamance and Guinea-Bissau. In addition, Professor Vansina has been kind enough to make further corrections based on his recent research. None of these people, however, can be held responsible for the possible errors or uncertain identifications that remain, and several differences persist between this version and that of Professor Dalby. In most instances these are not crucial. Dalby sought to give the correct name of the language in each instance, while this version seeks to give the most common ethnic, linguistic, or place name found in the literature. For linguistic purposes, therefore, Dalby's list will be the more accurate.

An asterisk after a name indicates an uncertain or probable identification. R. before a date indicates beginning of residence in Sierra Leone, rather than date of capture. Italics indicate that the informant was not a liberated African.

(1) *Informant's name for his country*	(2) *Modern name*	(3) *Location*	(4) *Number present in Sierra Leone*	(5) *Informant's date of capture*
I. WEST ATLANTIC LANGUAGES				
A. First Group				
1. Fulup	Diola (Huluf)	Senegal	1	1839
2. Fliham or Filhol	Diola (Fogny)	Guinea-Bissau	3	1836
B. Second Group				
3. Bola	Bram	Guinea-Bissau	1	1813
4. Sarar	Bram (Manjacu)	Guinea-Bissau	1	1833
5. *Pepel*	*Papel*	Guinea-Bissau	1	R. 1831
C. Third Group				
6. Biafada	Biafada	Guinea-Bissau	6	1829
7. Padsade	Badiaranke	Guinea-Bissau	2	<1809
D. Fourth Group[1]				
8. *Baga*	*Baga*	Guinea-Bissau and Guinea-Conakry	1	R. 1824
9. *Timne*	*Temne*	Sierra Leone	many	—
10. *Bulom*	*Bullom (Kafu)*	Sierra Leone	many	R. 1834
11. *Mampua* or *Mampa-Bulom*	*Bullom (Sherbro)*	Sierra Leone	many	R. 1846
12. *Kisi*	*Kisi*	Guinea-Conakry	many	R. 1838
II. MANDINKA LANGUAGES				
13. Mande or Mandinka	Mandinka[2]			
a. *Mande* proper	*Malinke*	Guinea-Conakry	—	R. 1840
b. Kabunga	Kabunke	Guinea-Bissau	13	1820
c. *Toronka*	*Toronke*	Guinea-Conakry	3	R. 1838
d. *Dsalunka*	*Dialonke*	Guinea-Conakry	30	R. 1837
e. *Kankanka*	*Kankanke*	Guinea-Conakry	10 residents, many transients	R. 1842
14. *Bambara*	*Bambara*	Mali	1	R. 1834
15. Kono	Kono	Sierra Leone[3]	few	1819
16. *Vei*	*Vai*	Liberia	few	R. 1844
17. Soso	Susu	Sierra Leone and Guinea-Conakry		
a. Sulima dialect—Sierra Leone			4	1819
b. *Furodugu* dialect—Guinea-Conakry			—	R. 1819

[1]Languages 9, 10, 11, and 12, being in the immediate hinterland of Sierra Leone, were represented by a fluctuating population which came and went between the colony and the home country. This is why Koelle's informants could not give the number of fellow countrymen present at the time of the interview. The Sierra Leone census of 1848, however, gave a total of 3889 'Natives' (excluding liberated Africans and Kru people), representing about 8 per cent of the colonial population.

[2] This linguistic group included many African traders, who were merely transient in the colony.

[3] Not to be confused with another group with the same name in Guinea-Conakry.

(1) *Informant's name for his country*	(2) *Modern name*	(3) *Location*	(4) *Number present in Sierra Leone*	(5) *Informant's date of capture*
18. Tene	Tene*[4]	Guinea-Conakry	2	1831
19. Gbandi	Bandi	Sierra Leone and Liberia	1	1846
20. *Landoro*	*Loko*[5]	Sierra Leone	many	—
21. Mande	Mende[5]	Sierra Leone	many	1822
22. Gbese or Gbrese	Kpelle	Liberia	many	1829
23. *Toma* or *Buse*	*Toma*	Guinea-Conakry and Liberia	—	R. 1839
24. Mano or Ma	Manon	Liberia	2	—
25. Gio	Gyo	Liberia	3	1827
III. UPPER GUINEA LANGUAGES				
A. Liberian or Kru Languages				
26. *Dewoi* or *De*	*De*	Liberia	1	R. 1848
27. *Basa*	*Basa*[6]	Liberia	1	R. 1845
28. *Kra* or *Kru*	*Kru*[7]	Liberia	many	R. 1843
29. *Krebo* or *Grebo*	*Grebo*	Liberia	—	R. 1844
30. Gbe	Ge or Sikon[8]	Liberia	3	1822
B. Dahomean or Slave Coast Languages				
31. Adampe	Ewe	Ghana	1	1823
32. Anfue or Adsa	Adja	Dahomey	few	1820
33. Hwida	Hueda or Aizo	Dahomey	6	1834
34. Dahome or Popo	Fon	Dahomey	—	1844
35. Mahi	Mahi	Dahomey	30	1825
C. The Aku-Igala Languages				
36. Yoruba[9]		Nigeria		
a. Ota	Egbado		21	1834
b. Egba	Egba		many	1827
c. Idsesa or Igesa	Ijesha		many	1843
d. Yoruba proper	Oyo		several thousand	1821
e. Yagba	Yagba		many	1832
f. Ki or Eki	Ekiti		many	1823
g. Dsumu	Jumu		many	—
h. Oworo	Aworo		3	<1819
i. Dsebu or Idsebu	Ijebu		—	1829
k. Ife	Ife		6	1825
l. Ondo	Ondo		30	1841

[4] Modern name is not known. Linguistically, Koelle's sample vocabulary is that of a Susu dialect.

[5] Languages 20 and 21 are spoken in the immediate hinterland and were represented in the colony by a relatively large, but fluctuating, population.

[6] Not to be confused with two other West African groups sometimes called Basa. One of these is in northern Nigeria, the other in Cameroons. There is no connection between the three, other than the chance similarity of the names.

[7] Kru people had been coming to Sierra Leone for many decades in search of temporary employment. The Kru population in 1848 was 743. (R. R. Kuczynski, *Demographic Survey*, p. 82.)

[8] The two neighboring groups, now called Ge and Sikon, were formerly referred to jointly as Gbe.

[9] Since speakers of Yoruba dialects were by far the largest group among the liberated Africans, the informants were unable to give an accurate estimate of the numbers. See, however, Table 71.

(1) *Informant's name for his country*	(2) *Modern name*	(3) *Location*	(4) *Number present in Sierra Leone*	(5) *Informant's date of capture*
m. Dsekiri	Itsekiri		3	1823
37. Igala	Igala	Nigeria	13	1829
IV. NORTH-EASTERN HIGH SUDAN LANGUAGES				
A. First Group				
38. Mose	Wagadugu Mossi	Upper Volta	1	1823
39. Dselana	Kilir	Dahomey	5	1844
40. Guren or Guresa	Gurensi	Ghana and Upper Volta	—	1843
41. Gurma	Gurma	Upper Volta	5	1843
B. Second Group				
42. Legba	Logba	Togo	3	1844
43. Kuare	Kabre	Togo	8	1819
44. Kiamba or Dsamba	Temba or Kotokoli	Dahomey	few	1826
C. Third Group				
45. Koama	Isala[10]	Ghana	3	1845
46. Bagbalan	Isala[10]	Ghana	1	1844
D. Fourth Group				
47. Kasm	Kasena	Upper Volta and Ghana	1	1846
48. Yula	Kasena[11]	Upper Volta and Ghana	none	—
V. NIGER DELTA LANGUAGES				
A. First Group				
49. Ibo Dialects[12]				
a. Isoama	Igbo (Isu-Ama)	Nigeria	many	1819
b. Isiele	Igbo (Ishielu)		4	1838
c. Abadsa	Igbo (Abaja)		40	1819
d. Aro	Igbo (Aro)		none	—
e. Mbofia	Igbo (Mbofia)		6	1819
B. Second Group				
50. Sobo	Urhobo	Nigeria	2	1815
51. Egbele	Etsako	Nigeria	—	1827
52. Bini	Benin	Nigeria	few	1827
53. Ihewe or Isewe	Ishan*	Nigeria	7–9	1818
54. Oloma	Olomo (north-west Edo)	Nigeria	1	1831

10 These closely related languages (45 and 46) are now considered to be dialects of a single language spoken in northern Ghana.

11 Koelle obtained his sample of this language from the same informant as 47. It is therefore not shown on the maps. The language itself is now considered to be a dialect of Kasena.

12 Koelle notes that the Ibo were recognized as having a common culture and similar language, but they did not call themselves Ibo. Instead, they identified their home countries by more local names, of which he listed fifteen, giving samples of five. Since the Ibo were second only to the Yoruba as the most numerous group among the liberated Africans, the best indication of their numbers will be found in the census figures, Table 71.

(1) *Informant's name for his country*	(2) *Modern name*	(3) *Location*	(4) *Number present in Sierra Leone*	(5) *Informant's date of capture*
C. Third Group				
55. Okuloma	Delta Ijaw	Nigeria	12	1829
56. Udso or Utso	Western Ijaw	Nigeria	1	1834
VI. NIGER-DSHADDA (NIGER-BENUE) LANGUAGES OR NUPE GROUP				
57. Nupe	Nupe	Nigeria	60	1825
58. Kupa or Ekupu	Kupa	Nigeria	40	1834
59. Esitako	Dibo	Nigeria	30	1825
60. Musu	Gbari	Nigeria	4	1819
61. Goali or Gbali	Gbari	Nigeria		
a. Gugu dialect	South-west Gbari		3	1846
b. Kuta dialect	North-east Gbari		20	1815
62. Basa[13]	Kakanda or Basange	Nigeria	100	1836
63. Ebe	Ebe[14]	Nigeria	12	1820
64. Opanda or Egbira	Igbira-Panda	Nigeria	25	1830, 1828[15]
65. Egbira-Hima	Igbira-Hima	Nigeria	9	1827
VII. CENTRAL AFRICAN LANGUAGES				
A. First Group—Chad Languages				
66. Buduma	Buduma	Nigeria	1	1845
67. Bornu dialects	Kanuri	Nigeria		
a. Kanuri proper	Kanuri	Nigeria	30	1812
b. Munio or Manga	Manga	Nigeria and Niger	3	1845
c. Nguru	Nguru[16]	Nigeria	1	1844
d. Kanem	Kanem	Chad	2	1845
B. Second Group				
68. Pika or Fika	Bolewa	Nigeria	5	1845
69. Karekare	Karekare	Nigeria	2	1845
				<1819
70. Bode dialects	Bede*	Nigeria	8	
a. Bode or Abunogo	Bede*		2	1842
b. Ngodsin	Ngizim		2	1809
c. Doei	Doei*		4	1812

[13] Not to be confused with the quite different Basa groups in Cameroons and in Sierra Leone, or with the true Basa of northern Nigeria, language 75. The language is, in fact, a riverine dialect of Nupe, and Basange, the alternative name for the people, means 'We are not Basa.'

[14] All of the Ebe arrived in Sierra Leone in a single ship, no others having come either before or since.

[15] Here and below, where more than one date is given, Koelle obtained his information from several informants.

[16] Nguru was the seat of government of the Galadima of Bornu, or the warden of the Western Marches. The name reported is therefore a geographical, rather than an ethnic or linguistic, designation.

(1) *Informant's name for his country*	(2) *Modern name*	(3) *Location*	(4) *Number present in Sierra Leone*	(5) *Informant's date of capture*
VIII. SOUTH AFRICAN LANGUAGES				
A. First Group	Ekoi	Eastern Nigeria	30[17]	
71. Ekamtulufu	Nde		1	1829
72. Udom	Nde		12	1827
73. Mbofon	Nde		1	1835
74. Eafen	Ekoi		31	1829
B. Second Group				
75. Basa	Basa Komo	Nigeria	1	1842
76. Kamuku	Kamuku	Nigeria	1	1843
C. Third Group				
77. Dsuku	Jukun	Nigeria	9	1809, 1816
IX. MOKO LANGUAGES				
A. First Group				
78. Isuwu	Su	West Cameroons	1	1831
79. Diwala	Duala	East Cameroons	2	1829
80. Orungu	Rungu	Gabon	11	1831, 1819
81. Bayong or Pati	Banggot	East Cameroons	50	1822, 1829, 1819
82. Kum or Bakum	Bakom	East Cameroons	3	1826
83. Bagba	Bagba*	Cameroons	1	1834
84. Balu	Bali	Cameroons	1	1831
85. Mom or Bamom	Bamum	East Cameroons	1	1826
86. Ngoala	Banggola	Cameroons	3	1826
87. Bamenya	Bamenyam	East Cameroons	12	1830
88. Papiah	Baba	East Cameroons	30	1831
89. Param	Bagam	Cameroons	8	1827
B. Second Group				
90. Ngoten	Ngoteng	West Cameroons	3	1819
91. Melon or Mellommesie	Bongkeng	East Cameroons	1	1829
92. Nhalemoe	Kossi	East Cameroons	3	<1819
93. Seke or Baseke	Seke	Rio Muni and Gabon	11	1835
X. KONGO-NGOLA LANGUAGES				
A. First Group				
94. Kabenda	Vili[18]	Cabinda and Congo-Brazzaville	2	1819
95. Bambona	Mboma (Kongo)	Congo	20	1809
96. Musentandu	Ntandu (Kongo)	Congo	4	1836
97. Mbamba or Babamba	Obamba	Gabon	11	1835

[17] The inconsistency here is Koelle's. He reports thirty members of the Ekoi group as a whole but the numbers reported for the subdivisions add up to forty-five.

[18] This informant had been a slave, but he was not a recaptive. Following his original capture, he spent fifteen years as a slave in Brazil, then came to Sierra Leone as a free immigrant about 1835.

(1) *Informant's name for his country*	(2) *Modern name*	(3) *Location*	(4) *Number present in Sierra Leone*	(5) *Informant's date of capture*
98. Kanyika	Kaniok	Congo (Katanga)	2	1835
99. Ntere or Nteke	Teke (Tio)	Congo-Brazzaville	1	1832
100. Batsaya	Tsaye	Congo-Brazzaville	21	1832
B. Second Group				
101. Babuma or Badongo	Boõõ (Tio)	Congo	6	1829
102. Bumbete	Mbeti	Gabon and Congo-Brazzaville	4	1822
103. Kasands or Kasandsi	Imbangala	Angola	6	1834
104. Nymobe or Bayombe	Yombe (Kongo)	Congo	13	1831
105. Sunde or Basunde	Nsundi	Congo	50	1840
C. Third Group				
106. Ngola	Ambundu	Angola	many	1839
107. Benguela or Pangela	Ovimbundu[19]	Angola	11	1832
108. Lubalo or Balubalo	Lweno	Angola	2	1841
109. Ruunda or Runda	Lunda	Congo (Katanga)	3	1840
110. *Songo*	*Songo*[20]	Angola	4	1794
111. Kisama	Sama	Angola	4	1837

XI. SOUTH-EASTERN LANGUAGES

112. Veiao	Yao	Malawi and Mozambique	1	—
113. Kiriman	Cuabo	Mozambique	1	1829
114. Marawi	Maravi	Malawi	5	1828
115. Meto	Makwa	Mozambique	1	—
116. Matatan	South Makwa	Mozambique	11	1828
117. Nyamban	Inhambane (Tonga)	Mozambique	21	1831

XII. UNCLASSIFIED OR ISOLATED LANGUAGES

A. Unclassified West Atlantic Languages				
a. With final inflection				
118. Wolof	Wolof	Senegal	2[21]	1820
119. Bidsogo	Bijago	Guinea-Bissau	3	1834

[19] This informant had been a slave in Demerara for six years before coming to Sierra Leone in about 1838, after the emancipation of the slaves in the British West Indies. Koelle's notes throw no light on the problem of his apparent sale to Demerara in 1832, when the enforcement of the British anti-slave-trade legislation was supposedly effective in British colonies. See also number 126 below.

[20] The early date of capture for this informant is accounted for by the fact that he served some twenty-one years as a slave, then as an agent for the slave trade in Luanda and Brazil. He came to Sierra Leone in 1821 as a crew member of a captured slaver and stayed on as an immigrant.

[21] The informant, however, reported that there had once been fifty Wolof in Sierra Leone, but the others had emigrated, presumably returning to Senegal.

(1) *Informant's name for his country*	(2) *Modern name*	(3) *Location*	(4) *Number present in Sierra Leone*	(5) *Informant's date of capture*
120. *Gadsaga*	*Soninke*	Mali and Senegal	1	1839
121. Gura	Gola	Liberia	few	—
b. With initial inflection				
122. Banyon	Banyun	Guinea-Bissau	—	—
123. Nalu	Nalu	Guinea-Bissau Guinea-Conakry	4	1824
124. Bulanda	Bolanta	Guinea-Bissau	7	1835
125. Limba	Limba	Sierra Leone	many	1836
126. Landoma	Landuma[22]	Guinea-Conakry	1	1833
B. Unclassified High Sudan Languages				
127. Asante	Ashanti[23]	Gold Coast	—	1825
128. Barba	Bariba	Dahomey	50	1812
129. Boko	Boko	Dahomey	1	1841
C. Unclassified Central African Languages				
130. Kandin	Agadès Tamashek	Niger	1	1842
131. *Tumbuktu*	*Songhai*	Mali	1	1839
132. Bagermi or Bagrmi	Bagirmi	Chad	1	1842
133. Hausa	Hausa	Nigeria		
a. Kano dialect[24]			—	1845
b. Katsina dialect			8	1834
134. Pula	Fulbe or Fulani			
a. *Futa Jallon* dialect		Guinea-Conakry	6	1839
b. *Salum* dialect[25]		Senegal and The Gambia	—	1813
c. Gobir dialect[26]		Nigeria and Niger	—	1805
d. Kano dialect		Nigeria	—	1845
D. Unclassified Niger Delta Languages				
135. Yala	Iyala	Nigeria	1	1829
E. Unclassified South African Languages				
136. Anan or Kalaba	Anang or Western Ibibio	Eastern Nigeria	>200	1831
137. Dsarawa	Jarawa	Nigeria	1	1817

[22] This informant, like number 107, had been sold to Demerara about 1833. After being emancipated in 1838, he came to Sierra Leone as a free immigrant.

[23] This informant was initially a prisoner of war, rather than a slave in a strict sense. He was imprisoned by the British in Accra about 1825, during the Ashanti War. Later he was enlisted in the British army and served on the Gold Coast and the Gambia before settling in Sierra Leone.

[24] This informant, together with 134b below, was captured by the Gobirawa while resisting the Habe invasion of Kano in 1844–5.

[25] The informant in this case was a recaptive, but many Fulbe from the Gambia region came to Sierra Leone as free immigrants.

[26] This informant was not a liberated African, though he had been a slave. He was initially captured by the Hausa in the early years of the Fulani *jihad* and sold to Jamaica before the British slave trade became illegal. There he apparently obtained his freedom and enlisted in the forces, which brought him to Sierra Leone in about 1814. On his discharge from the army about 1829 he settled down as a free immigrant.

(1) *Informant's name for his country*	(2) *Modern name*	(3) *Location*	(4) *Number present in Sierra Leone*	(5) *Informant's date of capture*
138. Koro	Koro	Nigeria	4	1844
139. Ham or Dsaham	Ham or Jaba	Nigeria	4	1842
140. Akurakura	Akunakuna	Eastern Nigeria	6	1829
141. Okam	Yakö	Eastern Nigeria	few	1818
142. Yasgua	Yeskwa	Nigeria	5	1839
143. Nki	Boki	Eastern Nigeria	2	1827
144. Kambali	Kambari	Nigeria	15	1815
145. Alege	Gayi	Eastern Nigeria	2	1835
146. Penin	Nen	East Cameroons	7	1819
147. Bute	Wute	East Cameroons	3	—[27]
148. Murundo or Barundo	Lundu	West Cameroons	12	1827
149. Undaza	Ndaza	Gabon	1	1838
150. Ndob or Burukem	Bandobo	West Cameroons	4	1827
151. Nkele or Bakele	Kalai	Gabon	17	1822
152. Knoguin or Okui	Anyang	West Cameroons	100	1833
153. Mbarike	Zumper	West Cameroons	7	1823
154. Tiwi or Midsi	Tiv	Nigeria	20	<1829, 1839
155. Boritsu	Boritsu[28]	Nigeria	2	1828
156. Afudu	Afu*	Nigeria	—	1827
157. Mfut or Bafut	Bapet (Bafia)	West Cameroons	2	1814
158. Mbe	Bakongwang	Cameroons	6	1838
159. Nso or Banso	Nsaw	Cameroons	5	1825
F. Africanized Arabic				
160. Arabic				
a. Wadai dialect[29]		Chad	1	R. 1837
b. *Adrar* dialect		Mali	1	1846
c. Beran dialect[30]		Mali	none	—

[27] Date of capture not given. The informant arrived in Sierra Leone in about 1846, but he had already spent some time as a slave in other parts of Africa, first of the Fulani who captured him, then in Hausa, and finally in Yoruba before he was sold to a Portuguese slave dealer.

[28] The informant reported that he came from a small chiefdom with only two towns, about one day's travel north of the Benue river. The language is not known to be recorded in recent linguistic literature, and it is possible that Boritsu disappeared after the Fulani raid of about 1828, in which the informant was captured.

[29] Koelle's notes are unclear as to whether this informant was a recaptive or a free immigrant.

[30] Not shown on map. Informant was a native speaker of the Adrar dialect, who also supplied vocabulary of his own language, 160b.

BIBLIOGRAPHY

Adams, Capt. John. *Remarks on the Country Extending from Cape Palmas to the River Congo. . . .* London, 1823.

Aguirre Beltrán, Gonzalo. *La poblacíon negra de México, 1519–1810.* Mexico, D.F., 1946.

———. "The Slave Trade in Mexico," *Hispanic American Historical Review,* 24:412–31 (1944).

Aimes, Hubert H. S. *A History of Slavery in Cuba, 1511–1868.* New York, 1907.

Ajayi, J. F. Ade and Ian Espie, eds. *A Thousand Years of West African History: A Handbook for Teachers and Students.* Ibadan, 1965.

Akinjogbin, I. A. "The Oyo Empire in the Eighteenth Century—A Reassessment," *Journal of the Historical Society of Nigeria,* 3:449–60 (1966).

Alden, Dauril. "The Population of Brazil in the Late Eighteenth Century: A Preliminary Study," *Hispanic American Historical Review,* 43:173–205 (1963).

Azevedo, João Lucio de. *Epocas de Portugal económico.* Lisbon, 1929.

Balandier, Georges. *Daily Life in the Kingdom of the Kongo.* Tr. by Helen Weaver. New York, 1968.

Ballagh, James C. *A History of Slavery in Virginia.* Baltimore, 1902.

Bancroft, George. *History of the United States of America. . . .* 3rd ed., 3 vols. New York, 1892.

Barreto, João Melo. *Historia da Guiné.* Lisbon, 1938.

Basauri, Carlos. "La población negroïde Mexicana," *Estadistica,* 1:96–107 (1943).

Birmingham, David. *Trade and Conflict in Angola: The Mbundu and Their Neighbours under the Influence of the Portuguese, 1483–1790.* Oxford, 1966.

Blake, John W. *European Beginnings in West Africa, 1454–1578.* New York, 1937.

Booth, Alan R. "The United States African Squadron 1843–1861," in J. Butler, ed., *Boston University Papers in African History,* vol. 1 (Boston, 1964), pp. 77–117.

Boxer, Charles R. *The Dutch Seaborne Empire 1600–1800.* London, 1965.

Brito Figueroa, Federico. *La estructura económica de Venezuela colonial.* Caracas, 1963.

Buarque de Hollanda, Sergio, ed. *História geral da civilização brasileira.* 4 vols. São Paulo, 1960—.

Buxton, Sir Thomas Fowell. *The African Slave Trade.* Philadelphia, 1839.

Carey, Henry C. *The Slave Trade, Domestic and Foreign.* Philadelphia, 1872.

Chaunu, Huguette and Pierre. *Séville et l'Atlantique (1504–1650).* 8 vols. Paris, 1955–60.

Chaunu, Pierre. "Pour une 'geopolitique' de l'espace américain," in R. Konetzke and H. Kellenbenz, eds., *Jahrbuch für Geschichte von Staat, Wirtschaft, und Gesellschaft Lateinamerikas,* 1:3–26 (Cologne, 1964).

Chemin-Dupontès, Paul. *Les petites Antilles: Etude sur leur évolution économique.* Paris, 1909.

Chiché, Marie-Claire. *Hygiène et santé à bord des navires négriers au XVIIIe siècle.* Paris, 1957.

Chilver, E. M., P. M. Kaberry, and R. Cornevin, "Sources of the Nineteenth-Century Slave Trade: Two Comments," *Journal of African History,* 6:117–20 (1965).

Coelho de Senna, Nelson. *Africanos no Brasil.* Belo Horizonte, 1938.

Collins, Robert O., ed. *Problems in African History.* Englewood Cliffs, N.J., 1968.

Congresso afro-brasileiro, Recife, 1934. *Estudos afro-brasileiros.* Trabalhos apresentados ao 1^{0} congresso afro-brasiliero reunido no Recife em 1934, vol. 1. Rio de Janeiro, 1936.

———. *See also* Freyre, Gilberto, and others.

Coolen, Georges. "Négriers dunkerquois," *Bulletin de la Société de la Morinie,* 19:289–320, 321–23 (1960).

Cornevin, Robert. *Histoire du Dahomey.* Paris, 1962.

———. *Histoire du Togo.* Paris, 1959.

Correia Lopes, Edmundo. *A escravatura.* Lisbon, 1944.

Cortés, Hernando. *Documentos inéditos relativos a Hernán Cortés.* Mexico, D.F., 1935.

Corwin, Arthur F. *Spain and the Abolition of Slavery in Cuba, 1817–1886*. Austin, Tex., 1967.

Coupland, Sir Reginald. *The British Anti-Slavery Movement*. London, 1964.

Curtin, Philip D., ed. *Africa Remembered: Narratives by West Africans from the Era of the Slave Trade*. Madison, 1967.

———. "Epidemiology and the Slave Trade," *Political Science Quarterly*, 83:190–216 (1968).

———. *The Image of Africa: British Ideas and Action, 1780–1850*. Madison, 1964.

———. " 'The White Man's Grave': Image and Reality, 1780–1850," *Journal of British Studies*, 1:94–110 (1961).

———, and Jan Vansina. "Sources of the Nineteenth Century Atlantic Slave Trade," *Journal of African History*, 5:185–208 (1964).

Dalby, David. "Provisional Identification of Languages in the *Polyglotta Africana*," *Sierra Leone Language Review*, 1:83–90 (1964).

Dardel, Pierre. *Navires et marchandises dans les ports de Rouen et du Havre au xviiie siècle*. Paris, 1963.

Davidson, Basil. *Black Mother: The Years of the African Slave Trade*. London, 1961.

Davidson, David M. "Negro Slave Control and Resistance in Colonial Mexico, 1519–1650," *Hispanic American Historical Review*, 46:235–53 (1966).

Davies, Kenneth G. *The Royal African Company*. London, 1957.

Davis, David Brion. *The Problem of Slavery in Western Culture*. Ithaca, 1966.

Debien, G. "Au sujet des origines ethniques de quelques esclaves des Antilles," *Notes africaines*, No. 106, p. 58 (1965).

———, J. Houdaille, R. Massio, and R. Richard. "Les origines des esclaves des Antilles," *Bulletin de l'IFAN*, série B, 23:363–87 (1961); 25:1–41, 215–66 (1963); 26:166–211, 601–75 (1964); 27:319–71, 755–99 (1965); 29:536–58 (1967).

Deerr, Noel. *The History of Sugar*. 2 vols. London, 1949–50.

Delafosse, M. "La Rochelle et les îles au xviie siècle," *Revue d'histoire des colonies*, 36:238–277 (1949).

Delcourt, André. *La France et les établissements français au Sénégal entre 1713 et 1763*. Dakar, 1952.

Denoix, L. "La Compagnie des Indes au xviiie siècle, ses activités diverses," *Revue d'histoire économique et sociale*, 34:141–57 (1956).

Díaz Soler, L. M. *Historia de la esclavitud en Puerto Rico, 1493–1890*. 2nd ed. Rio Piedras, 1965.

Dike, K. Onwuka. *Trade and Politics in the Niger Delta 1830–1885: An Introduction to the Economic and Political History of Nigeria.* Oxford, 1956.

Donnan, Elizabeth. *Documents Illustrative of the History of the Slave Trade to America.* 4 vols. Washington, 1930–35.

———. "The Slave Trade into South Carolina before the Revolution," *American Historical Review,* 33:804–28 (1928).

Du Bois, W. E. B. "The Negro Race in the United States of America," *Papers on Inter-Racial Problems Communicated to the First Universal Races Congress.* London, 1911.

———. *The Suppression of the African Slave-Trade to the United States of America, 1638–1870.* New York, 1896.

Ducasse, A. *Les négriers, ou le trafic des esclaves.* Paris, 1948.

Duffy, James. *A Question of Slavery: Labour Policies in Portuguese Africa and British Protest, 1850–1920.* Oxford, 1967.

Duignan, Peter and Clarence Clendenen. *The United States and the African Slave Trade 1619–1862.* Stanford, 1963.

Dunbar, Edward E. "History of the Rise and Decline of Commercial Slavery in America, with Reference to the Future of Mexico," *The Mexican Papers,* 1:177–279 (No. 5, April, 1861).

Edwards, Bryan. *An Historical Survey of the Island of Saint Domingo.* . . . London, 1801.

———. *The History, Civil and Commercial, of the British Colonies in the West Indies.* . . . 2nd ed., 2 vols. London, 1793–94.

Elkins, Stanley. *Slavery: A Problem in American Institutional and Intellectual Life.* Chicago, 1959.

Escragnolle de Taunay, Affonso. *See* Taunay.

Fage, John D. *Ghana: A Historical Interpretation.* Madison, 1959.

———. *An Introduction to the History of West Africa.* Cambridge, 1955.

Faro, Jorge. "O movimento comercial do porto de Bissau de 1788 a 1794," *Boletim cultural da Guiné Portuguesa,* 14:231–58 (1959).

Faulkner, Harold U. *American Economic History.* 8th ed. New York, 1960.

Faure, Claude. "La garnison Européene du Sénégal (1779–1858)," *Revue d'histoire des colonies,* 8:5–108 (1920).

Forde, C. Daryll, ed. *Efik Traders of Old Calabar.* London, 1956.

———. "The Nupe," in D. Forde, ed., *Peoples of the Niger-Benue Confluence* (London, 1955), pp. 17–52.

Franco, José L. *Afroamérica.* Havana, 1961.

Franklin, John Hope. *From Slavery to Freedom: A History of American Negroes.* New York, 1947.

Freyre, Gilberto, and others. *Novos estudos afro-brasileiros.* Trabalhos apresentados ao 1° congresso afro-brasiliero reunido no Recife em 1934, vol. 2. Rio de Janeiro, 1937.

Fyfe, Christopher, ed. "The Transatlantic Slave Trade from West Africa." Edinburgh: Centre of African Studies, University of Edinburgh (mimeographed), 1965.

Gamble, David P. *The Wolof of Senegambia.* London, 1957.

Garnault, Emile. *Le commerce rochelais au xviiie siècle. . . .* 5 vols. La Rochelle, 1888–1900.

Garzón Maceda, Ceferino and José Walter Dorflinger. "Esclavos y mulatos en un dominio rural del siglo XVIII en Córdoba: Contribución a la demografía histórica," *Revista de la Universidad Nacional de Córdoba,* 2 (2nd series): 627–40 (1961).

Gisler, Antoine. *L'esclavage aux antilles françaises (17e–19e siècle): Contribution au problème de l'esclavage.* Fribourg, 1965.

Gomes, Alfredo. "Achegas para a história do tráfico africano no Brasil —Aspectos numéricos," in Instituto Histórico e Geográfico Brasiliero, *IV Congresso de História Nacional, 21–28 Abril de 1949, Anais,* vol. 5 (Rio de Janeiro, 1950), pp. 29–78.

Goulart, Mauricio. *Escravidão africana no Brasil.* São Paulo, 1950.

Gray, Lewis Cecil. *History of Agriculture in the Southern United States to 1860.* 2 vols. Washington, 1933.

Great Britain Parliamentary Sessional Papers. 1833, xxvi (700), "General Summary of the Slave Population of the District of Demerara and Essequibo Colony of British Guiana. . . ."

———. 1845, xlix (73), "Return of the Number of Slave Vessels Arrived in the Transatlantic States since 1814," pp. 593–633.

———. 1847–48, xxii (623), "Fourth Report from the Select Committee on the Slave Trade."

———. 1865, v (412), "Report of the Select Committee on the Western Coast of Africa."

Great Britain, Privy Council. *Report of the Lords of the Committee of Council for Trade and Foreign Plantations . . . Concerning the Present State of Trade to Africa, and Particularly the Trade in Slaves. . . .* London, 1789.

Greene, Evarts B. and Virginia D. Harrington. *American Population before the Federal Census of 1790.* New York, 1932.

Guerra y Sanchez, Ramiro. *Sugar and Society in the Caribbean: An Economic History of Cuban Agriculture,* trans. from the Spanish by Marjory M. Urquidi. New Haven, 1964.

———, and others. *Historia de la nación cubana.* 10 vols. Havana, 1952.

Guillot, Carlos Federico. *Negros rebeldes y negros cimarrones: Perfil afroamericano en la historia del Nuevo Mundo durante el siglo XVI.* Buenos Aires, 1961.

Hair, P. E. H. "The Enslavement of Koelle's Informants," *Journal of African History,* 6:193–203 (1965).

———. "Ethnolinguistic Continuity on the Guinea Coast," *Journal of African History,* 8:247–68 (1967).

Hargreaves, John D. "The Slave Traffic," in Natan, Alex, ed., *Silver Renaissance: Essays in Eighteenth-Century English History* (London, 1961), pp. 81–101.

———. *West Africa: The Former French States.* Englewood Cliffs, N. J., 1967.

Harlow, Vincent T. *A History of Barbados 1625–1685.* Oxford, 1926.

Hartog, Johannes H. de. *Geschiedenis van de Nederlandse Antillen.* 4 vols. Orangstad, 1964.

Helps, Sir Arthur. *The Conquerors of the New World and Their Bondsmen, being a narrative of the principal events which led to Negro slavery in the West Indies and America.* 2 vols. London, 1848–52.

Herskovits, Melville J. *The Myth of the Negro Past.* 2nd ed. Boston, 1958.

———. "On the Provenience of New World Negroes," *Social Forces,* 12:247–62 (1933).

———. "Social History of the Negro," in *Handbook of Social Psychology* (Worcester, Mass., 1935).

Higham, Charles S. *The Development of the Leeward Islands under the Restoration 1660–1688.* Cambridge, 1921.

Howard, Warren S. *American Slavers and the Federal Law, 1837–1862.* Berkeley, 1963.

Humboldt, Alexander von. *Personal Narrative of Travels to the Equinoctial Regions of the New Continent . . . 1799–1804,* translated from the French by Helen Maria Williams. 7 vols. London, 1814–29.

Jaramillo Uribe, Jaime. "Esclavos y señores en la sociedad colombiana del siglo XVIII," *Anuario Colombiano de Historia Social y de la Cultura,* 1:3–55 (1963).

Jeulin, Paul. *L'Evolution du port de Nantes: Organisation et trafic depuis les origines.* Paris, 1929.

Johnston, Sir Harry H. *The Negro in the New World.* New York, 1910.

Jones, Gwilym I. *The Trading States of the Oil Rivers: A Study of Political Development in Eastern Nigeria.* London, 1963.

Karasch, Mary. "The Brazilian Slavers and the Illegal Slave Trade, 1836–1851." Unpublished M.A. thesis, University of Wisconsin, 1967.

Kay, Frederick G. *The Shameful Trade.* London, 1967.

Kent, R. K. "Palmares: An African State in Brazil," *Journal of African History,* 6:161–75 (1965).

King, James F. "The Negro in Continental Spanish America: A Select Bibliography," *Hispanic American Historical Review,* 24:547–59 (1944).

———. "Negro Slavery in New Granada," in *Greater America: Essays in Honor of H. E. Bolton.* Berkeley, 1945.

———. "Negro Slavery in the Viceroyalty of New Granada." Unpublished Ph.D. thesis, University of California, 1939.

Klein, Herbert S. *Slavery in the Americas: A Comparative Study of Virginia and Cuba.* Chicago, 1967.

Koelle, Sigismund W. *Polyglotta Africana. . . .* Edited by P. E. H. Hair and D. Dalby. Sierra Leone, 1963; first ed. London, 1854.

Kuczynski, Robert R. *Demographic Survey of the British Colonial Empire.* 3 vols. London, 1948–53.

———. *Population Movements.* Oxford, 1936.

La Courbe, Michel Jajolet de. *Premier Voyage du sieur de La Courbe fait à la coste d'Afrique en 1685,* ed. P. Cultru. Paris, 1913.

Lasascade, Pierre. *Esclavage et immigration: La Question de la main-d'oeuvre aux Antilles.* Paris, 1907.

Lawrence, Arnold W. *Trade Castles and Forts of West Africa.* Stanford, 1964.

Lecky, William E. H. *A History of England in the Eighteenth Century.* 8 vols. London, 1892–1920.

Le Moal, G. "Note sur les populations 'Bobo'," *Bulletin de l'IFAN,* série B, 19:418–30 (1957).

Le Page, Robert B., ed. *Jamaican Creole.* London, 1960.

Lier, Rudolf A. J. van. *The Development and Nature of Society in the West Indies.* Amsterdam, 1950.

———. *Samenleving in een Grensgebeid: een sociaal-historische studie van de Maatschappij in Suriname.* The Hague, 1949.

Lloyd, Christopher. *The Navy and the Slave Trade: The Suppression of the African Slave Trade in the Nineteenth Century.* London, 1949.

Lockhart, James. *Spanish Peru, 1532–1560: A Colonial Society.* Madison, 1968.

Lowenthal, David. "The Population of Barbados," *Social and Economic Studies,* 6:445–501 (1957).

Luttrell, Anthony. "Slavery and Slaving in the Portuguese Atlantic (to about 1500)" in C. Fyfe, ed., "The Transatlantic Slave Trade from West Africa." Edinburgh: Centre of African Studies, University of Edinburgh, 1965. Mimeographed.

Ly, Abdoulaye. *La Compagnie du Sénégal.* Paris, 1958.

Macedo, Sergio D. T. *Apontamentos para a história do trafico negreiro no Brasil.* Rio de Janeiro, 1942.

Machat, Jules. *Documents sur les établissements français et l'Afrique occidentale au xviii*[e] *siècle.* Paris, 1906.

MacInnes, Charles M. *England and Slavery.* Bristol, 1934.

Mackenzie-Grieve, Averil. *The Last Years of the English Slave Trade, Liverpool, 1750–1807.* London, 1941.

Macpherson, David. *Annals of Commerce. . . .* 4 vols. London, 1805.

Malvezin, Théophile. *Histoire du commerce de Bordeaux.* 4 vols. Bordeaux, 1890–93.

Mannix, Daniel P. and Malcolm Cowley. *Black Cargoes: A History of the Atlantic Slave Trade, 1518–1865.* New York, 1962.

Martin, Gaston. *Histoire de l'esclavage dans les colonies françaises.* Paris, 1948.

———. *Nantes au XVIII*[e] *siècle: L'Ere des négriers (1714–1774).* Paris, 1931.

———. *Négriers et bois d'ébène.* Grenoble, 1934.

Martin, P. A. "Slavery and Abolition in Brazil," *Hispanic American Historical Review,* 13:151–96 (1933).

Matson, Henry James. *Remarks on the Slave Trade and African Squadron.* London, 1848.

Mauro, Frédéric. *L'expansion européene (1600–1870).* Paris, 1964.

———. *Le Portugal et l'Atlantique au xvii*[e] *siècle (1570–1670): Etude économique.* Paris, 1960.

Mellafe, Rolando. *La esclavitud en Hispanoamérica.* Buenos Aires, 1964.

———. *La introducción de la esclavitud negra en Chile: Trafico y rutas.* Santiago de Chile, 1959.

———. "Problemas demográficos e historia colonial hispanoamericana," *Nova Americana,* 1:45–55 (1965).

Melo Barreto, João. *See* Barreto.

Menkman, W. R. *Geschiedenis van de West-Indische Compagnie.* Amsterdam, 1942.

Meyer, Jean. "Le commerce négrier nantais (1774–1792)," *Annales, Economies, Sociétes, Civilisations,* 1:120–29 (1960).

Mintz, Sydney. "Labor and Sugar in Puerto Rico and in Jamaica, 1800–1850," *Comparative Studies in Society and History,* 1:273–83 (1959).

———. Review of S. M. Elkins, *Slavery,* in *American Anthropologist,* 63:579–87 (1961).

Mörner, Magnus. *Race Mixture in the History of Latin America.* Boston, 1967.

———. "The History of Race Relations in Latin America: Some Comments on the State of Research," *Latin American Research Review,* 1:17–47 (1966).

Moreau de Jonnès, Alexandre. *Recherches statistiques sur l'esclavage colonial et sur les moyens de le supprimer.* Paris, 1842.

Moreau de Saint-Méry, Médéric Louis Elie. *Descripción de la parte española de Santo Domingo,* trans. from the French edition of 1796, by C. Armando Rodríguez. Santo Domingo, 1944.

———. *Description . . . de la partie française de l'isle Saint-Domingue.* 3 vols. New ed., revised from the original mss. by B. Maurel and E. Taillemite. Paris, 1958. (First published 1797.)

Morel, Edmund D. *The Black Man's Burden.* London, 1920.

Morton-Williams, Peter. "The Oyo Yoruba and the Atlantic Trade 1670–1830," *Journal of the Historical Society of Nigeria,* 3:25–45 (1964).

Murdock, George Peter. *Africa: Its Peoples and Their Culture History.* New York, 1959.

Neumark, Solomon D. *Foreign Trade and Economic Development in Africa: A Historical Perspective.* Stanford, 1964.

Newbury, Colin W. *The Western Slave Coast and its Rulers: European Trade and Administration among the Yoruba and Adja-Speaking Peoples of South-Western Nigeria, Southern Dahomey, and Togo.* Oxford, 1961.

Newton, John. *The Journal of a Slave Trader (John Newton), 1750–1754,* edited with an introduction by B. Martin and M. Spurrell. London, 1962.

Oldendorp, C. G. A. *Geschichte der Mission der Evangelischen Brüder auf den Caraibischen Inseln S. Thomas, S. Croix and S. Jan.* 2 vols. Barby, 1777.

Oliveira Martins, Joaquim P. *O Brazil e as colonias portuguezas.* 6th ed. Lisbon, 1953.

Oliver, Roland and J. D. Fage. *A Short History of Africa.* London, 1962.

Ortiz Fernández, Fernando. *Hampa afro-cubana. Los negros esclavos.* Havana, 1916.

Otte, Enrique and Ruiz-Burruecos, Conchita. "Los portugueses en la trata de esclaves negros de las postrimerias del siglo XVI," *Moneda y Crédito* (Madrid), 85:3–40 (1963).

Parkinson, C. Northcote. *The Rise of the Port of Liverpool.* Liverpool, 1952.

———. *The Trade Winds: A Study of British Overseas Trade during the French Wars, 1795–1815*. London, 1948.

Patterson, Orlando. *The Sociology of Slavery: An Analysis of the Origins, Development and Structure of a Negro Slave Society in Jamaica*. London, 1967.

Pereda Valdés, Ildefonso. *Negros esclavos y negros libres: Esquema de una sociedad esclavista y aporte del negro en nuestra formación nacional*. Montevideo, 1941.

Peytraud, Lucien. *L'Esclavage aux Antilles françaises avant 1789*. Paris, 1897.

Phillips, Ulrich B. *American Negro Slavery*. New York, 1918.

Pi-Sunyer, Oriol. "Historical Background of the Negro in Mexico," *Journal of Negro History*, 42:237–46 (1957).

Pitman, Frank Wesley. *The Development of the British West Indies, 1700–1763*. New Haven, 1917.

———. "Slavery on British West India Plantations in the Eighteenth Century," *Journal of Negro History*, 11:584–668 (1926).

Pollitzer, W. S. "The Negroes of Charleston (S.C.); A Study of Hemoglobin Types, Serology, and Morphology," *American Journal of Physical Anthropology*, 16:241–63 (1958).

Pope-Hennessy, James. *Sins of the Fathers: A Study of the Atlantic Slave Traders, 1441–1807*. London, 1967.

Posada, Eduardo, and Carlos Restrepo Canal. *La esclavitud en Colombia: Leyes de manumisión*. 2 vols. Bogotá, 1933–38.

Potter, J. "The Growth of Population in America, 1700–1860," in D. V. Glass and D. E. C. Eversley, eds., *Population in History: Essays in Historical Demography*. Chicago, 1965.

Rambert, Gaston, ed. *Histoire du commerce de Marseille*. 7 vols. Paris, 1949–66.

Rinchon, Dieudonné. *Les Armaments négriers au xviiie siècle*. Brussels, 1956.

———. *Pierre-Ignace-Liévin van Alstein, capitaine négrier*. Dakar, 1964.

———. *Le Trafic négrier, d'après les livres de commerce du capitaine gantois Pierre-Ignace-Liévin van Alstein*. Vol. I. Paris, 1938.

———. *La Traité et l'esclavage des congolais par les européens*. Brussels, 1929.

Roberts, George W. *The Population of Jamaica*. Cambridge, 1957.

Rodney, W. "Portuguese Attempts at Monopoly on the Upper Guinea Coast, 1580–1650," *Journal of African History*, 6:307–22 (1965).

Rodriques, José H. *Brazil and Africa*. Trans. Richard A. Mazzara and Sam Hileman. Berkeley, 1965.

Romero, Emilio. *Historia económica del Perú.* Buenos Aires, 1949.

Romero, Fernando. "The Slave Trade and the Negro in South America," *Hispanic American Historical Review,* 24:368–86 (1944).

Roncal, Joaquín. "The Negro Race in Mexico," *Hispanic American Historical Review,* 24:530–40 (1944).

Rose, J. Holland. "The Royal Navy and the Suppression of the West African Slave Trade," *Mariner's Mirror,* 22:54–64, 162–71 (1936).

Rosenblat, Angel. *La población indígena y el mestizaje en América.* Buenos Aires, 1954.

Rotberg, Robert I. *A Political History of Tropical Africa.* New York, 1965.

Rottenberg, Simon. "The Business of Slave Trading," *South Atlantic Quarterly,* 66:409–23 (1967).

Ryder, A. F. C. "Dutch Trade on the Nigerian Coast during the Seventeenth Century," *Journal of the Historical Society of Nigeria,* 3:195–210 (1965).

———. "The Re-establishment of Portuguese Factories on the Costa da Mina to the Mid-Eighteenth Century," *Journal of the Historical Society of Nigeria,* 1:157–81 (1958).

Saco, José Antonio. *Historia de la esclavitud de la raza africana en el Nuevo Mundo y en especial en los países américo-hispanos.* New ed. 4 vols. Havana, 1938.

Sandoval, Alonso de. *De instauranda aethiopium salute; el mundo de la esclavitud negra en America.* Bogota, 1956 (facsimile of Seville, 1627 ed.).

Scelle, Georges. *La traite négrière aux Indes de Castille. . . .* 2 vols. Paris, 1906.

Sherrard, Owen A. *Freedom from Fear: The Slave and His Emancipation.* New York, 1959.

Simonsen, Roberto. *História econômica do Brasil 1500–1820.* São Paulo, 1937.

Smith, T. Lynn. "The Racial Composition of the Population of Colombia," *Journal of Inter-American Studies,* 8:23–35 (1966).

Spears, John R. *The American Slave Trade: An Account of its Origin, Growth and Suppression.* London, 1901.

Stetson, Kenneth Winslow. "A Quantitative Approach to Britain's American Slave Trade, 1700–1773." Unpublished Master's thesis, University of Wisconsin, 1967.

Stewart, Watt. *Chinese Bondage in Peru: A History of the Chinese Coolie in Peru, 1849–1874.* Durham, N.C., 1951.

Studer, Elena F. S. de. *La trata de negros en el Río de la Plata durante el siglo xviii.* Buenos Aires, 1958.

Sutherland, Stella. *Population Distribution in Colonial America.* New York, 1936.
Tannenbaum, Frank. *Slave and Citizen: The Negro in the Americas.* New York, 1946.
Taunay, Affonso Escragnolle de. *Subsídios para a história do trafico africano no Brasil.* São Paulo, 1941.
Tauxier, Louis. *Histoire des Bambara.* Paris, 1942.
Thornton, A. P. "The Organization of the Slave Trade in the English West Indies, 1660–1685," *William and Mary Quarterly,* 12 (3rd ser.):399–409 (1955).
United States, Bureau of the Census. *Historical Statistics of the United States, Colonial Times to 1957.* Washington, D.C., 1960.
Vansina, Jan. *Kingdoms of the Savanna.* Madison, 1966.
———. "Long-Distance Trade-Routes in Central Africa," *Journal of African History,* 3:375–90 (1962).
Verger, Pierre. *Bahia and the West Coast Trade, 1549–1851.* Ibadan, 1964.
———. *Flux et reflux de la traite des nègres entre le golfe de Benin et Bahia de Todos os Santos du 17ᵉ et 19ᵉ siècles.* The Hague, 1968.
———."Mouvement de navires entre Bahia et la Golfe de Benin (xviiᵉ–xixᵉ siècles)," *Revue française d'histoire d'outre-mer,* 55:1–36 (1968).
———. "Rôle joué par le tabac de Bahia dans la traite des esclaves au Golfe du Bénin," *Cahiers d'études africaines,* 4:349–69 (1964) (No. 15).
Vianna Filho, Luís. "O trabalho do engenho e a reacção do índio. Establecimento de escravatura africana," *Congresso do Mundo Portugues,* 10:12–29 (1940).
Vrijman, L. C. *Slavenhalers en Slavenhandel.* Amsterdam, 1937.
Waddell, D. A. G. "Queen Anne's Government and the Slave Trade," *Caribbean Quarterly,* 6:7–10.
Weber, Henry. *La Compagnie française des Indes (1604–1875).* Paris, 1904.
West, Robert C. *Colonial Placer Mining in Colombia.* Baton Rouge, 1952.
Westergaard, Waldemar. *The Danish West Indies Under Company Rule (1671–1754).* New York, 1917.
West Indische Encyclopaedie. Amsterdam, 1927.
Wiedner, Donald L. *A History of Africa South of the Sahara.* New York, 1962.
Williams, Eric. "The Golden Age of the Slave System in Britain," *Journal of Negro History,* 25:60–106 (1940).

———. *Capitalism and Slavery*. Chapel Hill, 1944.

Williams, Gomer. *History of the Liverpool Privateers and Letters of Marque with an Account of the Liverpool Slave Trade*. London, 1897.

Wolff, Inge. "Negersklaverei und Negerhandel in Hochperu 1545–1640," in R. Konetzke and H. Kellenbenz, eds., *Jahrbuch für Geschichte von Staat, Wirtschaft, und Gesellschaft Lateinamerikas,* 1:157–86. Cologne, 1964.

Wyndham, Hugh A. *The Atlantic and Slavery*. London, 1935.

Young, Sir William. *The West-India Common-Place Book. . . .* London, 1807.

Zelinsky, Wilbur. "The Historical Geography of the Negro Population of Latin America," *Journal of Negro History,* 34:153–221 (1949).

Zimmermann, Matilde. "The French Slave Trade at Moçambique, 1770–1794." Unpublished M.A. thesis, University of Wisconsin, 1967.

INDEX